Movements and Issues in American Judaism

Movements and Issues in American Judaism

AN ANALYSIS AND SOURCEBOOK OF DEVELOPMENTS SINCE 1945

Edited, with an Introduction,
By BERNARD MARTIN

 GREENWOOD PRESS
WESTPORT, CONNECTICUT • LONDON, ENGLAND

Library of Congress Cataloging in Publication Data
Main entry under title:

Movements and issues in American Judaism.

  Bibliography: p.
  Includes index.
  1. Judaism—United States—History—Addresses,
essays, lectures. 2. Jews in the United States—
History—Addresses, essays, lectures. I. Martin,
Bernard, 1928-

BM205.M67   296'.0973   77-87971

ISBN 0-313-20044-0

"God the Life of Nature" on pages 223-25 is reprinted
with the permission of the Jewish Reconstructionist
Foundation.

Library of Congress Catalog Card Number: 77-87971
ISBN: 0-313-20044-0

First published in 1978

Greenwood Press, Inc.
51 Riverside Avenue, Westport, Connecticut 06880

Printed in the United States of America

10 9 8 7 6 5 4 3 2 1

Contents

Preface _____

This volume is intended to provide a portrait of the Jewish community in America and a discussion of the major movements and issues in its corporate life since the end of World War II. It was in this period, undoubtedly the most eventful and momentous in its entire history, that this community emerged as the largest and most powerful in world Jewry.

All the chapters were commissioned and written expressly for this volume by recognized authorities in their respective fields of specialization in the study of American Jewry. In most cases the authors submitted selected bibliographies, some annotated, which should prove useful to the reader desiring to pursue further study. (I have augmented these bibliographies to a very considerable degree.)

In the introductory essay I have presented an overview of the history of American Judaism in the period since 1945 in the hope that it will provide a framework that may facilitate comprehension of the more specialized themes discussed in the chapters that follow. Because the Jewish community of Canada has always had a particularly close relationship with American Jewry and has been deeply influenced by the latter, it seemed appropriate to conclude the volume with an essay on the Canadian Jewish experience.

I wish to express my sincere gratitude to all the contributors to this book, which, it is anticipated, will furnish the reader with the possibility of a fuller understanding of a crucial era in the life of the American Jewish community.

Bernard Martin

Case Western Reserve University
Cleveland, Ohio

Movements and Issues in American Judaism

Bernard Martin _____

AMERICAN JEWRY SINCE 1945: AN HISTORICAL OVERVIEW

In 1945 the Jews of America joined their fellow citizens in jubilation over the end of World War II. Their joy, however, was far from unadulterated; mingled with it was a profound sorrow generated both by the knowledge of how many of their own sons and daughters had been killed or maimed and by the realization of the enormity of the tragedy that had befallen European Jewry during the years of the conflict. As early as 1942, three years before the guns were silenced, a great deal of information about the atrocities being committed against Jews in Nazi-occupied Europe was already reaching America. However, the full dimensions of these atrocities—the fact that from 1939 to 1945 six million Jews had been systematically and brutally murdered at the command of Adolf Hitler—became common knowledge only after the liberation of the German concentration camps by Allied forces and the cessation of hostilities.

The revelation of the magnitude and effectiveness of the Nazis' program of genocide as the "final solution of the Jewish problem" came as a terrible, but not a paralyzing, blow to the American Jewish community. Quickly recovering from the initial shock, the community marshaled its energies and resources to assume the tasks it perceived as having been thrust upon it by historical destiny: relief of the "brand plucked from the fire," the remnant of European Jews who had somehow survived the Holocaust and now found themselves transformed from the miserable status of inhabitants of Nazi concentration camps into a hardly more enviable position—inmates of displaced persons camps; support for the intensive struggle of the *Yishuv*, the Jews resident in Palestine, to establish a sovereign and independent Jewish state that would exercise complete control over its own immigration policies and serve as a place of refuge not merely for displaced persons but for Jews anywhere suffering persecution; and acceptance of its responsibility, as henceforth the most numerous, prosperous, and secure Jewry in the world, to assume the burden of maintaining and advancing Jewish religious life and learning that had been borne for centuries chiefly by the now decimated communities of central and eastern Europe.

Certain social and economic developments that had been proceeding for some time and had achieved their culmination in the postwar period facilitated the undertaking of these tasks. By 1945 American Jewry was well on the way to becoming fairly homogenized in its social composition. Large-scale immigration from Europe had ceased more than two decades earlier. The now mainly native-born children and grandchildren of the immigrants from eastern Europe of the period 1881-1924 had become quite Americanized; the social, cultural, and economic distinctions that once sharply separated Jews of east European origin from the descendants of the German-Jewish immigrants who had arrived a generation or two earlier were becoming ever more blurred. To be sure, there were still social classes, based primarily on degrees of wealth, within the Jewish community. Furthermore, a considerable number of Jews continued to earn their living through manual labor and other lower-income occupations, especially in New York and other large cities. Increasingly, however, Jews were gravitating toward business and the professions and enjoying a rising level of prosperity that, before long, was to place them, as a group, among the most affluent elements of the entire population. At a time when not only a cohesiveness and sense of unity deriving from a large measure of social homogeneity but huge sums of money as well were to be required of them, American Jews were in a position to respond with both.

In the realm of religious belief and practice nothing approaching a comparable degree of homogenization had developed. Strong differences of opinion on numerous issues persisted among those who identified themselves as Orthodox, Conservative, Reform, Reconstructionist, or secularist Jews. Nevertheless, the mutual rancor and hostility that had once generally characterized the attitudes toward one another of the adherents of the various religious (and anti or nonreligious) ideologies had subsided to a marked extent. More tolerant moods were coming to the fore, except among the extremists at either end of the religious spectrum—the ultra-Orthodox and the ultra-Reform. When a group of rabbis representing the former assembled in New York City in 1945 to pronounce a *herem*, or religious ban, against the recently issued Reconstructionist prayerbook and to consign it to the flames, their act was widely condemned as a reversion to outmoded and pernicious attitudes and regarded with revulsion even by a great many Orthodox Jews.

Most importantly, on the issue that was obviously of greatest consequence at the moment, namely, the religious legitimacy of Zionism and the desirability of establishing a Jewish state in Palestine, virtual unanimity had now been achieved, with only the extremists declining to abandon their doctrinaire opposition. The Conservative movement, almost from its inception, had been practically unanimous in championing the Zionist cause. As for Orthodoxy, its followers initially remained aloof from Zionism, clinging to the traditional view that human activity toward the restoration of an independent Jewish state constituted an impious "forcing" of the messianic consummation that ought properly to be left in God's hands. Over the years, however, growing numbers of Orthodox Jews in America had come to either join or give their tacit support to *Mizrahi*, the religious Zionist organization that had been founded in 1902 by the eminent Lithuanian Rabbi Isaac Jacob Reines. *Mizrahi* approved Zionist activism on the condition that the state ultimately to be established would be organized on a religious foundation and governed by *halachah*, the corpus of traditional Jewish law. By 1945 only far right-wing Orthodox Jewry persisted in refusing to give any sanction whatever to human efforts to build a Jewish commonwealth in Palestine.

American Reform Judaism, too, had been generally opposed to Zionism. The great majority of its adherents perceived in the movement organized by Theodor Herzl a denial of Reform's long-held conviction that Jews constitute not an *ethnos*, or people, but a religious community only. Moreover, they regarded Jewish nationalism as an unnecessary abandonment of Reform Judaism's cherished universalism and of the doctrine, inherited from its nineteenth-century German founders, that the worldwide dispersion of the Jews was an act of divine providence in furtherance of the "mission of Israel" to bring knowledge of God to all mankind. These theories, however, could not withstand the forces of historical reality. Under the impact of Hitler's attack on German Jewry immediately after his rise to power in 1933 they had to crumble. Zionism had never been without ardent defenders in the American Reform rabbinate; indeed, such eminent Reform rabbis as Stephen S. Wise and Abba Hillel Silver were among the foremost leaders of the world Zionist movement. By 1937 the majority of their colleagues had become persuaded that anti-Zionism was no longer defensible and that on humanitarian grounds alone, if on no other, the creation of a Jewish state as a haven for persecuted Jews was a moral imperative.

In that year the national Reform rabbinical association, the Central Conference of American Rabbis, adopted a new set of guiding principles that came to be known as the Columbus Platform. Among its major points was the following: "In the rehabilitation of Palestine, the land hallowed by memories and hopes, we behold the promise of renewed life for many of our brethren. We affirm the obligation of all Jewry to aid in its upbuilding as a Jewish homeland by endeavoring to make it not only a refuge for the oppressed but also a center of Jewish culture and spiritual life." Five years later, in 1942, Zionist sentiment had become so strong in its ranks that the American Reform rabbinate adopted a resolution favoring the organization of a Palestinian Jewish army. By 1945 the overwhelming majority of Reform Jews in the United States, not only in the rabbinate but among the laity, were advocates of the immediate establishment of a Jewish state. Only a numerically insignificant group of rabbis and laymen, banded together in the American Council for Judaism, persevered in espousing an embittered and implacable opposition to Zionism.

Thus, at the end of World War II virtually all American Jews, whatever their particular religious (or nonreligious) identification may have been, were united in their determination to support the *Yishuv* in its efforts to create a sovereign state in Palestine as quickly as possible. This determination was strengthened by the realization that the majority of the survivors of the Holocaust, many of whom continued to languish in various displaced persons camps in Europe for months and—in some cases—years, had set their hearts on joining their Jewish brethren in Palestine and would not hear of being resettled anywhere else, although ultimately a considerable number came to the United States. Hence, the relief of these survivors, prevented from realizing their desire by the adamant refusal of the British government (which still held mandatory power over Palestine and persisted in its prewar policy of placating the Arab population of the country) to open its doors to Jewish immigration, and the struggle for the establishment of an independent state were merged into a single cause, one which American Jewry made its own and to which it devoted itself with enormous energy and enthusiasm.

The sums of money contributed to this cause by the Jews of the United States reached unprecedented levels. In 1946 the United Jewish Appeal, the joint fund-raising instrument for rescuing and rehabilitating needy Jews overseas and for aiding the Zionist struggle, collected $101 million. In 1947 $117 million was raised, and in 1948, the year in which the State of Israel was proclaimed, $148 million. Formal affiliation with Zionist institutions also increased dramatically. The membership of the Zionist Organization of America grew from somewhat less than 50,000 in 1940 to 225,000 in 1948, and in the same period the membership of Hadassah, the women's Zionist organization of America, more than tripled. American Zionist leaders, foremost among them Rabbi Abba Hillel Silver, played a major role in fashioning world Zionist policy and in rallying support for the creation of an independent Jewish commonwealth not only in the United States Congress but among the representatives of the recently established United Nations as well. Several thousand Jewish volunteers from the United States and Canada served on the "illegal" ships that sailed across the Mediterranean from European ports to Palestine in attempts to smuggle Jewish refugees into the country past British patrols. Many of them also fought in the 1948-49 War of Independence that broke out immediately after the proclamation of the State of Israel.

After reaching a peak of intensity in the period 1947-50, American Jewry's interest in the Jewish state leveled off. But it did not, by any means, cease. It may have declined somewhat when Israel seemed secure, but it could be counted on, as we shall see, to manifest itself with renewed vitality and even greater power in the years to come whenever Israel was confronted with a threat to its existence. From the day of its birth to the present moment, the State of Israel has continued to be among the central concerns of the American Jewish community.

Even at its peak, the preoccupation of American Jews with bringing relief to the survivors of the Holocaust and with lending maximum assistance to the struggle for the creation of a Jewish state was not so all-engrossing as to preclude involvement in the third of the major tasks noted above—the maintenance of, and infusion of new vigor into, American Jewish religious life and learning. Indeed, very soon after the end of the war, the Jewish community of the United States showed signs of being caught up in what has since frequently been referred to as a "revival" of Judaism.

Judaism, that is, Jewish religion and its institutional embodiments, had not been in particularly vibrant health in the decades preceding the war. Only a minority of Jews maintained even so much as nominal affiliation with a synagogue, whether Orthodox, Conservative, or Reform, and even fewer participated regularly in the traditional religious disciplines of worship, Torah study, and ritual observance. Secularism appeared to be the dominant mood of the time. In fact, a good many Jews who were themselves alienated from the synagogue and convinced that Judaism (like all religions) was in a state of irreversible decline but who, nonetheless, felt a strong commitment to the preservation of the Jewish people had been advocating various secular substitutes for Judaism— for example, Yiddish or Hebrew culture, Jewish nationalism or socialism—as the only possible substance of an enduringly viable Jewish life in America.

The period immediately following the war witnessed a dramatic reversal of this attitude. The proponents of the various forms of Jewish secularism suddenly found themselves virtually bereft of any following and were forced to concede that their programs no longer appeared to have any relevance or attractive power. At the same time Judaism, long neglected and scorned, enjoyed an accession of extraordinary strength. This revival manifested itself chiefly in the following phenomena: a very substantial increase in the number of synagogues and of families affiliated with them; a similarly substantial rise in the number of children receiving some form of Jewish education, especially the intensive form provided by the rapidly expanding day school movement; a reappropriation of ceremonial observance, to a greater or lesser degree, among many families that had either abandoned it altogether or had never engaged in it, and, finally, something hitherto practically unknown in the history of American Jewry—the publication, and the reading by a significant body of adult Jews, of serious works on Jewish religious thought. Each of these phenomena deserves brief discussion.

Soon after the end of the war a massive relocation of the Jewish population of the United States began. Hundreds of thousands of families abandoned the aging and crowded neighborhoods of the large cities in which they had been concentrated and moved to the suburbs. Some urban centers, such as Cleveland, Detroit, Washington, and Newark, saw practically all of their Jewish population resettle in suburban outskirts. A considerable number of congregations that had long been established in the central city realized that if they were to survive they would have to follow their constituencies, relocate in a suburban area, and construct new synagogue buildings there. More than a few of the congregations that acted upon this realization quickly found their membership rosters swelling; twofold and even threefold increases were not uncommon. In addition, hundreds of new congregations were founded, mainly in suburbia, and many of these soon grew to substantial size.

The Conservative movement, which in 1937 had claimed only some 250 congregations and approximately 75,000 affiliated families, reported in 1956 that the total of its congregations had more than doubled and the number of families holding membership in them had come close to tripling. The Reform movement claimed that it had grown in the same period from somewhat less than 300 congregations with a total of about 50,000 member families to 520 congregations with over 250,000 families. Some of the Jews joining Conservative and Reform congregations in the decade after the war came from Orthodox synagogues, but far more had not previously been identified with any religious institution. Furthermore, whatever losses Orthodoxy sustained were compensated to a significant degree by new recruits into its ranks from the several hundred thousand European Jews, most of them traditionally minded and religiously observant (in fact, a sizable segment of them were Hasidim), who immigrated to the United States in the years immediately preceding and following the war. Far from being fated progressively to diminish in strength and ultimately to lose its followers entirely to the less traditional branches of Judaism, as many observers had predicted, Orthodoxy proved very much alive and flourishing. Not only did it participate fully in the postwar religious revival, but it continues to manifest extraordinary vigor to the present day. Indeed, there are grounds for believing, as some of its protagonists urge, that it may, in the long run, turn out to be more durable than its liberal rivals on the American Jewish scene.

Paralleling the large growth in synagogue affiliation was an increase in the number of children receiving one or another form of religious education. Jewish school enrollment rose from 268,000 in 1950 to a peak of 589,000 in 1962. This rise was due, in part, to the postwar "baby boom," but perhaps a more important factor was the desire of Jewish parents, in unprecedented numbers, to provide their children with at least a minimal exposure to religious tradition—an exposure which a good many of the parents had themselves never experienced in their own youth. That most parents were content with giving their offspring a rather limited and superficial education in Judaism is attested by the fact that more than half the children attending Jewish schools during the period indicated were in Sunday schools meeting only once a week for no more than two or three hours. However, a considerable number of students, estimated at approximately a third of the total enrolled, were attending weekday afternoon communal or congregational (mostly Conservative) schools, where they received from six to ten hours of instruction per week. Not surprisingly, the most intense concern for Jewish education was manifested within Orthodoxy. Orthodox rabbis and lay leaders were the chief promoters of the Jewish day school, in which roughly equal amounts of time are alloted in the curriculum to Jewish and general studies. Since 1945 Orthodox day schools have enjoyed a phenomenal growth. Long after other types of Jewish schools reached a peak in enrollment and began to decline, these schools have continued to expand. By 1977 there were more than 450 in the United States, claiming a total of more than 90,000 students. Conservative Judaism began to establish its own day schools in the early 1950s; presently there are about sixty Solomon Schechter Schools functioning under Conservative auspices. Within the last few years even Reform congregations have founded a handful of day schools.

The postwar upsurge in synagogue membership and religious school enrollment was accompanied by a perceptible rise in personal religious observance. Although the great mass of previously non-practicing American Jews did not suddenly begin to observe the Sabbath in the way prescribed by tradition or to follow the dietary laws in all their details, in more than a few homes which had formerly been completely devoid of religious practice a certain minimal standard of observance did emerge. Frequently under the prodding of their children, who had been taught Jewish customs and ceremonies and indoctrinated with a sense of their importance in the religious schools to which they were being sent, parents began to do such things as light candles regularly on Friday evening, attend an occasional Sabbath worship service, and observe the major Jewish holy days by staying away from work and going to the synagogue. In other families a similar pattern was adopted without any special pressure from the side of its juvenile members. Even in Reform Judaism, which had long minimized the importance of ritual, there was a revival of interest in *halachah*, and a number of rabbis published "guides" for ceremonial observance that were based to a greater or lesser degree on traditional Jewish law. Certainly no large-scale renaissance of intense personal piety occurred among the non-Orthodox sectors of the American Jewish community, but there was a definite rise in the degree of religious observance.

Concomitant with this rise was the development of an interest in Jewish religious thought on the part of a small but growing number of adult Jews other than rabbis and scholars. Heretofore very few American Jewish thinkers (Mordecai Kaplan, the founder of Reconstruction, was a notable exception) had made an effort to grapple with the problems of Jewish faith in the modern, secular world or to write on Jewish theology. Undoubtedly they sensed there was little, if any, concern with theological issues among the generality of Jews or—for that matter—even among the intellectual elite. Beginning in the early 1950s, however, a series of books that marked a new era in American Jewish religious thought appeared. Will Herberg's *Judaism and Modern Man* (1951) and Abraham Joshua Heschel's *Man Is Not Alone* (1951) and *God in Search of Man* (1956) were perhaps the most original and influential of these works. The fact that they sold quite well and went into several printings indicated that a certain readership for such books had come into existence. In the years following this readership increased slowly but steadily; its interest was fed by a considerable number of serious and important works for laymen written by other theologians and philosophers.

How to account for the postwar revival of Judaism, whose chief manifestations have been sketched here? A plausible sociological explanation is offered by Nathan Glazer in his *American Judaism* (Chicago: University of Chicago Press, 1957; second, revised edition, 1972). According to Glazer, the revival was due primarily to the wholesale migration of Jews to the suburbs and their consequent tendency to conform to the set of values and attitudes, conveniently grouped under the heading of "respectability," espoused by their non-Jewish neighbors. Since, as a result of the general religious revival taking place in the United States, church membership and attendance were prominent elements in the life-style of the typical middle-class Protestant and Catholic suburbanite, Jews, many of whom had previously identified themselves mainly—if not solely—in ethnic or secularist terms, now felt compelled to join synagogues and attend worship services, at least occasionally. Furthermore, Jewish children in suburbia found themselves in constant contact, in school and at play, with non-Jewish children. Under these circumstances questions such as Why am I a Jew?, or What does it mean to be Jewish?, or What are Jews supposed to believe and do? were bound to arise. Incapable of dealing with these questions themselves either because they had received no Jewish education or only a kind that had not prepared them to give adequate answers, many parents were glad to send their children to Sunday and weekday afternoon schools where, they hoped, the youngsters would learn why they were Jews and come to have positive feelings about their Jewishness.

The factors emphasized by Glazer no doubt contributed significantly to the revival of Judaism, especially to the phenomena of burgeoning synagogue membership and school enrollment. But they do not seem fully to account even for these, much less for the phenomena of intensified personal religious observance and the awakening of interest in questions of Jewish theology. More widely invoked as explanations for the revival in all its manifestations have been the impact on American Jewry of the creation of the State of Israel and of the Holocaust. What shall we say to these explanations?

The cause of bringing into being a Jewish state in Palestine, as noted above, powerfully engaged the sympathies and energies of American Jewry at large in the years immediately following the war. The Zionism so eagerly embraced at the time was based, in most cases, on humanitarian considerations—providing a haven for homeless and persecuted Jews. But a good deal of rhetoric was also heard in certain Zionist circles about the great revitalization of Jewish religious life throughout the world that could be expected to occur as a direct result of the establishment of a Jewish state in which Judaism was the dominant religion. This expectation, however, proved largely illusory. Judaism in Israel, it quickly became apparent, was essentially only a rather rigid Orthodoxy practiced by a minority of the population and rejected, either with indifference or hostility, by the majority of the Jews living there. There was little, if anything, new or exciting that such a Judaism could teach American Jews, whether Orthodox, Conservative, or Reform, nor did it seem to have much capacity to inspire emulation, especially among the non-Orthodox. Nevertheless, the creation of the Jewish state did exercise a definite and specifiable influence on American Judaism. Thus, for instance, many Conservative and Reform congregations, and even some Orthodox, eventually adopted the Israeli pronunciation of Hebrew and popular Israeli songs and melodies both in their religious schools and in their worship services. More significantly, Israelis who emigrated to the United States (and a substantial number did) came to constitute a large segment of the teachers of Hebrew in American Jewish schools, which were never able to muster a sufficient number of natively trained Hebrew teachers. Of even greater importance, it may justifiably be argued, the very existence of the Jewish state, with its triumphs and achievements, instilled a large measure of pride in American Jews, as well as in Jews throughout the Diaspora, and strengthened their resolve to remain Jewish—a point of obvious and far-reaching religious significance.

If Israel contributed substantially to the revival in American Jewry—and it appears rather perverse to deny that it did—its contribution was matched, I believe, by the impact of the Holocaust. Strangely, the Holocaust was not, in the late 1940s and during the 1950s, a topic of widespread and intensive discussion among Jews in the United States; it became so only in the 1960s, after the enormous amount of publicity accompanying the trial and execution of Nazi mass murderer Adolf Eichmann by the Israeli government in 1961. The immediate reaction to the Holocaust, on the part of both the majority of the survivors who experienced it directly and the mass of American Jews who had only secondhand knowledge of its horrors through the reports of witnesses, seems to have been an attempt to repress it, to expunge it from conscious memory. The murder of six million Jews was an event of such incomprehensible barbarity and still of such recent occurrence that it apparently constituted something too frightful to keep deliberately in mind or to remain a subject of sustained reflection and discussion.

However, the Holocaust undoubtedly lived in the subconscious of the Jews, continuing to exercise enormous power. Personally I am persuaded that, even while suppressed, it contributed to drawing many Jews to a renewed affirmation of Judaism at the same time that it made the God of traditional Jewish theism totally untenable for others. The subconscious "reasoning" of the former group, one may conjecture, is likely to have been something like the following: Hitler's plan to exterminate the Jews achieved a large measure of success; even though the Nazi dictator was finally defeated, he managed in a few years to destroy more than a third of all the Jews in the world. Had not my parents or grandparents decided to leave Europe and emigrate to the United States when they did, I might well have been one of his victims. Since, by an accident of fate, I am one of the survivors, have I not an obligation both to the martyrs who perished and to my fellow Jews who remain alive to do all I can to make sure that the diabolical purpose Hitler conceived is not ultimately realized? Is it not my duty to frustrate his intention of wiping Jews and Judaism completely off the face of the earth and to contribute as much as I personally can to the survival of the Jewish people? And how better to do this than by affirming, and incorporating into my life to the maximum extent possible for me, that which has unquestionably been the major force in keeping my people alive—its religious faith and way of life?

The large-scale resettlement of the Jewish population in suburbia, the enthusiasm generated by the phenomenon of an independent Jewish state reborn after a hiatus of nineteen hundred years, the trauma of the

Holocaust and the soul-searching it engendered both consciously and subconsciously—all these factors contributed to the postwar revival of Judaism in America. Historians will probably continue to differ as to their relative weight and importance. There will also, no doubt, be conflicting views even regarding the very authenticity of the revival— whether it was fundamentally a genuinely religious phenomenon (as I believe) or mainly the response of Jews to a felt constraint to relocate themselves in an American society of the late 1940s and the 1950s which had come to prefer a religious over an ethnic-secularist identification on the part of its various components. Be that as it may, by the early 1960s it was clear that the revival itself, as far as its overt manifestations are concerned, showed unmistakable signs of having reached a peak and had already begun to fade. The continuous growth in synagogue membership then came to an end, although perhaps close to half the Jews of the United States still remained unaffiliated. Enrollment in Jewish schools reached its highest point in 1962, when, as was noted previously, 589,000 pupils were reported; four years later the number had declined to 554,000, and only the Orthodox and Conservative day schools showed continued growth. Interest in Israel and concern for its security and welfare remained generally high, fanned by the unremitting hostility of its Arab neighbors and their frequent terrorist raids into its territory. Nevertheless, the initial excitement over the Jewish state had been waning for some years; to many Jews the existence of Israel was increasingly becoming a routine fact, and the threats to it did not seem terribly serious.

By and large, American Jewry in the first half of the 1960s constituted a community at ease with itself and troubled by no great anxiety over its future. Racist anti-Semitism had been at a low ebb for some years, and few expected it to erupt again with any degree of intensity. Considerable progress also had been made in promoting an atmosphere of goodwill and mutual toleration among the adherents of the different religious faiths in the United States. Judaism was now generally accorded the status of the "third religion of America," along with Protestantism and Roman Catholicism. In 1965 there was exhilaration in certain Jewish circles over the adoption, after several years of deliberation and much behind-the-scenes maneuvering, of the new declaration by Vatican Council II on the relation of the Catholic Church to the Jews that seemed to offer "absolution" from the charge of "deicide," an absurd accusation that had nevertheless caused an incalculable amount of Jewish suffering over the centuries. While some Jews saw no particular reason for exulting at the cautiously worded and carefully limited declaration that the crucifixion of Jesus "cannot be charged against all Jews then alive, nor against Jews of today" and that the Church "decries hatred, persecution, displays of anti-Semitism, directed against Jews at any time and by anyone," others hailed it as the beginning of a golden new era of fruitful interreligious dialogue and mutual appreciation of each other's faith on the part of Christians and Jews.

Themselves enjoying a rising level of prosperity and generally unencumbered by serious apprehension over their own position in American society, many Jews—mainly secularist liberals, but also a considerable number belonging to congregations in the Reform movement whose leadership had come to stress activity for the promotion of social justice as one of the central pillars of Judaism—threw themselves in the later 1950s and early 1960s, along with non-Jewish liberals, into the cause of securing greater opportunities for disadvantaged elements of the population, especially Negroes (who soon made it clear that they preferred the designation "blacks"). Both adult Jews and Jewish college and university students participated in the civil rights movement in numbers altogether out of proportion to their representation in the total population. By the later 1960s the older and younger generations of Jews concerned with social activism also found themselves united in a common and passionate opposition to America's involvement in the Vietnam War.

By that time, however, these generations discovered that they were also drifting apart, even in the form and substance of their activism. The older Jews generally continued to operate within the framework of traditional liberalism, emphasizing such methods as nonviolent protests and demonstrations, attempts to persuade political leaders of the irrationality or immorality of their policies, efforts to effect change in public opinion or to influence voting decisions, and the like. But a certain segment of the younger generation, especially students on the elite college and university campuses, scorned such tactics and proceeded to organize radical groups based on the revolutionary doctrines of Marx, Lenin, Trotsky, Stalin, and even Mao Tse-tung. These groups were not at all averse to violence; they preached the necessity of a complete destruction and rebuilding of American society, which, in their view, was repressive, exploitative, and imperialistic. The various radical groups were loosely associated in a movement that styled itself "New Left" but was, in fact, nurtured by a resurrected collection of old and well-known revolutionary ideas. In denouncing America, more than a few of the New Left's non-Jewish members also denounced its so-called client states, notably Israel, as "agents of American imperialism." This was especially true of black militants, who tended to side with the Arab nations against Israel. Jewish students, who constituted a considerable part of the total membership of the New Left, did not demur to any perceptible degree; many even joined in the denunciations.

In the spring of 1967, however, an event occurred that was to have an enormous emotional effect on virtually all of American Jewry, including many of the radical and revolutionary-minded of its youth, among whom it was to produce a particularly striking reversal of attitudes. This was the trauma preceding and following the Six-Day War in the Middle East. As the armies of Egypt and other Arab countries, massively equipped by the Soviet Union with the most advanced and lethal weapons, prepared for war on Israel, it seemed to most observers that the very existence of the Jewish state was now hanging in the balance and that it was more than likely to sustain a crushing defeat. Israel, it was obvious, was isolated and alone in a world that manifested either indifference or hostility. The governments of the Western powers that it had regarded as its friends for years—the United States, Great Britain, and France—were standing neutral and aloof, while Russia was providing unlimited support to its enemies, whose declared intention was to drive all Israelis into the sea.

American Jews, sensitized in the preceding years by the Nazi Holocaust, asked themselves agonized questions: Was another Holocaust now impending? Were Israel and its Jewish population doomed to annihilation? Would the world at large look on with the same equanimity as it had a generation before toward Hitler's murderous onslaught against European Jewry? There was a great upsurge of deeply felt anxiety among Jews not only in the United States but all over the world in the terrible weeks before the outbreak of the war. Simultaneously there was also a determination that this time, at least, they themselves would not rightly be charged with apathy or inactivity. Thousands of American Jewish students made persistent attempts to fly to Israel at once, either to fight in the army or to assume the jobs of Israelis called to military duty. The older generation, among them some who had heretofore been negative or indifferent to Israel, responded with unparalleled contributions of funds to the United Jewish Appeal and purchases of Israel bonds.

The unexpected, lightning-like victory of the Israeli armed forces in the Six-Day War in June 1967 immediately transformed the anxiety of American Jewry into grateful rejoicing. But the joy was quickly marred by the realization that, in the wake of Israel's triumph, many Americans, not merely the young radicals of the New Left, had become Arab sympathizers. During the weeks when it appeared that Israel might be overwhelmed, the silence of the clergy, especially the liberal Protestant clergy, was almost total, despite the "interreligious dialogue" that had been carried on for some years between the clergy and American rabbis. Now, when the defeated Arabs had become the "underdogs," they evoked fervent expressions of commiseration and repeated condemnations of Israeli "militarism" from ecclesiastical circles. Many others joined the chorus of the clergy, although it is likely that the majority of

Americans remained more favorably disposed to Israel than to the Arab states.

Parenthetically, when the bitterly fought Yom Kippur War broke out six years later in October 1973, probably the majority of Americans again supported Israel. Furthermore, this time the United States government soon compensated for the Soviet Union's wholesale supply of airplanes and tanks to the Arabs by a large airlift of military equipment to Israel. Nevertheless, it was clear that many Americans were more exercised about the possibility of a reduction in Arab oil shipments to the United States than about the survival of Israel. Once again it seemed to American Jews that, except for the United States government (whose support might also eventually be eroded), the Jewish state could confidently rely on no resources other than its own and the aid of world Jewry in its struggle for continued existence. Perceiving the situation in this way, they responded with support, both personal and financial, in even greater measure than six years previously.

The year 1967, it has been urged (and, I believe, properly so), must be regarded as a turning point in the recent history of the American Jewish community. The imminent threat to Israel's survival that suddenly erupted in that year gave the masses of American Jews a renewed awareness of how much they really cared about the fate of their brethren in that little state created through so much toil and sacrifice. Whatever other causes in which they may have invested their energies, none, it became clear, meant so much as this one. It is probably no exaggeration to say that American Jews saw in the threat to Israel an indirect, if not immediate, threat to themselves. They appear to have been powerfully gripped by a sense of the shared destiny of the Jewish people worldwide and to have become imbued with an intensified resolve to survive.

These feelings engaged many even among the alienated and indifferent young Jews who had embraced the New Left. Some of these activists continued to spout the movement's line on Israel, but a substantial number of others discovered, frequently to their own surprise, that their latent Jewishness was too strong to permit them to do so. Soon after the Six-Day War a large gathering of radical groups connected with the New Left met in Chicago in a Convention for a New Politics. When the black militants in attendance managed to push through a resolution condemning the "Zionist imperialist war," many Jewish leftists found that they could not stomach this and left the convention in angry protest.

Some of the erstwhile Jewish leftists even joined other Jewish students, who had previously been largely indifferent to both radical politics and Israel, in forming new Zionist societies on college and university campuses. These societies tended to call themselves, in the accepted fashion of the youth counter-culture, "radical" or "liberation" movements. A considerable number of these societies carried their Zionist convictions to their logical conclusion and proceeded to make *aliyah* to Israel. Between July 1967 and January 1971 more than 17,000 American Jews, most of them young, emigrated to Israel.

Borrowing a leaf from the black militants, who had been subjecting college and university administrations to intense pressure to introduce Black Studies into the curriculum, many Jewish students also began pushing for the introduction of Jewish Studies—particularly courses in Hebrew, Yiddish, and Jewish history. Prior to the 1960s only a relatively few of the more prestigious universities in the United States had offered courses in Judaica. In the years after 1967 the number of colleges and universities doing so multiplied dramatically. By 1975 more than 300 American institutions of higher learning had inaugurated more or less extensive programs in Jewish Studies, and students by the tens of thousands were taking advantage of the new offerings. This phenomenon was not merely the result of Jewish imitation of the new ethnic consciousness and pride that had come to dominate the black community; it was also the result of a genuine desire on the part of many Jewish students, aware of the total inadequacy of their prior Jewish education, to reappropriate more of their Jewish cultural and religious heritage.

In the period following the Six-Day War a sizable group of young American Jews emerged who took up as their major causes the survival and welfare of the State of Israel, the alleviation of the plight of the more than 2 million Jews living in the Soviet Union and particularly the fostering of their right to emigrate from the country whose regime continued to subject them to prejudice and discrimination, and the strengthening of the debilitated condition of the American Jewish community. With regard to the last of these causes, their diagnosis of the chief ills affecting the community included the superficiality of Jewish education to which, they contended, neither sufficient attention nor funds were being devoted; the misplacement of priorities on the part of Jewish community federations which, they argued, had been lavishing money on such peripherally significant institutions as "Jewish" hospitals while starving vital Jewish cultural and educational enterprises; and the impersonality and preoccupation with the organizational efficiency and success of the American synagogue which, with rare exceptions, had failed to create any genuine sense of community among its members.

In protest against the impersonality of the synagogue and its failure to develop a feeling of community, some young Jews in recent years have established *havurot*, or Jewish "fellowships," on university campuses and in the larger cities for the purpose of providing themselves with an opportunity to live together in a kind of commune and to participate in a shared quest for a deeper knowledge of Jewish tradition and an inten-

sified self-awareness as Jews. A few large synagogues have also attempted to develop within their organizational structure *havurot* consisting of
small groups of individuals and families with common interests that
meet regularly to study together, pray together (at times in new liturgical
forms which they have themselves created), and to celebrate the Jewish
festivals. Some of the original *havurot* have already dissolved, but others
continue to flourish. What their long-range capacity for endurance and
effectiveness may be is difficult to predict, but that their fundamental
purpose is to promote among their members a more meaningful experience of Judaism is not to be questioned.

In recent years also some younger Jewish women, no doubt influenced
by the general Women's Liberation movement, have been pressing for
equalization of religious rights and for an amelioration of the second-
class status implicitly accorded them by certain aspects of traditional
Jewish law. Little pressure of this kind has been exerted in Orthodox
circles. Some years ago, however, the Conservative movement granted
women the right in principle to participate in the conduct of public
worship in the synagogue, especially the right to be given an *aliyah*, that
is, a summons to the reading of the Torah. More recently, the Conservative Rabbinical Assembly's Committee on Jewish Law gave official sanction to the counting of women toward the *minyan*, the minimum of ten
adult persons required for the holding of a public worship service. Each
Conservative congregation is autonomous, free to accept or reject the
national organization's recommendations in these matters.

A sizable segment of the Conservative rabbinate and laity has also
been urging the ordination of women as rabbis, but to date the majority
of the faculty of the Jewish Theological Seminary, which in general is far
more tradition-minded than the congregational rabbinate, has success-
fully resisted the admission of female applicants to its rabbinic training
program. The Reform Hebrew Union College-Jewish Institute of Religion, despite the fact that Reform Judaism proclaimed the complete
religious equality of women more than a century ago, ordained its first
female rabbi only a few years ago. At the time of this writing more than
ten women have been ordained by the Reform seminary as well as by the
Reconstructionist Rabbinical Seminary of Philadelphia. In the years
ahead a far larger proportion of women seems likely to be ordained by
both these schools. However, signs are emerging that even the most
liberal congregations are not quite comfortable with the idea of having
women in their pulpits; female rabbis will probably not achieve total
acceptance for a long time.

Perhaps the central fact about American Jewry in the 1970s is its
general determination that Jewry and Judaism will survive—a determination that may now be even stronger and more widespread than in the

period immediately after World War II. This is no doubt due, in considerable measure, to the revived sense of ethnicity and the resurrected notion of "cultural pluralism" presently riding the crest of the wave of popularity in the United States at large, and not merely to the traumas of the Six-Day War of 1967 and the Yom Kippur War of 1973. That American Jewry has been redirecting its energies from a universalist concern with the general social problems of the nation and the world to a particularist concern with issues affecting its own welfare and survival is evidenced by the fact that even that element of the synagogue-affiliated community, Reform Judaism, which, a few years ago, was most active in the struggle for civil rights and in the opposition to America's involvement in the Vietnam War has, of late, largely abandoned the social-action program it pursued in the 1950s and 1960s. It has begun to concentrate on specifically Jewish problems—the maintenance and enhancement of a sense of Jewish identity, the strengthening of Jewish education in the United States, the promotion of the security and interests of Israel, the alleviation of the situation of the Jews in the Soviet Union, and other related issues.

Nevertheless, two major threats to Jewish survival in America are present and appear to be gaining strength. The first is the extremely low birth-rate among Jews and the second is the rising incidence of intermarriage.

Jews currently have the lowest birth rate of any ethnic group in the United States; Jewish families are barely reproducing themselves. Only among Orthodox, and especially Hasidic, Jews is the old tradition of large families maintained. While Zero Population Growth has become a favorite ideal of "environmentalist" and "conservationist" groups in America, for the Jews it poses a serious danger. The Jews of the world have not recouped the enormous losses sustained during the years of the Nazi Holocaust. With a total global population of barely 14 million, they seem to be excellent candidates for being an "endangered species." Given the present general tendency in America to postpone marriage, to begin childbearing and childraising at a later age, and to limit the number of children to one or two per family (all fostered, in part, by the "new consciousness" of the Women's Liberation movement which contends that, to have a meaningful and fulfilled life, a woman must have some career other than that of wife and mother), the Jewish population of America appears likely to decline both in absolute numbers and as a proportion of the general population. Such a result cannot but weaken the position of the Jews and negatively affect both their ethnic and religious viability.

The growing rate of intermarriage points to the same consequence. While a considerable number of the non-Jewish partners in an intermarriage convert to Judaism and many of the children of such marriages are brought up as Jews, it seems likely that large numbers of these children are lost to the Jewish community within a generation or two. The statistical evidence regarding present or recent intermarriages is by no means complete or unambiguous, but the historical evidence is instructive. Hardly any of the descendants of intermarriages that took place in America four or five generations ago are still in the Jewish fold today.

The ongoing acculturation of American Jewry presents still another threat to its survival. Professor Joseph L. Blau of Columbia University recently wrote with great perceptivity: "A small minority, without physical distinction from the majority, increasingly like the majority in language, behavioral traits, education, range of occupational distribution, and other matters making up the complex called 'culture,' can easily disappear into that majority, losing the last remaining shreds of differentiation." From this Blau concludes that only Judaism, that is, loyalty to the Jewish religious tradition, can promote survival, but correctly notes that Judaism and Jewishness, that is, Jewish ethnicity, are inextricably intertwined: "The preservation of Judaism, the last difference, is essential to the survival of the Jews of America. Paradoxically, however, the preservation of the Jewish people as an ethnic minority within the culturally plural setting of the United States is essential to the perpetuation of Judaism within the religiously plural setting of the United States. In ultimate terms, Judaism and Jewishness support and maintain each other." (Blau, *Judaism in America: From Curiosity to Third Faith*, Chicago and London: The University of Chicago Press, 1976, p. 117.)

Jewishness, or Jewish ethnicity, expresses itself at present among American Jews primarily—though certainly not exclusively—in ardent support for Israel. There is a visceral feeling among Jews not only in America but throughout the world that the end of Israel would probably mean their own end as a people. Irving Kristol gave eloquent utterance to this widespread feeling at the time of the Yom Kippur War: "Should Israel be extinguished in a blood bath, it could be the end of 3,000 years of Jewish history. In the course of World War II, two out of every five Jews on this earth were slaughtered for no other reason than that they were Jews. But that holocaust was in part redeemed—was given some meaning—by the astonishing emergence of the State of Israel, a sudden and unanticipated answer to 2,000 years of daily prayer. If that fantastic dream, now realized, should turn into just another Jewish nightmare, a great many Jews are going to conclude—reluctantly but inevitably—that the burden of Jewish history is just too grievous to bequeath to one's descendants, and they will opt out." (Kristol, "Notes on the Yom Kippur War," *The Wall Street Journal*, October 18, 1973.)

Nevertheless, there are still Jews, among the now tattered remnants of the New Left, who are uncompromisingly anti-Israel. And there are several hundred other Jews—among them a good sprinkling of Reform and Conservative rabbis—belonging to an organization called *Breira* (Alternative), established in 1973, who are vociferously critical of Israeli government policy, particularly its administration of the territories occupied in the Six-Day War, its rejection of the establishment of a new Palestinian Arab state on the Jordan, and its refusal to enter into negotiations for a peace treaty with any Arab delegation that includes members of the terrorist Palestinian Liberation Organization which is officially committed to the destruction of the Jewish state. Members of *Breira* note that their positions are echoed by certain Israeli citizens. They also point out that there is far more criticism of Israeli government policy in the Israeli press than in American Jewish newspapers which are largely owned or dominated by the Jewish community federations of the larger cities and are hardly free to express anything but the "establishment" view. On both points they are quite correct. Nevertheless, it may be noted that there is an important difference between the permissibility of criticism of their own government by Israeli citizens who may have to pay with their lives for the policies adopted by this government and the moral legitimacy of criticism by secure and unaffected Jews 6,000 miles away who bear no practical responsibility whatever for their moralistic, gratuitous, and often fatuous counsel of suicide offered to the authorities in Israel. The dissent expressed by *Breira* and other like-minded American Jews is, to a degree, healthy and ought not to be stifled, but its moral irresponsibility, insofar as it may weaken the already precarious position of Israel vis-à-vis its hostile Arab neighbors and the world at large, may not be overlooked.

Despite their worries about the increasing isolation of Israel in the world and the possible withdrawal of support for the Jewish state by the United States government, as well as their continuing concern for the persecuted Jews of the Soviet Union, Syria, and other countries, American Jews face the future with confidence and with a sense of satisfaction over their accomplishments in the period since the end of World War II. It may be appropriate to conclude by summarizing the most important of these.

Even though the religious revival may not have been as intense and spiritually authentic as it seemed at the time, the synagogue has certainly been strengthened and remains the most important institution in American Jewish life. Even Jewish community federations, which sometimes claim hegemony and have been competing with the synagogue for volunteer manpower and funds, recognize that without the loyalty to Judaism fostered by the synagogue their own continued vitality is highly problematic.

Jewish education, while still beset with numerous unsolved problems, has shown a definite improvement in quality. Though much of what is offered in Sunday schools and weekday afternoon schools is incredibly superficial and simplistic, the still-growing day schools are providing a substantial segment of American Jewish youth with an opportunity to acquire a genuine knowledge of the classical sources of Jewish tradition. Some of these schools, to be sure, continue to follow old-fashioned methods of rote learning and heavy-handed indoctrination, but others utilize the most advanced pedagogical techniques in both their general and Jewish studies programs. Increasingly the day schools are receiving generous subventions from the Jewish community federations. Furthermore, some 7,000 young men, it has been estimated, are presently studying in American post-high school *yeshivot*, and a similar number of American-born youths are enrolled in Israeli *yeshivot*. Even Orthodox young women, whose Jewish education was long neglected, are now studying by the thousands in the intensive Beth Jacob and Beth Rivkah schools and teachers' seminaries.

American college and university campuses which, a generation ago, were justifiably characterized as a "Jewish wasteland" are now teeming with Jewish activities—formally accredited courses in Hebrew and Judaica, free Jewish university courses, *havurot*, student-edited Jewish magazines, Zionist societies, groups organized to aid Soviet Jewry, and the like.

In the realm of higher Jewish learning American Jewry is no longer dependent on European-born and European-trained scholars. The recent installation of Rabbi Norman Lamm as the first American-born president of Yeshiva University symbolizes the fact that American Jewry has matured to the point of being able to take full possession of the mantle of Jewish learning left by the destroyed Jewish communities of eastern Europe. Unlike the situation thirty years ago, the faculties of American rabbinical seminaries and university departments of Jewish studies (established more recently) are now dominated by American-born or American-trained teacher-scholars. While Jewish elementary and secondary schools in the United States are still heavily dependent on Israeli emigrants to the United States for Hebrew instruction, it is interesting to note that more than a few chairs of Jewish studies at leading universities in Israel are now occupied by scholars born or trained in America.

In both quality and quantity, the Jewish scholarship produced in the United States within the last generation has been remarkable. Hundreds of books and thousands of articles of high Jewish scholarly value have been published since 1945. To these must be added scores of translations into English of major works originally written in Hebrew, Yiddish, German, and other languages. It is probably safe to venture the guess that more has been produced in the field of American Jewish scholarship in the last generation than in the whole of the three preceding centuries of Jewish settlement. While many of the monographs and essays have been written by scholars merely for reading by other scholars, it is surprising to note how many volumes of authentic learning are accessible to the intelligent Jewish lay leader. Very few books of Jewish scholarship become best sellers, but the fact that even profit-motivated trade publishers issue such works indicates that there is a readership for them outside the academic environment.

That a thirst for Jewish knowledge has been created among the masses of Jews in the United States is attested by the sensational success of *The Jewish Catalog*. Without special fanfare and an all-out advertising and promotion campaign, this admittedly naive and superficial guide to Jewish life and learning has sold almost 250,000 copies in just a few years. *The Second Jewish Catalog* by the same authors, published in 1976, is likely to become even more of a best seller, even though a competent and highly sympathetic reviewer (Rabbi Arnold Jacob Wolf, Jewish chaplain at Yale University) properly characterizes it as "the very apotheosis of the non-book . . . too cute, too ambitious, too pseudo-encyclopedic, too media-intoxicated, too unserious" and then adds, "I loved it . . ." (in a forthcoming review in *The Journal of Reform Judaism*).

One more point must be mentioned. It has already been noted that the very existence of the State of Israel has injected a new élan into the communal activity of American Jewry and instilled a heightened sense of pride in the minds of millions of Jews. While relatively few American Jews have become so wholeheartedly devoted to Israel that they have decided to settle there permanently, hundreds of thousands in recent years have made long or short—and, in some cases, repeated—tours of the country. The quantity of Judaic knowledge and the degree of "Jewish inspiration" derived from this experience naturally run the gamut from the most superficial and trivial to the most thorough and meaningful. But few American Jews have returned from a trip to Israel without some strengthening of their sense of Jewish identity or some intensification of their desire for the survival of the Jewish people.

What of the future? During the thirty-year period under discussion in the present volume American Jewry, by and large, has tended to define itself more in religious than in ethnic-communal terms. But there may be a reversal of this tendency in consequence of certain trends signs of whose emergence may already be discerned. America appears to have entered upon what has frequently been called a "post-Christian era." The attractive power of Roman Catholicism and the main-line Protestant churches seems to be declining; only the more fundamentalist and evangelical churches continue to enjoy vigorous growth. If this trend persists, many American Jews who now identify themselves fundamentally as adherents of the Jewish religion may become more inclined toward a primarily ethnic self-definition, with only the committed Orthodox minority maintaining a strong religious identification. Furthermore, Israel, whose security and welfare presently constitute the substance of the "religion" of a great many American Jews, may strengthen their sense of Jewish identity, but Jewish nationalism, it must surely come to be realized in the end, is largely an *ersatz* Judaism. Jews whose Judaism is expressed exclusively, or almost so, in enthusiasm for the State of Israel may arrive at the recognition that theirs is certainly not the Judaism of the Bible and the Talmud and may, out of considerations of intellectual integrity, redefine themselves in purely secular and ethnic terms. Finally, should there be a serious recrudescence of anti-Semitism in the United States and Canada, it may be that Jewish ethnicity will be strengthened at the expense of Jewish religiosity in reaction to the phenomenon, although it is also possible that Jews may respond with a heightened commitment to traditional Jewish belief and practice.

All specific predictions about the future of the American Jewish community are hazardous, if not foolhardy. But one general conjecture may safely be ventured on the basis of past history: Jews will continue to be a significant part of the American scene in the foreseeable future and manifest a vibrant and fascinating life uniquely their own.

Erich Rosenthal _____

THE JEWISH POPULATION OF THE UNITED STATES: A DEMOGRAPHIC AND SOCIOLOGICAL ANALYSIS

INTRODUCTION

This study is designed to present a description of the Jewish population of the United States in demographic terms. Thus, to the extent that it is possible to discern trends in the rather narrow time span from 1957 to 1970, the size of this population, its regional distribution, secular education, occupations and income, fertility patterns, and age composition will be presented and analyzed.

Since the end of World War II, our knowledge of the demographic structure of the Jewish population of the United States has expanded considerably. This progress has become possible through the application of sampling techniques to the study of human populations. Just as a physician is able to judge the health of his patient from a sample of blood, so the demographer or survey specialist can describe the social characteristics or social attitudes of a total population by studying a sample drawn from the total universe.

DATA SOURCES

PREVIOUS APPROACHES TO THE STUDY OF THE JEWISH POPULATION OF THE UNITED STATES

The progress that has taken place since World War II will become all the more apparent after a brief review of the state of our knowledge about American Jews before 1957, the date of the first sample survey. The United States government has had a long-standing policy of abstaining from inquiring into the religious beliefs or religious backgrounds of its citizens in the decennial population censuses.[1] The United States shares this practice with—among others—Belgium, France, and Great Britain. The USSR, Tunisia, and Rumania enumerate Jews as members of an ethnic group, while Canada gives its Jewish population an opportunity to identify themselves as members of a religious community as well as of an ethnic group.[2]

Repeated efforts to include a question on religion in the United States Census have met strenuous and consistent opposition. The organized Jewish community has always been strongly opposed to the inclusion of such a question in the decennial population census. While the early history of this issue and its attempted partial resolution by including a question on "mother tongue" has been sketched by Goldberg, the controversy surrounding the 1960 census has been recorded by Foster.[3]

Any demographic data published before 1957, including figures concerning the size of the total Jewish population in the United States, were estimates derived from a variety of nongovernmental sources. The local community survey was a favorite tool first developed by the National Jewish Welfare Board and later applied by the Council of Jewish Federations and Welfare Funds, both national philanthropic roof organizations. To generate the information needed for local planning purposes such as the location of community centers, social service agencies, health facilities, synagogues and temples, a variety of techniques were developed. Among the older ones are the "Yom Kippur Absence" method which compares public school attendance before and after this holiday, the utilization of death certificates, and the employment of membership and official voters' lists.[4] More recently, a technique combining membership lists with random sampling proved especially effective.[5] However, none of these methods is capable of yielding national data.

There are three major sources on which this presentation is based. The most important is a 1957 sample survey undertaken by the U.S. Bureau of the Census which included a question on religion.[6] Its significance derives from its being the first such survey ever undertaken and thus being a bench mark for all subsequent surveys.

The second source consists of three sample surveys for 1969, 1971, and 1972, again by the Census Bureau, in which the Jewish population appears in the guise of persons of Russian origin or descent.[7] The third is a 1970-71 sample survey sponsored by the Council of Jewish Federations and Welfare Funds (a private, nonprofit organization) and designed to determine a variety of attributes and attitudes found among American Jews.[8]

In 1957 the U.S. Bureau of the Census included a question on religion in its Monthly Sample Survey. Monthly Sample Surveys differ from decennial population censuses in that replies to questions in sample surveys are voluntary, while the refusal to answer a question in the decennial population census is subject to punishment by a fine. The bureau claims that the 1957 survey was executed with great care and resulted in a high degree of accuracy.

[The 1957 survey] of religious affiliation was part of the Bureau's monthly sample survey. This "Current Population Survey"—as it is officially known—goes back to 1942, has been under constant critical observation and revision, and probably owes its meticulousness to the fact that it is primarily devoted to the collection of data on employment and other important aspects of the labor force—data which can also be used as political weapons. In the end, the accuracy of any survey—whether complete census or sample survey—depends on the interviewer's integrity and his ability to collect the desired data. Hence, the results of a well-conducted sample survey may be more accurate than those of a complete census, since in the first instance it is feasible to pay the price necessary to collect a smaller volume of data with a higher degree of accuracy and to cut down the number of refusals. According to the Census Bureau, refusals to cooperate have averaged only a fraction of one per cent since the inception of the monthly surveys, even though they are conducted on a *voluntary* basis.[9]

Although the 1957 survey is nearly twenty years old, it still commands our attention. It was the first attempt to determine the size and characteristics of the major religious groups in the United States and it thus made possible the study of likenesses and differences between Jews, Protestants, and Catholics.

The ethnic data (Russian origin or descent) are also derived from current population surveys. These samples were taken in November 1969 and in March of 1971 and 1972. The Census Bureau describes the sampling procedures for the 1972 survey as follows:

Most of the data for this report were based on results obtained in the March 1972 Current Population Survey of the Bureau of the Census. The sample was spread over 449 areas comprising 863 counties and independent cities with coverage in each of the 50 States and the District of Columbia. Approximately 47,000 occupied households were eligible for interview each month. Of this number 2,000 occupied units, on the average, were visited but interviews were not obtained because the occupants were not found at home after repeated calls or were unavailable for some other reason. In addition to the 47,000, there were also about 8,000 sample units in an average month which were visited but were found to be vacant or otherwise not to be interviewed.

The estimating procedure used in this survey involved the inflation of the weighted sample results to the independent estimates of the civilian noninstitutional population of the United States by age, race, and sex. The independent estimates were based on statistics from the previous decennial census of population; statistics of births, deaths, immigration and emigration; and statistics on the strength of the Armed Forces.[10]

This study, in its substantive part, also analyzes the demographic characteristics of American Jews in terms of census data for persons of "Russian" origin or descent. This is done because the category "Russian" became a residual one, that is, reserved for Jewish emigrants from the Russian Empire and because at least two-thirds of American Jews trace their origin to Russia. Every demographer who has ever worked with United States Census data for the foreign-born or the native-born of foreign parentage has been forced to recognize that dealing with the category of Russian stock (as the immigrants and their children are technically called) is, in effect, dealing with Jews who had left the Russian Empire between 1870 and 1914.

Because of immigration restrictions by the Tsar and the application of certain statistical categories by U.S. immigration authorities and the U.S. Bureau of the Census, the Russian category became a residual for American Jews. Of course, not all American Jews hail from the territories of the Russian Empire, but at least two-thirds do. Since Jews, like other American religious-ethnic groups, have a tendency to congregate in neighborhoods of their own, these settlements are identified in small-area statistics as census tracts in which Russian stock predominates. To the extent that census tracts are homogeneous in land use, monthly rentals, family size, education, and occupation, it can be assumed that those Jews who are from countries other than Imperial Russia share a variety of characteristics with the latter who form the majority in such tracts.[11]

Under the auspices of the Council of Jewish Federations and Welfare Funds a group of demographers developed a sample design and conducted a survey in 1970 and 1971 aimed at gathering information about the Jewish population of the United States. A preliminary analysis of the "United States National Jewish Population Study" (NJPS) has been published.[12] It appears that fairly complex sampling procedures were applied. In addition to "area probability samples," membership lists of Jewish organizations were utilized, as were lists of so-called distinctive Jewish names. While this sample survey does not yield any comparative data for other religious or ethnic groups, it provides data on the demography of American Jews as well as on religious practices and social psychological matters such as group identification.

OPERATIONAL DEFINITION OF JEWISHNESS

To provide valid statistical data it is necessary to count identical units (persons or things). This is done with the help of an operational definition. An unemployed person, for example, is operationally defined as one who is out of work, seeking work, and able to work.

In its first attempt to delineate the religious composition of the American people in 1957, the Census Bureau asked, What is your religion?, and enumerated this attribute in the same manner in which it collects age, sex, and marital status data. There was no room for being Jewish with an explanation, such as "I don't practice the Jewish religion, but am an ardent Zionist," or "But I support the Yiddish language movement." (The Canadian decennial population census allows Canadian Jews to respond to three separate categories: religion, nationality, and language.)

The U.S. Census Bureau was well aware that the question regarding religion was poor in terms of an operational definition, since it elicited a multidimensional response. In the introductory remarks of the census release we read that "the question did not relate to church membership, attendance at church services or gatherings, or religious belief." While the questionnaire undoubtedly tapped these three major sources of religious affiliation, "many persons," in the words of the bureau, "in addition to those who maintain formal affiliation with a religious organization, associated themselves with such a group and reported its name." In other words, the question elicited a fourth dimension, namely, religious and cultural, or religio-cultural, background.[13]

This lack of precision is well suited to the situation of American Jews whose Jewish identification ranges from practicing the Jewish religion, to ethnicity, to family background. Of course, in many instances these dimensions overlap. Defining who is a Jew gets into the way of such a seemingly simple task as counting the Jewish population of the United States. A fairly valid answer is that a Jew is a person who considers himself to be one, and is treated by others as if he were one. While self-identification does not always coincide with identification by others, it seems (at any rate to me) that in cases where there is such a discrepancy, self-identification should be given greater weight. Since the bureau's question was aimed at eliciting the respondents' own view, the validity of the response cannot be questioned.

The National Jewish Population Study of 1970 (NJPS) employs virtually the same criteria as the 1957 sample survey. The interviewers for the NJPS were told that "For the purpose of the study, anyone is Jewish who says he is Jewish, or of whom it is said that he is Jewish, or who is reported to have a Jewish mother or father."[14] In addition,

A screening section in the interview provided a formal basis for determining whether a person was to be considered Jewish, and whether the household, therefore, was to be included in the study. For eligibility, the respondent had to provide an affirmative reply, for himself and/or for one or more household members, to one or more of the following questions: (1) Was person born Jewish? (2) Is person Jewish now? (3) Was person's father born Jewish? (4) Was person's mother born Jewish? The application of this definition often made possible a rapid determination that the entire household was Jewish—particularly if the replies to all four screening questions were affirmative for all household members—or alternatively, that the household clearly was not Jewish.

A more narrow or halakhic definition would exclude certain households, some of whose members may, however, satisfy sociological (ideological and/or behavioral) definitions of Jewishness.

Given these considerations, the concepts "persons in Jewish households" and "Jewish persons in Jewish households" are clearly not synonymous. The former includes persons who do not meet screening section criteria—as, for example, nonconverted partners in intermarriages—or the criterion of present minimal identification as Jews. [15]

THE FINDINGS

THE SIZE OF THE JEWISH POPULATION IN THE UNITED STATES

How many Jews are there in the United States? The result of the sample survey yielded a total of 5 million Jews in 1957. If children under fourteen years from religiously mixed marriages (one partner Jewish) are excluded, the total is 4,975,000; if included, 5,039,000.

How does this finding from the sample survey compare with existing estimates? The *American Jewish Year Book,* which is the major source for such estimates, states that "The Jewish population of the United States approximated 5,000,000 in the summer of 1955." This estimate is the result of the cumulative total of estimates for the states of the union. According to the compiler of this data, "these estimates are very approximate."[16] How can one explain this striking congruence between the 1955 year book estimate and the 1957 sample survey? In an earlier analysis of this material I strongly suggested that the similarity of the estimates was not due so much to chance as to the sustained effort of conducting increasingly sophisticated *local* Jewish population surveys since the thirties.[17]

It is most interesting to learn that the preliminary analysis of the results of the 1970-1971 National Jewish Population Survey does not present a total figure for the Jewish population of the United States. Apparently, the total was, and is, a most difficult matter. However, in a companion article it is claimed that the "NJPS preliminary evaluation indicates a total of no less than 6,000,000" for 1970-71.[18] A year later, however, Massarik reported that "the total number of Jewish residents in households" was 5,370,000 in 1970, much lower than the "no less than 6,000,000" preliminary figure.[19] The phrase "in households" needs two explanations. Excluded from this total are non-Jews in households with at least one Jewish person. A household is defined as a private household; persons in institutions are not included.

How reasonable is this figure of 5,370,000 for 1970? The size of a population is determined by births, deaths, and migration. In addition, conversion to and from Judaism must also be considered. Data on the conversion of American Jews to Christianity has always been scant. Whatever has come to light gives the impression that conversions are numerically insignificant. From contemporary obituaries and wedding notices one gets the impression that the passage to Christianity is smoothed through intermarriage. It is also known that the recent and current vogue to embrace Far Eastern religions and cults has not by-passed Jewish youth. However, I do not know of any attempt to assess the numerical strength of this current.

Rabbi D. M. Eichhorn in a study published in the 1950s suggests that conversions to Judaism do occur and mainly in the context of a marriage to a Jewish man or woman. Eichhorn, in his survey of Reform and Conservative rabbis, found that from 1,000 to 1,400 conversions to Judaism took place annually between 1948 and 1953.[20] He claimed that the number of conversions was increasing steadily. Assuming 2,000 conversions annually, 28,000 persons must be added to the Jewish population for the years 1957-70. This gain consisted overwhelmingly of women since the ratio of male to female proselytes was one to four among Reform, and one to six among Conservative rabbis. To the extent, however, that these converted women replace Jewish women and keep the latter from marrying Jewish men or marrying at all, the gain, which is small in any case, is rather spurious.

The section on fertility, presented below, confirms earlier findings by myself and Bogue that fertility among American Jews may be at or slightly below the replacement level. In other words, births and deaths cancel each other out.[21]

The impact of immigration to and emigration from the United States cannot be assessed with any degree of accuracy. Reports published in the *American Jewish Year Book* covering the years 1957 through 1968 suggest that an average of 8,000 Jews annually entered the country as immigrants. Since this data was collected by HIAS, the agency to aid Jewish immigrants, the figures are too low, because persons who arrived here unaided may have escaped the statistical net of the agency.

As for emigration from the United States, a personal communication from the Israel Aliyah Center indicates that between 1968 and 1971 an annual average of 5,000 persons were "processed" for emigration to Israel. Assuming a net immigration of 10,000 Jews a year to the United States for the period 1957 through 1970, 140,000 would be added to the 5,000,000 as of 1957 for a total of 5,130,000. This figure is still 240,000 below Massarik's latest downward revision to 5,370,000.

Another way of assessing the revised Massarik estimate of 5,370,000 for 1970 is to compare the growth rate of the white population with that of the Jewish population. According to the *Statistical Abstracts of the United States*, the white population increased by 11.9 percent between 1960 and

1970.[22] Massarik's estimate constitutes a gain of 370,000, or only 7.4 percent since 1957. For the reasons enumerated earlier the growth rate of the Jewish population should be smaller than that of the total white population. Therefore, Massarik's downward revision is a step in the right direction. For the same reasons, I feel that his estimate is still too high and that a figure of 5,200,000 for the year 1970 is more realistic.

REGIONAL AND URBAN DISTRIBUTION

In 1957 the Jewish population constituted 3.2 percent of the population fourteen years old and over. However, as is well known, the Jewish population is not evenly distributed throughout the country. Rather, Jews are heavily concentrated in the Northeast region of the United States. This region consists of: (1) the middle Atlantic states (New York, New Jersey, and Pennsylvania) and (2) New England from Connecticut to Maine. As will be seen from Table 1, 69 percent of the total Jewish

Table 1.   Region of Residence of Persons 14 Years Old and Over by Religion Reported: Civilian Population, March 1957

Percentage Distribution

	RELIGION				
Region	Total, 14 years old and over	Jewish	White Protestant	Roman Catholic	All Other[a]
United States	100.0	100.0	100.0	100.0	100.0
Northeast	26.2	69.1	17.1	46.0	21.6
North Central	29.2	11.9	32.1	28.0	30.0
South	30.6	7.7	35.1	13.9	29.9
West	14.0	11.3	15.8	12.1	18.5

"All Other includes "Other Religion," "No Religion," and "Religion not Reported."

SOURCE: U.S. Bureau of the Census, *Current Population Reports*, "Religion Reported by the Civilian Population of the United States: March 1957," Series P-20, no. 79, Table 2.

population resided in this region. The heaviest concentration was found in the New York-northeastern New Jersey area, where an estimated 52.3 percent of the total Jewish population was located. A further study of Table 1 reveals that Roman Catholics were also concentrated in the

Northeast but not to the same extent as Jews (46.0 percent as compared with 69.1 percent). The North Central region (better known as the Midwest) and the West each had about 11 percent of the total Jewish population, while the remaining 7.7 percent resided in the South.

Has the regional distribution been altered since 1957? Since the preliminary report of the National Jewish Population Survey did not give any information on this topic, we are dependent on estimates of the Jewish population for each state (as published in the *American Jewish Year Book*). We find that some southern and western states have made substantial gains in Jewish population between 1957 and 1971. Most prominent are Florida, California, Arizona, and Colorado.

The most important finding of the 1957 survey is that 96.1 percent of the Jewish population resides in urban areas (Table 2). Since the rural, nonfarm area resembles urban culture more than rural life, we are justified in adding the 3.6 percent found in such areas to the urban popula-

Table 2. Urban-Rural Residence of Persons 14 Years Old and Over by Religion Reported: Civilian Population, March 1957 (Percent)

RESIDENCE	TOTAL POPULATION	WHITE PROTESTANT	ROMAN CATHOLIC	JEWISH
United States	100.0	100.0	100.0	100.0
Total urban	63.9	55.2	78.8	96.1
Urbanized areas of				
250,000 or more	36.6	24.5	53.9	87.4
Other urban	27.3	30.7	24.9	8.7
Rural nonfarm	24.4	30.1	15.8	3.6
Rural farm	11.7	14.7	5.4	0.2

SOURCE: *Current Population Reports*, Series P-20, no. 79, Table 3.

tion. Altogether, then, 99 percent of the Jewish population is urban. It is fair to state, then, that the Jewish population of the United States is an urban population *par excellence*. Table 2 further reveals that Jews are not randomly distributed over small or middle-sized towns, but that 87.4 percent resides in the most highly urbanized areas of 250,000 inhabitants or more. (An urbanized area—according to the Census Bureau's definition—is a central city of 50,000 or more inhabitants with its suburban fringe.) By contrast, only one-fourth of the white Protestants and one-half of the Roman Catholics were found there. As the analysis of the data proceeds, it will become evident that the urban character of the Jewish population has an overriding influence on other social attributes of this group, such as education, occupation and income, and fertility pattern.

SECULAR EDUCATION

The love for secular education, the concern for its quality, is a well-known trait of American Jews. Some observers have interpreted this desire for lengthy exposure to secular learning as an extension of the tradition of religious instruction in Europe. Others have attributed this passion to the need to adapt to an industrial urban society. A third group of analysts has suggested that the embrace of scientific and modern thought was a reaction to the suppression of such knowledge in the *shtetl* of Eastern Europe. Irving Howe has expressed it as follows: "Uneducated, ill-educated, narrowly educated, or educated according to premises that seemed not to bear on American life, the immigrant Jew now wanted to learn at least a fraction of what had long been denied him."[23]

This yearning for education can only be satisfied if there are opportunities, that is, large numbers, great variety, and graduated levels of educational institutions to meet the variety of needs in a democratic society. Compared to Europe before the end of World War II, the United States has offered virtually unlimited educational opportunities. The returns of the 1957 survey show the extent to which American Jews have availed themselves of these opportunities. The educational level of the adult population twenty-five years and over is presented in Table 3. We find that the median number of school years completed is 12.5 years for Jewish men as compared to only 10.9 and 10.3 years for white Protestants and Roman Catholics, respectively. It means that just about half of all Jewish men twenty-five years and over had graduated from high school in 1957. This table also reveals that Jewish men graduate from college to a much greater extent than do white Protestants and Roman Catholics. About one-fourth (26.3 percent) of Jewish men had four or more years of college education; the rest graduated from college or had done postgraduate work, while only 10.5 percent of white Protestants and 8.2 percent of Roman Catholics had had that much formal education.

The educational achievement of Jewish women is even more remarkable, for it must be viewed in the light of the virtual absence of educational facilities for women in Europe in general and in the Jewish culture in particular, reflecting the low status of women. *Kinder, Kirche, Küche* expresses in a phrase the widespread European denial of educational opportunities to young girls and women. This practice in the larger

Table 3. Years of School Completed by Persons 25 Years and
Older, by Religion Reported and Sex, for the United
States: Civilian Population, March 1957

YEARS OF SCHOOL COMPLETED AND SEX	WHITE PROTESTANT		ROMAN CATHOLIC		JEWISH	
	Number	%	*Number*	%	*Number*	%
Male, 25 years and over: *Total*	26,183,000		11,731,000		1,574,000	
School years not reported	336,000		154,000		44,000	
Total	25,847,000	100.0	11,577,000	100.0	1,530,000	100.0
Elementary:						
0 to 7 years	4,897,000	18.9	2,683,000	23.2	231,000	15.1
8 years	5,050,000	19.5	2,212,000	19.1	206,000	13.5
High school:						
1 to 3 years	4,731,000	18.3	2,140,000	18.5	153,000	10.0
4 years	6,283,000	24.3	2,809,000	24.3	339,000	22.2
College:						
1 to 3 years	2,161,000	8.4	778,000	6.7	198,000	12.9
4 years or more	2,725,000	10.5	955,000	8.2	403,000	26.3
Median school years completed	10.9		10.3		12.5	
Female, 25 years and over: *Total*	29,154,000		12,556,000		1,711,000	
School years not reported	274,000		134,000		31,000	
Total	28,880,000	100.0	12,422,000	100.0	1,680,000	100.0
Elementary:						
0 to 7 years	4,586,000	15.9	2,653,000	21.3	283,000	16.8
8 years	5,121,000	17.7	2,379,000	19.1	224,000	13.3
High school:						
1 to 3 years	5,499,000	19.0	2,309,000	18.6	175,000	10.4
4 years	9,177,000	31.8	3,946,000	31.8	613,000	36.5
College:						
1 to 3 years	2,590,000	8.9	625,000	5.0	219,000	13.0
4 years or more	1,907,000	6.6	510,000	4.1	166,000	9.9
Median school years completed	11.6		10.5		12.3	

SOURCE: U.S. Bureau of the Census, "Tabulations of Data on the Social and Economic
Characteristics of Major Religious Groups, March 1957." Xeroxed. Table 3.

society dovetailed with the Jewish custom—based on the religious tenets of Judaism—of giving girls only the most limited education. Table 3 reveals that in 1957 9.9 percent of all Jewish women twenty-five years old and over had either graduated from college or taken graduate work. This is more than double the rate for Roman Catholic women (4.1 percent) and 3.3 percent higher than for white Protestants.

The returns from the 1957 survey are not strictly comparable to the returns which elicited information on ethnic origin or descent in 1969, 1971, and 1972. Instead of dealing with the category "Jewish" we have to rely on "Russian origin or descent." Furthermore, the more recent data was not tabulated by sex, thus making it difficult to chart the progress Jewish women may have made since 1957. However, a breakdown by age is a welcome refinement. What does Table 4 reveal? There are two important findings: One is that the median number of school years completed for persons of Russian origin or descent between the ages of twenty-five and thirty-four had advanced to sixteen years by 1971. In other words, half of the Jewish persons in this age group have completed college. The second important finding is that, for this age group, the gap between persons of Russian origin or descent and members of other ethnic derivations has not been closed; the percentage of Jewish persons with at least a college education (51.6 or 51.8 percent) is at least double that of persons with other ethnic backgrounds.

The returns of the 1957 sample survey (Table 3) as well as the data in the bottom half of Table 4 show that these patterns of differential education achievement had been set a long time ago. For the persons thirty-five years and over (who were born before 1935) Table 4 shows that, with the exception of the English, Scottish, and Welsh, the percentage of persons of Russian origin or descent who had completed four years of college or more was twice that of members of the other ethnic groups included in the table.

While Tables 3 and 4 highlighted the differences in educational achievement between Jews and other religious or descent groups, returns from the National Jewish Population Survey as presented in Table 5 illuminate the generational differences in educational achievement *within* the Jewish population. Three distinct achievement levels characterize the age group twenty-five to thirty-nine years, forty to sixty-four years, and sixty-five years and over. Under forty years of age about 25 percent of all persons had graduated from college, as compared to about 12 percent of persons forty to sixty-four years old and about 5 percent of the older population.

The data presented in Table 5 also makes it possible to follow the educational progress of Jewish women. According to the returns, the percentage of Jewish women who graduate from college is about equal to

Table 4. Years of School Completed by Persons 25 Years Old
and Over, by Ethnic Origin and Age: November 1969;
March 1971; March 1972

Percent Distribution

NATIONAL ORIGIN	NOVEMBER 1969	MARCH 1971		MARCH 1972	
	College: 4 Years or More Percent	*College: 4 Years or More Percent*	*Median School Years Completed*	*College: 4 Years or More Percent*	*Median School Years Completed*
25 to 34 Years Old					
English[a]	17.6	24.1	12.8	26.3	12.9
German	17.5	19.8	12.7	19.2	12.7
Italian	11.9	16.0	12.6	16.5	12.6
Irish	13.9	15.5	12.6	16.3	12.6
French	No Inf.	9.9	12.5	13.2	12.6
Polish	16.3	16.8	12.7	24.1	12.8
Russian	52.6	51.6	16.0	51.8	16.0
35 Years Old and Over					
English[a]	13.6	14.6	12.4	15.4	12.4
German	8.5	10.5	12.1	10.2	12.2
Italian	5.9	6.3	11.0	6.0	11.1
Irish	9.3	8.9	12.0	9.5	12.1
French	No Inf.	7.8	11.5	8.0	11.9
Polish	7.2	7.8	10.9	7.0	11.2
Russian	18.4	18.9	12.5	20.6	12.6

[a] For 1971 and 1972 "English" includes Scottish and Welsh.

SOURCE: U.S. Bureau of the Census, *Current Population Reports*, "Ethnic Origin and Educational Attainment: November 1969," Series P-20, no. 220, p. 8; "Characteristics of the Population by Ethnic Origin: March 1972 and 1971," Series P-20, no. 249, Tables A-6 and 6.

that of Jewish men. This suggests that the enthusiasm for secular education among American Jews has been extended to females, so that whatever educational inequality there may have been has been overcome. An unexpected confirmation of this gain comes from a survey of the membership of Hadassah, a Jewish women's organization. It was found that "three out of every four current members attended college, compared with one of every two a dozen years ago."[24] Last, but not least, Table 5 permits us to explore in some detail the extent of postgraduate education,

Table 5. Individuals Aged 25 and Over, Level of Secular Education, by Age and Sex, in U.S. Jewish Population:* 1971 (Percent)

EDUCATIONAL LEVEL	25-29	30-39	40-49	50-64	65 & OVER	AGE NOT KNOWN	TOTAL[a]
			Total				
Not high school graduate	2.6	3.1	8.8	12.4	47.9	12.7	15.6
High school graduate	19.5	18.5	32.4	40.1	22.8	30.8	29.2
Some college	18.8	23.1	23.3	20.6	8.9	17.2	19.2
College graduate	23.8	25.4	12.6	12.1	4.3	11.5	14.2
Graduate work through master's	18.8	16.3	11.5	5.5	1.6	6.9	9.3
Beyond master's through Ph.D.	3.3	4.0	2.5	2.3	1.0	0.6	2.5
Professional degree	12.4	8.1	7.6	4.0	4.6	2.1	6.4
Other	0.5	0.9	0.6	1.7	3.7	5.7	1.6
NR	0.4	0.6	0.7	1.4	5.2	12.4	1.9
Total	100.0	100.0	100.0	100.0	100.0	100.0	100.0
(Sample size)	(2,046)	(3,761)	(4,671)	(6,481)	(3,950)	(331)	(21,240)
			Male				
Not high school graduate	0.8	3.9	11.7	13.3	42.6	13.5	15.2
High school graduate	10.0	13.4	22.9	32.3	19.1	23.1	22.5
Some college	16.5	13.1	19.4	21.3	12.2	7.7	17.3
College graduate	24.7	22.7	14.0	13.5	5.2	22.1	14.9
Graduate work through master's	17.2	21.8	13.8	5.2	1.7	8.7	10.5
Beyond master's through Ph.D.	5.8	6.8	4.1	3.7	1.4	1.9	4.1
Professional degree	24.6	15.9	12.7	7.1	9.6	4.8	11.9
Other	—	1.6	0.7	1.8	3.7	3.9	1.7
NR	0.3	0.8	0.8	1.8	4.5	14.4	1.8
Total	100.0	100.0	100.0	100.0	100.0	100.0	100.0
(Sample size)	(976)	(1,743)	(2,188)	(3,322)	(1,747)	(104)	(10,080)
			Female				
Not high school graduate	4.3	2.4	6.3	11.4	52.1	12.3	16.0
High school graduate	28.0	22.9	40.7	48.2	25.7	34.4	35.3
Some college	20.8	31.7	26.8	19.8	6.2	21.6	21.0
College graduate	22.9	27.7	11.3	10.6	3.6	6.6	13.6
Graduate work through master's	20.3	11.5	9.5	5.8	1.5	6.2	8.2
Beyond master's through Ph.D.	0.9	1.5	1.1	0.8	0.7	—	1.0

Table 5 (continued)

EDUCATIONAL LEVEL	25-29	30-39	40-49	50-64	65 & OVER	AGE NOT KNOWN	TOTAL[a]
Professional degree	1.3	1.4	3.2	0.7	0.7	0.9	1.4
Other	0.9	0.3	0.5	1.7	3.7	6.6	1.6
NR	0.5	0.5	0.6	1.0	5.8	11.5	1.9
Total	100.0	100.0	100.0	100.0	100.0	100.0	100.0
(Sample size)	(1,070)	(2,017)	(2,483)	(3,158)	(2,201)	(227)	(11,156)

N.B. Details may not add to 100.0 because of rounding.
NR-Not reported
*Data are exclusive of institutional population.
[a]Totals include four respondents for whom sex was not reported.

SOURCE: *American Jewish Year Book* 74 (1973), p. 280.

what the Census Bureau categorized as "Four or more years of college." The increasing professionalization of Jewish men is very pronounced. The percentage of males with a professional degree rises from 7.1 percent for fifty to sixty-four years old to 24.6 percent for the age group twenty-five to twenty-nine. Similarly, the percentage of men with a master's degree which is required for positions in welfare and educational fields rises from 5.2 percent for fifty to sixty-four-year-old men to 21.8 percent for the thirty to thirty-four year age group and declines slightly to 17.2 percent for the twenty-five to twenty-nine-year-old category. If this increase in the professions should be linked to a shift from traditional activities in business and trade and especially to a shift from self-employment, the American Jewish community is faced with a serious change in its economic structure.

OCCUPATION AND EMPLOYMENT STATUS

The Jewish occupational structure is the result of the interaction of traditional Jewish values, accessibility to economic opportunities, and the effect of educational achievement upon occupational choice. In the past, occupational choice was primarily determined by the desire for group survival and the limitations imposed by discrimination. Self-employment in business and the professions was the means by which to arrange one's work schedule in accordance with religious precepts, the daily prayers, and the Sabbath and festival calendar. The troubles that Sabbath observers encounter in the working world testify to the wisdom of engaging in economic activity which is under one's own control.

Discriminatory practices against Jews in employment also forced Jews to turn to self-employment, thus reinforcing group cohesion.

Table 6.　Percent Distribution of Employed Persons, 18 Years Old and Over By Major Occupation Group, By Religion Reported and Sex for the United States: March 1957

	MALE			FEMALE		
MAJOR OCCUPATION GROUP	*Jewish*	*White Protestant*	*Roman Catholic*	*Jewish*	*White Protestant*	*Roman Catholic*
Total employed, 18 years and over	100.0	100.0	100.0	100.0	100.0	100.0
Professional and white-collar workers	77.5	38.2	34.6	83.7	60.3	57.7
Professional, technical, and kindred workers	20.3	10.9	8.9	15.5	13.7	11.4
Wage and salary workers	12.8	9.5	7.5	15.1	12.8	11.0
Self-employed and other workers	7.5	1.4	1.3	0.4	0.9	0.4
Managers, officials, and proprietors, except farmers	35.1	14.1	12.5	8.9	6.5	4.3
Wage and salary workers	10.8	7.3	5.7	3.2	3.0	1.3
Self-employed and other workers	24.3	6.7	6.8	5.7	3.5	3.0
Clerical and kindred workers	8.0	6.8	8.4	43.9	32.1	35.6
Sales workers	14.1	6.0	4.8	14.4	8.0	6.4
Farmers and blue-collar workers	22.5	61.8	65.4	16.3	39.7	42.3

SOURCE: U.S. Bureau of the Census. "Tabulation of Data on the Social and Economic Characteristics of Major Religious Groups, March 1957." Xeroxed. Table 15.

The extent to which self-employment was still practiced in 1957 will be seen from Table 6. The largest percentage of Jewish men (over one-third) is found in the occupation group of managers, officials, and proprietors, except farmers, which includes, of course, owners of businesses. In this category 24.3 percent out of 35.1 percent (or 70 percent) were self-employed. Table 6 shows that among white Protestants and Roman Catholics self-employment was only one-quarter of that of Jewish men in this category, 6.7 and 6.8 percent among white Protestant and Roman Catholics, respectively, as compared with 24.3 percent for Jewish men.

Self-employment in the category of "Professional, technical and kindred workers" was considerably lower, with 7.5 percent out of 20.3 percent (or 37 percent) in the category of self-employed. Still, Jewish self-employment for this group is five to six times higher than for white Protestants and Roman Catholics. Of equal importance is the finding that in 1957 only 22.5 percent of employed Jewish men were found in the blue-collar categories of craftsmen, foremen, operators, and the like. If one takes into account that over 60 percent of white Protestant and Roman Catholic men were found in these categories in 1957, the statement that for American Jews the role of industrial worker was a temporary adaptation of immigrants appears fully justified.

An inspection of the data for employed women reveals that the differences that were found between Jewish men and white Protestant and Roman Catholic men also hold for the women. At the same time, the differences are considerably smaller, which may be attributed to the special conditions of the labor market for women in the late 1950s.

It will be recalled that the census surveys of 1969, 1971, and 1972 revealed that over half of the men of Russian origin or descent had extended their education to four or more years of college (Table 4). The National Jewish Population Survey showed in greater detail (Table 5) the progressive increase in professional education among American Jews. One should expect that this shift toward professionalization would be reflected in the occupation statistics. This expectation is borne out, as Table 7 demonstrates. The percentage of professional, technical, and kindred workers increased from about 20 percent in 1957 to about 30 percent in 1971 and 1972, according to both the U.S. Bureau of the Census Survey and the National Jewish Population Survey. This increase in professional workers was accompanied by a decline in the category of managers, officials, and proprietors, except farmers, from 35 percent to 24 percent in the census surveys. However, it will be noted that the return of the National Jewish Population Survey does not confirm this shift, since it yielded 40 percent for this category. It is important to state here that the returns from the various surveys are not strictly comparable. The figure for managers from the NJPS may be due to differences in the classificatory scheme of occupations. The 1957 survey deals with males eighteen years and older, the 1971 and 1972 surveys with men fourteen years and over, while the National Jewish Population Survey used twenty-five years as the cutoff point. The 1957 survey and 1971 NJPS survey deal with Jews, the 1971 and 1972 surveys with men of Russian origin or descent. From a perusal of the methodological notes to the census surveys it appears that there have been no changes that would affect the major occupation groups presented in Table 7.

Table 7. Percent Distribution of Male Employed Persons by Major Occupation Groups for the United States: 1957, 1971, and 1972.

	U.S. BUREAU OF THE CENSUS			NJPS
	18 Years Old and Over	14 Years Old and Over	25 Years Old and Over	
MAJOR OCCUPATION GROUP	Jewish	Russian Origin or Descent		Jewish
	1957	1971	1972	1971
TOTAL EMPLOYED	100.0	100.0	100.0	100.0
Professional, technical and kindred workers	20.3	30.2	31.7	29.3
Managers, officials, and proprietors, except farmers	35.1	24.2	23.6	40.7
Clerical and kindred workers	8.0	6.5	9.1	3.2
Sales workers	14.1	14.1	13.4	14.2
All others	22.5	25.0	22.3	12.6

SOURCES: For 1957, Table 6, *supra:* for 1971 and 1972, *Current Population Reports* P-20, no. 249, Tables A-7 and 7; for 1971 "United States National Jewish Population Study: A First Report," *American Jewish Year Book*, vol. 74, 1973, p. 284.

It will be recalled that the most distinctive economic attribute of the Jewish population is the high degree of self-employment. Therefore, the question arises whether and to what extent the shift towards professionalization has affected the percentage of persons who are self-employed. Since the 1971 and 1972 census returns do not present any tabulations on this item, and since the National Jewish Population Survey has not yet published any data on this topic, the question cannot be answered at the present time. It stands to reason, however, that shifts in secular education beget shifts in the occupational structure, so that I am inclined to accept as genuine the shift toward professionalization between 1957 and 1971 and 1972 as expressed in Table 7.

EDUCATION, OCCUPATION, AND INTERMARRIAGE

Table 8 is of extraordinary significance. Unexpectedly, it sheds light on the effect of occupational homogeneity upon the facilitation of intermarriage. It appears that this factor of occupational homogamy has not received the attention it deserves.

Table 8. Percent Distribution of Employed College Graduates in Urban Areas by Major Occupation Group, by Religion Reported for the United States: March 1957

MAJOR OCCUPATION GROUP	JEWISH	WHITE PROTESTANT	ROMAN CATHOLIC
Total employed	100.0	100.0	100.0
Professional and white-collar workers	97.0	93.2	92.0
Professional, technical, and kindred workers	58.2	62.0	66.1
Wage and salary workers	39.2	53.5	56.4
Self-employed and other workers	19.0	8.5	9.7
Managers, officials, and proprietors, except farmers	22.1	17.1	12.4
Wage and salary workers	11.3	11.9	8.3
Self-employed and other workers	10.8	5.3	4.1
Clerical and kindred workers	8.9	8.3	7.4
Sales workers	7.8	5.8	6.1
Blue-collar workers	3.1	6.7	8.1

SOURCE: U.S. Bureau of the Census, "Tabulations of Data . . . March 1957." Table 16. Xeroxed.

Table 8 presents data on major occupation groups for the three religious groups, but differs from Table 6 by limiting the tabulation to: (1) urban residents and (2) college graduates. If the bureau had presented the data for males and females separately, this table would fulfill a sociologist's dream. It will be seen that the substantial differences that were observed between Jews, on the one hand, and white Protestants and Roman Catholics for all professional and white-collar workers, on the other, have virtually disappeared. In urban areas over 90 percent of persons with a college education are in this group, regardless of religion.

As a matter of fact, for the category "Professional, technical, and kindred workers," Jews show a slightly lower percentage, 58.2 percent versus 62.6 and 66.1 percent for white Protestants and Roman Catholics, respectively. For "Managers, officials, and proprietors, except farmers," Jews have a slightly higher percentage than the two other groups but a substantially smaller percentage than Jews regardless of type of residence and college education, 22.1 percent versus 35.1 percent (Table 6). For clerical and sales workers the percentages are virtually identical for all three groups.

It will be recalled that self-employment was found to be the most outstanding economic characteristic of the Jewish community. Table 8 suggests some interesting shifts, with the result that even this trait loses some of its Jewish specificity. It appears that among urban college graduates self-employment increases significantly among members of all three religious groups, with the result that Jewish professionals and managers contribute only twice as high a percentage as white Protestant and Roman Catholic professionals and managers: 19 percent versus 8.5 and 9.7 percent among the former, and 10.8 percent versus 5.3 and 4.1 percent among the latter. For the total population, regardless of residence and education (Table 6), Jewish self-employment was five and four times higher than among the Christian groups. In other words, in term of both occupational grouping and employment status, Jews and non-Jews resemble each other more closely with a college education and in an urban setting. How does this relate to facilitating religious intermarriage?

Studies in mate selection (who marries whom) have shown that men and women who share certain background characteristics are more likely to marry each other than a person whose background is different. The technical term for this preference is homogamy (marriage of spouses with similar background characteristics). Within the framework of this paper, studies of educational and occupational homogamy are relevant. Winch cites a study of educational homogamy by Paul C. Glick, who found that persons with similar educational levels are more likely to marry each other than would occur by chance. Similarly, an analysis of the occupation of the groom's father and the bride's father showed strong homogamous tendencies.[25] My thesis is that educational homogamy (college education) and the resulting occupational homogamy (as revealed in Table 8) are stronger than Jewish-Gentile heterogamy and result in increases of intermarriage. In other words, the 1957 data as presented in Table 8 were predictive of increased Jewish-Gentile intermarriages in the 1960s and 1970s.

INCOME DISTRIBUTION

The collection of income data by the Bureau of the Census was started on a limited basis in connection with the 1940 census. Since then, many sample surveys, as well as the 1950 census, not only have built up a continuous record of the income of Americans but have also made it possible to relate size of income to a number of social and physical characteristics. The 1950 census returns were analyzed in a monograph by Herman P. Miller, who found that incomes tend to increase with size of city, length of education, proximity to the apex of professional status, and increasing age up to fifty-four years.[26] All of these factors help explain the relatively high income of the Jewish population.

Table 9.   Median Income in 1956 of Urban Men 14 Years Old and Over in the Civilian Noninstitutional Population with Income, by Religion Reported and Years of School Completed.

YEARS OF SCHOOL COMPLETED		WHITE PROTESTANT	ROMAN CATHOLIC	JEWISH
Elementary:	0 to 7 years	$2,812	$2,819	$2,609
	8 years	3,712	3,729	3,844
High school:	1 to 3 years	3,850	4,170	4,672
	4 years	4,684	4,567	4,913
College:	1 to 3 years	4,712	4,361	5,026
	4 years or more	6,375	5,727	8,041

SOURCE: U.S. Bureau of the Census. "Tabulations of Data . . . March 1957." Table 19. Xeroxed.

Table 9 demonstrates clearly and in detail the effect of education upon earnings. With added years of education the median income rises. At least as of 1957, the median income of men who had graduated from college was considerably higher than that of men who had graduated from high school. The increment was $1,600 for white Protestants, $1,400 for Roman Catholics and about $3,000 for Jewish men. Table 9 also shows that attending college without graduation does not significantly improve income over that received by high school graduates, a fact which under-scores the pressure to attain that college diploma. The high differential of $3,000 between the incomes of high school and college graduates among Jewish men can be explained by the fact that for a considerable number of Jewish men "four years or more of college" means more than four years.

Table 10 permits us to examine whether and to what extent the income pattern and distribution of the Jewish population corresponds to those of the major religious groups. First, in all three religious groups income declines after age fifty-five, ranging from 18.3 percent for Roman

Table 10. Percent Distribution of Families by Total Family
Income in 1956, for the Urban United States, by
Religion Reported.

TOTAL MONEY INCOME URBAN UNITED STATES	WHITE PROTESTANT	ROMAN CATHOLIC	JEWISH
Total families	100.0	100.0	100.0
Under $1,000	2.6	3.4	2.7
$1,000 to 1,999	5.9	5.7	5.1
$2,000 to 2,999	8.1	6.9	5.9
$3,000 to 3,999	11.8	10.8	8.1
$4,000 to 4,999	16.0	16.9	12.2
$5,000 to 5,999	14.6	10.2	12.2
$6,000 to 6,999	10.9	11.9	9.1
$7,000 to 9,999	19.9	19.6	19.6
$10,000 and over	10.2	8.8	25.1
Median Income			
Total families	$5,384	$5,389	$6,418
By age of head			
Under 35 years	$5,024	$5,077	a
35 to 54 years	$6,713	$5,826	$7,500
55 years and over	$4,504	$4,762	$4,909
Decline	32.9%	18.3%	25.9%
By number of earners			
1 earner	$4,626	$4,491	$5,561
2 or more earners	$6,455	$6,631	$7,534
Added income	28.3	32.2	26.2
Percent of families with 2 or more earners	46.6	48.2	38.6

[a]Median not shown

SOURCE: U.S. Bureau of the Census. "Tabulations of Data . . . March 1957." Table 20.
Xeroxed.

Catholics to 25.9 percent for Jewish heads of households to 32.9 percent
for white Protestants. Declining income after age fifty-five is most likely
due to deterioration of health or the difficulty of rebuilding a career that
may have met with reverses of one sort or another. It will also be seen
from Table 10 that an additional earner raises family income 26.2 percent
for Jews and 28.5 percent for white Protestants and 32.2 percent for
Roman Catholics. It will also be noted that in 1957 nearly 50 percent of
white Protestants and Roman Catholics relied on a second earner for

additional income, as compared with only 38.6 percent for Jewish families.

The top part of Table 10 is devoted to a description of the income distribution among the three religious groups. Since the median family income for the Jewish population was about $1,000 higher than for the white Protestants and Roman Catholics ($6,418 versus $5,384 and $5,389), it can be expected that Jewish family incomes are concentrated in the higher income brackets. The table shows that in 1957, 25.1 percent of Jewish families had an income of $10,000 or more, as compared with 10.2 percent for white Protestants and 8.8 percent for Roman Catholics.

POVERTY AMONG AMERICAN JEWS

It will be recalled that poverty in contemporary America was "rediscovered" by Michael Harrington in 1962.[27] Jewish poverty in America was "discovered" by Ann G. Wolfe a decade later in an article titled "The Invisible Jewish Poor."[28] By the time Wolfe's paper appeared the Federal government had launched a war on poverty and had initiated several programs to alleviate it.

Governmental action had to be based on the following operational definition of "poverty": "At the core of this definition of poverty is a nutritionally adequate food plan ('economy' plan) designed by the Department of Agriculture for 'emergency or temporary use when funds are low' . . . Annual revisions . . . are based on price changes of the items in the economy food budget."[29] However, when "funds are low" for more than a temporary span of time or a state of emergency, "poverty" becomes a permanent abject condition. It appears that the poverty budget does not make any provisions for maintaining the dignity of the individual by including items for cultural, religious, or social needs, such as votive candles, tuition for parochial school, or dues for the Golden Age Club.

Were there any poor Jews in 1956? According to the census report mentioned above, the poverty threshold for a nonfarm family of four was $2,973 in 1959.[30] Well over 90 percent of Jewish families were nonfarm in 1956. Table 10 shows that 13.7 percent of Jewish families had family incomes of less than $2,999 in 1956. Since the 1956 income data in Table 10 has not been broken down by size of family and employment status (retired couples, for instance), it is only fair to state that 13.7 percent is too high an estimate of the proportion of Jewish families living in this officially designated state of "poverty." In the absence of more precise information one may be justified in stating that families with an income of less than $2,000, constituting 7.8 percent of all Jewish families, were "poor" or economically marginal in 1957.

To assess the extent of "poverty" among American Jews in 1970, Table

11 has been prepared. Remember that the 1957 survey revealed that Jews had a higher median income than white Protestants and Roman Catholics (Table 10). Therefore, the returns for ethnic groups, presented in Table 11, should not come as a surprise. Families with a head of

Table 11. Median Family Income and Persons Below Low-Income Level in 1970 by Ethnic Origin of Head

ETHNIC ORIGIN OR DESCENT	MEDIAN INCOME	RANK	PERSONS BELOW LOW- INCOME LEVEL PERCENT	RANK
Russian	$13,985	1	4.5	1
Polish	11,619	2	5.3	2
Italian	11,089	3	6.1	3
English, Scottish, Welsh	10,727	4	8.6	4.5
German	10,402	5	8.6	4.5
Irish	9,964	6	10.5	6

SOURCE: U.S. Bureau of the Census. Series P-20, no. 249, Table A-9 and "Characteristics of the Low-Income Population 1970," Series P-60, no. 81, Table 6.

Russian origin or descent had the highest median income in 1970 ($13,985) as compared with medians ranging from below $12,000 to below $10,000 for other European descent groups.

Table 11 further shows that there is a perfect inverse rank order correlation between median income and extent of poverty, with the expected result that families with heads of Russian origin or descent exhibit the smallest percentage of persons below the "poverty" line (4.5) as compared with 5 percent or more for the other groups. Assuming a Jewish population of 5,200,000 in 1970, 4.5 percent translates into 234,000 Jewish persons living in "poverty" in that year.

Who are the Jewish poor? Two-thirds of them are women as Table 12 shows—66.3 percent, to be precise. Unrelated females are beset with "poverty" twice as much as female heads of households—45.3 percent as compared with 21.1 percent. Why do women show this affinity? First, women suffer from the considerable wage and salary differential between men and women.[31] Second, widows may not have been adequately provided for or may have exhausted whatever resources were left to them. For Jewish men the pattern of poverty is reversed. Table 12 shows that male heads of household outnumber unrelated individuals. A clue to the understanding of this reversal may be found in the following: In the City of New York, in the borough of Brooklyn, the local community of Williamsburg in 1966 was an officially designated poverty area.[32] We also know that Williamsburg is the home of a considerable number of Hasidic families, some of whom fall below the low-income threshold. It must, therefore, be inferred that among the heads of household below

Table 12. Background Characteristics of Jewish Persons, 14 Years Old and Over, Below Low-Income Levels, 1970

BACKGROUND CHARACTERISTICS	NUMBER	PERCENT
Male		
Heads of families	44,000	18.8
Unrelated individuals	34,630	14.8
Female		
Heads of families	49,370	21.1
Unrelated individuals	106,000	45.3
TOTAL	234,000	100.0

SOURCE: U.S. Bureau of the Census. Series P-60, no. 81, Tables 4 and 6.

the poverty threshold there are an undetermined number who belong to the Hasidic community.

While all the other waves of Jewish immigrants to the United States have overcome poverty through the maximum utilization of secular education and family planning, the Hasidim are opposed to both of these devices. At this time there is no telling whether subsequent generations will adopt the general American Jewish culture pattern and will get on the escalator that would lift them out of poverty. When the issue received considerable attention in the news media, CBS focused on the situation of the Hasidic community in a telecast on February 21, 1972, at 6:15 P.M. in New York City. A Hasid told the viewers that he was forty years old, had eight children and an income of $7,000, which was supplemented by $80 worth of food stamps. He had studied in *yeshivot* until he was twenty-two years old and had no special skills. He claimed that the tuition fee for a child in a *yeshivah* was $250, and that kosher food was 50 percent more expensive than ordinary food.

ADEQUACY OF INCOME

Clearly, persons who live below the poverty threshold suffer from a lack of adequacy of income. Adequacy of income is the concern of the Bureau of Labor Statistics. Each year the bureau figures out the annual costs for maintaining a family of four at a lower, intermediate, and higher level of living. In 1970 these estimates were $7,183, $12,134, and $18,545, respectively, in the New York-northeastern New Jersey area, where nearly half of the Jewish population of the country is located.[33] Three levels of budgets are also available for retired couples.[34] I cannot resist the temptation to view the income distribution in the light of the adequacy of income levels as determined by the Bureau of Labor Statistics. To this end Table 13B has been prepared. Note, however, that this allocation must be of a tentative nature for two reasons: (1) the family income data presented in Table 13A is not detailed for size of family and

Table 13

A. Family Income in 1970 of Family Heads of Russian Origin or Descent		B. Estimated Level of Living of Jewish Families, 1970	
FAMILY INCOME	PERCENT	BUDGET LEVEL	PERCENT OF FAMILIES
Total families	621,000		
Percent	100.0	TOTAL	100.0
		Below lower level (Below $7,183)	20.0
Under $7,000	19.9		
$7,000 to $9,999	8.8	Between lower and	
$10,000 to $14,999	27.5	intermediate	25.0
$15,000 to $24,999	27.9	($7,183 to $12,134)	
$25,000 and over	15.9	Between intermediate	
		and higher	25.0
Median income	$13,895	($12,134 to $18,545)	
		Above higher	30.0
		($18,545 and above)	

SOURCE FOR A: U.S. Bureau of the Census, P-20, no. 249, Table A-9

SOURCE FOR B: 1970 budget levels from U.S. Department of Labor, Bureau of Labor Statistics, news release, December 21, 1970 (processed)

employment status, and (2) the income groupings in the stub of Table 13A do not dovetail with the budget levels that prevailed in 1970. With these limitations in mind, Table 13B presents an estimated breakdown of adequacy of income among Jewish families in 1970. It will be seen that 20 percent of Jewish families are found below $7,183, the lower level of adequacy. Between lower and intermediate levels ($7,183 to $12,134) and between intermediate and high levels ($12,134 and $18,545), 25 percent each of the total of Jewish families are found. Above the higher level of $18,545 are 30 percent of the families.

Since the National Jewish Population Survey enumerated data on income, a comparison of its returns with those of the sample survey for persons of Russian origin or descent should be most welcome. Apart from differences in income classes used, the major difficulty arises from the fact that about 30 percent of the households in the NJPS failed to furnish information on income. This forced the sponsors of the survey to allocate the nonrespondents. "They were assumed, for each age and family composition category, to have the same income distribution as those reporting income. [It is promised that] these data will be refined further by correlating non-response figures with occupation, education and other factors."[35] In spite of these limitations, the income data from NJPS is presented in Table 14A and compared with the 1970 sample

Table 14. Family Income in 1971 of Jewish Households and in 1970 of Family Heads of Russian Origin or Descent, the United States

A. JEWISH HOUSEHOLDS		B. HEADS OF RUSSIAN ORIGIN OR DESCENT	
Family Income	*Percent*	*Family Income*	*Percent*
TOTAL	100.0	TOTAL	100.0
Under $6,000	19.4	Under $7,000	19.9
$6,000 to $9,999	13.5	$7,000 to $9,999	8.8
$10,000 to $15,999	23.8	$10,000 to $14,999	27.5
$16,000 to $19,999	10.9	$15,000 to $24,999	27.9
$20,000 and over	32.4	$25,000 and over	15.9

SOURCE: "U.S. National Jewish Population Study," *American Jewish Year Book*, vol. 74, 1973, p. 288; U.S. Bureau of the Census, P-20, no. 249, Table A9.

census data for persons of Russian origin or descent in Table 14B. It will be seen that there is considerable similarity between the two distributions, especially in the lowest income group under $6,000 or $7,000, with about 20 percent of families in each survey, and in the highest income group of $16,000 or more and $15,000 or more, with about 44 percent in each survey.

FERTILITY

The enthusiasm of immigrant Jews and their children for secular education was matched by their strong participation in, and support of, the birth control and planned parenthood movement.[36] In Chicago, for example, Rabbi Louis L. Mann, the rabbi of Sinai Congregation, which was the most prestigious temple in the city in its time, was a leader in the local birth-control movement. The Chicago Women's Aid, a charitable club founded by members of the congregation, sponsored or cosponsored the first birth-control clinics in Chicago. It supported the clinic at the Jewish People's Institute, a community center in the heart of the largest Jewish community. In my opinion, the symbolic presence of this clinic was more important than its concrete delivery of advice and services.[37]

In the United States, residence in an urban area, a high level of secular education, and a white-collar occupation for the husband depress the level of marital fertility. This is well documented in Table 15. Panel A shows that a rural farm wife over forty-five years of age (whose fertility is completed) had nearly four children as compared with only 2.5 children for urban ever-married women. Panel B reveals that with increasing urbanization the number of children declines slightly from 2.4 to 2.2 in the largest urbanized areas. The effect of college education on fertility is considerable: Panel C shows that wives with four or more years of college have one child less than wives who finished only three years of high school (1.5 versus 2.3 children). Finally, Panel D shows that wives whose husbands are sales workers or professionals have just about two children, 2.1 and 1.9 respectively.

From this presentation of the preference of the Jewish population for urban residence, of the high value placed on secular education, and of the predilection for white-collar occupations it should follow that the Jewish population has developed a rather low level of fertility. This is indeed the case. Panel E shows that for 1,000 Jewish wives over forty-five who had completed their childbearing, the number of children was 2,218, virtually identical with the fertility observed in urbanized areas with more than three million residents. For 1,000 women fifteen to forty-four years of age, the number of children was 1,749, identical with the fertility of wives who had had four or more years of college education.

Panel E of Table 15 presents the fertility patterns of the three major religious groups in the United States and shows that Jews have a lower fertility than Protestants and Roman Catholics. However, this particular set of data is misleading and has led to a great deal of misunderstanding. Since (as has been pointed out) the Jewish population is virtually entirely urban, a *valid* comparison can only be obtained if data is available for the fertility of urban white Protestants and Roman Catholics. Therefore, the fertility rates for Protestants (all races) and Roman Catholics in their present form (as presented in Panel E of Table 15) must be disregarded. We are much closer to the true levels of fertility in Panels A to C where the

Table 15. Cumulative Fertility Rate (Number of Children Ever Born Per 1,000 Women Ever Married) by Type of Community, Years of School Completed, Major Occupation Group, and Religion, March 1957

Characteristic	UNSTANDARDIZED CUMULATIVE FERTILITY RATE	
	15 to 44	*45 and over*
A. Type of community		
Rural farm	3,009	3,910
Rural nonfarm	2,356	3,069
Urban	2,035	2,514
B. Type of urban community		
Total urban	2,035	2,514
In urbanized areas	1,990	2,386
Areas of 250,000 to 1,000,000	1,993	2,410
Areas of 1,000,000 to 3,000,000	1,981	2,367
Areas of 3,000,000 or more	1,877	2,228
C. Years of school completed		
Total urban	2,035	2,514
High school: 1 to 3 years	2,164	2,280
4 years	1,857	1,923
College: 1 to 3 years	1,748	1,865
4 years or more	1,746	1,498
D. Major occupation group of husband		
Total with employed civilian husband	2,343	2,708
Managers, officials, and proprietors, excluding farmers	2,209	2,273
Sales workers	2,056	2,090
Professional, technical, and kindred workers	1,996	1,908
Clerical and kindred workers	1,884	2,270
E. Religious groups		
Jews	1,749	2,218
Protestants (all races)	2,220	2,753
Roman Catholics	2,282	3,056

SOURCE: U.S. Bureau of the Census, Series P-20, no. 84, Tables 4 and 5.

urban factor is held constant. These rates justify two conclusions: (1) fertility differences between Jews and all other urban residents are minimal, and (2) as more and more Americans are drawn into the urbanized way of life, fertility differences between American Jews and members of other religious or ethnic groups will become smaller and smaller.

There arises the question whether the level of Jewish fertility is sufficient to insure that the size of the American Jewish population be maintained in the future. Demographers have devised a measure called a "replacement index" which can project the future growth of the population from current fertility and mortality rates. This index tells us that under present mortality conditions 1,000 women—unmarried as well as married—need about 2,100 children to replace themselves.[38]

The returns of the 1957 survey show that 2,216 children were born to 1,000 married Jewish women forty-five years old and over, while 1,749 children were born to married Jewish women fifteen to forty-four years old.[39] To compute the replacement index properly, we would need to know the number of children per 1,000 married *as well as* unmarried Jewish women. In the absence of this information the conclusion may be drawn that for women over forty-five, the actual replacement quota was slightly below the required figure of 2,100. Since women fifteen to forty-four years had not yet completed their families, there is a chance that their completed fertility may come close to 2,100. At the same time it should be pointed out that in the year 1957 the "baby boom" crested and later receded to lower levels.

A sample survey conducted by the U.S. Bureau of the Census in November of 1969 allows us to explore whether the replacement index had changed since 1957.[40] Since this survey was aimed at an ethnic composition of the population rather than a religious one, it may bear repeating that the census analyst in his introductory remarks to one of the bulletins emphasizes the equivalence of data for persons of Russian origin or descent with American Jews in this manner: "Since very few persons have migrated to this country from Russia in 1930, when two-thirds of the Russian-born Americans reported that they had spoken Yiddish in their childhood, it is likely that most persons of Russian origin had a Jewish cultural heritage."[41]

The replacement index for women of Russian origin or descent is presented in Table 16. It will be seen that the index has been tabulated for three age groups separately. For the oldest group, women born between 1910 and 1924 who were from forty-five to fifty-nine years old and who had completed their families, the index stood at 1,891, about 200 children short of the needed 2,100 for replacement. However, because of sampling variability, the real rate could be as high as 2,169 which would meet the required number for replacement, or as low as 1,613, about half a child per woman short of replacement. Women born between 1925 and 1934, who were from thirty-five to forty-four years old in 1969, showed the best

Table 16. Children Ever Born per 1,000 Women of Russian
Origin or Descent, November 1969.

	WOMEN		
Year of Birth	Age	Rate	Two Standard Errors[a]
1910-1924	45-59 years	1,891	± 278
1925-1934	35-44 years	2,386	± 470
1935-1944	25-34 years	1,480	± 494

[a]The Standard Error was computed by the U.S. Bureau of the Census for this tabulation.

SOURCE: U.S. Bureau of the Census, Series P-20, no. 226, Table 2, p. 12.

level of fertility with 2,386 children. They participated in the "baby
boom" after World War II. Although, because of sampling variability,
their replacement index may have been as low as 1,916, they came closer
to replacement than the older age group and the younger. The younger,
born between 1935 and 1944 and from twenty-five to thirty-four years old
in 1969, had the lowest fertility with 1,480 children. Of course, their
families were not yet complete by 1969. However, because of the currently low birth rate, there is serious doubt that the younger age group
will come up to the replacement level. Altogether, Table 16 confirms the
earlier finding, based on the returns of the 1957 survey, that the fertility
level among American Jews is slightly below the replacement level.

AGE COMPOSITION

There is considerable evidence that the age composition of a population is "almost entirely" the result of past fertility.[42] The low fertility
among American Jews described in the previous section extended over
two generations and has left its mark on the age distribution of this
group, as will become evident in an analysis of Table 17.[43] A comparison
of the age composition of the Jewish population with that of the white
Protestant and Roman Catholic populations for the year 1957 is presented
in Part A of Table 17. This table reveals two significant facts: (1) the
Jewish population is older than the other two groups, and (2) differences
in age between Jews and Roman Catholics are more pronounced than
between Jews and white Protestants. Up to the age of thirty-five years,
Jews constitute a smaller percentage for each age group than do white
Protestants and Roman Catholics. The difference is most pronounced for
children under fourteen years of age, with at least a 5 percent differential.
Correspondingly, a higher proportion of Jews (at least 6 percent more) is
found among the middle-aged (forty-five to sixty-four years). The pro-

Table 17. Age Composition
(Percentage Distribution)

A. Major religious groups: March 1957

	JEWISH		WHITE PROTESTANT		ROMAN CATHOLIC	
AGE GROUP	*Male*	*Female*	*Male*	*Female*	*Male*	*Female*
Under 14	22.9	21.6	27.9	25.6	28.4	27.0
14-19	6.6	7.4	8.5	8.3	8.8	8.7
20-24	5.3	4.1	5.2	6.1	5.8	6.7
25-34	12.8	13.7	13.9	13.7	15.3	15.6
35-44	13.9	15.3	13.9	13.7	15.1	15.1
45-64	28.9	27.1	21.4	21.7	19.6	19.4
65 and over	9.5	10.6	9.2	10.7	6.8	7.6
Total	100.0	100.0	100.0	100.0	100.0	100.0

SOURCE: Erich Rosenthal, "Jewish Fertility in the United States," *American Jewish Year Book,* vol. 62, 1961, p. 5.

B. American Jews and white urban population: 1970

	JEWISH		URBAN WHITES	
AGE GROUP	*Male*	*Female*	*Male*	*Female*
Under 15	22.4	21.7	28.2	25.3
15-19	10.1	8.9	9.5	8.8
20-24	8.7	8.7	8.7	8.6
25-34	10.5	10.6	12.6	12.0
35-44	11.7	12.0	11.5	11.2
45-64	25.8	24.8	20.7	21.7
65 and over	10.2	11.9	8.4	12.0
Not reported	0.6	1.2	—	—
Total	100.0	100.0	100.0	100.0

SOURCE: "National Jewish Population Study," *American Jewish Year Book* 74, 1973, p. 271; U.S. Bureau of the Census. Census of Population: 1970. General Population Characteristics. Final Report PC(1) B1 United States Summary Table 52, pp. 1-271.

portion of "senior citizens" (sixty-five years old and over) is virtually the same for Jews and white Protestants but smaller for Roman Catholics.

That the age composition of the Roman Catholic population in 1957 was comparatively younger than that of the Jews or white Protestants can be attributed to the position of the Church on birth control for practicing Catholics. Once "Roman Catholic" is translated into concrete ethnic groups such as Americans of Polish, Italian, or Irish descent, other factors, mainly socioeconomic in nature, may be adduced to help explain higher levels of fertility in the past.

For the year 1970 we have available the returns of the NJPS and the returns of the decennial population census, both of which are presented in Part B of Table 17.[44] The age distribution used in 1957 for the Jewish and Christian populations is largely repeated in 1970. Likewise, the differences between the two groups are found again: smaller youth and larger middle-age age groups among Jews as compared with the other groups. However, the "baby boom" after World War II has made an identical impact on both populations. The proportion of persons who in 1970 were twenty to twenty-four years old, that is, born between 1946 and 1950, rose by about three percentage points among Jews. The differences between the Christian groups in 1957 and the urban whites in 1970 are just about as large for this age group. If data was available for urban residence for 1957, the differences would be at least the same, if not higher.

Finally, the age group sixty-five years and over ("senior citizens") needs attention. It will be seen that among the Jewish population the increase for men was only from 9.5 percent in 1957 to 10.2 percent in 1970. The corresponding percentages for women were 10.6 and 11.2. This is the time to state that neither the NJPS nor the 1970 decennial census in its tabulation included the institutional population. This omission, of course, distorts the true age composition. In the light of the long-standing low levels of fertility among the Jewish population, I think that the exclusion of institutionalized persons presents a more serious distortion for the true age composition of the Jewish population than for the total population as a whole.

CONCLUSION

Demographic data has been utilized to present a current profile of the Jewish population of the United States. At the same time, sociological factors such as attitudes and values have been incorporated into the analysis to give greater meaning to the demographic material. This combined approach is leading to the development of a new theoretical framework whose outlines are beginning to emerge, using the concepts of adaptation to urban life, similarity of response, demographic lag, and social and cultural integration. Since these concepts reflect the social processes at work with greater specificity, they should begin to complement the older terms of acculturation and assimilation.

It will be recalled (from Table 2) that in 1957, 96.1 percent of American Jews lived in urban areas. Urban residence is the most outstanding attribute of members of this group. This concentration in urban areas is not so much the result of migration from rural areas of the United States to cities as it is the result of settlement in cities, especially in northern industrial cities, upon immigration to this country. American Jews, then, have had a relatively long exposure to urban life and an opportunity to work out a favorable adaptation to it. Secular education is the most potent device for survival in an urban-industrial complex. With regard to participation in the labor force, its value is self-evident for both men and women. There is, however, an additional value for women, since secular education is linked to the acceptance and practice of efficient birth control.

The term "similarity of response" is designed to indicate that American Jews are in the mainstream of American life and that their position in the social structure and their response to social changes are basically the same as those of other groups. Participation in the postwar "baby boom" may serve as an example of similarity of response. In an analysis of the fertility of the population as of 1957, the Census Bureau found that "women 35 to 44 years old had already borne more children, on the average, than women 45 to 49 years old. This is the first time that the fertility rate for an age group still in the reproductive period had exceeded that of a group already beyond the reproductive period."[45] Since age-specific data for Jewish women for the year 1957 is not available, we must be satisfied with the returns of the 1969 sample survey. An analysis of the fertility of women in Russian origin or descent (Table 16) showed an identical pattern, with women thirty-five to forty-four years having a higher fertility than women forty-five to fifty-nine years old. This pattern is matched by women of Polish, Italian, Irish, German, and English origin or descent, supporting the "similarity of response."

The significance of the above concept was highlighted in a recent controversy concerning poverty among American Jews. Earlier in this discussion (p. 47) it was stated that Ann G. Wolfe, a social worker, "discovered" poverty among American Jews ten years after Michael Harrington had explored its extent among the total population. Other social workers took issue with Ms. Wolfe over the extent of poverty among American Jews. However, behind the debate over the magnitude of poverty, there was a larger issue, namely the "similarity of response." A subheading in the article which aired these matters reads: "Are Jews not unlike other ethnic groups in prevalence of poverty?"[46]

It is suggested that differences in social characteristics and attributes between American Jews and other groups be interpreted as cultural lags between the groups rather than intrinsic differences. When fertility differences between the Jewish population and other groups were first noted, some observers argued that these differences were due to specific Jewish values arising from being a minority. We now know better. Such differences can be attributed mainly to residence patterns, and as groups shift their locale to an urban area the level of fertility approaches the level that prevails seemingly among Jews but, more truly, in an urban environment of which the Jews are an integral part. As the urban way of life envelops ever larger sectors of the population, the two-child pattern which has been typical of the Jewish population will become more and more acceptable. According to the Census Bureau, "by 1971 the percentage of wives expecting 2 children or less had risen to about 65 percent."[47]

It was also observed earlier (Table 8) that differences in occupation and employment status declined substantially once comparisons between Jews and other groups were limited to college-educated persons in urban areas. This convergence can be expected to lead to a decline of social boundaries and to an increase in social integration, namely, intermarriage. This expectation is borne out by data collected by the National Jewish Population Study which found that the formation of intermarriages began to rise steeply in the 1960s.[48]

NOTES

1. *The Census of Religious Bodies* which used to be published by the U.S. Bureau of the Census in the seventh year of each decade was nothing more than a compilation of membership and financial data furnished by churches, synagogues, and temples on a voluntary basis.

2. Erich Rosenthal, "Jewish Populations in General Decennial Population Censuses, 1955-61: A Bibliography," *The Jewish Journal of Sociology* II (June 1969), pp. 31-39.

3. Nathan Goldberg, "Forty-Five Years of Controversy: Should Jewish Immigrants be Classified as Jews?" *The Classification of Jewish Immigrants and Its Implications* (New York: YIVO-Yiddish Scientific Institute, 1945), pp. 90-102, and Charles R. Foster, *A Question on Religion,* Inter-University Case Program, no. 66 (University of Alabama Press, 1961).

4. Erich Rosenthal, "The Jewish Population of Chicago, Illinois," in Simon Rawidowicz, ed., *The Chicago Pinkas* (Chicago: College of Jewish Studies, 1952), pp. 23-42.

5. Stanley K. Bigman, *The Jewish Population of Greater Washington in 1956* (Washington, D.C.: The Jewish Community Council of Greater Washington, 1957).

6. U.S. Bureau of the Census, Current Population Reports, "Religion Reported by The Civilian Population of the United States: March 1957," Series P-20, no. 79 (Washington, D.C.: U.S. Government Printing Office, 1958); and U.S. Bureau of

the Census, "Tabulations of Data on the Social and Economic Characteristics of Major Religious Groups, March 1957" (no date, Xeroxed, and privately distributed).

7. U.S. Bureau of the Census, Current Population Reports, "Ethnic Origin and Educational Attainment: November 1969," Series P-20, no. 220 (Washington, D.C.: U.S. Government Printing Office, 1971).

_____. "Characteristics of the Population by Ethnic Origin: November 1969," Series P-20, no. 221 (Washington, D.C.: U.S. Government Printing Office, 1971).

_____. "Fertility Variations by Ethnic Origin: November 1969," Series P-20, no. 226 (Washington, D.C.: U.S. Government Printing Office, 1971).

_____. "Characteristics of the Population by Ethnic Origin: March 1972 and 1971," Series P-20, no. 249 (Washington, D.C.: U.S. Government Printing Office, 1973).

8. Fred Massarik and Alvin Chenkin, "United States National Jewish Population Study: A First Report," *American Jewish Year Book* 74 (1973), pp. 264-306.

9. Erich Rosenthal, "Five Million American Jews," *Commentary* 26 (December 1958), p. 500.

10. "Characteristics of the Population by Ethnic Origin: March 1972 and 1971," Series P-20, no. 249, pp. 13-14.

11. A detailed exploration of the equivalence of persons of Russian origin or descent with American Jews will be found in Erich Rosenthal, "The Equivalence of United States Census Data for Persons of Russian Stock or Descent with American Jews: An Evaluation," *Demography* 12 (May 1975), pp. 275-90.

12. Massarik and Chenkin, "U.S. National Population Study . . .," *American Jewish Year Book* 74 (1973), pp. 264-305.

13. "Religion Reported . . .," Series P-20, no. 79, p. 1.

14. Fred Massarik, "National Jewish Population Study: A New United States Estimate," *American Jewish Year Book* 75 (1974-75), p. 303.

15. *Ibid.*, p. 298.

16. "Jewish Population of the United States, 1955," *American Jewish Year Book* 56 (1955), pp. 119, 123.

17. Erich Rosenthal, "Five Million American Jews," *Commentary* 26 (December 1958), p. 501; Sophia M. Robison, ed., *Jewish Population Studies* (New York: Conference on Jewish Relations, 1943).

18. Alvin Chenkin, "Jewish Population in the United States," *American Jewish Year Book* 74 (1973), p. 307.

19. Fred Massarik, "National Jewish Population Study: A New United States Estimate," *American Jewish Year Book* 75 (1974-75), p. 297.

20. David M. Eichhorn, "Conversions to Judaism by Reform and Conservative Rabbis," *Jewish Social Studies* 16 (October 1954), pp. 299-318.

21. Erich Rosenthal, "Jewish Fertility in the United States," *American Jewish Year Book* 62 (1961), p. 25; reprinted in *Eugenics Quarterly* 8 (December 1961), pp. 198-217; reprinted in *Population and Society* (a textbook of readings) edited by Charles B. Nam (Boston: Houghton Mifflin Co., 1968), pp. 541-59; Donald J. Bogue, *The Population of the United States* (Glencoe, Ill.: The Free Press, 1959), pp. 696-97; S. Joseph Fauman and Albert J. Mayer, "Jewish Mortality in the U.S.," *Human Biology* 41 (September 1969), pp. 416-26.

22. U.S. Bureau of the Census, *Statistical Abstracts of the United States:* 194, 95th edition (Washington, D.C.: U.S. Government Printing Office, 1974), p. 17.

23. Irving Howe, *World of Our Fathers* (New York: Harcourt, Brace, Jovanovich, 1976).

24. *New York Times*, 12 August 1976, p. 8.

25. Robert F. Winch, *The Modern Family*, 3rd ed. (New York: Holt, Rinehart and Winston, Inc., 1971), pp. 280-83.

26. Herman P. Miller, *Income of the American People* (New York: Wiley, 1955), pp. 39, 54, 67.

27. Michael Harrington, *The Other America* (New York: Macmillan, 1962).

28. Ann G. Wolfe, "The Invisible Jewish Poor," *Journal of Jewish Communal Service* 48 (Spring 1972), pp. 259-65.

29. U.S. Bureau of the Census, Current Population Reports, "Characteristics of the Low-Income Population, 1970," Series P-60, no. 81, p. 19. According to the introduction to this report (p. 1), the terms "low-income" and "poverty" are used interchangeably.

30. "Characteristics of the Low-Income Population, 1970," Series P-60, no. 81, p. 19.

31. It is a well-known fact that American women earn less than men and that women are usually employed in the less-skilled and lower-paying jobs and often receive unequal pay for equal work. In 1955 the median wage of a working American woman was nearly 64 percent of that of her male counterpart. By 1970, the median earnings of an American woman had dropped to 59.4 percent of a man's salary. The imbalance between men and women was greatest for sales workers, where female earnings were only 43 percent of men's. In the professional and technical fields women earned 67 percent of the salaries paid to men. (*New York Times*, 11 February 1972, p. 41.)

32. *New York City Poverty Areas*, as designated by the Council Against Poverty, processed, maps, 1966.

33. U.S. Department of Labor, Bureau of Labor Statistics, Middle Atlantic Regional Office, news release, 21 December 1970, p. 1.

34. U.S. Department of Labor, Bureau of Labor Statistics, *Three Budgets for a Retired Couple in Urban Areas of the U.S., 1969-70*, Supplement to Bulletin 1570-6 (no date).

35. Fred Massarik and Alvin Chenkin, "United States National Jewish Population Study: A First Report," *American Jewish Year Book* 74 (1973), p. 286.

36. It is my opinion that there is a likelihood that the positive attitude toward birth control has its roots in European sex codes and practices. See David M. Feldman, *Marital Relations, Birth Control and Abortion in Jewish Law* (New York: Schocken Books, 1974). The practice by oppressive secular European powers of severely limiting marriages of Jews may have been a second contributory factor toward accepting family limitation. See Stefan Behr, *Der Bevölkerungsrückgang der deutschen Juden* (Frankfurt-am-Main: 1932), p. 26.

37. To the best of my knowledge, the history of Jewish participation and leadership in the American birth control and planned parenthood movement has not been recorded. Since the record of social movements depends to a large extent on information furnished by the participants, it may already be too late to

render a good account. Rabbi Mann, for example, left instructions that his papers be destroyed after his death, a wish that was carried out by his family.

38. U.S. Bureau of the Census, Current Population Reports, "Fertility of the Population: March 1957," Series P-20, no. 84 (Washington, D.C.: U.S. Government Printing Office, 1958), p. 4.

39. U.S. Bureau of the Census, *Statistical Abstracts of the United States: 1958* (Washington, D.C.: U.S. Government Printing Office, 1958), p. 41.

40 "Fertility Variations by Ethnic Origin: November 1969," Series P-20, no. 226.

41. "Ethnic Origin and Educational Attainment: November 1969," Series P-20, no. 220, p. 1.

42. Clyde V. Kiser, "The Aging of Human Populations: Mechanisms of Change," in Charles B. Nam, ed., *Population and Society* (Boston: Houghton Mifflin, 1968), p. 364.

43. The reader should be reminded that the enumeration of age is a very sensitive matter. When the comedian Jack Benny refused to grow older than thirty-nine years, he expressed this widespread sensitivity. His refusal to turn forty was an expression of what census technicians call "age heaping." Hyman Alterman, *Counting People, The Census in History* (New York: Harcourt, Brace & World, 1969), p. 76.

44. It should be noted that comparability may be somewhat limited, since the data were collected by different agencies. Since the NJPS presents the age distribution only in the form of a percentage distribution, an adjustment for the .6 and 1.2 percent of persons whose age is not known cannot be made.

45. U.S. Bureau of the Census, Current Population Reports, "Fertility of the Population: March 1957," Series P-20, no. 84 (Washington, D.C.: U.S. Government Printing Office, 1958), p. 1.

46. Saul Kaplan and James P. Rice, "Comment on 'The Invisible Jewish Poor'," *Journal of Jewish Communal Service* 48 (Summer 1972), p. 349.

47. U.S. Bureau of the Census, Current Population Reports, "Fertility History and Prospects of American Women: June 1975," Series P-20, no. 288 (Washington, D.C.: U.S. Government Printing Office, 1976), p. 2.

48. Massarik and Chenkin, "U.S. National Population Study . . ." *American Jewish Year Book* 74 (1973), p. 295.

Sidney Z. Vincent _____

JEWISH COMMUNAL ORGANIZATION AND PHILANTHROPY

In Jewish life, commitments to the community and to *tzedakah* (loosely, philanthropy) are almost as ancient as the Jewish people itself. But the era that began with the close of World War II brought new dimensions to both these basic traditions.

The most obvious measure of the growth and complexity of American Jewish communal life after 1945 is the spectacular increase in philanthropic giving through organized communal activity. There has been nothing before in Jewish life—nor, for that matter, anywhere else—to match this voluntary but organized outpouring of gifts. Throughout their long and, for the most part, tragic history, Jewish communities had certainly come to the rescue of fellow Jews in trouble; the paying of ransoms was a normal and expected component of the Jewish condition. But never to this extent. In the thirty-year period from 1945 through 1975, the organized Jewish communities of America raised in their annual community campaigns (generally called Welfare Fund drives) more than six billion dollars.[1] Nor was this the complete record. These funds were raised to help meet overseas needs and the operating expenses of local and national beneficiary agencies. Massive additional sums were raised for needs not included in the communal drives—most notably for synagogues, capital fund campaigns, and for institutions that for various reasons elected to raise their own funds or were not eligible for such support. Since the thirty-year period was one of extraordinary mobility, in virtually every community in the country there was a major (and often, a total) change in the locale of Jewish neighborhoods as Jews moved from the central city to the suburbs. The resulting construction costs for new buildings during the three decades also ran into the billions. So did the continuing campaign for the sale of Israel Bonds which, while not constituting a philanthropic enterprise, clearly appealed to more than business interests.

The sums raised by the organized Jewish community are of a dimension usually associated with government actions or high finance. Certainly they are rarely raised by private charity—particularly from so small a part of the total American community. Jewish giving in the postwar period to meet human needs overseas has been characterized as the largest and most sustained philanthropic enterprise in history. The following table of year-by-year giving reflects in matter-of-fact, statistical

Table 1. Amounts Raised in Central Jewish Community Campaigns
1945-1975
(Estimates in Millions of Dollars)

YEAR	TOTAL
1945	57.3
1946	131.7
1947	157.8
1948	205.0
1949	161.0
1950	142.1
1951	136.0
1952	121.2
1953	117.2
1954	109.3
1955	110.6
1956	131.3
1957	139.0
1958	124.1
1959	129.1
1960	126.0
1961	124.4
1962	128.1
1963	123.4
1964	125.2
1965	131.3
1966	136.5
*1967	317.5
*1968	232.6
*1969	261.9
*1970	298.9
*1971	359.8
*1972	380.0
*1973	380.0
*1974	660.0
*1975	480.0
Total 1945-1975	6,238.3

*From 1967 to 1975, these totals represent a combination of regular fund-raising and the Israel Emergency Fund.

SOURCE: This table is based on information supplied by S. P. Goldberg.

form what has been in actuality a prodigious, vitalizing communal effort. From a national total of $57 million pledged in 1945 (then itself a record), giving almost quadrupled to over $200 million in 1948.[2] Then followed two decades when annual gifts leveled off at near the $125 million mark, until the outbreak of the Six-Day War in 1967 led to a new record achievement of over $300 million. Then came six years at a new plateau at and above that high level, until the Yom Kippur War once again resulted in a still higher achievement—about $650 million in 1974. At each of these successive transitions to higher standards of giving, it was common to hear predictions that now at last the ultimate in contributions had been reached and it would not be possible for the community to sustain such exemplary giving. In 1946 there was even considerable emphasis on "one-time gifts" on the optimistic assumption that a unique emergency existed that, once met, could be succeeded by "normal" giving.

Life decided otherwise. The responsibilities history imposed on the American Jewish community were continuous, and few facts of Jewish life became more widely accepted than the obligation to make an annual contribution to the communal fund for meeting needs overseas and at home. The traditional *pushkeh* (coin box for charity) of the *shtetl* found its modern counterpart in the computerized pledge card of the community Jewish Welfare Fund drive. The results reflected the change from old-style giving to technological efficiency. What has been called "The Jewish Gross National Project," including all expenditures from whatever source for support of Jewish communal agencies, has been estimated at exceeding two and a half billion dollars annually. For every dollar contributed by the Jewish community itself, four additional dollars come from fees, third party payments, grants, and the like. These figures somewhat distort the practical situation, since of this total amount more than half goes for the support of hospitals and, if they are deducted, about one-third of the remaining costs are borne by the local welfare funds. Nevertheless, the total enterprise now constitutes "big business." And the shareholders, so to speak, are numerous. It is estimated that of the approximately two million Jewish families in America in 1973, more than half were contributors to such funds, with the number rising to 90 percent or better in some of the smaller communities,[3] where it is less possible to avoid communal responsibilities.

What is the explanation for such a dramatic, widespread, and sustained response? It cannot be found only in economic terms—though the Jewish community certainly became more affluent. In the case of philanthropy by the general community, there has been virtually an identity between the graph representing increases and decreases in the level of philanthropic gifts and the graph depicting the ups and downs of the economy. That has not been the case with Jewish philanthropy. According to S. P. Goldberg, outstanding communal researcher, the correlation of Jewish giving has been with "Jewish *tzuris* (troubles)." The high peak of 1974 is typical; it was not a good year economically, but the trauma of the Yom Kippur War led to a breaking of all records for giving.

The deeply rooted and continuing tradition of responsibility of Jews for each other took place in the postwar period at a time of encounter between unprecedented challenges and unprecedented resources to meet them. The challenges are obvious. Indeed, it has become commonplace to point out that the two most flaming Jewish events in millennia occurred within a single decade—the Holocaust and the establishment of the State of Israel. But there was nothing commonplace about their decisive effect on Jewish life everywhere—not least on both philanthropy and the nature of the Jewish community in America.

The work of rescue and rehabilitation differed not only in quantity but in quality from comparable efforts of the past. For the first time Jews were in a position to be masters of their own fate, instead of the puppets of historical forces beyond their control. The giving was not merely to finance a shuffling of refugees from one point to another in the Diaspora, but the ingathering of the remnants of Hitlerism and the relatively newly discovered Jewish communities of the Moslem world into a Jewish homeland—with continuing responsibilities for their welfare accepted by the contributors. The sense of purpose, of having a hand in historic developments, of being front and center on the world stage, with daily headlines testifying to the impact of events the communities themselves helped fashion—these were new and heady experiences.

So too was the fact that Jewish philanthropy had become, so to speak, big business, calling upon the talents of a new class of status professionals and sophisticated laymen. The annual campaigns set formidable goals, demanded sacrifices not only of resources but of time and energy, and in return promised the dividends of tangible Jewish results, with a highly visible impact. These were elements that captivated the interest of laymen. To some cynics, the fringe benefits of being involved in "the best show in town" explained some of the dramatic appeal of the campaigns. Most communities sought to foster a feeling of "family"; the ties that bound contributor to contributor in the yearly joint efforts (that frequently became year-long efforts, so complex did the drives become) were sometimes more responsible for increased levels of giving than the ties that bound contributor to an impersonal beneficiary.

But the spirit animating the campaigns involved more than a desire to advance one's own status by participating in a prestigious communal exercise:

One has only to work in a Federation campaign to understand how it creates a sense of common purpose and action. The atmosphere is one of tension and excitement, of doing something important, being related to Jews wherever they may be. . . . All of the fragmentations of Jewish life seem to disappear when Jews band together in their annual welfare fund campaigns.[4]

Salo Baron, eminent historian, goes further. Taking issue with those who "sneer at such 'pocketbook' Judaism," he draws an only partly tongue-in-cheek parallel between the ritual sacrifices of ancient times and the modern rites of fund-raising in which money, presumably now the most precious possession, is "sacrificed" for the common good. He concludes, more seriously, by stressing that though modern fund-raising is more efficient and vastly more organized, it is an ancient and honorable tradition:

At all times (in Jewish history) major contributors or taxpayers have played a more or less preponderant role in communal affairs. Even in the so-called democratic communities of medieval and early modern Europe wealth carried great weight. In many cases rabbinic decisions emphasized that in communal action a balance must be struck between the will of the majority of constituents and that of the largest financial contributors.[5]

Many critics of the performance of the American Jewish community in the postwar period are less kindly in their evaluations. Almost unanimously, they agree that the outpouring of money was and is critically needed; the remarkable development of Israel and the absorption of millions of immigrants, in the face of massive problems, could hardly have been so successful without the gifts of resources and manpower, as well as the moral and political backing, of the organized American Jewish community. But, they ask, at what price? Although the criticisms are varied, most derive in some fashion from the fear, despite Baron's thesis, that the urgent need for funds will cause the community to be dominated by a plutocracy. The position has been sharply articulated by one critic:

The establishment, for all its rhetoric about being sensitive and appreciative of the total Jewish community, is dominated by a small aristocracy of rich, peripheral Jews, and assimilated Jewishly illiterate, who have arrogated to themselves, by virtue of their wealth, the right to speak for the Jewish community. Their Jewishness is expressed in pseudo-religious terms of a self-proclaimed liberal dogmatism that is somehow equated with prophetic Judaism. . . . The Jewish establishment worships a humanistic, liberal value system that it defines in new terms daily, depending on the vogue of the day, and it calls that "Jewishness."[6]

The claim of lack of representation in decision-making and the charge of elitism in general are most commonly raised by members of the Orthodox community, by women, and by young people (and less responsibly by sloganeers who demand "One Jew, one vote"). There is some evidence to support the complaints. In his study of one major American community, Dr. Arnold Gurin found that although 17 percent of the community designated their Jewish affiliation as Orthodox, only 2 percent of the members of its board of trustees were Orthodox.[7] Such gaps are usually explained by suggesting that representation from the Orthodox or any other section of the community increases in direct proportion to greater involvement in communal activities. Nevertheless, the problem of attaining fuller representation persists, despite the validity of the explanation. Women do occasionally serve as presidents of federations, but it still is a rare occurrence and, despite the importance of "Women's Divisions" in the Welfare Fund drives and the fact that women increasingly control a substantial portion of the community's wealth, women rarely head the annual fund-raising campaigns.

As far as youth is concerned, the 1969 General Assembly of the Council of Jewish Federations and Welfare Funds was picketed by young representatives demanding greater participation in the communal enterprise and changes in the direction of communal life. They charged that the priorities of communal philanthropy were, if not anachronistic, at least obsolescent. Jewish hospitals are the agencies most often pointed to by those advancing this criticism, on the assumption that the rationale for subventing them disappeared once discrimination and difficulties in *kashrut* observance in general hospitals largely ended. Instead, it is argued, community funds should be reserved for those activities that have to do more directly with Jewish commitment, such as Jewish education and culture. (For a full presentation of this viewpoint see Eli Ginzberg, *Agenda for American Jews.*)

The slow pace of change has also been a target of criticism. The social turmoil of the period, with its insistent demands for dramatic action, deeply affected the Jewish community. The tasks of philanthropy were primarily assumed by local federations, whose very name bore witness to the premium placed on accommodation, on compromise, on reaching a consensus that would not alienate significant sections of the community, including important individual contributors. But the times called, it was claimed by critics, for decisive, clear-cut action, with willingness not only to be flexible but to undertake risks in a society insecure and adrift and facing unprecedented new conditions. From a Jewish standpoint, such conditions were often defined as the danger of assimilation, the spread of intermarriage (which was sometimes estimated at close to 50 percent), and the alleged growth of Jewish illiteracy. The organized community had failed to address itself imaginatively to these challenges with the forthrightness that changing times required, the critique concluded.

The leadership of the organized communities tended to agree with the definition of the problems but to deny the charge of indifference or even slowness in addressing them. Certainly the annual meetings of the Council of Jewish Federations and Welfare Funds (CJFWF), the coordinating national agency of the federations, were devoted in significant measure to problems of Jewish commitment and survival and to methods of widening the base of community participation. So were a number of its major committees. The period was not noted for establishment of new national organizations, but those that were created by actions of the organized communities—the National Foundation for Jewish Culture, the Institute for Jewish Life, the Large City Budgeting Conference, the Joint Cultural Appeal—were overwhelmingly aimed at serving these purposes.

Agencies traditionally subvented by the organized Jewish communities were also significantly affected by changing priorities. The national Jewish health agencies (City of Hope, National Jewish Hospital, and so forth) were almost completely phased out of support by the organized Jewish community and became, in fact as well as in program, overwhelmingly nonsectarian. In other cases, notably the community relations agencies, concern with Jewish commitment became a markedly more significant part of their program, one result being increased validation of their claims for continuing communal support. On the local level, there were comparable developments, as will be outlined below.

Moreover, what was seen by the critics as faults was frequently perceived as a mark of communal maturation. The passion for consensus largely eliminated the querulous divisiveness of the earlier immigrant generation—a fragmentation vividly portrayed in Irving Howe's *World of Our Fathers*. Old disputes between Zionist and anti-Zionist (or non-Zionist), secularist and religionist, socialist and capitalist faded as completely as the older divisions between Galitzianer-Litvak-Hungarian. All sections of the community found a common basis of concern in meeting dramatic problems overseas.

Additional forces, both within and outside the Jewish community, also contributed to a growing sense of unity within the community. Most Jewish agencies were originally established in a spirit of "giver" and "taker"; that is, those with means established homes for the aged, summer camps, settlement houses, and various counseling services to help their less fortunate brethren. In the postwar period, almost no Jewish agency would accept so limited a definition of its function. Although service to those in need remained a prime motivation, "need" was redefined to include not only those who were financially troubled, but all those seeking the proferred services, which in effect meant everybody. As Jewish-sponsored homes for the aged attained high levels of quality, waiting lists for entrance contained applications from all sections of the community. Settlement houses became "Jewish Community Centers" with services attractive to all, so that not only their health clubs and swimming pools, but their classes in Jewish dramatics and arts were likely to include members from everywhere. Counseling services of all kinds offered by Jewish agencies of quality were utilized by parents concerned about the appeal of drugs or college admittance or their disturbed children or their own conflicts—all problems that cut across class distinctions. This universality of appeal and the growing affluence of the community reached such dimensions that criticisms were raised as to whether the Jewish community had now forgotten its own poor (most notably in "The Invisible Jewish Poor" by Ann G. Wolfe). No such question would have been raised at the earlier noblesse-oblige stage in Jewish philanthropy.

The general increase in Jewish affluence was, of course, another powerful factor tending to blur earlier class distinctions. In any case, the fact that the producers of the funds also became consumers of the local communal product made for greater involvement in fund-raising and, less universally, in decision-making. Participation in community activities became so widespread that Dr. Daniel Elazar, analyzing the Jewish community of the seventies, established categories not in the usual religious or economic or social terms, but rather in the degree of participation in Jewish life. He defines six levels of Jews: hard core (those living full Jewish lives); participants (those involved in Jewish life more than casually); members (Jews affiliated with Jewish institutions in some concrete way); contributors and consumers; peripherals (those recognizably Jewish but uninvolved); and quasi-Jews.[8]

The worldwide drive toward ethnicity, so vivid a feature of the postwar world, also profoundly affected the Jewish community. The universal resurgence of interest in ethnic heritage was vastly reinforced in the Jewish situation by the aftereffects of the Holocaust and the resurgence of anti-Semitism in new forms. Following a brief period when the shock of Hitlerian atrocities created an attitude of relative understanding for Jewish concerns, world conditions again produced unexpected hostilities, most dramatically symbolized by the United Nations resolution of 1975 equating Zionism and racism. The impact on the American Jewish community was to underline the need for strong and unified central organization, on both the national and local level, to deal with the common threat. Internally, the organized Jewish community placed greatly increased emphasis upon Jewish education and activities leading to Jewish commitment, although criticisms continued that Jewish educational offerings were frequently pallid and did not ward off assimilation. Education originally was not usually a beneficiary of the organized Jewish community, on the assumption that specific Jewish training was the function of the synagogue and the home and not the responsibility of the community as a whole.

That view changed radically during the thirty-year period. In 1975 allocations by federations for Jewish education exceeded $20 million, representing more than 22 percent of all allocations for local purposes and constituting the third largest subvention by Jewish communities to any field of service. Only youth services (including community centers and camps) and family and child services received greater support, and both contained educational components. If funds received from United Ways for operating Jewish agencies are excluded, the change becomes more apparent, since about one-quarter of all funds raised by the Jewish community itself for local services was earmarked for Jewish education. The most significant index of the gradual shift in emphasis toward education was the *rate* of increase by field of service. During the sixth decade of the twentieth century, there was an increase of $5.8 million in total allocations to local services not supported by the nonsectarian United Ways; of this increase, $4.3 million, or 74 percent, was allocated to Jewish education.

Much of this increase was to day schools. For all practical purposes there was no federation support for Jewish day schools at the conclusion of World War II; by 1975 every community in the country with a Jewish population of over 10,000 had a Jewish day school, and the great majority received support from federation funds. Programs of Jewish studies in general universities were confined in 1945 to Harvard and Columbia; by 1975 there were offerings on hundreds of campuses, many of them as a result of some form of cooperation with local federations.

EXPANSION OF COMMUNAL ACTIVITIES

The extraordinary growth in fund-raising during the three decades was paralleled by a comparable growth in responsibilities assumed by the organized Jewish community. The traditional agencies involved in the federated network of the organized community were family service associations, community centers, homes for the aged, hospitals, vocational services and, generally, the health and welfare fields. To these were now added various community agencies or projects concerned with community relations, cultural activities, a variety of programs aimed at reaching college youth, and a cluster of even more experimental and innovative programs—supervision of *kashrut,* employment of *shlichim* (emissaries) from Israel, neighborhood stabilization projects, administration of cemeteries, research programs, and public relations programs. And as third-party payments became increasingly the basis for maintenance of many essential services, more intimate relations with governmental and quasi-public agencies of all sorts grew substantially.

The result of all these influences has been to move the organized Jewish community far beyond its original purpose of raising and budgeting relatively modest funds for a few Jewish agencies into acting as—or aspiring to—the role of "central address" for the Jewish community. This process has been well described by a director of one of the agencies as follows:

In most instances, Federation began as a voluntary association of community services agencies. Its objectives and its functions were relatively mechanistic: to raise the level of financing, to eliminate competing fundraising, to improve the quality of service.

It was an idea that worked. It attracted people in programs that sought affiliation. In the process, Federation took on a personality which vested it with qualities which were partly real and partly wishful anticipation. The base of support broadened; the area of program interest widened. The dream of a future for Federation as "the organized Jewish community" in an organic sense and a drive for its fulfillment gained momentum.[9]

There can be little doubt that the vast fiscal responsibilities, primarily to meet overseas needs, accepted by local communities in the postwar period had the effect of substantially broadening its horizons in areas beyond fund-raising and establishing the federation as the place to turn for resolving problems and accomplishing a variety of Jewish objectives.

But what Jewish objectives? Since federations by definition are committed to include every viewpoint within the Jewish community, they are consciously nonideological. Questions soon arose as to the Jewish direction the community was taking—or indeed, whether the greatly expanded responsibilities were assumed with any clear sense of direction. Decisions made by federations, it was alleged, were taken on a pragmatic, case-by-case basis rather than in any organized or coherent fashion.

For the most part, Federations struggle with these proposals and tend to resolve them on a pragmatic basis, differing from community to community. This process usually takes place without the help of objective guidelines. Instead, there is the "gut feeling" on the part of local Federation leadership—lay and professional—that it would be "a good thing for the community."[10]

Certainly there has been variation from community to community on what constitutes "a good thing": whether to support this or that beneficiary, what action to take on any given project, what importance to assign to particular priorities. Such variations strengthen the hypothesis that communal judgments are basically pragmatic and sometimes erratic, determined by impulse and "gut feelings" and lacking in a shaping sense of direction.

And yet the similarities among the communities, in the decisions they reached and the course they followed during the quarter century, far overshadowed the variations. All became increasingly committed to the centrality of Israel in Jewish life; all increased their emphasis on Jewish commitment and promoting Jewish survival; all supported more or less the same network of local agencies (depending on the size of the community) and made roughly similar judgments in their allocations among the various fields of concern; all conceived of themselves as consensus operations and strove to broaden the base of participation in their activity and, sometimes almost against their will, the range of the activities they supported. Consciously or unconsciously, a sense of direction seemed to be at play. The period marked the end of the era dominated by services to immigrants or the children of immigrants, with its prime emphasis on health and welfare, and the emergence of a native-born, relatively secure community, prepared to take on worldwide responsibilities and at the same time, to serve its own needs.

Earlier visions of a more traditional and more authoritative Jewish community proved unable to adapt to the voluntary and sometimes chaotic American atmosphere. The *kehillah* of the second decade of the century in New York and Mordecai Kaplan's dream of an "organic community" ran counter to the prevailing patterns of decentralization and local autonomy. The Jewish community emerging in America would clearly be a new phenomenon, combining the ancient Jewish commitment to community with the organizational know-how and expertise of the American tradition. That union had produced by the third quarter of the century 215 federations in local communities and a number of national coordinating organizations for the various fields of service.[11] Debate would no doubt continue about the wisdom of decisions taken by the organized communities, but despite (or possibly because of) the lack of an ideology, there could be little doubt that a tacitly agreed sense of direction was at work.

This could be seen in the issues the communities were actively debating in the seventies. No doubt some communities would respond to them through "gut feelings," as charged, and others through deliberate planning. But all would be called on to wrestle with such issues as the half dozen outlined below, selected not as exhaustive but as representative of the many problems confronting them:

PRIORITIES

The most common critique of the organized community has been that its priorities are awry; the most common defense has been that there is no way to secure agreement on overall priorities with finality or objectivity. Moreover, any attempt to do so as part of a grand communal design might fragment the community. The simplest test proposed has been that activities, policies, agencies, and fields of service should receive support to the degree that they contribute to "creative Jewish survival." Such an approach, as suggested above, would increase grants to Jewish education and culture and decrease them to such institutions as Jewish hospitals. Practice has demonstrated that such a test is not only simple but simplistic, if it is administered absolutely and not directionally as a long-range goal. Philanthropy is a voluntary act, and the wishes of donors must be seriously taken into account. In addition, experience raises doubts about how Jewish commitment is created. Formal Jewish education, it is argued, can be highly effective but, if poorly conceived or administered or taught, it can also "turn off" the child. Association with a Jewish organization, including a hospital, can be either Jewishly mean-ingless or linked to the concerns of the Jewish community as a whole and result in increased Jewish commitment. Nevertheless, in practice, agencies are increasingly expected to produce "Jewish creden-tials" by the organized Jewish community. How to proceed further in this direction while retaining the support of all constituents will continue to be a major problem.

Demography complicates the issue of priorities. The Jewish popula-tion of the country is older than the general population, and the coming generation will inevitably have a substantially increased proportion of old people and a lesser proportion of young people. If priorities between fields must be established, this fact will have to be taken into account when hard questions arise as to whether to increase support of care of the Jewish aged or of services to youth; for both objectives there is strong Jewish validation.

National agencies complain that they have been overlooked in sub-stantial measure because the priorities of local and overseas needs are more dramatic and immediate and make it difficult for them to present their case adequately at the local level. Some undertake supplementary campaigns in local communities; this frequently raises involved ques-tions of the mutual obligations, prerogatives, and responsibilities of local and national organizations.

Finally, there is the perennial question of the relationship between the organized community, as represented by federation, and the cluster of direct service agencies. In some communities, the local federation ad-ministers the individual agencies with a strong hand and utilizes the powers implicit in budget control authoritatively. In others, the federa-tion is relatively weak and individual agencies tend to dominate and, in effect, strongly determine priorities by their influence. Most communities would define their procedures as falling between these two poles, but actual conditions require more than easy generalizations about mutual aims and responsibilities. Sharp questions arise: Shall the community as a whole be part of the search process when an agency seeks a new director? What procedures shall be followed when there is basic disagreement on a fundamental question between the agency and the federation? If the community is unable to provide adequate support, shall an agency be free to raise supplementary funds? What constitutes "adequate support" and what restrictions, if any, shall be placed on the fund-raising? Who should be responsible for capital fund-raising and for location of new facilities?

The problem of priorities is obviously a perennial one.

REPRESENTATIVENESS

If the community lodges considerable power within the federation, it has a right to expect that the decision-making will reflect the thinking of as broad a spectrum of viewpoints as possible. How can that be achieved? Is it possible, or even desirable, to achieve that kind of representativeness? A major task of the community at this point is to raise crucially needed funds, particularly for overseas needs. To what extent does this require some "weighting" for those who give well, either of their means or of their ability? Is the popular slogan "one man, one vote" a piece of demagoguery since membership in the community is voluntary and there is no taxing power, or can it be converted into a serious attempt to determine the views of the community? If so, how?

Almost every community has been concerned with this problem. Central community structures are constantly examined, constitutions are modified, and there is almost universal adoption of such policies as rotating officers, limiting terms of office for crucial chairmen, and providing increased points of entry for new talent. Composition of the membership of boards of trustees is examined to determine whether the obvious subdivisions (women, youth, the religious subgroups, "educationists," and the like) are adequately represented. But no completely satisfactory solution has been found to the problem of how to combine experience and responsibility with enthusiasm and full representativeness.

Attempts were made during the 1940s and early 1950s to establish parallel organizations to the federations, usually under the name "Jewish Community Council," that were presumably more representative. These largely lost their momentum as the pressing urgency of problems has led in the other direction—toward establishment of unified central organizations. But the problem of how to achieve greater representativeness remains. It becomes urgent when emergencies arise and the inevitable question is posed: "Who speaks for the Jewish community?" The answer is usually found through either the religious organizations or the federations, but the nature of American life makes it unlikely that any single voice will be accepted as authoritative.

On the national level, the Conference of Presidents of Major Jewish Organizations provides a vehicle for formulation of positions affecting Israel, and as other major issues arise—for example, in connection with Soviet Jewry—organizational structures have been formed to coordinate activities. But such organizations are informal and nonauthoritative, and national agencies (and sometimes local communities) feel free to express their own positions.

FINANCES

Although fund-raising has, under the spur of emergencies, achieved unprecedented levels, both overseas and local needs have simultaneously increased so dramatically that the gap between needs and funds available to meet them is, if anything, wider than at the beginning of the period. With inflation almost certain to remain a constant force for the foreseeable future, the problem of how to maintain adequate support for local services as well as overseas needs will remain a vexing one. If inflation holds at a 6 percent level, it will require a 50 percent increase in contributions in seven years merely to hold the present levels of support—a monumental problem.

Secondary sources of financing, already important, will take on even more urgency. The Jewish community historically lagged behind the general community in the acquisition and use of endowment funds; in recent years, however, these efforts have received increasing priority, as evidenced by the fact that retiring executive directors of federations are frequently kept in service as directors of endowment funds.

For services requiring maintenance of individuals, notably homes for the aged and institutions for children (as well as hospitals), third-party payments have become the major source of support. Clearly, only governmental funds can provide adequately for such maintenance. But agencies that receive public funds are required to extend their services to all citizens, regardless of religion or race. This requirement is no problem to the Jewish hospital, but it is to Jewish homes for the aged and Jewish institutions servicing children. They were founded and exist today primarily to provide a Jewish atmosphere ("a home away from home") and were not designed, as the hospitals were, to serve the general community. To a somewhat lesser degree, the same problem arises in connection with Jewish agencies supported in part by funds derived from the United Fund.

RELATIONS WITH SYNAGOGUES

The American environment is dynamic and mobile and does not lend itself to permanent power centers. Moreover, Jewish communities are highly decentralized; both local federations and local congregations are autonomous and do not adapt easily to central authority or sometimes even to coordination. Both may formulate strong positions on problems of the day and on decisions the community is called on to make. Both are deeply concerned with Jewish education and with nurturing Jewish commitment. Both extend a variety of services to their constituents in times of trouble. Both seek to enlist top leadership in their activities.

Are these two sectors of Jewish life complementary or competitive? Here are two somewhat conflicting views:

This growth (of congregations in the postwar period) in the local communities was accompanied on the countrywide plane by attempts on the part of the national synagogue bodies to lay claim to a larger voice in the affairs of the American community than they had heretofore commanded. Though the challenge that the national synagogue bodies threw out to the federations was only partly successful, this struggle for supremacy bespoke a continuing area of contention within American Jewish life. As leaders of the synagogue bodies sought to bring additional functions into their synagogues (i.e., under their jurisdiction), they increasingly came into conflict with the leaders of the federation bodies, whose conception of the tasks of the community as a whole was expanding at the same time. . . . Organizationally speaking, the first task of the American Jewish community for the final quarter of the century is to deal with the problems brought on by this conflict. [12]

A second, differing view was expressed by the executive vice president of the Council of Jewish Federations and Welfare Funds at a national meeting of the Central Conference of American Rabbis:

Federations and synagogues serve the same communities, serve the same people—the synagogue directly its own members but in a deeper and a true sense serving, too, to enhance the quality of the total Jewish community. And the federations manifestly are committed to serve the well-being and the advancement of the total community. Both are part and parcel of the same community and both reinforce the other. In that collaboration there is much that we can and must do together, and much that each must do distinctively, not in competition, but complementing each other in what each can do best in its own special role. . . . It is a fact that we can have and we do have the strongest federations and the strongest synagogues in the very same cities. [13]

Many of the larger communities of the country have appointed committees on the relationship of synagogues and federations; on the national level, a joint committee is exploring the problem. It may not turn out to be, as predicted, the single most pressing issue, organizationally, in the final quarter of the twentieth century, but there can be no doubt about its major significance. Finances also will play a role in sharpening the problem. As memberships in synagogues decrease, as they inevitably will with the continuing drop in child population, budgeting problems become formidable, and they are turning to federations and communal funds for support, particularly for the Jewish education of the children of their congregants. However, financing by the community usually requires supervision and budgeting, and whether the traditionally totally independent congregations will submit to that discipline remains to be seen.

RELATIONSHIP WITH THE GENERAL COMMUNITY

There are broad constructionists and narrow constructionists in Jewish organizational life. The broad constructionists are prepared to extend the Jewish communal mandate. The well-being of the society as a whole, they argue, is a prime determinant of Jewish status, since times of turmoil produce religious hostility, whereas relatively peaceful times diminish the danger. Therefore, the spectacular leadership provided by the Jewish community for civil rights in the fifties and sixties should now be directed toward other ameliorative measures. It is not sufficient to have fair employment if there is not full employment; the right to purchase a home without discrimination means little unless one can afford the purchase; decay of the cities breeds social disease that in turn will infect society as a whole, with the end result that scapegoats will be sought—often Jewish scapegoats.

Therefore, the Jewish community as such, and not simply interested Jewish individuals, has a stake in fighting pollution and crime, and becoming involved in such measures as gun control and improved transportation and general reconstruction of decaying cities. Not only these pragmatic considerations but traditions of social justice require the organized Jewish community to accept such responsibilities. Unless there is such involvement, there is a lessened likelihood of retaining the interest of young people who are presumably committed to social improvement.

The opposite contention, by the narrow constructionists, warns that to become involved in everything is to dissipate energies and lose sight of the essential and unique responsibility of the Jewish community—to be vigorous in specifically Jewish undertakings, where no one else assumes responsibility. To continue broadening the mandate in the directions urged by the broad constructionists is to fragment the community, since on all these issues there are deep divisions within the Jewish community, and in any event, no specific Jewish expertise exists, nor is it likely that actions taken by the Jewish community will have any significant impact.

RELATIONS WITH ISRAEL

The effects of the establishment of the State of Israel have clearly dominated the actions and the thinking of the organized Jewish community during the period and profoundly affected its function and even its structure. The most prevailing slogan throughout the fund-raising campaigns was "We Are One," stressing the solidarity of the American Jewish community with the Jewish community of Israel. Fund-raising campaigns of the period always included in their appeals the importance of meeting local needs, but the spectacular rise in giving was motivated primarily by the Holocaust and its aftereffects, and the need to provide for "the ingathering of exiles." But local agencies also benefited by the generous outpouring of gifts. The greatly increased giving at the outbreak of the Six-Day War led to the creation of a special Israel Emergency Fund to assure that the additional amounts raised went primarily to meet overseas needs, but with the passing of the years, there was a return in most cities to a single gift, incorporating local, national, and overseas beneficiaries.

There had always been questions as to how to divide the funds equitably between local needs and overseas needs. Early in the period debates as to the proper distribution were sharp and at times acrimonious, even extending in the mid-forties to the division between the two major partners that made up the United Jewish Appeal: the Joint Distribution Committee, primarily responsible for help to communities outside Israel, and the United Palestine Appeal (subsequently, after the founding of the state, the United Israel Appeal) for the work in Israel.[14] By the end of the period, the temperature of such debates decreased markedly. There continued to be variations from community to community but, by and large, a pattern emerged of allocating approximately two-thirds of the funds raised for overseas needs.

But deeper questions of the relationship between the two communities remained. As long as the future of Israel hangs precariously in the balance and the Arab nations are, for various reasons, joined by many other countries in displaying deep hostility, the American Jewish community rallies to Israel's defense, not only through fund-raising but through various forms of political action and enlisting of manpower. Complicated questions of relationships have been postponed. Conservative and Reform Jewry from time to time have voiced dissatisfaction with their lack of legal status in Israel; differences of opinion have emerged as to what position to take in regard to help for emigrants from Soviet Russia leaving Israel for a less arduous life in the United States. But confrontations have been avoided, although issues were constantly debated: Did American Jewry (or, for that matter, other sections of the world) properly have a right to suggest how Israel should conduct itself in closing the social gap between Sephardic and Ashkenazic Jews, or in its relationship with its own Arab citizens? Did Israel properly have the right to intervene in Jewish educational and cultural undertakings in America? American Jewry during the seventies played a key role in reorganization of the Jewish Agency, achieving a greater voice in the agency's decision-making bodies, on the thesis that it should have more than a perfunctory role in determining how the funds it had raised were actually expended. Constant pleas were made by leaders in Israel to American Jewry and its federations to become involved in *aliyah* on the assumption that, although material support was important, the greater need was for people. Various mechanisms were worked out involving high-level coordination of authorities in both countries to control multiple appeals by Israeli organizations.

Underlying all these and other questions was the fundamental issue of the relationship between the two communities. Was Diaspora Jewry a sometime phenomenon, with the only assured Jewish future belonging to the country where Jewish life was primary? Or was Jewish life in America a permanent and creative locus of Jewish life for the foreseeable future? In the latter case, the problem of working out mutual responsibilities (and areas of mutual abstention from interference) would undoubtedly continue to constitute in the last quarter of the century perhaps the major concern and the major undertaking of the American Jewish community.

CONCLUSION

The American Jewish community faced problems in 1977 more complex than those of 1945. The establishment of the State of Israel put major concerns of Jewish life, deeply involving the American Jewish community, front and center on the world stage. At home, the organized Jewish community had greatly expanded its interests and its responsibilities and was looked to as the primary medium for solving, or at least addressing, most problems of Jewish interest. But if there were major issues to be faced, there was also the security derived from a solid past record of accomplishment; the disparate elements of the community had been welded together more coherently than ever before in the American Jewish experience. A Jewish civil service was in the process of emerging as increased attention was being devoted to the planned training of a corps of professionals, and leadership development courses and programs for laymen proliferated. The record of accomplishment of the organized Jewish community and its growing awareness of the many adjustments it still had to make constituted the best assurance that the perhaps even more demanding problems of the last quarter of the century would be met with competence and vigor.

NOTES

1. S. P. Goldberg, *Jewish Communal Services, Programs and Finances,* 17th ed. (New York: Council of Jewish Federations and Welfare Funds, January 1973). Material on the years 1973 through 1975 has also been supplied by Goldberg.

2. Figures reflecting fund-raising are usually stated in terms of the amounts pledged. Experience over the 30-year period would indicate that shrinkage in the amount actually collected was approximately 5 to 6 percent.

3. Charles Miller, *An Introduction to the Jewish Federation* (New York: Council of Jewish Federations and Welfare Funds, 1976).

4. Daniel J. Elazar, "Decision Makers in Communal Agencies: A Profile," *Journal of Jewish Communal Service* (Summer 1973), p. 284.

5. Salo W. Baron, "The American Experience," in Leo W. Schwartz, ed., *Great Ages and Ideas of the Jewish People* (New York: Random House, 1956), p. 461.

6. Bernard Weinberger, "Confessions of an Orthodox Rabbi," *Jewish Life,* Tishrei 5736 (September 1975), p. 25.

7. Arnold Gurin, *The Functions of a Sectarian Welfare Program in a Multi-Group Society: A Case Study* (Ann Arbor, Michigan: University of Michigan, 1965; doctoral dissertation).

8. Daniel J. Elazar, *Community and Polity* (Philadelphia: The Jewish Publication Society of America, 1976), pp. 72ff.

9. William Avrunin, "Can the Future of Federation Be Shaped by the Community Organization Process and the Grand Design?" (unpublished paper, 1976).

10. *Ibid.*

11. The leading national coordinating agencies are the Council of Jewish Federations and Welfare Funds, for the federations; the National Jewish Welfare Board, for the Jewish Community Centers; the National Jewish Community Relations Advisory Council, for the field of community relations; the Jewish Occupational Council, for the vocational service field.

12. Elazar, "Decision Makers . . .", p. 178.

13. Phillip Bernstein, *Federation-Synagogue Relations* (unpublished address delivered to the Central Conference of American Rabbis, San Francisco, 1976).

14. One of the significant developments of the period was the change in the relationships between the two major partners in the annual United Jewish Appeal (UJA). Immediately after the war, the major beneficiary was the Joint Distribution Committee, which had the responsibility of caring for the remnants of the Holocaust. However, as Palestine and then, after the founding of the state, Israel became the most important locus of Jewish settlement and rehabilitation,

the United Israel Appeal became dominant. At times, early in the period, the debates concerning the proper distribution of funds grew so sharp as to threaten the continuance of the joint overall fund-raising mechanism, the UJA. An attempt was made in the mid-40s to create a National Advisory Budgeting Formula that would establish an agreed standard for the division of funds. This specific procedure was defeated, but the two organizations arrived at an amicable understanding and, by the end of the period, little vestige of the early divisions remained.

Shubert Spero ───────────

ORTHODOX JUDAISM

If the religion that the earliest Jewish settlers in America brought with them was Orthodox Judaism, it might be expected that Orthodox Judaism would have been the first to meet the challenge of the American scene. In point of fact it was the last to do so, lagging far behind the Reform and Conservative movements. "It is only in the last few decades since World War II that Orthodoxy has seriously come to grips with the problem of its own future."[1] But this and other important facts about Orthodox Judaism in America, let alone a grasp of their significance, have until recently remained fairly unknown for few serious studies were undertaken prior to the 1960s. The editors of the *American Jewish Year Book* of 1965 introduced Charles Liebman's study of Orthodoxy in America as "a vital but hitherto neglected area of American Jewish life."[2] The primary reason for this was the generally accepted notion, in which even some Orthodox leaders concurred, that Orthodox Judaism simply had no future in America. The open texture of American society, the educational demands of acculturation, the requirements of the economic structure, and all the implications of the melting-pot theory militated against retention of either the religious or the ethnic component of Judaism. If there was any hope for Judaism at all, it was felt, it would have to take the form of some drastically liberalized or modified version of the traditional religion, an "Americanized" form such as Reform or Conservative Judaism.[3] As far as the old Orthodoxy was concerned, good taste required that one avert his gaze from the aimless thrashings of a body in its death throes.

However, Nathan Glazer, writing in the 1950s, reported that "Orthodoxy, despite the fact that it feeds the growth of the Conservative and Reform groups, has shown a remarkable vigor."[4] Glazer viewed this revitalization as a part of the general religious revival that he found in the American Jewish community in the years 1940 to 1956. There was an impressive increase in the number of congregations, of synagogue-affiliated families, and proportion of children attending Jewish schools. Glazer perceived this partly as a result of the Holocaust and the establishment of the State of Israel and partly as a consequence of the movement of Jews to the so-called third area of settlement where social influences that simultaneously strengthened Judaism and weakened *Jewishness*, that is, the secular-ethnic component of Jewish identity, were felt.[5]

Liebman, however, claims that the revival of Orthodoxy was primarily due to the influx of Orthodox immigrants to the United States in the years before and immediately after World War II, an influx which included a leadership more militant than the native Orthodox. Whatever the cause, there is general agreement that in the 1940s Orthodoxy in America seemed to undergo a revitalization and exhibit a remarkable vigor and creativity in a number of areas. Not only had Orthodoxy decided to live rather than die, but it reasserted its claim to being "the true conservator and guardian of Jewish tradition."[6]

The "dignified Orthodoxy" of the earlier Sephardic settlers in America, who were mainly merchants and traders rather than scholars, could stand up neither to the social pressures of the early nineteenth century nor to the intellectual demands for reform introduced by the German immigration of the 1840s and 1850s. By 1881, of the approximately 200 major congregations in existence in the United States, only about a dozen were still Orthodox.[7] For all practical purposes, therefore, the self-conscious struggle of Orthodoxy in America must be seen as starting not earlier than 1880-90, with the large-scale immigration of Jews from Eastern Europe. However, here, too, an important qualification must be entered. The prevailing notion has been that the masses of eastern and central European Jews who came to the United States between 1880 and 1924 were overwhelmingly Orthodox. Under the impact of economic necessity and cultural challenge most of these immigrants and their descendants supposedly abandoned religion completely or joined Reform and Conservative congregations; the minority who remained Orthodox were generally the aged, the poor, and the poorly educated. What we are inclined to question today is the propriety of identifying these masses as "Orthodox."[8] The evidence suggests that most of the nominally Orthodox immigrants to the United States during those years possessed primarily an ethnic commitment to elements of Jewish tradition rather than a religious commitment. Those who emigrated first, often against the advice of their local rabbis, can be expected to have been the least traditional. There was, indeed, a marked paucity of distinguished rabbis and scholars among these immigrants. The American life-style that the immigrants adopted did not entail a decision to opt out of traditional Judaism but rather a decision to substitute new social and cultural mores for the older ones.

How shall we define an Orthodox Jew? In institutional terms we may consider as an Orthodox Jew anyone who affiliates with a nominally Orthodox synagogue. Alternatively, an Orthodox Jew may be defined as one who views the *Halachah*, or Jewish Law, as binding for all Jews, or one who actually behaves in accordance with *Halachah*. In numerical terms, the best estimate in 1965 placed the number of known Orthodox synagogues in the United States at 1,603 with a total affiliation of 205,640 men, or a total of well over one million individuals.[9] An educated guess put the figure of committed Orthodox Jews (those who conduct their lives within the framework of the *Halachah*) at 200,000. In terms of social characteristics, studies indicate that income and educational and occupational levels of the American Orthodox Jew are rising relative to other Jews.

Two groups included among the Orthodox but who are not quite committed to Orthodox Judaism have been identified as the "residual Orthodox" and the "nonobservant Orthodox."[10] The former refers to the remnants of the East European immigrants who remained nominally Orthodox and are responsible for the statistical picture which shows a higher percentage of older persons among the Orthodox. These people form the bulk of the membership of the older Orthodox synagogues in areas of first and second settlement in such cities as Chicago, Philadelphia, Boston, Baltimore, Cleveland, Detroit, and Springfield. The communal structure in these cities was headed by older, European-trained rabbis who formed the membership of the Union of Orthodox Rabbis of the United States and Canada (Agudath Harabanim). This group, which claimed a membership of 600 in 1964, is still active, having allied itself with the heads of the advanced *yeshivot*. However, its influence and prestige has declined greatly. Since the 1940s some of the grandchildren of the residual Orthodox have become committed Orthodox via the day schools.

The non-observant Orthodox are another substantial element. "They are Jews who are affiliated with Orthodox synagogues but have no commitment to even those parts of the *Halachah* practiced by the residual Orthodox."[11] Some of the most affluent among the Orthodox are to be found in this group. Reasons why the non-observant Orthodox affiliate with Orthodox institutions vary. It may be because the Orthodox synagogue has a monopoly in a certain neighborhood, or it may be out of a sentimental attachment to the synagogue to which one's parents belonged; sometimes it is the attraction of a charismatic rabbi or an association developed by sending one's child to the local day school. Liebman observes that "in the older generation the residual Orthodox were Jewishly better educated than the non-observant but the reverse is true of their children."[12] This is because the latter are more likely to be drawn into the network of day schools which exist today.

The committed Orthodox tend to be geographically concentrated. Orthodox Jewish life is dependent upon a number of institutions in proximity to one's home, institutions which require a community for their establishment and maintenance. Included among these are a *mikveh*, a kosher butcher and bakery, a day school at both the elementary and high school level and, of course, a synagogue. Most of the committed Orthodox are to be found in the greater New York area, with smaller centers in some of the larger cities such as Boston, Cleveland, Detroit, St. Louis, Denver, Los Angeles, and Washington, D.C. In none of these areas do all the Orthodox Jews constitute one community in a structural sense. The smallest unit for differentiated grouping among the Orthodox is the synagogue or congregation. Several congregations may have the same *kashrut* system. An even larger combination of congregations may support the same day school. Among the more distinctive Orthodox communities are the densely Hasidic ones in the Williamsburg, Boro Park, and Crown Heights sections of Brooklyn, the Breuer Kehilla in Washington Heights (Manhattan) which continues the Hirschian philosophy of the Frankfurt group, and the diverse community in Monsey, New York.

In terms of synagogue practice, one finds a wide variety of types included within the Orthodox camp. Among the constituents of the Union of Orthodox Jewish Congregations of America are large, stately synagogues which are almost indistinguishable from right-wing Conservative temples. In these synagogues men and women sit together at worship or are separated by a partition that is mainly symbolic. Worshipers wear uniform prayer shawls and skull caps, use a uniform prayerbook, relax in padded, theater-type seats, and respond in hushed tones as prescribed by Western notions of decorum. The cantor is professional and uses a microphone. At the other end of the spectrum is a *shtiebel*-type synagogue in which none of those who perform the duties of cantor, sexton, or preacher are professionals, where the worship services, the decor, and the decorum are characterized by informality, spontaneity, and individuality. Here, in strict accordance with the *Halachah*, no microphone is used and the men are separated from the women in such a manner that they (the women) cannot be seen during services. Between these two extremes there is an entire continuum of mixed types.

As already stated, the revival of Orthodoxy in America may be traced to the influx of Orthodox immigrants to the United States before and immediately after World War II. These included prominent scholars, heads of well-known *yeshivot* in Europe and Hasidic *rebbes* such as Rabbi Aaron Kotler of Kletsk, Rabbi E. M. Bloch of Telshe, and the *rebbes* of Lubavitch and Satmar. These leaders were not only more militant than those who had come before but they carried the sober realization that, with the destruction of European Jewry, the American Jewish community had to become Jewishly self-sufficient. The life-sustaining sources of Jewish existence had to be transferred and built anew in the United States. What followed was a two-pronged educational movement to create simultaneously institutions of Jewish learning on the highest as well as on the elementary level. Rabbi Kotler himself organized the Beth Medrish Govoha, a school for advanced Talmudic study on a post-high school level in Lakewood, New Jersey, with an original enrollment of twenty students. Although it did not at first seem that America was a likely place from which to draw students to a traditional *yeshivah*, others soon followed his lead. Today Lakewood has an enrollment of 450 students, many of them married men living on subventions from the *yeshivah*. There are in America today more than forty academies of varying sizes for advanced Talmudic study with a total enrollment of more than 6,500 students.[13] Some of them, like Telshe Yeshivah in Cleveland, are transplanted European *yeshivot*; others are newly organized in America. Although most are in greater New York, there are thriving *yeshivot* in Baltimore, Boston, Philadelphia, Chicago, Detroit, St. Louis, Denver, and Los Angeles. Graduates of these schools provide the major source of staff for the growing number of day schools.

In 1944, under the initiative of Rabbi S. F. Mendelovitz of Yeshivah Torah Vodaath, Torah U'Mesorah, a national society for Hebrew day schools, was organized. Its purpose was not only to service existing day schools but to encourage, through financial aid and intensive field work, the establishment of new day schools in the larger Jewish communities of the country. Between 1917 and 1938, twenty-eight day schools had been founded mainly in New York; among them were two post-high school *yeshivot*—Torah Vodaath in Brooklyn and Tiffereth Jerusalem in lower Manhattan.[14] The period after 1940 saw remarkable growth, with increases in the number of day schools, students, and communities served by day schools. In 1965 there were 306 Orthodox day schools with 65,000 students located in thirty-four states and provinces in the United States and Canada; 64 percent of the enrollment was in metropolitan New York, and 27½ percent of the enrollment and 44 percent of the schools in other United States communities. Over 70 percent of all Jewish day schools were founded after 1940.[15] In its report of October 1976, Torah U'Mesorah listed a total of 446 Hebrew day schools in the United States (with an additional thirty-two in Canada) with a total enrollment of 92,000 students. Of these, 302 are elementary schools and 144 are high schools.

It should be noted in connection with this post-World War II surge in the development of both advanced *yeshivot* and elementary day schools, that their prototypes already existed quite early in this country. During the first decades of the twentieth century four pioneering *yeshivot* had been established in New York: Rabbi Jacob Joseph School, Rabbi Chaim Berlin School, the Talmudic Institute of Harlem, and the Rabbi Isaac Elchanon (Etz Chaim) School which set the pattern for the future development of both the American *yeshivah* and day school.[16] Under the

leadership of Dr. Bernard Revel, the Rabbi Isaac Elchanon Yeshiva grew
in various ways. In 1921 it formed a Teachers Institute. In 1928 it expanded to include Yeshiva College, a liberal arts college for men, and
added the Bernard Revel Graduate School in 1937. By 1939 about 800
students were enrolled in the various departments of Yeshiva College.
Resembling the Yeshiva in many respects was the Hebrew Theological
College in Chicago which was established in 1921 and which combined a
liberal arts program with Talmudic studies leading to rabbinic ordination.

The growth in Orthodox Jewish education institutions triggered by the
postwar immigration was facilitated by the support of the committed
Orthodox who were already here. These were generally the American-
born children of those who had weathered the acculturation process of
the first two decades of the twentieth century. This element is
exemplified by the Young Israel movement, a lay group dominated by lay
leadership organized in 1912 with a model synagogue on the lower East
Side of Manhattan. Consisting mainly of college-educated, American-
born, middle-class young men and women, Young Israel synagogues
became known for decorum at services, an attractive social and youth
program, adult education, and the requirement that the officers of every
Young Israel branch be Sabbath observers. Reporting ninety-five
synagogues and branches and about 23,000 affiliated families in 1965, the
Young Israel movement "was the one successful effort to bridge the gap
between the faith of the old world and the faith of the new."[17] Young
Israel was among the first Orthodox organizations to seek to raise the
level and dignity of kashrut supervision, to work with the American
military chaplaincy, and to lend support to Zionism and to youth and
collegiate work. It is no accident that a day school will be found in every
community today where a Young Israel synagogue exists.

It seems, therefore, fair to conclude that if we seek to explain the revival
of Orthodoxy after 1940, it should be basically in terms of a working
alliance between a more militant Orthodoxy among the World War II
immigrants and the small group of residual, native-born, committed
Orthodox clustered around Young Israel and the pioneering yeshivot like
Rabbi Isaac Elchanon and the Hebrew Theological College.

The growth of day schools and advanced yeshivot has resulted in an
increased emphasis on halachic observance within the entire Orthodox
community. Thus, Young Israel, which at one time was proud of the fact
that it relied on lay leadership and did not need rabbis to officiate, has
changed its policy to the point where almost every branch has its own
rabbi. It has been noted that these spiritual leaders tend to be more
aggressive and less compromising than their colleagues in other Orthodox synagogues.[18] Young Israel no longer tolerates mixed dancing at

its conventions. The Union of Orthodox Jewish Congregations reports that since 1955 some thirty synagogues which formerly had mixed seating have installed *mechitzot* (separations between the men's and women's sections of the synagogue).[19]

One of the most successful efforts of the Union is its *kashrut* program which, together with the Rabbinical Council of America, the largest association of Orthodox American-trained rabbis, supervises and certifies over 5,000 products. The (U) symbol unobtrusively printed on the label is looked for and relied upon by thousands of consumers from coast to coast.[20] Observance of the traditional dietary laws no longer entails the sacrifices and restrictions that it once did. Kosher food at no extra cost is now available on all the major airlines, in many hospitals, and in some national motel chains. Today Orthodox Jews can vacation at resorts in Miami or in the Caribbean which combine the usual luxury features with scrupulous adherence to Jewish ritual law. More recently New York has seen a proliferation of fancy kosher restaurants and something which has been called Orthodoxy's answer to McDonald's and Colonel Sanders: the Kosher King drive-in restaurant!

Symptomatic of the increased sensitivity to *Halachah* is the growing demand for even higher, extrahalachic standards in food preparation such as *Glatt Kosher* and *Cholov Yisroel.*[21] But perhaps the most surprising development of all is a reawakened interest in what until recently was surely considered the most archaic of Jewish halachic requirements and the one least expected to survive the onslaught of the American spirit. I refer to a married woman's monthly immersion in a ritual bath known as a *mikveh* and the prohibition of marital relations in the period which precedes it. The *New York Times* recently reported a renaissance of this ancient ritual based on "the proliferation of seminars and lectures on the subject, in tours of *mikvaot,* open discussions of the practice from the pulpit and in Jewish women's organizations."[22] In 1965 there were 177 public *mikvaot* in the United States.

So far we have emphasized *Orthopraxis* —the shift to traditional practice and observance. How has Orthodoxy fared with focus on its doctrines and creeds? In describing the devastating effects of the intellectual attacks against traditional religion which took place in the middle of the nineteenth century, Nathan Glazer notes the special plight of Orthodoxy: "The defenders of Traditional Judaism, accepting neither the rationalism of the enlightenment nor the reaction of romanticism, were thus left without intellectual weapons of any force among Jewish intellectuals and had to battle the Jewish rationalism of the 19th century with the weapons of the Middle Ages."[23] Of course, it was not quite that bad. Glazer ignores the work of Samson Raphael Hirsch and the school that formed around him. The fact is that by this time almost all the writings of Hirsch have been translated into English and Hebrew, testifying to their relevance to at least some of the intellectual problems that Orthodoxy faces today.

Oddly enough, however, the problem of theology, or the need to present a rational reconstruction of the creedal aspects of Judaism, seems to have receded in importance. Writing in 1965, Charles Liebman reported that "the main body of Orthodoxy in the United States appears at present to be doctrinally untroubled" and that those who abandon Orthodoxy because of intellectual problems are "quantitatively insignificant."[24] At least some of this change should be attributed to the effects of the existentialist movement in philosophy and in the arts that reached America in the 1950s. The assumptions of rationalism and naturalism came under attack, the human predicament was seen as filled with tensions and contradictions and, in seeking a philosophy of life, contemporary man was urged to look for "authenticity" and "subjective truth" and not to fear "paradox."[25] It is no wonder that Reform and Reconstructionist Judaism on the whole rejected existentialism.[26] For Orthodoxy, however, existentialism created the philosophic climate and popularized certain categories of thought wherein the classical biblical concepts could again be spoken and appreciated. In general Jewish thought the way was prepared by such writers as Martin Buber and Franz Rosenzweig, whose work had been made available to the English-speaking public. Among Orthodox writers the existentialist approach is reflected by Rabbi Joseph B. Soloveitchick and Abraham J. Heschel. Theological writing of a more analytic nature is to be found in the pages of the journals *Tradition* and *Judaism* by a coterie of Orthodox rabbis and professors of Jewish Studies who hold advanced degrees in philosophy and utilize the conceptual tools of modern thought to explicate the principles of Judaism and critically evaluate the attacks made on it.[27]

Evidence of Orthodoxy's ability to have worked through many of its doctrinal problems is seen in the replies of the Orthodox respondents to a symposium conducted by *Commentary* in 1966.[28] The journal addressed four basic questions of Jewish belief, including revelation and the concept of the chosen people, to fifty-five Orthodox, Conservative, and Reform rabbis. Thirty-eight replies were received—fifteen from Reform rabbis, twelve from Conservative rabbis, and eleven from Orthodox. In analyzing the replies it was found that the true division was between the Orthodox and the non-Orthodox. The Reform and Conservative replies were indistinguishable on any basis of content. The replies of the Orthodox rabbis, however, were unanimous in upholding the traditional viewpoint and yet were formulated in a manner which revealed their awareness of, and struggle with, the challenges of modern thought.[29]

The divergences within Orthodoxy have been described in different ways. Liebman at one time suggested the typology of the church-sect dichotomy, in which these ideal types are set up as end-points on a continuum along which religious groups can be placed and evaluated.[30] The *church*, recognizing the strength of the secular world (in our case the larger Jewish society as well as the non-Jewish society), accepts the main elements of the social structure and works within its framework. The *sect* repudiates the compromises of the *church*, is hostile or indifferent to the secular order, and seeks primarily to satisfy individual religious needs rather than societal ones. Using this framework, we can identify a church wing of Orthodoxy that would comprise the so-called modern Orthodox and which would include the Rabbinical Council of America with its close to 1,000 members whose spiritual leader is Rabbi Joseph B. Soloveitchick, the Union of Orthodox Jewish Congregations of America, the National Council of Young Israel, the Religious Zionists of America, Yeshiva University, the Hebrew Theological College, and the Sephardic community (consisting in 1965 of sixty-three congregations and an estimated 25,000 members).

The sect wing of Orthodoxy would include the Hasidic communities, the *yeshivah* world, the Breuer community, Agudath Israel, the Rabbinical Alliance of America, and the Agudath Harabanim. An alternative way to describe these differences is in terms of the interplay of integration-survival forces.[31] The majority of Jews in modern times are torn between two desires. On the one hand, there is the wish for acceptance by gentile society and the attraction of non-Jewish values and attitudes. At the same time, there is a strong desire for group identity and survival as a distinct community. Clearly, an extreme survival position is incompatible with integration and an extreme integration position is incompatible with survival. Even as Orthodox Jews differ from Conservative and Reform Jews in their understanding of the most effective strategy to insure both integration and survival, so, too, do the Orthodox differ among themselves. Thus, for example, some Hasidic groups can be viewed as taking an extreme survival position, tending to be quite indifferent to the rest of the American Jewish community and seeking only a minimal economic relationship with the non-Jewish society.

To explain these differences becomes a bit more difficult. It is certainly to be doubted that the differences between the two wings of Orthodox Jewry are to be attributed to their differing degrees of acculturation. The reverse seems closer to the truth. The lack of acculturation among the sectarian Orthodox seems to be the result of their conscious rejection of integration.[32] Most of the students in the advanced *yeshivot* will not attend college on principle or will take courses of study that are narrowly vocational.

The most plausible explanation for the church-sect difference within

Orthodoxy is the differing perceptions of certain principles of Judaism along lines which seem to approximate a fundamentalism-liberalism scale. The issues in the Orthodox community today which reflect these differences and which evoke the most heated debates are the following:[33]

RELATIONSHIP TO GENERAL CULTURE

This, of course, is an old controversy that goes back to the Maimunist-anti-Maimunist split of the fourteenth century and to even earlier roots.[34] The issue is not whether Judaism is compatible with this or that philosophy, but whether Judaism is ever in any need of being understood in terms of categories other than its own. In the nineteenth century the issue was raised anew in the teachings of Samson Raphael Hirsch (1808-1888), who called his approach *Torah im Derech Eretz,* meaning "Torah with secular education."[35] While Hirsch proclaimed the supremacy of the Torah over the civilization of the passing age, he insisted on the need for acquiring the best of the knowledge that the age had to offer. The community established by Hirsch in Frankfurt, strengthened by the work of Israel Hildesheimer and David Hoffman in Berlin, had produced by World War II three generations of Western European Orthodox Jews who included in their ranks an imposing list of physicians, lawyers, and industrialists who were knowledgeable and observant of Jewish tradition and yet involved in modern life. Infiltrated by the *yeshivah* world, the upholders of Hirsch's views on secular learning today are very much on the defensive even in the Breuer community. In a pamphlet published in 1966, Rabbi Shimon Schwab, associate rabbi of the Breuer Kehilla, felt impelled to present both the "Torah-only" view of the *yeshivah* world and the *Torah im Derech Eretz* view of Hirsch as possible and valid options for the Orthodox Jew. However, Schwab courageously pointed out that, contrary to *yeshivah* attempts to rewrite history, for Hirsch the obligation to study general knowledge was not a one-time concession to stem the tide of assimilation but the ideal Jewish outlook to be pursued at all times and under all conditions.[36]

The issue seems to depend upon one's perception of Torah. Is the Jew to regard the body of doctrine found in the written and oral tradition as the sum total of all necessary wisdom, as sufficient to meet all of his intellectual needs? Or is the Torah merely the prescription of *Halachah,* directives as to how a Jew is to live ritually and morally and the basic insights into the nature of God, man, and sacred history? And were these meant to be supplemented by a growing body of knowledge and ideas as man exercises his reason, explores his world, and deepens his insights through experience? As Maimonides taught, the more man learns about himself and his world, the more will he learn to appreciate and love the

Creator of his universe and the better will he understand God's Torah. Thus doing and studying science and acquiring an understanding of the regnant philosophy is not only permitted for a Jew but is a religious obligation.

The only concession that the *yeshivah* world (except, of course, for Yeshiva University and the Hebrew Theological College) makes toward college education is if it can be justified as necessary for making a living. It denies that knowledge from sources outside of Torah has any intrinsic value. Others in the *yeshivah* world agree that knowledge of the world, if it could be acquired in an antiseptic form of "pure facts," might be permissible. However, they claim that today's milieu and the form in which this knowledge must be experienced is so permeated with naturalistic bias and irreligious attitudes that the religious cost for a Jewish student to go to college is prohibitive. The astonishing fact is that many American-born young men and women have been persuaded by the *yeshivah* that they can find complete intellectual fulfillment in Torah alone. Involved here is not only the question of a college education but one's attitude toward the arts and the cultural life of America as a whole. The modern Orthodox Jew is interested in the theater, literature, music, and the visual arts not only as consumer but as creator; not merely as entertainment but as another dimension of emotional and intellectual fulfillment as a human being. The followers of the *yeshivah* world and the Hasidic elements would see all of this as, at best, a waste of time.

The modern Orthodox have developed a variety of organizations designed to assist those in college and university. Under the sponsorship of Young Israel some fifteen kosher eating plans have appeared on campus, many of them in conjunction with Hillel Houses. Yavneh, a Jewish student organization, was founded in 1960 and in 1964 reported over forty chapters in American colleges and universities. Affirming its commitment to *Halachah*, Yavneh calls for an understanding of what the *Halachah* is and a decision by the individual. Yavneh sponsors many seminars, Shabbatons, and discussions on campus, as well as special study programs in Israel, and it emphasizes intellectual over social activity. It has also issued a number of interesting publications geared to college students.[37]

Reflecting Orthodoxy's involvement with secular knowledge and education is a group called the Association of Orthodox Jewish Scientists. Claiming a membership of 1,000, it issues a publication and at its periodic conventions conducts seminars on a variety of problems which touch upon the interaction of science and *Halachah*. The observation has been made that the overwhelming majority of its members are natural scientists with universities, government, or large corporations, and few are from the social sciences. This might explain their tendency to concentrate more on narrow technical problems rather than address themselves to some of the broader moral and philosophical issues which confront Orthodoxy. For, as Liebman correctly observes, "It is not difficult to dichotomize religious belief and scientific work, whereas the very assumptions of the social sciences are often thought to run counter to traditional Orthodox views."[38]

RELATIONS WITH THE NON-ORTHODOX

The second most important issue that divides the left and the right in Orthodox Jewry is the question of how to relate to the Reform and Conservative communities. The dilemma that these constitute for Orthodoxy may be understood in terms of two mutually exclusive mandates. Since it is a major tenet of Orthodoxy that it is the obligation of every Jew to observe the *mitzvot* (religious commandments), the Orthodox are doctrinally obligated to encourage the observance of Jewish law among all Jews here and now. On the other hand, Orthodoxy perceives itself as the only legitimate bearer of Jewish tradition with an exclusive claim to the truth. To the extent that Conservative and Reform doctrines and practices deviate from Orthodoxy, they must be seen as false and misleading. Thus Orthodoxy is always wary of appearing to accept or "legitimize" non-Orthodox versions of Judaism as valid alternatives. But since most of the reachable non-Orthodox Jews are affiliated with Reform and Conservative institutions, how can Orthodoxy relate to them without giving recognition and comfort to the existing institutions where they are to be found?[39] Moreover, overriding needs such as the plight of Soviet Jewry or the security of Israel, where a united effort on the part of all Jews is required, sometimes arise. There are virtually no Orthodox groups who would, at such a time, stop to question the doctrinal correctness of the Jews with whom they are working.

Modern Orthodoxy takes the position that, for the sake of Jewish unity and more effective action in matters of mutual concern, it should cooperate on a formal ongoing basis with Conservative and Reform Jews, rabbis, and organizations. Thus the Union of Orthodox Jewish Congregations of America and the Rabbinical Council of America are members of the Synagogue Council of America. Their presidents, as well as presidents of the National Council of Young Israel and the Religious Zionists of America, participate in the Presidents' Conference. Many members of the Rabbinical Council of America are also members of the New York Board of Rabbis and other local mixed rabbinical groups. They counter the arguments of the right by claiming that cooperation with the Reform and Conservative movements does not imply recognition; that Conservative and Reform laymen and rabbis are not to be classified as *minim*, or heretics; and that uncivil behavior on the part of the Orthodox will only serve to further alienate the masses of Jews from traditional Judaism.[40] The Orthodox right takes issue with every one of the aforementioned statements and appeals to the authority of the *gedolim* (masters of Jewish tradition) or heads of the advanced *yeshivot* who, in 1955, issued an *issur* (prohibition) against joining mixed groups such as the Synagogue Council of America.[41]

The modern Orthodox respond to the issue of authority by pointing to their own "master of Jewish tradition," Rabbi Joseph B. Soloveitchick, who had not signed the *issur* and tacitly approves the position of the Rabbinical Council of America.[42] But more importantly, it is argued that broad communal questions, such as cooperating with non-Orthodox Jews, are not strictly halachic questions but matters of policy which ought not to be decided simply by appealing to halachic authorities. In these matters the views of the individual rabbis in the field, as well as the views of intelligent lay leaders, ought to be considered.[43]

Historically there would appear to be a basis for both the policies of coalitionism and separatism in Orthodox ideology. It seems that separatism originated in the Orthodox experience in Western Europe, whereas participation and cooperation (coalitionism) was the dominant policy in Eastern Europe where different conditions obtained. "Where Jews chose the religious options, as in Western Europe, we find Reform Judaism, a high rate of intermarriage, deemphasis of the Hebrew language and an Orthodox religious group which favored secular education but separated itself from the non-Orthodox Jews. In those countries (Eastern Europe) where the communal option was chosen we find Jewish political parties, a demand for cultural separation, strong Zionist orientation . . . low rates of intermarriage and a traditional Judaism which opposed secular education . . . *but remained part of the total Jewish community vying for its leadership.*"[44]

American Orthodoxy would thus appear to be the heir to conflicting traditions on the question of cooperation with the non-Orthodox. Modern Orthodoxy continues to be open to suggestions for increased dialogue between the "three wings" of Judaism, and even for some kind of mutual acceptance based upon the recognition of a "common framework." However, with all the best intentions, severe difficulties seem to be involved in that even such basic concepts as God and Torah may already mean different things today for Orthodox, Conservative, and Reform theologians.[45] It has been noted that American Jewry has been able to abide its own religious divisions in the past because of the uniting force of a common ethnicity. The notion that "we are all nevertheless Jews" was supported by the fact that all unmarried Jews were able to intermarry with each other. However, with the deepening of religious differences—for example, the practice of remarriage without a *get* (religious divorce), or one improperly drawn, and the performance of conversion without regard to halachic norms—we may be approaching the time when not all individuals who believe that they are Jewish will be accepted as such by other Jews. The unity of American Jewry may be in jeopardy.[46]

RELATIONSHIP TO ZIONISM AND ISRAEL

There can be no question about the high reverence that all elements within Orthodoxy have for the Holy Land as such. There are, however, deep emotional and intellectual differences between the two wings of Orthodoxy in regard to their policy toward Zionism as an organized movement and toward the secular State of Israel. This goes back to the Mizrahi-Aguda controversy which started in the early part of this century. In part, the issue of Zionism can be viewed as an instance of the general question of relating to the non-Orthodox. Here again the right wing Agudath Israel, consisting of *yeshivah*, Hasidic, and Hirschian Orthodoxy, argued that any form of cooperation with the Zionist organizations constituted a legitimation of secular nationalism as a definition of Jewishness. Mizrahi, which has evolved into the Religious Zionists of America, and the Mafdal, the National Religious Party in Israel, replied that Orthodox Jews may work together with others toward the creation of an autonomous Jewish state in Israel without surrendering their ultimate goal of imparting to the state a religious character.

Zionism, however, involved the additional issue of messianism. Here, again, differing conceptions divide the right and the left wings in Orthodoxy. Sectarian Orthodoxy sees the return of Jews and Jewish independence to the land of Israel as one of the events involved in the process of redemption, which they conceive as directed by God and accompanied by a religious reformation on the part of all Jews. Events involving the land of Israel from which the overt hand of God and Jewish spirituality are absent are viewed with grave suspicion and ambiguity by the right wing of Orthodoxy. Although Agudath Israel refused to join the Zionist Organization during the pre-state period, it participated in the political process in Israel and at one time was a member of the government. Religious Zionists, such as the adherents of Mizrahi, justified their policies from the very beginning by a conception of the redemptive process which was gradual and called for the initiative to be taken by the Jewish people themselves.[47] The teachings of the first Chief Rabbi of Palestine in the pre-statehood era, the revered mystic, Rabbi Abraham Isaac Ha-Kohen Kuk, have been most influential in providing a complete rationale for the policies of religious Zionists in their struggle with the

Orthodox right. There are some religious Zionists today who believe that the Messianic activism of Rav Kuk is being misinterpreted in the efforts of such militant Orthodox groups as the Gush Emunim who are fighting for Jewish settlement in the Israeli-occupied territories of Judea and Samaria and oppose the return of any of these lands.

The most extreme negative view on Zionism is held by the Satmarer Hasidim and their Israeli followers, the Neturai Karta. In regard to changing the dispersed condition of the Jewish people, they are committed to a policy of "quietistic apoliticism" which implies that the very idea of an independent Jewish state before or without Messiah is heretical and must be viewed as an act of defiance by arrogant men.[48] Their extreme anti-Israel position, which periodically prompts them to denounce Zionism in paid advertisements in the *New York Times*, recently caused a bitter and acrimonious debate to break out between the followers of Satmar and the *Rebbe* of Lubavitch. This was over the question of whether the Entebbe rescue of 1976 should be viewed as a miraculous deliverance for which the Israeli army is to be praised. Satmar and their followers criticized the praise heaped upon the rescuers, whom they dubbed "godless men." In a public address the *Rebbe* of Lubavitch hailed the rescue as a miracle and stated that all those involved were assured of a portion in the world-to-come for risking their lives for their fellow Jews.

The fact remains that, for all the ambiguities that Orthodoxy finds in modern Zionism, almost all Orthodox elements continue to take a very active role in every aspect of the upbuilding of the State of Israel, from fund-raising to *aliyah*.[49]

ATTITUDE TOWARD HALACHAH

Writing in 1954, Emanuel Rackman, considered one of the foremost spokesman for modern Orthodoxy, stated that the greatest challenge which faces the movement "lies in the realm of the *Halachah*. . . . Is the *Halachah* viable in the modern age. . . . Is it relevant to our yearnings and aspirations?"[50] Since then this theme has been taken up periodically by Rackman, Irving Greenberg, Eliezer Berkovits, and others who, while not sanctioning any particular practice or sponsoring any specific deviation from the standard Orthodox rulings, have nevertheless urged that the Halachists show greater flexibility and creativity in their application of the *Halachah*. The modern Orthodox claim that the duly constituted authorities in Orthodoxy today have the power to make many necessary changes and that the principles exist within the *Halachah* to justify these rulings, but that they are prevented from so doing by various nonhalachic considerations. Berkovits in particular has marshaled a wealth of illustrations from classical sources to show that authentic *Halachah* in every historic period has been "the law applied in a given situation in such a manner as to render it (1) practically feasible, (2) economically viable, (3) esthetically significant, and (4) spirtually meaningful." He convincingly argues that these considerations are not social pressures existing outside the system which, if allowed to influence the *Halachah,* distort it. On the contrary, these concerns have always been an integral part of the halachic process and should continue to be so today.

The refusal by the traditional authorities to recognize these broad social concerns as operative principles in their decisions has resulted in a "freezing of the *Halachah.*"[51] The Orthodox left believes that a number of halachic problems over the past decade, such as the autopsy controversy in Israel, Jewish divorce problems, and the issue of conversion could be handled with greater attention to the humanitarian factors. Thus, in regard to the problem of conversion and the differences in procedures followed by the Conservative and Reform rabbis, Berkovits suggests that Orthodoxy should agree to some minimal procedure that could be accepted by all wings of Judaism. Adoption of more lenient requirements in this area would be justified by the important principles of "unity of Israel" and "love of Israel." Here again is reflected modern Orthodoxy's broader approach to *Halachah.* "It is not just a matter of conversion but rather the problem of how to decide in the case of a conflict between the laws of conversion and one's Torah obligation of preserving *Achdut Yisrael* and *Ahavat Yisrael.*"[52]

There is perhaps another and more subtle cleavage in the thinking of the Orthodox in regard to *Halachah.* The *yeshivah* world seems to view every ritual prohibition as another expression of piety; the more strict and rigorous one is in one's observance of the ritual *mitzvot,* the deeper one's religiosity. The modern Orthodox Jew, however, while committed to observance of the *Halachah,* seeks to do what is required in a conscientious and devoted way but sees no special merit or religious value in adopting the more stringent view in areas of ritual *Halachah.* For him true piety is to be sought in the affective areas of one's relationship to God and in one's attitude and relationship to one's fellowman.

In the United States there are few ideological differences between the main-line Hasidim and the non-Hasidic Orthodox of the right. The Hasidim have retained their traditional European dress and some special customs. There is also the institution of the *rebbe,* or Hasidic leader, around whom the Hasidim build their religious lives. In addition to their main centers in the Boro Park, Crown Heights, and Williamsburg sections of Brooklyn, the Hasidim are attempting to build insulated enclaves of Orthodox Jewish life outside the inner city in rural areas like New Square. Among the Hasidim the Lubavitcher movement, headed by

Rabbi M. M. Schneersohn, stands out by virtue of its militant missionary activity among nonreligious Jews. Although its day schools have not been too successful, it has been able to attract many young people to its retreats, Chabad Houses on campus, and weekend "encounters" with the *rebbe*. It would seem that the same social forces which brought forth the "hippie" movement, the "flower children," and the "drug culture" with its emphasis on the intrinsic value of immediate sensory experience and human fellowship, have created a congenial atmosphere for the exotica in Judaism-Hasiduth.

In general, there is little ongoing contact between the modern Orthodox and the Hasidic communities. Their cohesiveness and their growth potential, however, make them a highly visible group and an element that will have to be reckoned with by both the non-Orthodox and the non-Hasidic Orthodox. In 1965, Liebman estimated, "with 5000 families averaging perhaps seven or eight children, the Satmar community today numbers between 35,000 and 40,000 individuals."[53] In terms of their broader significance, they seem to constitute an interesting alternative to the approach of the modern Orthodox with their policy of cooperation with the non-Orthodox and integration into many areas of the general culture. The Satmar community goes its own way, remaining financially independent of the Jewish federations, and seems to have found a formula for Jewish survival in America while keeping acculturation to a bare minimum. However, we do not have sufficient information concerning their internal problems and tensions to make any judgment as to the success of their formula.[54]

There is no doubt that the old antagonisms, intellectual and social, to the world of Orthodoxy are largely gone. Orthodox Judaism is today a genuine option for American Jews. While, on the average, Reform Jews continue to be in the highest income bracket and Orthodox Jews in the lowest, the overlap between the "three wings" has been growing. An increasing number of Orthodox synagogues are now located in areas whose social characteristics are above those of some Conservative and Reform temples. There is no longer a social stigma attached to Orthodox affiliation.

There are forces operating today which appear to favor the Orthodox synagogue. The positive status which authentic religion, particularly of an individual and personal nature, enjoys today acts to its advantage. There is general admiration today for the strength and will which has motivated Orthodoxy to build its day schools, spread its *yeshivot*, keep its youth free of the aberrations of American society, and maintain its devotion to Israel at a sustained peak. The large size of many Reform and Conservative temples may actually repel some people. There is an anonymity and lack of warmth in large institutions, whereas a smaller congregation (which the Orthodox tends to be) gives a sense of intimacy and a feeling of fellowship.

An age which values authenticity and genuineness is bound to look with a certain approval upon Orthodox Judaism. Even if one does not personally embrace the Orthodox way of life, one is apt to agree with Irving Kristol: "I am not Orthodox—but I think that Orthodoxy is the most important segment of Judaism. It is the one segment that survives all ideologies. . . . Survival happens to be its strength. It has many weaknesses, I know, but that fanatical adherence to the Orthodox way of life is what permits it to survive. . . . Therefore, I think it behooves all Jews to pay a certain special attention both to Orthodoxy and to what I would call neo-Orthodoxy."[55]

NOTES

1. Emanuel Rackman, "American Orthodoxy—Retrospect and Prospect," *Judaism*, vol. 3, no. 4, Fall 1954, p. 302.

2. *American Jewish Year Book* 66, 1965, p. 2.

3. Marshall Sklare, "Judaism at the Bicentennial," *Midstream*, November 1975, p. 26.

4. Nathan Glazer, *American Judaism* (Chicago: University of Chicago Press, 1957), p. 109.

5. *Ibid.*, pp. 116-117.

6. Sklare, "Judaism . . . ," p. 26.

7. Glazer, *American Judaism*, p. 38.

8. Charles S. Liebman, "Orthodoxy in American Jewish Life," *American Jewish Year Book* 66, 1965, pp. 9-12.

9. Liebman, "Orthodoxy . . .," p. 5. The Union of Orthodox Jewish Congregations of America claims a total of 3,600 synagogues and to speak for three million Jews. See p. 37.

10. *Ibid.*, p. 12.

11. *Ibid.*

12. *Ibid.*, p. 18.

13. Liebman puts the number at 10,000. See his *The Ambivalent American Jew* (Philadelphia: Jewish Publication Society of America, 1973).

14. Alvin Schiff, *The Jewish Day School in America* (New York: Jewish Education Committee Press, 1966), p. 245.

15. *Ibid.*, p. 246.

16. *Ibid.*, p. 44.

17. Irving Howe, *World of Our Fathers* (New York: Harcourt Brace Jovanovich, 1976), p. 198.

18. Liebman, "Orthodoxy . . .," p. 41.

19. *Ibid.*, p. 42.

20. There are a number of other symbols of *kashrut* certification, both national and local, such as K and (K).

21. *Glatt Kosher* signifies a more meticulous inspection of the animal's lungs than is actually required. *Cholov Yisroel* refers to milk produced under Jewish supervision.

22. *New York Times,* 16 August 1976.

23. Glazer, *American Judaism,* p. 30.

24. Liebman, "Orthodoxy . . .," p. 29.

25. Shubert Spero, "The Meaning of Existentialism for Orthodoxy," *Perspective,* Winter 1959.

26. Eugene Borowitz, "Existentialism's Meaning for Judaism," *Commentary,* November 1959.

27. S. T. Katz, *Jewish Philosophers* (New York: Bloch, 1975), p. 250.

28. *The Condition of Jewish Belief* (New York: Macmillan, 1966).

29. Shubert Spero, "The Condition of Jewish Belief—A Review-Article," *Tradition,* Fall 1967.

30. Liebman, "Orthodoxy . . .," p. 22.

31. Liebman, *The Ambivalent American Jew,* p. 23.

32. Liebman, "Orthodoxy . . .," p. 28.

33. In a recent article ("Voices of Orthodoxy," *Commentary,* July 1974) David Singer accurately identifies the two main divisions within Orthodoxy today and correctly points to the different "voices" which reflect their respective views— *Tradition,* the publication of the Rabbinical Council of America, for the modern Orthodox, and the *Jewish Observer,* the organ of Agudath Israel, for the sectarians.

34. The issue may go back even further to the discussion in the Talmud between Rabbi Shimon ben Yochai and Rabbi Ishmael (*Berachot* 35b) on whether a man is to engage in a worldly occupation or take literally the words: "This book of the Torah shall not depart out of thy mouth, but thou shalt meditate therein day and night" (Josh. 1:8).

35. *Avot,* 2:2. Actually, "An excellent thing is study of Torah combined with a worldly occupation." See J. L. Blau, *Modern Varieties of Judaism* (New York: Columbia University Press, 1966).

36. Simon Schwab, *These and Those* (New York: Feldheim, 1966).

37. Liebman, "Orthodoxy . . .," p. 38.

38. *Ibid.,* p. 39.

39. *Ibid.,* p. 21.

40. See Shubert Spero, "Does Participation Imply Recognition?," *Tradition,* Winter 1966.

41. See the exchange between Rabbi R. Pelkovitz and Shubert Spero in *Tradition,* Fall 1967.

42. See Shlomo Riskin, "Orthodoxy and Her Alleged Heretics," and Joseph Lookstein, "Coalitionism and Separatism in the American Jewish Community," *Tradition,* Spring 1976.

43. Samuel Belkin, *Essays in Traditional Jewish Thought* (New York: Philosophical Library, 1956), p. 140.

44. Liebman, *The Ambivalent American Jew,* pp. 21-22.

45. Shubert Spero, "A Rejoinder," *Tradition,* Winter-Spring 1972.

46. Sklare, "Judaism. . . ."

47. Shubert Spero, "The Religious Significance of the State of Israel," *Forum* (24), 1976.

48. Norman Lamm, "The Ideology of the Neturai Karta," *Tradition*, Fall 1971.

49. Liebman, "Orthodoxy . . .," pp. 88, 94.

50. Rackman, "American Orthodoxy," p. 309.

51. Eliezer Berkovits, "Authentic Judaism and Halakhah," *Judaism*, Winter 1970; "Conversion 'According to Halakhah'—What Is It?" *Judaism*, Fall 1974.

52. Berkovits, "Authentic Judaism and Halakhah," p. 469.

53. Liebman, "Orthodoxy . . .," p. 66.

54. Israel Rubin, *Satmar, an Island in the City* (Chicago: Quadrangle, 1972), p. 231.

55. *Congress Bi-Weekly*, 13 April 1973, "Tenth American-Israel Dialogue."

Bernard Martin _____

CONSERVATIVE JUDAISM AND RECONSTRUCTIONISM

THE SUCCESS OF CONSERVATIVE JUDAISM

In the period since World War II, Conservative Judaism has clearly emerged, at least numerically, as the most successful branch of American Judaism. While Orthodoxy and Reform have also grown, Conservatism has outstripped both; in the last two decades or so, more American Jews have come to regard themselves as Conservative than as either Orthodox or Reform. The partiality to Conservative Judaism has become especially manifest in the larger urban centers of the northeastern section of the United States, where the majority (about two-thirds) of American Jews remain concentrated, although there is presently an increasing shift of Jewish population to the South and Southwest (particularly Florida and Arizona) and to the West Coast (particularly California).

A survey made in Boston in 1965, for example, discovered that 44 percent of the Jews residing in that city and its environs considered themselves Conservative in comparison with 27 percent who identified themselves as Reform and 14 percent as Orthodox.[1] Somewhat surprisingly, Conservative Judaism demonstrated even more attractiveness in the much smaller Jewish community of Providence, Rhode Island. A survey there in 1963 showed that 54 percent of the Jews regarded themselves as Conservative, 21 percent as Reform, and 20 percent as Orthodox.[2] Even in the Midwest, the heartland of what was once considered Reform preeminence, Conservatism has shown a remarkable accession of strength. Thus a study conducted in Milwaukee in 1964 found that 49 percent of its Jews identified themselves as Conservative and only 24 percent as Reform.[3] From all indications, some 350,000 families, totaling probably close to 1,500,000 individuals, are currently affiliated with more than 800 Conservative synagogues.

One of the leading students of the sociology of American Jewry attributes the enhanced popularity of Conservative Judaism in large part to the massive removal to suburbia of the Jews of the more populous cities in the postwar era.

Suburbanization brought with it the problem of the maintenance of Jewish identity, and it was to the synagogue that the new Jewish suburbanite tended to look for identity-maintenance. The result was that the synagogue emerged in the 1950's and 1960's as the crucial institution in Jewish life. And Conservatism exemplified the type of synagogue that was most appealing to the suburban Jew.[4]

Another distinguished sociologist of the American Jewish community[5] perceives in Conservative Judaism the most adequate expression of the "folk" religion[6] of the present-day American Jew. Charles Liebman defines *elite,* as distinguished from *folk,* religion as "the symbols and rituals (the cult) and beliefs which the leaders of a religion acknowledge as legitimate." But, he adds, elite religion "is also the religious organization itself, its hierarchical arrangements, the authority of the leaders and the source of their authority, and the rights and obligations of the followers to the organization and its leaders."[7] Folk religion, on the other hand, emerges when a sizable number of people "affiliate with a particular religious institution, and even identify themselves as part of that religion, without really accepting all aspects of its elitist formulation."[8] According to Liebman, "folk religion tends to accept the organizational structure of the elite religion but to be indifferent to the elite belief structure."[9] To be sure, he notes, its rituals and symbols necessarily presuppose a system of theological beliefs; however, he insists that this system "tends to be mythic rather than rational and hence not in opposition to the more complex theological elaboration of the elite religion."[10] Liebman observes that folk religion has certain definite advantages over elite religion, advantages that make it more attractive to large numbers:

. . . folk religion permits a more intimate religious expression and experience for many people, and may, in fact, integrate them into organizational channels of the elite religion. It is a mistake to think of folk religion as necessarily more primitive than elite religion. While its ceremonies and sanctums evoke emotions and inchoate ideas associated with basic instincts and primitive emotions, it is also more flexible than elite religion. Hence it is also capable of developing ceremonial responses to contemporary needs which may be incorporated into the elite religion.[11]

He further notes that folk religion is characterized by qualities that may endow it with a special lure not only for the masses but for the more cultured and sophisticated among the adherents of a religion.

The absence of an elaborate theology within folk religion and the appeal of folk religion to primal instincts and emotions does not mean that folk religion is less attractive to intellectuals than is elite religion. Quite the opposite may be true under certain circumstances. In secular America, elite religion[12] has been forced to retreat before the challenge of science, biblical scholarship, notions of relativism implicit in contemporary social science, and the whole mood of current intellectual life.[13]

. . . The problem for the religious elite has been that most intellectuals cannot accept dogmatic formulations which purport to be true or to have arisen independent of time and place. Hence intellectuals have special difficulty with elite religion. But the same intellectual currents which challenge religious doctrine can also serve to defend behavioral and even organizational forms against the onslaught of such secular doctrines as twentieth-century positivism or eighteenth-and nineteenth-century deism. Thus folk religion, with its stress on customary behavior and traditional practices, may be legitimized functionally without an elitist prop. An intellectual today may well be attracted to folk religion because it provides him with comfort and solace, a sense of tradition, a feeling of rootedness, a source of family unity. His world view may remain secular, and from the point of view of elite religion his beliefs will therefore be quite unsatisfactory. But it is, at least in the first instance, elite religion, not folk, which is challenged by his world view.[14]

It may be, as we shall see from our subsequent discussion, that Liebman's suggestion that Conservative Judaism should be seen as the most adequate expression of the "folk" religion of the contemporary American Jew is not far from the mark and contributes significantly to our comprehension of the movement's recent success. First, however, we must take a look at its origins and development, for to understand the recent or present condition of a religious movement one must have some knowledge of its beginnings.

THE ORIGINS AND DEVELOPMENT OF CONSERVATIVE JUDAISM

Regarding organization and ideology, Conservatism was the last of the major branches of American Judaism to come into being. Its official inception may properly be traced to the formal establishment of the Jewish Theological Seminary in New York City in 1886. The foundation of the seminary was chiefly the work of a group of prominent rabbis and laymen from Philadelphia, Baltimore, and New York, among them Rabbi Alexander Kohut, Rabbi Marcus Jastrow, Rabbi Benjamin Szold, Rabbi H. Pereira Mendes, Rabbi Bernard Drachman, Dr. Cyrus Adler,[15] and Dr. Solomon Solis-Cohen. The most charismatic figure in the founding group was Sabato Morais, the Italian-born and trained rabbi who served as *hazzan* of the aristocratic, primarily Sephardic congregation Mikveh Israel in Philadelphia from his arrival in the United States in 1851 until his death forty-six years later in 1897. Morais served as president of the seminary from its establishment until his demise.

The creation of the Jewish Theological Seminary was basically a response, in the form of a protest, to the proclamation of the Pittsburgh Platform by a small group of Reform rabbis in 1885. Earlier, some of the founders of the seminary had collaborated with the leaders of the Reform movement and participated in the work of the Hebrew Union College.

This institution had been established in Cincinnati in 1875 by Isaac Mayer Wise, accurately described by most historians as the master builder of the major institutions of American Reform Judaism. But the extremely radical nature of the Pittsburgh Platform made further cooperation with the Reformers on the part of the more traditional but no longer completely Orthodox rabbis, who thought of themselves as belonging to the Historical School,[16] impossible. It impelled them to establish the seminary for the purpose of counteracting what they perceived as the negative and destructive influence of Reform Judaism in general, which was then clearly the dominant movement in American Jewry, and the Hebrew Union College, the fountainhead of Reform, in particular.

The men who identified themselves with the Historical School and resolved to create the Jewish Theological Seminary had a positive attitude toward the political emancipation and westernization of the Jews that had been initiated and were continuing in Germany, France, England, Italy, the Netherlands, and other countries of central and western Europe. They were strongly devoted to American political ideals, especially the separation of church and state and the formal equality under the law of all citizens, including Jews. They realized that emancipation and westernization must inevitably entail alterations in certain aspects of traditional Jewish life, social and religious. But they were persuaded that the religious changes could and should be made on the basis of biblical and Talmudic precedent. Their view, like that of all the rabbis of Europe trained in the new scholarship known as *die Wissenschaft des Judentums* (the Science of Judaism), was that Judaism had always been an evolving religion, adapting itself to new environments and altered socioeconomic conditions. From their standpoint, the Jewish people was central in Judaism, and they regarded it as an entity that had continuously revitalized itself by a gradual and natural response to novel situations. The traditional practices and teachings were still, for them, fundamentally valid; whatever changes were required should be made slowly and cautiously and represent the collective will of the Jewish people as a whole.

In the first decade of its existence the Jewish Theological Seminary limped along with a handful of students (one of them, Joseph Herman Hertz, ultimately became Chief Rabbi of the British Empire) and a very small and generally rather undistinguished faculty. After the death of its first president the spark of life in the fledgling institution was snuffed out; for lack of support, it was compelled to close. The revival of the seminary a few years later resulted from the efforts of Jacob H. Schiff[17] and Louis Marshall, both prominently associated with Reform Judaism and the leading Reform congregation of New York City, Temple Emanu-El. To their own financial contributions to the renewed seminary was added the material support of some of the wealthiest Jewish families in the United States, including the Guggenheims, Lewisohns, and Lehmans. In 1902 Jacob Schiff and his associates succeeded in persuading the eminent scholar Professor Solomon Schechter to leave his comfortable and prestigious position as Reader in Rabbinics at Cambridge University in England and come to New York to preside over the reorganization of the seminary. They seem to have been primarily concerned with the slow pace of adaptation to American mores and manners by the masses of East European Jews who were then pouring into the United States. This, apparently, was a source of considerable embarrassment to them, and they hoped that a school training traditional, but English-speaking and university-educated, rabbis would speed the acculturation of their "uncouth" immigrant coreligionists. Naturally, they did not publicly articulate their patronizing views, which, had they been made explicit, would have greatly irritated a large segment of the clientele they anticipated for the reorganized seminary[18] and alienated it from their project.

Of Schiff and his colleagues, Marshall Sklare, in his excellent sociological study of Conservative Judaism, has written:

Although the members of the philanthropic group were affiliated with Reform, they agreed that no attempt should be made to change the traditional character of the Seminary. The philanthropists recognized that Reform had little appeal to the immigrants. They felt that a modified Orthodoxy, stripped of ghetto characteristics, would be the type of Judaism most suitable for the East Europeans. The connection between the Seminary and Conservatism came about because the third settlement congregations [consisting primarily of the first- and second-generation native-born children of the East European immigrants] . . . obtained their rabbis from this particular institution. Apparently Seminary policy was such that its graduates were better suited to act as their spiritual leaders than those who came from the various other rabbinical schools.[19]

Solomon Schechter recreated the Jewish Theological Seminary during his thirteen-year tenure as its president and set it solidly on the path of becoming the institution it is today. Born in 1847 into a Hasidic family in a Rumanian *shtetl*, he had studied as a young man at various *yeshivot* in the Austro-Hungarian empire. Schechter was also a student for several years at the University of Berlin and at the recently established Reform seminary of Germany, the Hochschule fuer die Wissenschaft des Judentums, located in the Prussian capital. There he acquired a critical methodology for his later work in Jewish literature. Somehow he managed to combine the historical-critical approach to the exploration of Jewish texts with an intense and unqualified love for the Jewish tradition in its entirety.

Essentially, Schechter's "philosophy" of Judaism was derived from the so-called Positive-Historical School of nineteenth-century German Jewry. Like the foremost protagonists of this school—Zacharias Frankel, Solomon Judah Rapoport, Heinrich Graetz, and the later Leopold Zunz—he vigorously defended the retention of all the traditional religious practices and customs that were still accepted by the Jewish people as a whole (what he liked to call "Catholic Israel"), along with a critical investigation of the Jewish past. Schechter was also positively disposed to Zionism, which had become a major and divisive issue in Jewish communities throughout the world just around the time he assumed the presidency of the Jewish Theological Seminary. To the openly expressed distress and disapproval of some of the seminary's anti-Zionist Reform trustees and chief benefactors, he encouraged Zionism as "the great bulwark against assimilation" among his students and opened the seminary's rooms to Zionist speakers and activity.

Although Schechter wrote a significant historical study under the title *Some Aspects of Rabbinic Theology*, he was by no means a systematic theologian and did not himself have any comprehensive, consistent, and neatly articulated theology of Judaism. Perhaps his clearest statement on what many would consider the most fundamental and crucial issue of Jewish theology, namely, the revelatory nature of the Torah and its contemporary authority in Jewish life, is one written when he was still living in England and obviously reflective of the position of Zacharias Frankel and the Positive-Historical School in general:

It is not the mere revealed Bible that is of first importance to the Jew, but the Bible as it repeats itself in history, in other words, as it is interpreted by Tradition. . . . Since, then, the interpretation of Scripture or the Secondary Meaning is mainly a product of changing historical influences, it follows that the center of authority is actually removed from the Bible and placed in some *living body*, which, by reason of its being in touch with the ideal aspirations and the religious needs of the age, is best able to determine the nature of the Secondary Meaning. This living body, however, is not represented by any section of the nation, or any corporate priesthood, or Rabbihood, but by the collective conscience of Catholic Israel, as embodied in the Universal Synagogue. . . . The norm as well as the sanction of Judaism is the practice actually in vogue. Its consecration is the consecration of general use—or, in other words, of Catholic Israel.[20]

Schechter managed to obtain for the Jewish Theological Seminary faculty a number of very distinguished scholars, among them Louis Ginzberg, perhaps the most eminent critical Talmudic and rabbinic scholar of the twentieth century, Israel Davidson, an authority on medieval Jewish poetry, Alexander Marx, a great bibliographer and historian, and Israel Friedlander, an outstanding Semitist, student of the Bible, and historian of the Jewish people who died tragically early in his career before he could achieve his full scholarly promise. The greatly admired president also appointed as principal of the seminary's new Teachers' Institute the then youthful Mordecai Kaplan, who is still living today and who, during more than half a century of service on the seminary faculty, exercised an enormous influence on American-Jewish life and thought.

Under Solomon Schechter's benign but forceful leadership, and with its remarkable faculty, the seminary quickly attained the status of one of the most important seats of Jewish learning in the world. The majority of its alumni became rabbis of congregations that no longer attempted to duplicate, without significant variation, the pattern of organization and worship of the East European synagogues, as did those of the Orthodox first-generation immigrants, but to accommodate Jewish tradition to the cultural milieu of the New World without the radical reformulation of worship and theology introduced by the earlier Reform movement in America. The emphasis in these congregations, which increasingly came to call themselves "Conservative," was on a worship service that would be traditional in content but dignified and decorous in form, that is, without the constant conversations, the random moving about of worshipers in the synagogue, the unsynchronized recitation of the prayers by congregants, the public auctioning of "Torah honors," and similar characteristics typical of both the East European and American *shul* that were repugnant to Western aesthetic sensibilities. The desired dignity and decorum were to be achieved mainly by having the rabbi actually *conduct* the service, make it more interesting and varied by preaching a sermon in English as well as including the recitation of some English prayers, and gently remind errant congregants that conversations with their neighbors and strolling about in the synagogue were not acceptable forms of behavior. Such functions had never been performed by the traditional Orthodox *rav*.

After graduating some ten classes of rabbis from the seminary, Schechter, his colleagues, and a group of committed lay leaders proceeded, in 1913, to found the United Synagogue of America, a national union of the Conservative synagogues, which has ever since (although, in recent decades, with signs of increasing restiveness and incipient rebellion) looked to the seminary and its faculty for guidance in all matters of Jewish law and practice. The aims of the United Synagogue were stated in explicitly traditionalist and implicitly anti-Reform terms:

The advancement of the cause of Judaism in America and the maintenance of Jewish tradition in its historical continuity; to assert and establish loyalty to the Torah and its historical exposition; to further the observance of the Sabbath and the Dietary Laws; to preserve in the service the reference to Israel's past and the hopes for Israel's restoration; to maintain the traditional character of the liturgy, with Hebrew as the language of prayer; to foster Jewish religious life in the home as expressed in traditional observances; to encourage the establishment of Jewish religious schools, in the curricula of which the study of the Hebrew language and literature shall be given a prominent place, both as the key to the true understanding of Judaism and as a bond holding together the scattered communities of Israel throughout the world. It shall be the aim of the United Synagogue of America, while not endorsing the innovations introduced by any of its constituent bodies, to embrace all elements essentially loyal to traditional Judaism and in sympathy with the purposes outlined above.[21]

Schechter hoped, as had Isaac Mayer Wise when he founded the Hebrew Union College, that, through the Jewish Theological Seminary and the United Synagogue, he would ultimately unite all of American Jewry into a single religious movement. That hope proved just as illusory as Wise's. Both men, however, left an enduring legacy to American Judaism in building institutions that fostered Jewish scholarship and trained rabbis who preached a more or less satisfying interpretation of Judaism to their respective constituencies.

When Schechter died in 1915 he was succeeded as acting president (this was his title for eight years; he was not appointed president until 1924) of the seminary by the indefatigable Dr. Cyrus Adler. Adler had been one of the significant personalities in the founding of the seminary almost thirty years earlier; he also played a leading role in practically every major national Jewish institution and organization in America at some time or other in his life. During his quarter-century tenure as its head (1915-1940), the seminary moved into its present buildings in New York City on Broadway between 122d and 123d Streets, in close proximity to Columbia University and the Protestant nondenominational Union Theological Seminary. It was also during Adler's administration that the seminary library came to be the largest collection of Jewish books in any single place in the world and obtained a charter as a separate corporation (1924). The ceaselessly activist president (who seemed to have endless energy but was, even as an administrator, little more than mediocre) was constantly on the alert to expand the scope of his institution's activities. In 1931 the seminary established a Museum of Jewish Ceremonial Objects as an addition to the library. Some time later, a substantial bequest from Mrs. Felix Warburg enabled the museum collection to be moved from Broadway into its own home in the former Warburg mansion on Fifth Avenue. There its name was changed to the simpler Jewish Museum. For a while, especially in the 1950s and 1960s, the Jewish Museum concentrated on exhibitions of modern art without any particular or even recognizable Jewish content; more recently it has refocused its major attention on Jewish ceremonial objects, as well as paintings and sculptures of a substantively Jewish character.

In his young manhood Cyrus Adler, born (in 1863) the son of a cotton planter in Van Buren, Arkansas (on his mother's side he was related to one of the leading Jewish families of Philadelphia, the Sulzbergers), had obtained a doctorate in Semitics from Johns Hopkins University and served there briefly as an assistant professor. However, with his predominantly administrative interests and political, bureaucratic temperament, he did not become a productive scholar. And he was certainly not a theologian. His conception of the nature of Conservative Judaism was simplistic in the extreme: "Conservative is a general term which nearly everybody uses but which is, I believe, technically applied to those congregations which have departed somewhat in practice from the Orthodox, but not to any great extent in theory."[22]

Upon Adler's death in 1940 the trustees of the Jewish Theological Seminary elected as his successor a very learned alumnus who had been associated with it for many years. This was Louis Finkelstein,[23] ordained at the seminary in 1919 and the recipient of a doctorate from Columbia University in 1918. Although Finkelstein served for more than a decade as rabbi of the Orthodox congregation Kehilath Israel of the Bronx, he maintained a close connection with his alma mater following his ordination. In 1919 he began teaching Talmudic literature at the seminary, and in 1924 theology. Seven years later, in 1931, he was appointed professor of theology. By that time he had already published his important book that was highly acclaimed by medievalists and scholars of post-Talmudic law and institutions, *Jewish Self-Government in the Middle Ages* (1924)[24] and his edition of the *Commentary of David Kimhi on Isaiah* (1926).[25]

Although strongly committed to scholarship and tirelessly continuing his research and publication,[26] Finkelstein assumed the burden of increasing administrative responsibility at the seminary, first as assistant to the president (1934), then as provost (1937), president (1940), and finally as chancellor (from 1951 until his retirement in 1972). Under Finkelstein's leadership the seminary became better known than ever before on the American Jewish scene, as well as in the Christian world, particularly in circles concerned with interfaith relationships. This was largely the result of his establishment, beginning in the late 1930s and continuing in later years, of an Institute for Religious and Social Studies, a Conference on Science, Philosophy, and Religion, and an Institute on Ethics, all of which brought together leaders of various religious faiths and nationally renowned scholars from different disciplines for a discussion of the crucial moral and social problems of the contemporary world. Finkelstein was also responsible for the sponsorship by the seminary of the widely acclaimed "Eternal Light" series presented nationwide on radio and television.

Among other projects sponsored by the seminary and inspired by Dr.

Finkelstein are the Herbert H. Lehman Institute of Talmudic Ethics, the Seminary Israel Institute, the Maxwell Abbell Research Institute in Rabbinics, the Universal Brotherhood Movement, and the Women's Institute. To cement bonds with the State of Israel, the Schocken Institute for Jewish Research and the American Student Center were established in Jerusalem. Finkelstein early realized that the Jewish population of the West Coast was burgeoning and that Los Angeles was destined to become the second largest Jewish community in the United States; hence, in 1947 he opened in that city a California branch of the seminary, to which the somewhat grandiloquent title, University of Judaism, was given. Realizing also the importance of camping as an invaluable educational instrument for youth, the head of the seminary and his faculty colleagues organized a number of summer camps in various regions of the United States and Canada; these camps, called Ramah, have proven, by and large, to be among the most innovative and successful experiments of the Conservative movement in recent years.

Compared with eight students in the first class in 1887 when instruction at the seminary began, the institution had expanded, under Finkelstein's vigorous leadership, to a point, a few years ago, where it enrolled over 800 students in its various classes and had almost 100 full-time and part-time faculty members. Although in its first decades the seminary restricted itself to the training of rabbis, it now also offers instruction to prospective cantors, teachers, and synagogue administrators. It also offers courses, in some cases in conjunction with Columbia University, to men and women aspiring to teach Judaica at college and university campuses as well as to other students who simply wish to pursue higher Jewish learning and have no particular professional goal in mind.

Throughout his career at the seminary Finkelstein has been generally a traditionalist, a staunch defender of what has not inappropriately been called the right wing of Conservative Judaism. Thus the curriculum of the rabbinical school has not differed radically, except in its emphasis on the historical-critical mode of analysis, from that of the more modern Orthodox *yeshivot*; there is far more emphasis on the study of ancient rabbinic texts and codes than on professional courses that may prove of practical use when the graduates enter the congregational rabbinate. Furthermore, worship in the seminary's synagogue is conducted in a thoroughly traditional fashion, hardly distinguishable from what one would find in a typical Orthodox *shul*.

Finkelstein was abetted in his traditionalism by Professor Louis Ginzberg,[27] who, during his fifty years at the Seminary (he was still a professor there when he died in 1953), was unquestionably the dominant figure on the faculty and served as the acknowledged authority on Jewish law for the Conservative rabbinate. Ginzberg was a descendant, albeit a collateral one, of the Gaon of Vilna who had learned the Talmud as a boy at the renowned *yeshivot* of Telshe and Slobodka and then gone on as a young man to study history, philosophy, and oriental languages at the universities of Berlin, Strasbourg, [28] and Heidelberg. Because of the immense scope and profound depth of his scholarship, [29] very few of his students had the temerity to question his decisions on Jewish law or practice either in their days at the seminary or later when they had entered the rabbinate.

Ginzberg, who could be extremely radical in his academic theories but was generally quite Orthodox in practice, rejected almost all the halachic changes or innovations proposed by various individual Conservative rabbis and by the Rabbinical Assembly of America, the national association of Conservative rabbis. Only on rare occasions did he manifest a mild liberalism. Thus, while disapproving of the mixed seating of men and women in the synagogue, he stopped short of condemning it totally. Professor Ginzberg also approved a minor modification of the traditional *halachah* permitting a female convert to Judaism to wear a loose, flowing robe instead of going completely nude for her ritual immersion in the *mikveh*. [30] Ginzberg's son, Professor Eli Ginzberg, candidly reports:

Since my father did not find a solution [to the general problem of adapting traditional *halachah* to the requirements of the contemporary situation] that appeared to be a clear improvement, he preferred to let others take the responsibility for modifying the law. The fact that many Orthodox rabbis refused to acknowledge the authority of the Rabbinical Assembly helps to explain Louis Ginzberg's caution. He saw little point to developing a solution that would not be acceptable beyond the confines of the Rabbinical Assembly. He wanted no part in further splintering authority. [31]

As far as Jewish theology was concerned, while Louis Ginzberg had profound competence in the history of the subject, he was disinclined to develop any specifically Conservative theology and did not believe it would contribute to any substantive revitalization of Jewish faith and practice among the members of Conservative synagogues. According to his son, "in one of his more sarcastic formulations, my father would ask, 'What point is there to revise Jewish theology for pants-makers?' "[32]

As has been noted, the pants-makers (needless to say, there were also many other occupations represented) who constituted the membership of Conservative congregations were organized in 1913, chiefly through the efforts of Solomon Schechter, into a national union of Conservative congregations, the United Synagogue of America. From twenty-two congregations in 1913, the United Synagogue swelled to a membership of more than 800 congregations in the middle 1970s. Nevertheless, the organization throughout most of its history has been, and to a large extent remains, relatively weak. Effective control over it has generally been exercised by the administration and faculty of the Jewish Theological Seminary. It is not without significance that its offices have almost always been located in one of the seminary buildings and have only recently been moved elsewhere.

The weakness of the United Synagogue is perhaps due mainly to the ambiguity and vagueness of its goals. The charter of the organization, while refraining from "endorsing the innovations introduced by any of its constituent bodies," proclaimed that it would "embrace all elements essentially loyal to traditional Judaism." A more ambiguous phrase than "essential loyalty to traditional Judaism" is scarcely conceivable. In the first years of the United Synagogue's existence there was interminable debate, for example, over whether one of the purposes of the organization was to persuade those member congregations that had mixed seating of the sexes at worship or used the organ at Sabbath and festival services to abandon these practices or not. Agreement could not be reached over whether such practices, common to the Reform synagogue but anathema to Orthodoxy, would continue tacitly to be condoned into the indefinite future and permitted to become part of the normative structure of Conservative Judaism.

Throughout its history the United Synagogue has largely confined its activity to providing support for the religious and educational activities of its constituent congregations. Over the years the Commission on Jewish Education of the United Synagogue has carried out scores of surveys on the scope and content of the religious schools conducted by Conservative congregations; this finally brought about the publication of a set of standards and curricula for the educational programs for boys and girls in these schools. However, each congregation, being totally autonomous, has felt no compunction whatever in accepting or rejecting the "official" standards and curricula. In practice, most Conservative synagogues have been eclectic, devising their own educational programs to suit their members' preferences and choosing their texts and materials from whatever source, including Orthodoxy and Reform, they pleased. This has been the case despite the fact that the Commission on Jewish Education has been instrumental in creating a plethora of textbooks on virtually every subject, guides for school administration, and audiovisual materials—some mediocre and some of very high quality, indeed. Following the successful lead of the Orthodox, the commission has also promoted the establishment of a network of Conservative day schools—the so-called Solomon Schechter schools—but without the same numerical success as Orthodoxy. Furthermore, the first Conservative day school was founded only in 1950 in Belle Harbor, New York, by Rabbi Robert Gordis.

The United Synagogue, through its National Academy for Adult Jewish Studies, has attempted to promote the development of meaningful and effective adult education programs in its member congregations. Here again its success can only be described as mixed. As far as liturgy is concerned, while in the formative years of the Conservative movement most of the synagogues affiliated with it used the traditional Orthodox *siddur*, the United Synagogue, in order to render prayer more relevant to present-day needs and conditions, has published, in conjunction with the Rabbinical Assembly, revised editions of the traditional prayerbook, with deletions of archaic and clearly outmoded materials and the addition of some extremely moving and effective new prayers and meditations. The Conservative *Sabbath and Festival Prayerbook*, the product of a joint commission of the Rabbinical Assembly and the United Synagogue, was published in 1946 as the first "official" liturgy of the movement. One of the latest of Conservative prayerbooks, the *Mahzor for Rosh Hashanah and Yom Kippur*,[33] has been hailed even in Reform circles as a masterpiece of modern liturgical creativity, although it has also had its detractors and critics.

The leadership of the United Synagogue manifested intermittent concern over the years with the variety of procedures and activities, some of a questionable character from the standpoint of traditional Jewish morality, carried on in its constituent congregations. Finally, in 1952 it made a laudable attempt to elevate the standards of synagogue behavior by adopting a "Guide to Standards for Congregational Life." In 1959 the United Synagogue published a "Statement of Standards for Synagogue Practice" that was declared obligatory for all congregations in its membership. Regrettably, some Conservative synagogues have honored the statement more in the breach than in the observance.

The enormous rise in affiliation with Conservative congregations in the years following World War II (Reform and Orthodoxy also enjoyed substantial growth in this period, but to a lesser degree) led to the establishment by the United Synagogue of fourteen regional offices in the larger Jewish communities of America to serve their local needs. It has collaborated closely with other national Conservative organizations sharing its purposes. The oldest and perhaps most important of these is the Women's League for Conservative Judaism, founded by the widow of Solomon Schechter in 1918. In 1931 the National Federation of Jewish Men's Clubs was established. The United Synagogue Youth serves the teen-agers belonging to the Conservative movement, and Atid its college-age young men and women. Also enjoying close, but at times strained, relationships with the Conservative movement are the Cantors Assembly, the Educators Assembly, and the National Association of Synagogue Administrators.

Given the strongly Zionist and ethnic character of the Conservative movement from its origin to the present day, it is hardly surprising that the United Synagogue has made energetic attempts to support Israel and world Jewry as a whole. More than half a century ago the United Synagogue was instrumental in presenting the renowned Yeshurun Synagogue in Jerusalem as a gift to the Jews of Palestine (a fact now ignored by this "establishment" synagogue). The United Synagogue has also become an affiliate of the World Zionist Organization. The Conservative movement as such, however, has made comparatively little progress in Israel since the establishment of the Jewish state in 1948. There are only a few Conservative congregations in Israel presently, and neither Conservative nor Reform rabbis are recognized by the Israeli chief rabbinate or authorized to perform such rabbinic functions as officiating at marriages and granting Jewish divorces. To strengthen links with congregations elsewhere in the world sharing an orientation similar to that of its own affiliates, the United Synagogue in 1959 was instrumental in founding the World Council of Synagogues. This organization periodically convenes lay and rabbinic congregational leaders from more than a score of different nations, along with observers from a number of others.[34]

While the national lay leadership of the Conservative movement has found scope for its interests and activities in the United Synagogue and the related women's and youth organizations mentioned above, the Conservative rabbinate has its forum in an organization presently known officially as the Rabbinical Assembly, the International Association of Conservative Rabbis.[35] Emerging out of an alumni association for graduates of the Jewish Theological Seminary established in 1901, the Rabbinical Assembly soon made membership available to rabbis who had received ordination from other seminaries but shared the general ideology (insofar as one could legitimately speak with any precision of such a thing) of Conservative Judaism. Its present membership of over 1,100 rabbis ministers to congregations in the United States, Canada, Europe, South America, Australia, Africa, and Israel, teaches at the Jewish Theological Seminary and at various colleges and universities as well as secondary schools, is involved in Jewish communal service, works in military and civilian chaplaincy programs, and is engaged in a variety of other spheres of Jewish activity.

It should hardly astonish anyone that one of the chief concerns of the Rabbinical Assembly over the years has been centered on practical, "bread-and-butter" issues (one more inclined toward euphemism would probably term this "enhancement of the status of the profession"). Thus its Joint Placement Commission—like the parallel agency of the national Reform rabbinical association, the Central Conference of

American Rabbis, and the Reform lay Union of American Hebrew Congregations—serves the not-to-be-underestimated role of marriage broker or *shadkhen*, bringing together congregations in quest of a rabbi and rabbis seeking congregations. Both rabbis and congregations have surrendered some of their freedom under the formal procedures and disciplinary powers of the Joint Placement Commission—a sacrifice that would seem to be very much justified insofar as the commission has generally succeeded in replacing with orderliness and dignity the anarchy and the unseemly (and at times unscrupulous) manipulations and scrambling for position that often prevailed in the area of placement before its creation.

The central religious concern of the Rabbinical Assembly has been with *halachah*, particularly with adapting traditional Jewish law to what appear to be the demands of contemporary life. This task has been assigned as the special province of the Assembly's Committee on Jewish Law and Standards. Since there has almost always been a deep cleavage within the Assembly's membership over the general question of the degree to which the *halachah* should be modified and substantial differences of opinion over specific legal issues, the Committee has usually reported both majority and minority opinions on all questions of Jewish law submitted to it by members of the Assembly. Individual rabbis and congregations, being autonomous, are free to follow either the majority or minority report. Among the chief areas with which the Committee has dealt are Sabbath observance, dietary regulations, matters relating to marriage and divorce, procedures in the formal conversion of proselytes to Judaism, and funeral and burial practices.

In the 1930s and 1940s many of the younger members of the Rabbinical Assembly, chiefly under the influence of Professor Mordecai Kaplan, by far the most radically minded member of the Jewish Theological Seminary faculty and the founder of the Reconstructionist movement (to be discussed below in the penultimate section of this chapter), fought vigorously for substantive changes in the Orthodox *halachah*. However, given the adamant objection of the majority of the seminary faculty, led by the formidable Professor Louis Ginzberg and President Louis Finkelstein, as well as congregational rabbis in the Assembly, their efforts were largely fruitless. In 1936 the Rabbinical Assembly did approve a proposal regarding the plight of the *agunah* (generally, a woman abandoned by her husband or whose husband has long been missing but whose death has not been legally established by the testimony of two competent witnesses).[36] Orthodox halachic authorities were well aware of the sorry situation of such a woman, and some were keenly sympathetic, but they insisted that their hands were bound and they could do nothing to alleviate her misery. Under a proposal put forth by Dr. Louis M. Epstein, one of the most scholarly and respected members of the Rabbinical Assembly, the Assembly voted to insert in the *ketubah*, the traditional marriage contract, a new clause that would enable a *bet din*, or court of Jewish law, to grant a *get* (a religious divorce) to an *agunah*. However, Dr. Epstein's proposal was withdrawn in consequence of bitter opposition on the part of the Orthodox rabbinate and the majority of the seminary faculty, as well as the more traditionalist members of the Assembly. This incident symbolizes a fundamental conflict within the Conservative rabbinate and, indeed, within the Conservative movement in general that persists to the present day.

For a long time the traditionalists held the upper hand in this conflict. Dr. Saul Lieberman, an eminent Talmudist who joined the seminary faculty in 1942 and acceded to the position of chief defender of the *halachah* held by Professor Louis Ginzberg upon the latter's death in 1953, did participate in 1952 in a minor halachic modification which added to the *ketubah* a provision under which the groom bound himself to obey the judgment of a duly constituted *bet din* if it ordered him to grant his wife a divorce. This modification, however, would have been quite acceptable to almost any Orthodox halachist, even of the most rigorous type, and it contributed little to mollifying those more liberal members of the Rabbinical Assembly who believed that far more substantive changes in many areas of the *halachah* were required. Only in 1950 was the dominance of the seminary over the Committee on Law clearly, if temporarily, broken and did the liberals in the Rabbinical Assembly score a major triumph. This occurred when a majority of the Committee proclaimed the permissibility of the use of electricity on the Sabbath and also endorsed vehicular travel to the synagogue on the Sabbath for the purpose of participating in worship as a meritorious act.

In 1969 the Committee on Law passed a resolution permitting individual congregations to cease observing the second day of all the festivals, with the exception of Rosh Hashanah.[37] This action provoked passionate opposition among the traditionalist members of the Rabbinical Assembly. Perhaps even more emotional controversies were engendered by the decisions of the majority of the Law Committee in the 1970s to permit the participation of women in the public worship of the Conservative synagogue, including the privilege of being regularly called up to the platform for the reading of the Torah (this privilege had been approved for "special occasions" as early as 1953), and their inclusion in the *minyan* (this decision was taken in 1973). Feelings rose to such a pitch of intensity that, at one point in 1970, the majority of the members of the Committee on Law resigned, and only after delicate maneuverings was the Committee reconstituted. In 1975 there was a rebellion of "rightists," led by Rabbi David Novak and others, against what they deemed excesses on the part of "leftist" members of the Committee on Law.

Following the admission of female students into the rabbinical school of the Reform Hebrew Union College-Jewish Institute of Religion, as well as the Reconstructionist Rabbinical College, and their ordination as rabbis in the first half of the 1970s, a movement was initiated by some of the alumni and students of the Jewish Theological Seminary advocating the adoption of the same policy by the seminary. At the seventy-seventh annual convention of the Rabbinical Assembly held in the spring of 1977, the question of admitting women to the seminary and ordaining them as rabbis was vigorously debated. While a majority of the faculty made it clear that the proposal held no appeal whatsoever to them, support for it was so extensive among the rabbis and current rabbinical students that the present head of the seminary, Chancellor Gerson Cohen, agreed to the establishment of an interdisciplinary committee to study all aspects of the idea of women as spiritual leaders of Conservative congregations and promised that the seminary would accept the findings and recommendations of the committee.[39]

In recent years the Rabbinical Assembly, and the national organization of the Reform rabbinate, the Central Conference of American Rabbis, have, in the realization that they share a considerable number of common problems (including the nonrecognition of their rabbis and opposition to the spread of their respective movements in Israel by the Israeli chief rabbinate and Orthodox establishment) held a number of joint meetings and enlarged the sphere of their cooperative activity. Simultaneously the Jewish Theological Seminary seems to be moving toward an even more traditionalist position than that which prevailed in the 1940s through the 1960s. However, as the prominent Conservative rabbi, member of the Columbia University history department faculty, and current president of the American Jewish Congress, Arthur Hertzberg, observes:

The Conservative movement has always shown great capacity for maintaining institutional unity amidst great conflict. To continue such unity amidst ever greater diversity is the problem which it, perhaps more than either Reform or Neo-Orthodoxy, will have to face in the next generation.[40]

THE CONSERVATIVE SYNAGOGUE: WORSHIP, RITUAL PRACTICES, AND IDEOLOGY

What have been the distinguishing characteristics of the worship service of the Conservative synagogue in recent years? No universally valid answer can be given, for, as we have seen, each Conservative congregation is a law unto itself. Consequently, a great variety of pat-

terns are followed. In a work published in 1954, the eminent Conservative rabbi, historian, and philosopher Jacob B. Agus attempted a description of Conservative worship in America that would be generally
accurate.

With rare exceptions, the women's gallery is abolished and families worship
together. Worshipers wear the "tallith" at their morning prayers and "t'fillin" at
the daily weekday services. The congregations sponsor an intensive program of
Hebrew education and employ either the Orthodox prayerbook or the one of the
United Synagogue. The main changes in the United Synagogue Prayer-Book
consist in the elimination of a petition for the renewal of the sacrificial system.
The prayers of the Mussaph services are retained but the tense is changed so that
it becomes a recitation of what our ancestors did in the past. The translation of
"m'hayeh hamaisim," is so phrased as to suggest God's creative power, not to
teach the dogma of the resuscitation of the dead.
  Prayers in English are included in the services. Many synagogues employ the
organ to aid the cantor and choir, but the cantillation is in the musical tradition of
the synagogue. Worshipers sit with covered heads. With the exception of one
synagogue, two days of every festival are observed, and all synagogues celebrate
the two days of Rosh Hashono. All boys are prepared for the Bar Mitzvah
ceremony; the Bas Mitzvah ceremony for girls is rapidly becoming a standard
procedure, while the ceremony of Confirmation is also included in the total
educational program. The dietary laws are observed in all public functions of the
synagogue. The approved pattern of Sabbath observance for Conservative
laymen includes permission to ride to the synagogue on the Sabbath, emphasizes
the practices making for the hallowing of the day and distinguishes clearly
between avoidable and unavoidable types of work. As of the present, Conservative rabbis do not perform marriages for divorcees without a Jewish bill of
divorcement ("get"); by a decision of the Committee on Jewish Laws and Standards a descendant of a priestly family (Cohen) is permitted to marry a divorcee
or a convert.[41]

  While the foregoing description is still largely valid, there are one or
two details, as the careful reader will have noted from what has been said
above, that no longer obtain.
  In the same volume Dr. Agus could write: "A century of Jewish scholarship has demonstrated the responsiveness of the law and its official
interpretation to the exigencies of life and the requirements of the contemporary spiritual climate. Thus, the validity of Halachah is reaffirmed,
but only as one of the factors of the rich and varied tradition of Israel."[42]
These are clearly statements that would no longer be accepted without
serious qualification by more than a few Conservative rabbis. These
would argue that the "responsiveness of the law" has by no means been
proven and they would not care to affirm the validity of *Halachah*, even
with the modification offered by Agus.

In a work published in 1958 Rabbi Mordecai Waxman, who has since served as president of the Rabbinical Assembly, derives Solomon Schechter's term "Catholic Israel" from the concept of *Klal Yisrael* (the totality of Israel) which he connects with a "theological equation of its own whose best statement is found in the words of the medieval sage— 'God, Torah, and Israel are one.' "[43] In the same essay Waxman writes that Conservative Judaism "asserts the right of its rabbinical body, acting as a whole, to interpret and to apply Jewish law."[44] However, he admits that relatively little in the way of interpretation and modification has been accomplished. The reader must bear in mind that Waxman wrote before 1960, when the Rabbinical Assembly's Committee on Jewish Law and Standards first began vigorously to assert its independence of the Jewish Theological Seminary.

Waxman insists that it is a fact that there is an undefined but generally sensed set of standards in the Conservative movement and its congregations.[45] Almost all of his contentions, however, have been rejected by Jacob Neusner, a Conservative rabbi and a distinguished scholar of Judaica at Brown University, in a more recent article, "Conservative Judaism in a Divided Community."[46] Neusner emphatically declares that, whether or not it be true that "Catholic Israel" actually existed in Solomon Schechter's day, "it certainly does not exist today. There is no consensus, no collective conscience, and hence no authority to be located within the 'Universal Synagogue.' Further, the collapse of Jewish observance among masses of Jews renders unacceptable the criterion of 'the practice actually in vogue.' "[47] The chief elements of the Conservative consensus, according to Neusner, have not yet been formulated. "Bingo and violations of Sabbath and dietary laws do not exhaust our conception of Conservative sins; but we have never said what else matters."[48]

Professor Neusner notes quite correctly that the *halachah* of Conservative Judaism is *different* from that of Orthodoxy. But he urges that Conservatism is distinguished from Reform in affirming "the continuing authority of Jewish tradition" and holding that *halachah* "is a matter of *mitzvah*."[49] One cannot help but wonder, in view of his statements cited previously, whether he is altogether consistent or, at least, whether he does not here fail to make the necessary distinction between ideal and reality.

Reform Judaism, according to Neusner, "has not yet taken a firm stand in favor of Jewish tradition. In no respect do Reform Jews start with a presumption in its favor."[50] However, he qualifies this apodictic judgment to a certain degree almost immediately afterward by referring to "each painful step taken by Reform Judaism towards a renewed dialogue with Jewish tradition, towards a recovered tension between the necessities of the tradition and the requirements of the current age, and towards the revived appreciation, which we have never lost, of the infinitely interesting potentialities of inherited theology and inherited practices.''[51] In point of fact, Neusner himself approaches a major element in the ideology of Reform Judaism, which has often been pleased to call itself "prophetic" Judaism, when he scores "other" Jewish religious movements (among which, in all fairness, some representatives of Conservatism would have to be included) for failing "to give the ethical aspect at least the weight of the ritual."[52]

Mordecai Waxman had written in 1958 of Conservative Judaism that it

is not a mass movement despite its numbers. Its one million members have not made or basically affected the thinking or the emphases of the movement. They are, rather, a response to the ideas proposed and supplemented by the rabbinic leaders of the movement over the last fifty years. The aims and the intellectual orientation of Conservative Judaism have been provided by a kind of elite which sought to mold the community without itself being molded.[53]

It seems to me quite doubtful that this statement is historically true, certainly not without serious qualification. From my own admittedly limited observations, the facts seem to be quite the contrary, namely, that in most instances the lay leadership of Conservative congregations have "called the tune" (the same appears true of Reform congregations but less so of Orthodox) and the rabbis have generally followed their bidding. Theoretically, this would not be at all inconsistent with the fundamental ideology of the founders of the nineteenth-century German Positive-Historical School who came rather close to propounding the view that *vox populi vox Dei.*

It is interesting to note that Professor Neusner agrees with Rabbi Waxman that the laity has not played a crucial role in the Conservative movement. However, he perceives in this not a phenomenon on which Conservatism should congratualte itself (apparently, this is Waxman's position) but rather a fact to be deplored and an error to be rectified.

In both the synagogues and the central institutions, the interest of the lay supporter is cultivated not for Conservative Judaism but for the institution that serves it. The centre of interest is the maintenance of budgets and not the creation of a movement. The lay leader is a leader because he can give and raise money. His words are solicited only when he can tell us how to realise the most practical necessities. A lay leader need not even adhere to Conservative Judaism, and the virtues of his leadership do not necessarily include his wisdom, understanding, concern and knowledge, which he has and which all so desperately require. The layman is expected to resolve at his conventions to say and do things which rabbis formulate for him. He is infrequently consulted about the things we must say and do. And it is therefore quite normal for him to respond in kind. He will quite naturally regard Conservatism, its synagogues and the central institutions, as merely another "good cause" to receive his generous contribution of funds, rather than as a movement in great and grievous need of his spirit, heart and soul.[54]

We must turn to our lay leadership with both an apology and a demand, an apology for having permitted them to be used for so many decades merely as objects of our ministry or as agents of mainly material value; and a demand to consider seriously what it is that becoming part of the Conservative movement is meant to represent. At the same time, we must recognise how little we have listened to the Conservative layman, how much we have said to him, but how rarely we have been heard with distinction among the many Jewish messages directed to his ears.[55]

The sociologically oriented student of Conservative Judaism Marshall Sklare disagrees with both Neusner and Waxman in their insistence that the laity has not played a crucial role in Conservatism. In his work on the movement, which first appeared in 1955, he writes: "Historically, Conservatism has been a movement led by *laymen* rather than by rabbis. In many of the synagogues built in the areas of third settlement, major changes were instituted by the laity themselves. This was done either with the consent of the rabbis, or, as frequently happened since many of these congregations were new institutions, functionaries were engaged *after* the innovations had been conceived of, if not implemented."[56]

One of Sklare's chief emphases is that Judaism in general, and the synagogue as an institution in particular, should be viewed sociologically as an "ethnic church"[57] and that one of its major purposes has been to contribute to the preservation of Jewish distinctiveness. The Conservative synagogue, he maintains, has been especially cognizant of this and has, in fact, concentrated on making its synagogues instruments for the maintenance and intensification of Jewish identity. "The special contribution of Conservatism has been its relatively uninhibited 'exploitation' of the new type of synagogue—the kind which is a house of assembly as much or more than it is a house of prayer—for the purposes of group survival."[58]

It was Dr. Mordecai Kaplan, the disciple of Émile Durkheim, who stressed this function when he founded the first of the Conservative "synagogue centers." Concerned as he was with stemming the tide of assimilation, Kaplan urged the establishment of synagogues that would bring Jews together not only for the purposes of worship and study but also to intensify their feeling of belongingness to the Jewish people.

It therefore seemed to me that the only way to counteract the disintegrative influences within, as well as without, Jewish life was to create the *conditions* that would not only set in motion socially and psychologically constructive forces, but that would also make them forces for religion. What was needed . . . was to transform the synagogue into a . . . neighborhood Jewish center. *Instead of the primary purpose of congregational organizations being worship, it should be social togetherness. . . .*[59]

The history of the Synagogue . . . is a striking illustration of the importance of creating new social agencies when new conditions arise that threaten the life of a people or of its religion. The integration of Jews into a non-Jewish civilization created such conditions. They, therefore, justify transforming the Synagogue into a new kind of social agent, to be known as a "Jewish center." The function of the Jewish center would have to be the all-inclusive one of developing around the leisure interests a sense of social solidarity through face-to-face association and friendship.[60]

The synagogue center, or "institutional synagogue," which became popular in Conservative Judaism in the 1930s and 1940s, conceived its purpose as bringing together as many as possible of the Jews residing in its neighborhood, no matter whether they were religiously or secularly oriented. It was the hope of the leaders of the *"shul* with a pool," as the synagogue center was first facetiously referred to by Joel Blau, that "those who came to swim would stay to pray." Whether or not this really happened was not all-important; the significant point was that Jews would be meeting as Jews with other Jews in a Jewish environment. The widely admired rabbi of the Brooklyn Jewish Center, Dr. Israel H. Levinthal, wrote in 1936:

If the Synagogue as a *Beth Hatefilah* has lost its hold upon the masses, some institution would have to be created that could and would attract the people so that the group consciousness of the Jew might be maintained. The name center seems to work this magic with thousands who would not be attracted to the place if we simply called it Synagogue or Temple. . . .

The center is a seven-day synagogue not a one-day synagogue. From early morning to late at night its doors should be open. It is true that many will come for other purposes than to meet God. But let them come. . . .[61]

As a matter of historical fact, the synagogue center did not lead to any greater religiosity on the part of those who frequented it, whether this religiosity was manifested in attendance at worship services or through heightened personal observance of traditional Jewish religious rituals and customs. The trend toward progressive abandonment of personal observance was abetted by the view, held by many Conservative laymen (and even promoted by some rabbis and official leaders of Conservative Judaism), that the purpose, for instance, of the observance of the Sabbath was not so much to fulfill God's command as to obtain certain specifiable benefits. "In appealing for a reinvigoration of the holiday, Conservatism . . . speaks in terms of *social utility* — in this case the potential contribution of observance to better mental health. Only secondarily is it suggested that the Sabbath may have something more than therapeutic significance, and, furthermore, no Divine sanctions for nonobservance are inferred."[62]

It should not, therefore, come as a matter of astonishment that Conservative Judaism has proven to be relatively unsuccessful in promoting the observance of the *mitzvot* of the *halachah* among the membership of its synagogues. In the new and augmented version of his book, published in 1972, Sklare puts the matter far more strongly: "Judged from this vantage point, Conservatism has been an abysmal failure: there has been a steady erosion of observance among Conservative Jews. And despite a strong desire to encourage observance, Conservatism has not succeeded in arresting the decline in observance among its adherents, much less in increasing their level of conformity to the Jewish sacred system."[63] Sklare perceives this as a general tendency among first, second, and third generation native-born Jews impelling them progressively to abandon the religious values and commitments of their immigrant forebears.

The growing prosperity of Conservative Jews and the near universality of the five-day work week in the period after World War II might have been expected to lead to increased Sabbath observance, particularly attendance at synagogue worship. Sabbath worship, it might also have been anticipated, should have grown in consequence of the bold innovation introduced in 1950 by the Law Committee of the Rabbinical Assembly permitting automobile and other forms of traditionally proscribed travel to the synagogue on the Sabbath. These expectations and anticipations, however, were not fulfilled. In the survey made some years ago of Providence, Rhode Island, which, as was noted above, has a Jewry dominated by a preference for Conservatism, no more than 12 percent of those who identified themselves as Conservative reported attending worship services once a week or more. And—what apparently bears out Sklare's theory—Sabbath worship seemed to decline with each generation. Whereas some 21 percent of the first generation attended services, only one tenth of this group, 2 percent of the third generation, did so.[64] Furthermore, the ritual of lighting Sabbath candles was practiced in only 40 percent of the Conservative households of Providence (52 percent of the first generation households, and 32 percent of the third generation).[65]

While even the most minimal observance of the Sabbath through attendance at a late Friday evening service in the synagogue has diminished among Conservative Jews, the observance of the dietary laws seems to have fared somewhat better. Thirty-seven percent of the Jews who designate themselves Conservative in Providence indicated that they buy kosher meat for their homes, but only 27 percent of the households have separate sets of dishes for meat and dairy products, as required by halachic tradition. Again following the pattern suggested by Sklare, the percentage of Conservative Jews of the first generation who keep two sets of dishes is 41 percent, while among the third generation it is only 20 percent.

Providence may perhaps be dismissed as an atypical Jewish community. But that cannot be done with Philadelphia, the city in which the Conservative movement was, in a sense, born and on which it has had a profound influence throughout the ninety years of the movement's formal existence. The Har Zion Congregation of Philadelphia, led for more than twenty years (1925-1946) by a traditionalist rabbi with a commanding and charismatic personality, Simon Greenberg, is considered the "religious standard-bearer" of Conservative Judaism in Philadelphia. However, as Sklare notes:

A recent study of this model congregation has uncovered the fact that, despite its seeming traditionalism, the level of observance of the *mitzvoth* is strikingly low. Sabbath candles are lit in only 52% of Har Zion households. The practice of *kashruth* is limited to a minority: only 41% purchase kosher meat, and only 33% utilize separate dishes for meat and dairy foods. A bare majority—51%—attend services other than on the High Holidays, and only a segment of this group— perhaps a quarter—are regular Sabbath worshipers.[66]

In the Summer 1977 issue of the quarterly *Judaism*, devoted largely to a series of articles dealing with Conservative Judaism on its ninetieth birthday (the date of birth is assumed to be the foundation of the Jewish Theological Seminary in 1886), Rabbi Wolfe Kelman, executive vice-president of the Rabbinical Assembly, criticizes "reputable social scientists like Marshall Sklare and his less talented mimics who keep repeating the stale cliches about the demoralization of the Conservative movement."[67] These social scientists, he might have added, argue that Conservatism is undergoing a crisis of morale because of its failure to promote religious observance among its laity, while (and because) Orthodoxy is alive and flourishing on the American scene. However, it seems to me that, on the objective evidence, it is difficult to quarrel with Sklare's rather pessimistic conclusion:

In recent years it has become increasingly clear that the problem of observance constitutes a permanent crisis in Conservatism—that the religious derelictions of Conservative Jewry are much more than a temporary condition traceable to the trauma of removal from the closed society of the *shtetl* to the open society of the American metropolis. The elite are losing faith in their belief that through liberalization, innovation, and beautification the mass of Conservative Jews can be persuaded to return to the observance of the *mitzvoth*. In lieu of a solution to the crisis, the movement has sought to insure the observance of the *mitzvoth* in public: in the synagogue, at the Seminary, at Ramah, and during the tours and pilgrimages of U.S.Y. Although such conformity is gratifying to the elite—particularly to the older men who were reared in Orthodoxy and who have a strong need to justify their defection—it does not serve to erase the suspicion that the movement has been a failure. And Conservatism's failure in the area of the suprasocial is heightened by its brilliant achievements in the social arena: its success in building synagogues, in promoting organizational loyalty, and in achieving primacy on the American Jewish religious scene.[68]

According to Sklare, to whose work on Conservative Judaism I refer so frequently because I believe it represents the actualities of the movement most accurately,[69] "the essence of the Conservative position . . . is liberalization. While Conservatism believes that liberalization is its own justification, it also holds that liberalization makes possible the promotion of observance."[70] Besides liberalization, the author maintains, Conservative Judaism stresses two other major points. One of these is innovation, which is defined as "the development of new observances or procedures that are required when there is a need to substitute for, modify, or extend the traditional *mitzvoth*."[71] The second point is beautification, understood as "the requirement that the *mitzvoth* be practiced in as esthetic a manner as possible—'the Jewish home beautiful.'"[72] Orthodoxy repudiates all three elements of the Conservative position—liberalization, innovation, and beautification. Liberalization is rejected because of the intrinsic constraints of the *halachah* and is regarded as self-defeating. From the point of view of Orthodox Judaism, liberalization can only lead to a lesser degree of observance and finally to total nonobservance. Innovation is also spurned on the grounds that it is contrary to the eternal validity and the adequacy to all situations of the halachic system. As for beautification, it, too, is rejected because the observance of the *mitzvot* should not be, according to Orthodoxy, primarily an esthetic experience but essentially and fundamentally a religious response to the command of God.

We have discussed the synagogue worship and the ritual observance of Conservative Judaism in recent decades. Now we must turn our attention to the ideological undergirdings of the movement. What is the ideology of Conservative Judaism?

This question is virtually impossible to answer. Unlike Orthodoxy, which maintains that the essence of Judaism is the observance of the *halachah* as the will of God, or Reform Judaism, which has spelled out its basic but changing ideology in such documents as the Pittsburgh Platform (1885) and the Columbus Platform (1937), Conservatism has never adopted an official theological position.

Jacob Agus has maintained that one of the fundamental ideological assumptions of Conservative Judaism is rejection of the literalist conception of divine revelation. In his own words: "The naive picture of revelation as consisting of the 'Lord dictating and Moses transcribing' is taken to be no more than a symbolic representation of the process of Divine inspiration, that is itself beyond the power of human comprehension."[73] To this he adds that, for Conservatism, "the Torah *contains* the Word of God, especially when it is understood by way of a total self-identification with the historic experience of Israel, but the detailed precepts, phrases and words of the Holy Scriptures are not all, in their bare literalness, the word of God."[74] The Conservative position is distinguished by Rabbi Agus from that of Reform Judaism, which he rather surprisingly takes as still authoritatively expressed in the Pittsburgh Platform of 1885 in a work he published in 1954, seventeen years after the promulgation of the Columbus Platform. This platform also clearly stressed the idea of the Torah as the source of divine revelation.

It is pointed out by Agus that for some decades the Conservative movement was adversed to the scientific-critical study of the Bible (the so-called higher criticism was described by Solomon Schechter as the "higher anti-Semitism").[75] Nevertheless, ultimately, even though reluctantly, a moderate scientific-critical approach to biblical studies was adopted in the Jewish Theological Seminary. For Agus the authority of the Bible in the contemporary world has a two-fold origin: "the truth of its central philosophy of monotheism and the interpretation that it enshrines of the enduring bent of mind of the Jewish people."[76] Precisely what this means is, unfortunately, rather difficult to ascertain. Rabbi Agus takes refuge in presenting a nebulously rhetorical and "homiletical" statement: "It is through our complete identification with the life of our people, in the tragic travail of the past as in the living aspirations of the present, that we come to experience the vibrant reality of the monotheistic way of life. Judaism is not only philosophy; it is also a complex of psychic attitudes, a structure of loyalties and sentiments and a pattern of living."[77]

Conservative Judaism is distinguished by Rabbi Agus from both Reform and Orthodoxy in a way that a great many present-day Reform and Orthodox Jews would regard as a misinterpretation, if not a rather bizarre distortion, of their position:

In the Conservative view, the historic unity of God (metaphysical ideas), Torah (the detailed precepts governing the life of the individual), and Israel (the consciousness of ethnic unity and oneness of destiny), has been disturbed by the Reformers in their overemphasis on philosophical abstractions and by the Orthodox in their exclusive concentration on the precepts of the Torah. The impetus of Conservative thought is definitely in the direction of the re-creation of the original tri-partite unity, recognizing in the living people of Israel the synthesizing agent between the testimony of revealed tradition and the growing light of contemporary thought.[78]

It is clear that this summary of Conservative theology, formulated by Agus almost a quarter of a century ago, is vulnerable today because it more than a little misrepresents the present actualities of both Reform and Orthodox Jewry; furthermore, it will not pass muster because of its vagueness and lack of directive force. More recently Professor Jacob Neusner asserted that there are four major areas of general consensus among the Conservative laity as well as the rabbinate, implying that these might serve as the foundation of a viable theology for the Conservative movement. Neusner is no Martin Luther thundering forth with ninety-five theses. He is content to state simply four points of "common agreement," in the form of two affirmations and two denials:

1. We affirm the continued vitality of Jewish tradition and the abiding relevance of its major apprehensions concerning God, Torah, and Israel.

2. We affirm with equal vigour the need rigorously and unsentimentally to investigate what these words and ideas mean in the light of reality as we perceive it in this time and place.

3. We deny that the tradition can continue intact without requiring an unacceptable division in our minds between the tradition and all our other sources of knowledge about the world, our other patterns of thinking about the truth.

4. We deny that the tradition, unmodulated by the right and proper contribution of this generation, can or ought to lay a claim upon the life of the next.[79]

Further on in his essay Neusner set forth a set of "values" for Conservatism. Here, like in the case of Agus (except that Neusner is implicit while his older colleague is explicit), there is an animadversion to the deficiencies of Orthodoxy and Reform. (Conservative ideologues seem to be greatly concerned with refuting the popular and frequently expressed view that Conservatism is "half Orthodox and half Reform.") However, it seems to me, from a long and intimate association with the Reform movement, that the values lucidly set forth below by Professor Neusner would be acceptable with little or no demurrer to the large majority of Reform rabbis and laymen today.

Within Jewish tradition, moreover, we are prepared to isolate a series of values to which greater weight needs to be given in this generation. High in any such scale of Jewish values we should place knowledge of the Torah in its classical forms; adherence to its ethical and moral teachings as they can be seen to apply to contemporary life; and acceptance of its priorities, which, of course, include adherence not only to ethical and moral laws, but also to ritual patterns meant to make men accessible to, or to express, or to embody, these fundamental teachings.

So far as other groups regard such patterns as ends in themselves, to be preserved for their own sake and without reference to their impact upon the formation of society and personality, we regard them as guilty of misinterpretation, for they fail to give the ethical aspect at least the weight of the ritual. They therefore produce an imbalance between the details of Halachah and its theological and moral purposes. So far as other groups seek to construct a Jewish life without reference to these patterns, or deprive these patterns of any generalized reference in society and render them merely matters of personal style or whim, we regard their constructions as only partial. We see ritual as conditioned upon right; but we see that it has a useful and in some ways central role in religious life, not only for earlier times but for our own.

Within Jewish tradition, we find and accept substantial emphasis upon love for Israel, upon the centrality of the Jewish people in the scheme of history, upon the unique capacity for sanctity embedded and embodied in our sacred community. Just as ritual is conditioned and not of absolute value, however, so also the community is measured by its sanctity; indeed, the very definition of the Jewish people includes attention to the spiritual *condition* of those who adhere to it. "Yehudim" are worshippers of the Lord. We are prepared, therefore, to measure the adherence of a man to the corporate body of Israel by significant standards inherent in the religion of Israel. We believe that love for Israel requires infinite tact and care in making such a measurement, but in the end it is to be made.[80]

The reader will have noted that "love for Israel" and the idea of the "centrality of the Jewish people in the scheme of history" are stressed by Neusner. Here he reflects the classical bond between Conservative Judaism and Zionism. However, it is clear that one of the major areas presently requiring thoughtful ideological clarification, rather than sloganeering, is the precise relationship between Conservative Judaism and Zionism in the post-State of Israel era that has now lasted for almost three decades.

Ever since the time of Solomon Schechter virtually every Conservative rabbi and the overwhelming majority of Conservative laymen[81] have been ardently pro-Zionist. Conservative rabbis provided a great deal of the leadership for the Zionist cause in the United States before the establishment of the State of Israel, although historically its most significant and distinguished champions in America were two Reform rabbis, Abba Hillel Silver and Stephen S. Wise. The species of Zionism most popular among the Conservative rabbinate and laity is that known as "Cultural Zionism," the brainchild of the thinker and Hebrew essayist Asher Ginsberg who wrote under the pseudonym Ahad Ha-Am.[82] (Although Professor Mordecai Kaplan has written much over the years in support of Cultural Zionism, it was another member of the Jewish Theological Seminary faculty, Professor Israel Friedlander, who must be given credit for first introducing the ideas of Ahad Ha-Am into the seminary community and the Conservative movement.) However, the undeniable fact that no profound or creative cultural interchange—whether in the realms of religion, art, or literature—has developed between Israel and American Jewry has called into question the fundamental validity of the premises of Cultural Zionism.

Furthermore, the predominant secularism of the State of Israel has created numerous problems for American Jews, including Conservative Jews, who tend to identify themselves in religious rather than in nationalist or ethnic terms (although the ethnic stress, as we have noted, has been powerful in Conservatism). "Love of Zion," in and of itself, can no longer serve as an adequate ideological summary of the relationship between Israel and Conservative Judaism. Some Conservative rabbis began to be troubled by the directions taken by the general Zionist movement and by developments in Israel almost immediately after the establishment of the state.[83] Although some eighty or more Conservative rabbis have decided in recent decades to settle in Israel (where they are not recognized as rabbis by the Orthodox establishment), many Conservative rabbis in America continue to be distressed to the present day by certain tendencies prevalent in the society and culture of the Jewish state. A pro-Israel ideology, which will include a frank critique of these tendencies, would certainly appear to be a desideratum.

In the postwar period calls for a clear formulation of a total and comprehensive philosophy for the Conservative movement were increasingly heard. The late Rabbi Albert I. Gordon, director of the United Synagogue in the 1940s, asserted:

There is much to be desired both from the point of view of the loyalties we elicit and the sense of discipline we have a right to expect. . . . I believe, therefore, that it is of tremendous importance that the Conservative congregations . . . undertake the arduous but all-rewarding task of formulating the program of Conservative Judaism . . . it is the most important task that confronts us. We must cease to be regarded as "middle-of-the-roaders" by our lay people and must instead evolve and develop a positive approach to Jewish life. . . .

We must help to overcome the confusion of thought with reference to the nature of Conservative Judaism. . . . I plead for the good-will of my colleagues and all those who guide the destiny of the . . . Seminary.[84]

Another prominent Conservative rabbi, the late Morris Adler of Detroit, stressed the same note in an address before the 1948 biennial convention of the United Synagogue:

No apology or defense is necessary therefore for the negations which were implicit in our position from the outset, although our positive formulations were by comparison pale and feeble. We spoke of the process of development. . . . We stressed the integrity of the Jewish motive in refutation of those who favored an easy and convenient capitulation to the environment. In the same breath we spoke of the flexibility and fluidity of our social heritage as Jews. . . .

. . . we must face the truth that we have been halting between fear and danger; fear of the Orthodox and danger of Reform. . . . The time has come for our emergence from the valley of indecision. For one thing, there is a growing grass-root demand for . . . clarification of our position. There is a growing impatience on the part of our people. . . .[85]

The demands for ideological (or, if one prefers the term, theological) clarification voiced by Gordon, Adler, and many other leading Conservative rabbis were given scant support by the administration and faculty of the Jewish Theological Seminary. The seminary not only gave little encouragement to the development of a distinctively Conservative theology but has at times even made sedulous attempts to avoid using the word "Conservative." A Conservative rabbi complained in the late 1940s: "The Seminary which regards us as its children, when it comes to the question of helping the Seminary . . . very often refuses to permit us to recognize it as our mother. . . . The very fact that in the Seminary the word 'Conservative' doesn't appear in the literature, is, I think, humiliating. . . .[86]

It may be noted here parenthetically that while the Jewish Theological Seminary has trained a good many rabbis who have become serious and productive scholars in various fields of Jewish study, one is hard-pressed to think of a single original or even consequential Jewish theological or philosophical thinker that the seminary itself has produced, apart from Mordecai Kaplan and the late Milton Steinberg. This has not been the case with either the Reform Hebrew Union College-Jewish Institute of Religion or the Orthodox *yeshivot*, notably the Rabbi Isaac Elchanan Theological Seminary of Yeshiva University, from which have emerged such significant theologians and philosophers as, for instance, in the Reform camp, Jakob Petuchowski, Lou Silberman, Eugene Borowitz, Levi Olan, Bernard Martin, and a number of others who might be mentioned, and, in the Orthodox camp, such men as Norman Lamm, Michael Wyschograd, Shubert Spero, Walter Wurzburger, and others.[87]

While the Jewish Theological Seminary has not been greatly concerned—to put it mildly—with developing a distinctively Conservative theology, more than a few Conservative laymen have also believed, and continue to believe, that theology is not really terribly important and that theological discussion, in and of itself, represents something of a danger inasmuch as it may provoke dissension within synagogues and thereby inhibit the growth of the Conservative movement. Professor Marshall Sklare presents some interesting exerpts from an interchange between two lay leaders recorded in the minutes of a United Synagogue national board meeting in 1947:

Mr. Rothschild: . . . the people when they come into a synagogue do not philosophize, and the important thing is to get them interested in synagogue life.

Mr. Sachs: I feel like Mr. Rothschild . . . I was the president of a synagogue for many years . . . very few laymen have ever approached me to discuss the philosophy of the Conservative movement; they have simply joined because they have lived there; they wanted their children to go to school.

We have to take a definite stand. This is the Conservative movement; if you are a rightist you belong to the Orthodox; if you are a leftist you belong to the Reform. This is our philosophy; this is our tradition; these are our rituals. . . .[88]

Not all Conservative laymen agreed even in the late 1940s with this kind of anti-intellectualism and opposition to theological discussion. At the 1948 biennial convention of the United Synagogue Julian Freeman spoke out plainly: "No amount of talk will dissipate the fact that there is confusion throughout our movement. Some people insist on saying 'don't bring it up in public—time will help out.' Well, the Conservative movement is about fifty years old. Some of us are getting pretty well along in life, and we want a scheme for living today."[89]

With the increased level of education and the higher degree of general sophistication characteristic of the membership of Conservative congregations in recent years, demands for a lucid and consistent formulation of the fundamental religious ideas, policies, and goals of the Conservative movement have been on the increase. I think Jacob Neusner spoke for a large segment of both the Conservative rabbinate and the Conservative laity when he wrote:

Jews are Conservative by reason of convictions, though these now are mostly inchoate. If this is the case, then it is time to spell out in considerable detail, and not merely in slogans and vague generalities, the content of these convictions. Having done so, we shall have the right to turn to the divided community with a programme and a policy, a policy aimed not merely at the support of another organisation, but at the reconstruction, by the Conservative design, of the whole Jewish community in its various organisations and institutions. . . .[90]

THE PRESENT CRISIS IN CONSERVATIVE JUDAISM

Although many Conservative rabbis, especially those professionally associated with the national organizations of the movement, would deny its existence, Marshall Sklare seems to me generally justified in maintaining that a grave crisis presently confronts Conservative Judaism in America.[91] A major element of that crisis, I believe, consists in the fact that the survival and increasing vitality of Orthodoxy have nullified the claims made by Conservatism almost from its inception that it is, in fact, "normative" or "catholic" Judaism and the only kind of "traditional" Judaism that had a genuine potentiality for survival in the American milieu. Another element of the crisis is that the Conservative rabbinate as well as lay leadership are becoming even more aware that they will have to take personal responsibility for the future of their movement (for example, Conservative synagogues will have to recruit rabbis, not as they did largely in the past from among those who were born and reared in Orthodox homes and *yeshivot*, but from young Jews who obtained their spiritual nurture in Conservative homes, synagogues, and schools). Still another aspect is the odd circumstance that the real power within the Conservative movement has not resided, and still does not reside, in the Conservative rabbinate, or the lay members of Conservative congregations, or the United Synagogue. Effective power to mold the future of Conservatism lies mainly in the Jewish Theological Seminary, and the seminary appears to be divorced to a considerable degree in ideology and practice from both the Conservative rabbinate and the laity.

The growing doubts and disappointments in regard to their movement felt by a good many Conservative rabbis was reflected more than a decade or so ago by the then president of the Rabbinical Assembly, Rabbi Max Routtenberg of Rockville Center, New York, who told his colleagues:

During these past decades we have grown, we have prospered, we have become a powerful religious establishment. I am, however, haunted by the fear that somewhere along the way we have become lost; our direction is not clear, and the many promises we have made to ourselves and to our people have not been fulfilled. We are in danger of not having anything significant to say to our congregants, to the best of our youth, to all those who are seeking a dynamic adventurous faith that can elicit sacrifice and that can transform lives.[92]

Rabbi Routtenberg, who came from an Orthodox home, as did most of the Conservative rabbis of his generation, had broken with Orthodoxy and gone to the Jewish Theological Seminary because of his conviction that Orthodoxy as he had known it could not possibly survive in America and that the only form of traditional Judaism that could do so was Conservatism. In the same address he spoke poignantly of the feelings and motivations that led to his abandonment of Orthodox Judaism:

I think back to the period when my fellow students and I, at the *yeshivah*, decided to make the break and become Conservative rabbis. . . . We were breaking with our past, in some cases with our families who had deep roots in Orthodoxy. We broke with beloved teachers who felt betrayed when we left the *yeshivah*. It was a great wrench . . . but we had to make it. . . . We loved the Jewish people and its heritage, and as we saw both threatened we set out to save them. We saw the future of Judaism in the Conservative movement.[93]

However, as Professor Sklare has rightly noted, the Orthodox students who left the *yeshivah* to enter the Jewish Theological Seminary out of the conviction that Orthodoxy must inevitably die out in America, or—at best—become a feeble and numerically insignificant movement, proved to be profoundly mistaken. "Unaccountably, Orthodoxy has refused to assume the role of invalid. Rather, it has transformed itself into a growing force in American Jewish life. It has reasserted its claim of being *the* authentic interpretation of Judaism."[94] The distinguished sociologist adds: "To Conservative leaders, each new Orthodox success seemed to provide another instance where the laws of religious gravity had been repealed."[95] The final consequence, Sklare concludes, was "that the Conservative understanding of the American Jewish present, together with the Conservative expectation of the American Jewish future, became confounded. The ground was prepared for the development of a kind of conservative *anomie*."[96] Anyone who has had something more than a nodding acquaintance with Conservative rabbis will find it difficult, from his own experience, to dissent from Sklare's conclusion. The *anomie* of which he speaks is perhaps reflected in the fact, already mentioned above, that close to 10 percent of the Conservative rabbis in the United States in recent years have left their congregations and homes here and have made *aliyah* to Israel, where most of them have found employment in vocations that are not, strictly speaking, rabbinical.

Conservative rabbis and laymen are also assailed by profound doubts about the future viability of their movement (this is also the case in Reform Judaism, and perhaps to an even sharper degree) in view of the increasing rate of intermarriage among the young people reared in their synagogues. The question that has been raised with growing intensity in recent years is not, Can Conservative (or Reform) Judaism survive?, but rather, Can Judaism in America survive? The answer cannot be a categorical yes. It is highly probable that American Judaism will live on, though the number of Jews may decline drastically; but one cannot overlook the historical fact that large and flourishing Jewish communities have vanished in the past without leaving even a trace of their existence.

Conservative Judaism also seems in recent years to have lost its conviction that it possesses the magic formula that will win and maintain the allegiance of younger American Jews. Professor Sklare seems to me indubitably correct when he writes:

In addition to pessimism about whether the battle against intermarriage could be won, Conservatism in recent years has lost its older confidence of being in possession of a formula that can win the support of younger Jews. Despite interest in the *shtetl* and the East European milieu, many younger Jews—including those reared in Conservative congregations—have little connection with the Jewish culture of the immediate past. Inasmuch as Conservatism assumes some continuity with the East European past and some familiarity with Jewish culture generally, it has been deeply affected by such Jewish deculturation. If the mission of Conservatism has been to show how it was possible to practice selected aspects of Jewish culture in an American milieu, the result of Jewish deculturation has been that the movement no longer has its older foundation of Jewish culture on which to build its synagogal loyalties. Rather than having an assured constituency as before, Conservatism finds itself placed under the uncomfortable necessity of winning adherents to its cause, and having to do so without the undergirding of cultural compulsions. Thus, if Conservative leaders seem less assured by Conservative prosperity than they have a right to be, in one sense they are justified in their insecurity.[97]

Sklare properly notes that while "the problem of enlisting the loyalty of . . . young people is encountered by all religious movements, the issue is a particularly knotty one for Conservatism, with its stress on cultural reconciliation and the blending of Jewish and general culture."[98]

This most competent and eminent of present-day sociological students of the Conservative movement makes reference in his work to a significant incident in Conservatism's attempt to establish a rapprochement with contemporary youth, particularly those who have been attracted to the so-called counter-culture, that has been largely hushed up by the leadership of the movement. The incident took place at the Ramah Camp in Palmer, Massachusetts, during the summers of 1969 and 1970.

There has been considerable controversy in Conservatism as to what actually happened at Palmer: the extent of drug use, the degree to which campers absented themselves from religious services, the extent of laxity about the dietary laws, the amount of non-attendance at classes, and the implications of an English-language presentation of "Hair." Some claim that the outcome of the Palmer experiment was a greater Jewishness, while others contend that it resulted in heightened alienation. Whatever the case, the movement decided not to open Palmer in 1971. Palmer represented the first closing in Ramah's history; it was understood that the experiment was not to be continued at any other Ramah camp.[99]

A prominent scholar and member of the Rabbinical Assembly, Rabbi Edward Gershfield, several years ago pointed out to his colleagues how closely associated the Conservative movement has been with the American middle-class culture that preceded the emergence of the "youth culture" in the latter half of the 1960s and how large is the disjunction between this middle-class culture and the values and mores of the youth culture espoused by a considerable number of young people raised in Conservative homes and synagogues.

Our services of readings in fine English, correct musical renditions by professional cantors and choirs, and decorous and dignified rabbis in elegant gowns arouse disdain and contempt in our young people. They want excitement and noise, improvisation and emotion, creativity and sensitivity, informality and spontaneity. On the other hand, they feel guilty about the spending of large sums of money for synagogue buildings rather than for social services (generally for non-Jews). And they are "turned off" by the very beauty and decorum which we have worked so hard to achieve.

Of course, the youth do not wish to go into the reasons why these aspects of our life have been created. They are impatient with our explanations that most people are not dynamic and creative, and look to religious leaders for directions and instructions; that we who have managed to survive the rigors of youth appreciate regularity and stability in life, that we honestly want to endow our heritage with dignity and beauty, and that a congregation of a thousand persons cannot have a prayer service in a coffeehouse to the accompaniment of a guitar... we seem to be doomed to having to watch as our youth relive the same self-destructive impulses that we have seen long ago, and have thought could not happen again. Our appeals to reason and history . . . go right past them and we are for the most part helpless.[100]

That a crisis exists in Conservative Judaism is, it seems to me, undeniable. That a crisis of similar but perhaps somewhat less explosive proportions also exists within contemporary Reform Judaism can provide little in the way of comfort to rabbis and laymen concerned for the continued viability of the Conservative movement.

RECONSTRUCTIONISM

In any discussion of Conservative Judaism, the numerically largest religious movement in American Jewry, Reconstructionism, its smallest offshoot but intellectually a significant movement, must be included. Reconstruction is intimately associated with Conservative Judaism; for more than forty years it was not a separately organized movement but merely an approach to Judaism advocated at the Jewish Theological Seminary by a member of its faculty, Professor Mordecai M. Kaplan, who was the ideologist of Reconstructionism, the founder of its institutions, and its energetic propagandist. Until just about ten years ago, Reconstructionism, while also exerting a considerable ideological influence on Reform Judaism, was primarily a form of Conservative Judaism, differing from the latter mainly in its radical reformulation of Jewish theology. Although it has now assumed separate institutional and organizational forms, Reconstructionism continues to be a vital influence on a considerable segment of the Conservative rabbinate which has not officially allied itself with the new Reconstructionist institutions.

In a very real sense, Reconstructionism is the creation of this one man. Kaplan, now in his nineties, has written voluminously ever since the middle 1930s.[101] It must be said that much of Kaplan's work, while original and creative, is repetitive. He is prone to constant reformulation of his fundamental ideas, with minor variations, in most of his works.[102] The central idea in Kaplan's theology is his mature definition of Judaism as a changing religious civilization evolved by the Jewish people. In so defining Judaism he was explicitly rejecting the classical Reform Judaism represented by the Pittsburgh Platform of 1885 which had reduced Judaism to a set of dogmas about God and His relationship to individual Jews. Simultaneously he was reacting to Orthodoxy, according to which Judaism is essentially observance of the *mitzvot* of the *halachah*, itself the product of divine revelation and therefore not to be repealed or even slightly tampered with by the Jewish community of the present.

When Kaplan defines Judaism as the civilization of the Jewish people, he means to assert that like every other civilized people, the Jews have a unique history, literary and artistic heritage, languages, forms of social and communal organization, norms of conduct for the individual and the community, and—most important of all—religion. Professors Sidney Morgenbesser and David Sidorsky[103] point out that Reconstructionism has been deeply influenced by both European and American philosophical and sociological ideas. In my judgment, the most important of these is the view of the great French Jewish sociologist, Émile Durkheim,[104] that religion is fundamentally the expression of the social existence of a group and the instrument of its cohesion and survival. In addition to Durkheim's view, Morgenbesser and Sidorsky also mention the influence of W. Robertson-Smith's related theory of religion; Simon Dubnow's emphasis on the importance of the local Jewish community in the Diaspora; Ahad Ha-Am's contention that creative Jewish life outside of the independent Jewish state that he envisioned would depend on the emergence in that state of a "spiritual center" that would radiate its influence throughout the Diaspora, as well as his secularist reinterpretation of Jewish ethics; and the insistence of the nineteenth-century Historical School that Judaism's major institutions evolved naturally out of the changing historical situation and the emergent needs of the Jewish people.

According to Morgenbesser and Sidorsky, however, the chief influence in the development of Kaplan's Reconstructionism has been America, with its tradition of political democracy, social egalitarianism, naturalist and humanist philosophy, and Jamesian pragmatism. It is the American ideas, the two Columbia University philosophy professors insist, that are crucial in Reconstructionism inasmuch as they serve as the criteria whereby Reconstructionism assesses and reevaluates any American Jewish movement or proposal.[105]

That American ideals are predominant in Reconstructionism is, I believe, undeniable. Thus, in a formulation by Rabbi Ira Eisenstein, Mordecai Kaplan's son-in-law, faithful disciple, and exponent of his views, it is made clear that the Reconstructionist rejection of the classical Jewish idea that Jews are the "chosen people" is motivated basically by American ideas of equalitarianism and democracy.

We Jews have a remarkable history. In some respects we have been more preoc-
cupied than other peoples with the belief in God and with the conception of God,
with problems of life's meaning and how best to achieve life's purpose. But we
should not boast about it. Humility is more befitting a people of such high
aspirations. We ought not to say that God gave the Torah to us and to nobody
else, particularly at a time when mankind seeks to foster the sense of the equality
of peoples. We should be old enough and mature enough as a people to accept
our history with dignity, without resort to comparisons which are generally
odious. [106]

Other, more immediately obvious influences of prevalent American
ideology on Reconstructionism may be cited. Thus, for instance, *The
Reconstructionist*, the magazine of the movement, has published articles
strongly opposing Jewish day schools because, in the view of Reconstructionist leaders, such schools do not prepare students for American
democracy but, instead, indoctrinate them with a particular ideology. [107]
Mordecai Kaplan has also strongly supported the Jeffersonian principle
of strict separation of church and state. Apparently he believes that in
maintaining this separation and aiding in the development of a uniquely
American religion, that is, a "civic religion" independent of any church
or ecclesiastic organization and free of all supernaturalism, American
Jews might make a singular contribution to American civilization. [108]

Clearly and unequivocally Kaplan stated in his first major work that
"since the civilization that can satisfy the primary interests of the Jew
must necessarily be the civilization of the country he lives in, the Jew of
America will be first and foremost an American, and only secondarily a
Jew." [109] In that same work Kaplan was obviously influenced by the
dominant American climate of opinion even on so fundamental and
emotionally charged a Jewish issue as intermarriage. He contended the
Jews cannot legitimately object to intermarriage since America

is certain to look with disfavor upon any culture which seeks to maintain itself by
decrying the intermarriage of its adherents with those of another culture. By
accepting a policy which does not decry marriages of Jews with Gentiles, provided the homes they establish are Jewish and their children are given a Jewish
upbringing, the charge of exclusiveness and tribalism falls to the ground. [110]

I am not aware, though I may have missed the point in some of
Kaplan's later writings, that he ever subsequently recanted this position.

In view of the fact that Kaplan apparently gives primacy to
Americanism over Judaism in the life of the American Jew, the question
may be raised why Kaplan and Reconstructionism should be strongly
concerned with strengthening Judaism. Dr. Kaplan offers a number of
answers to this question. First, he contends that anti-Semitism links

Jews to each other whether they wish it or not. If for no other reason than that Jews do not obtain wholehearted acceptance among non-Jews and consequently suffer from feelings of inferiority and a diminished sense of self-worth, they should seek to strengthen Jewish civilization and make Jewish life more meaningful. Elsewhere Kaplan refers to the obligations imposed by the accident of Jewish birth and asserts that every historic group has a definite responsibility toward mankind at large to maintain "its own identity as a contributor to the sum of knowledge and experience."[111]

The great Protestant theologian Louis August Sabatier (1839-1901) distinguished various types of religion, among them the "religion of salvation." According to Kaplan, the core of Judaism is the quest for salvation, which he defines as the "progressive perfection of the human personality and the establishment of a free, just and cooperative social order."[112] Kaplan admits that the longing for salvation, which has persisted throughout the history of Judaism in all of its evolutionary stages, rests on faith rather than empirical evidence. However, he insists that there are powers and resources in the world and in human history, as well as potentialities in man, that are empirically discoverable and that make it possible for him to achieve salvation, that is, integrate his personality and establish a free, just, and cooperative social order.[113]

The "power that makes for salvation"[114] is what Kaplan terms God. Deity, he insists, is not deduced through logic or inferred from nature and history but actually experienced, since "we sense a power which orients us to life and elicits from us the best of which we are capable or renders us immune to the worst that may befall us."[115] Needless to say, it has been noted by more than one critic that such an experience may be merely subjective and in no way correspond to objective reality. Moreover, it has been observed that if God is identical with those forces in nature and history that make it possible for man to achieve salvation, He may be real in an objective sense but is not the unitary God of Jewish tradition. He is merely a term denoting many diverse forces in nature.[116] Furthermore, the question has been raised whether, if God, as Kaplan frequently asserts, is the name for the set of powers and processes that enable man to achieve salvation, is He "religiously available"? Can one, for instance, pray "To Whatever Processes and Powers It May Concern"?[117]

Kaplan's theology has been subjected to numerous and incisive criticisms in recent years on the part of many other Jewish thinkers, particularly those with a personalist and existentialist theological orientation. However, even those who object most strenuously to Kaplan's conception of God have found considerable value in his notion of the "organic community." If Judaism is properly defined as a civilization, as Kaplan repeatedly asserts that it is, then, he maintains, its several parts can function only in interrelationship: "The organic character is maintained so long as all elements that constitute the civilization play a role in the life of the Jew."[118] The founder of Reconstructionism applied the notion of organicity to the structure of the Jewish community which, he argued, should also strive to become organic: "The basic unit of Jewish life cannot be any one agency. The entire aggregate of congregations, social service agencies, Zionist organizations, defense and fraternal bodies, and educational institutions, should be integrated into an organic or indivisible community."[119] The concept of the organic community, in which Kaplan included, among other elements, the establishment of democratic organizations in local Jewish communities and a democratically elected national leadership, proved quite attractive to a substantial number of rabbis, educators, communal workers, and laymen in American Jewry and still retains much of its appeal to the present day. It drew to Reconstructionism a considerable number of people who dismissed Kaplan's naturalist theology as irrelevant or religiously and philosophically untenable but perceived in his advocacy of an organic Jewish community the potentiality for a necessary democratization and revitalization of organized Jewish life in America.

In 1936 Reconstructionism published the first[120] of several platforms it has subsequently issued, all essentially similar. This platform affirmed the necessity for reinterpreting the traditional supernatural beliefs of Judaism in naturalist fashion and of modifying traditional practices. It also advocated the establishment of a Jewish commonwealth in Palestine as "indispensable to the life of Judaism in the Diaspora" because Jewish civilization requires rootage in the soil of Palestine. It further declared itself unyieldingly opposed to fascism and economic imperialism, "the dominant cause of war in modern times," and in favor of peace, of the promotion of the labor movement and social justice against "an economic system that crushes the laboring masses and permits the existence of want in an economy of potential plenty," and of a "cooperative society, elimination of the profit system, and the public ownership of all natural resources and basic industries."

Mordecai Kaplan presented most of the radical reinterpretation of the structure of traditional Jewish belief that he believed was essential to bring it into harmony with modern scientific knowledge in his *The Meaning of God in Modern Jewish Religion* (1937). As the rabbi of a congregation in New York City, the Society for the Advancement of Judaism, whose membership was in sympathy with his views, Kaplan and his associate Ira Eisenstein who, as has been noted, is his son-in-law as well, also insisted on the need for liturgical change and creativity. In 1941 they published the *New Haggadah*. In 1945 they published a *Sabbath*

Prayer Book,[121] and later prayerbooks for the festivals, the High Holy Days, and for everyday use. In consonance with Kaplan's ideology as set forth in *The Meaning of God in Modern Jewish Religion,* all references to the Jews as a chosen people, to the idea of the direct revelation of the Torah by God to Moses at Mt. Sinai, to the notion of a personal messiah, to the rebuilding of the Temple in Jerusalem and the reinstitution of the sacrificial cult, and to resurrection of the dead and reward and punishment in an afterlife — all significant elements in traditional prayerbooks — were removed. The authors and editors were not, however, entirely consistent, retaining some traditional passages which conflicted with the Reconstructionist ideology professed by its creator. In these cases the introduction and notes suggest how these passages are properly to be understood. Prayers for the restoration of Israel, for instance, are not to be interpreted "as the return of all Jews to Palestine."[122] The reader is also informed that references to the immortality of the soul are to be understood as meaning that "the human spirit, in cleaving to God, transcends the brief span of the individual life and shares in the eternity of the Divine Life."[123]

We have already noted that the whole enterprise of worship becomes highly problematic on Kaplan's theological premises. He defends worship by saying that it "should intensify one's Jewish consciousness. . . . It should interpret the divine aspect of life as manifested in social idealism. It should emphasize the high worth and potentialities of the individual's soul. It should voice the aspiration of Israel to serve the cause of humanity."[124] Rather oddly, Kaplan adds that, for the attainment of these purposes, "the language and the atmosphere of the worship should be entirely Hebraic."[125]

In their *Guide to Jewish Ritual*[126] the leaders of the Reconstructionist movement categorically rejected the authority of traditional Jewish law. Eugene Kohn suggested the Jewish law must not be treated as though "the traditional *Halakah* was a viable legal system capable of developing adequate norms and standards."[127] According to the *Guide to Jewish Ritual,* ritual should not be treated as law but as "a means to group survival and enhancement on the one hand, and on the other, a means to the spiritual growth of the individual Jew."[128] The individual is given total freedom to decide for himself which rituals or "folkways" to practice and which to discard. In the exercise of his freedom he is urged to strive for a balance between his personal needs and the needs of the Jewish group. It is emphasized, however, that the "circumstances of life are so different for different Jews, their economic needs and opportunities, their cultural background, their acquired skills and inherited capacities are so varied that it is unreasonable to expect all of them to evaluate the same rituals in the same way."[129] The final criterion for the choice of ritual observance, it is noted, should be the self-fulfillment of the individual Jew. Thus, for example, the *Guide* suggests that work is permitted on the Sabbath "which the individual is unable to engage in during the week, and which constitutes not a means to making a living but a way of enjoying life."[130] What matters, according to the *Guide*, "is not the ceremonial observance of the Sabbath but the extent to which these ceremonies help one to live and experience the Sabbath."[131]

The Reconstructionist *Guide to Jewish Ritual* is quite in harmony with Kaplan's earliest work in which he insists that Jewish rituals, or "folkways," as he prefers to call them, should be practiced "whenever they do not involve an unreasonable amount of time, effort, and expense."[132] Though Kaplan was deeply influenced by Émile Durkheim's *The Elementary Forms of the Religious Life* (1912), he does not seem to have fully absorbed the importance of Durkheim's doctrine that religion is essentially a matter of ceremony and ritual and the values attached by the group to ceremonial and ritual acts. He does, however, pay lip service to Durkheim's view and, according to Milton Steinberg, he did learn (though he does not seem to me to have absorbed the lesson fully) that ritual functions "to preserve the integrity of the group and to protect those *sancta*, those holy devices by which the group was enabled to survive."[133]

In the practical program of Kaplan's Reconstructionism Zionism is a central element. From the beginning the author of the Reconstructionist ideology insisted that a full Jewish civilization could only be developed in Palestine and that an essential prerequisite for a civilizational revival throughout the Jewish communities of the world was the building of a Jewish commonwealth in *Eretz Yisrael.* The enterprise of establishing a Jewish state, in Kaplan's view, was extremely important because it added content and excitement to Jewish life without which that life was pallid, indeed. "Take Palestine out of the Jew's life, and the only spheres of influence that remain to him as a Jew are the synagogue and the cemetery."[134]

Kaplan recognized that Zionism is in fact the substantive religion of many Jews, including Reconstructionists, and he attempted in many of his works to give this religion an ideological foundation. However, as Charles Liebman has pointed out, Kaplan's Zionism

is typically American. He rejects the necessity for '*aliyah* (immigration to Palestine or Israel), *kibbutz galuyot* (the ingathering of exiles in Israel), and *shelilat ha-golah* (negation of the diaspora). An editorial in the magazine [*Reconstructionist*] attacks the Ashkenazi chief rabbi of Israel for giving "religious sanction to the mischievous policy of . . . associating the call for return of Jews to Zion with the state rather than some vague messianic period." In typically American Zionist fashion, Kaplan declares that Israel must not seek *kibbutz galuyot* but should be a "haven of immigration for all Jews who are not able to feel at home in the lands where they now reside." His ambitions for Palestine were modest. Jews, he felt, should be permitted to constitute a majority within a Jewish commonwealth, although they need not have exclusive responsibility for military defense and foreign policy. Before the creation of Israel many other Zionists, too, were prepared to accept such conditions, but few made a virtue of it. According to Kaplan, "relief from exclusive responsibility in these matters should be welcome." In other words, Jews do not "require the sort of irresponsible and obsolete national sovereignty that modern nations claim for themselves."[135]

Liebman suggests that what Kaplan with his Reconstructionism attempted to do was "formulate the folk religion in elitist terms."[136] But this attempt was doomed to failure for "the very nature of folk religion makes it unsuitable for elitist formulation. In an elitist formulation folk religion is often unrecognizable to the folk."[137] Liebman further suggests that Kaplan drew certain unwarranted (from a practical as well as a logical point of view) conclusions from his theological definitions.

If there was no traditional God, one could not pray to Him for help or direct intervention. But what follows for Kaplan does not necessarily follow in folk religion. One may admit in one's living-room that there is no supernatural God, no miracle, no divine intervention in the affairs of men. But this, after all, is living-room talk. When a folk Jew's child is sick, or when he is concerned about the safety of Israel, or even when he is grateful and elated to be alive, he can still open his *siddur* and pray to God—not a living-room God, but the traditional God. Who can say that conclusions reached in one's living-room are more compelling than what one *knows to be true* when one prays? If one has doubts as to which is the more compelling, one must reject Reconstructionism—precisely because it demands the supremacy of rational formulations of ideology. On the other hand, complete reliance on intellectual consistency, the rejection of what one's heart knows to be true, also leads to a rejection of Reconstructionism—because its very foundation lies in undemonstrable sentiments about man, progress, Judaism, Zionism. Reconstructionism is midway between religious belief and intellectual rigor, based on a minimum of axiomatic postulates. It is most likely to appeal precisely to those who waver. In fact, it has served as a two-way bridge between Jewish commitment and marginalism.[138]

After many years of wavering and irresolution, the leaders of Reconstruction finally decided to institutionalize the "movement." In 1968 they opened the Reconstructionist Rabbinical College in Philadelphia. Dr. Kaplan was the founder and Rabbi Ira Eisenstein was, and continues to be, the president of this small institution which has now ordained a number of graduates, including several women rabbis. Professor Liebman takes the view that the institutionalization of Reconstructionism was a serious error on the part of its leadership. "Reconstructionism can demand that its ideology be taken seriously, but it cannot make the same demand for its distinctive institutional claims without asserting that differences between itself and other denominations are significant. And this is precisely what folk religion abjures. This is also what caused special difficulty for Reconstructionism among many close friends when it decided to establish a rabbinical college."[139]

Whether an institutionalized Reconstructionism can look forward to a bright future on the American scene or not, there is little doubt that its ideology has been of prime importance in molding, during the past four decades, the religious thinking of many American Jews and—most significantly in the context of the present discussion—a considerable segment of the Conservative rabbinate.

CONCLUSION

If Professor Liebman is correct in his assertion that Reconstructionism committed a fundamental error in attempting to formulate a folk religion in elitist terms, then perhaps Conservative Judaism should learn something from this error and abjure the effort to specify its program in concrete, detailed, and consistent form, particularly if it wishes to remain, as it apparently has become, *the* folk religion of American Jews. However, demands for ideological clarification and theological formulation continue to be made by leaders of Conservatism. Thus the present head of the Jewish Theological Seminary, Dr. Gerson D. Cohen, recently asserted: "Ideologically, it is imperative for Conservative Judaism to develop a clear and unequivocal set of religious and national goals—a long term program—which is apposite to America in the latter part of the 20th century."[140] Rabbi David Novak, who also maintains the desirability of theological clarification on the part of the Conservative movement, it seems to me, offers a more appropriate proposal when he suggests that Conservatism should seek clarification both in the area of *halachah* and of theology. He is very much aware that there are grave difficulties in relating concern with the *halachah* to theological clarification, and prudently asserts that the best way to do this is for individual theologians to expound their personal positions.

This is problematic because halakhah and theology are structured differently. Whereas halakhah is meant to be authoritative for the group, theology is only the expression of an individual opinion. Nevertheless, though the Jewish theologian does not speak prescriptively, it does not mean that his statements have no frame of reference. His frame of reference is the traditional Jewish life of which halakhah is the *conditio sine qua non.* Therefore, if the Conservative movement is concerned with theological clarification, and if such clarification can be enunciated only descriptively by individuals rather than dogmatically by any authoritative body, then, it seems to me, the only course open is to encourage individual Conservative theologians to clarify *their* positions. A theologian can be considered Conservative not only by virtue of his organizational affiliation, but, more importantly, by his use of Conservative halakhic opinions, by his attempt to discern both their intellectual antecedents and consequences.[141]

Obviously a central issue that remains troublesome to Conservatism is the decline of halachic observance among its professed adherents. Gerson Cohen blithely asserts, without offering a shred of evidence, that ritual observance is on the upswing among Conservative Jews. He cites the example of the dietary laws, which he insists are becoming more widely observed in Conservative *homes* because—*mirabile dictu*— Conservative *synagogues* persisted in observing them on their premises. "Kashrut has become increasingly fashionable—and economically viable—owing not to the handful of Orthodox families that persisted in their loyalty to traditional Jewish dietary laws a generation ago but because Conservative congregations were insistent on the maintenance of the dietary laws in their own synagogues and wherever possible in the Jewish community at large."[142] Rabbi Stanley Rabinowitz, current president of the Rabbinical Assembly, however, states, with what strikes me as considerably greater realism, that the distinctions between Conservatism, Orthodoxy, and Reform have become increasingly blurred. "The differences in Jewish observance which once divided the Reform, Conservative, and Orthodox have . . . narrowed, for each of the movements has influenced the other. To a large extent it is institutional loyalties and social class rather than ideological differentia which dictate the groups to which we belong and the institutions with which we identify."[143] Rabinowitz's view is seconded by Rabbi Joseph Lookstein, the distinguished Orthodox leader and former chancellor of Bar-Ilan University in Israel, who has certainly not been a fighter *cum studio et ira* against Conservative Judaism and who writes: "If these [the present] trends continue, it will not be long before Conservative Judaism will be indistinguishable from Reform Judaism."[144]

The chancellor of the Jewish Theological Seminary insists upon the marked influence that has been exercised by Conservatism on Reform Judaism. "The *tallit*, the bar mitzvah ceremony, the reading of the Torah, the increased use of Hebrew in the synagogue service and, yes, even *kashrut* have made their way increasingly into Reform synagogues and schools, thanks to Conservative influence."[145] It is rather strange that Dr. Cohen has nothing to say about the influence of Reform Judaism on Conservatism and fails to point out that such significant characteristics of the present-day Conservative synagogue as the confirmation ceremony, family pews, the use of the organ and other instrumental music, and the attempt to grant religious equality to women, to mention only a few items, have all clearly been borrowed by Conservatism from Reform. Writing from the historical point of view, Professor Jakob Petuchowski of the Hebrew Union College-Jewish Institute of Religion is unquestionably correct when he writes: "On the whole . . . and not meaning to belittle the achievements of Solomon Schechter, his co-workers and disciples, it may well be said that antecedents of American Conservative Judaism include German *Liberales Judentum* as well as Frankel's 'historical school,' Geiger's 'progressive revelation' as well as Schechter's 'catholic Israel.'"[146]

Instead of speaking, in the fashion of many other Conservative rabbis, about the need for bringing traditional *halachah* into harmony with the demands of modern life as a fundamental desideratum for Conservative Judaism at this juncture in its history, Rabbi Mordecai Waxman, the immediate past president of the Rabbinical Assembly, states that one of the major tasks of Conservative Judaism is to develop a proper Conservative "life style" and "an authentic Conservative Jewish layman." Of Conservatism Waxman writes that it "has been quite successful in creating a Jewish professional elite who have an identifiable Conservative style, but it has not had much success with the laity."[147] He also insists that Conservative Judaism "must recognize that the intellectual and emotional scene are changing radically, that an openness to emotion and a willingness to rethink educational content and goals are becoming part of American Jewish life style. Sensitivity and response to these developments are the price of future vitality."[148]

Rabbi Waxman's insistence on the need for rethinking education content and goals is also stressed by Jacob Stein, the immediate past president of the United Synagogue, who notes: "Our educational goals are left undeveloped."[149] One cannot help but feel that the educational goals of Conservative Judaism are likely to remain not only undeveloped but confused if one peruses (and takes seriously) the recently issued "Statement of the New Curriculum Design for the Congregational Religious School"[150] proposed for implementation by 1977. The curriculum outlined in this brochure provides that in grades three through five every child enrolled in Conservative congregational schools will choose one of four curricular options that are described as follows:

A. Judaism: Sources—familiarity with major Biblical texts in either Hebrew or English (as the school needs dictate), selections from Rabbinic and Haskalah and Modern Hebrew literature, with a view towards understanding the major themes, concepts and ideas of the Jewish tradition and religious heritage.

B. Tefilah-Mitzvah—the ability to lead weekday and Shabbat services, comprehension of major themes and types of prayers, to intelligently follow Festival and High Holiday Services, to read (any) Haftorah and Torah portion publicly, to perform with skill and comprehension home, synagogue and personal Mitzvah rituals, to understand Mitzvot as reflecting God's will, as a means of introducing and incorporating Kedusha into one's life and as a force in preserving Judaism on a personal and collective level. Therefore, specific attention to Mitzvah concepts and observances related to: prayer, Torah study, mezuzah, tefilin, Festivals, pidyon haben, shekhitah, Shabbat, tzedek, mishpat, din, hashavat aveydah, proper treatment of the widow and orphan, tza'ar ba'alay hay'im, marriage, Kiddush Hashem, Hillul Hashem, and the like.

C. Modern Hebrew—the ability to converse with reasonable fluency in Hebrew, involving functional knowledge and use of conversational Hebrew related to school, home, family and daily personal and social activities.

D. History—familiarity with objective historical material and data and the ability to relate such information to concepts and ideas related to our growth and development as a people.[151]

It is impossible not to wonder whether the foregoing is to be taken soberly or whether it is an elaborate hoax. Will reading of selections from *Haskalah* literature (assuming that these will actually be included in the curriculum—a highly dubious assumption) really help an American Jewish child to relate positively to his Jewish heritage? Will any school (even one staffed by the most capable teachers) actually be able, given the five or six hours available in the weekday afternoon school, to fulfill all the goals listed under the rubric *Tefilah-Mitzvah*? And what about modern Hebrew? Will three years of study provide the child with the "ability to converse with reasonable fluency in Hebrew, involving functional knowledge and use of conversational Hebrew related to school, home, family and daily personal and social activities?" And, if by some miracle, a school should actually succeed in providing a few especially gifted and diligent pupils with such fluency, how would this promote their loyalty to Judaism in general and Conservative Judaism in particular?

One also notes with sadness the repeated use of the term "skills" in connection with *mitzvot* and the absence of any reference to *kavvanah*, or religious emotion, in discussing *mitzvot* which are, to be sure, described, in what strikes me as mere rhetoric, as "reflecting God's will, as a means of introducing and incorporating *Kedusha* into one's life and as a force in preserving Judaism on a personal and collective level." To reduce *mitzvot* to skills, I am utterly convinced, spells the death knell of Judaism. As one who ardently wishes Conservative Judaism to survive, even though I am not formally affiliated with the movement, I can only hope that this curriculum is to be taken as a jester's prank and no attempt will be made to implement it in any serious and self-respecting Conservative congregational school.

We have discussed the continuing and unresolved problems of Conservative Judaism with *halachah*. One not yet mentioned and, it seems to me, a very important one has been the relative unconcern of Conservatism with the moral aspects of the *halachah* and an overemphasis on its ritual and ceremonial aspects. It is therefore heartening to see that at least some Conservative rabbis are beginning to recognize this as a serious problem. Rabbi Ben Zion Bokser, rabbi of the Forest Hills Jewish Center and adjunct professor at Queens College, writes:

One senses a certain failure in the Conservative movement to stress the ethical and moral dimension of Judaism. Our culture is contaminated with opportunism, in which material gain supersedes all other values, and Jews have often been drawn into the whirlpool of general corruption. . . . One misses a prophetic strain in the preoccupations of contemporary Jewish religious leadership. Instead, the focus falls on sociological aspects of Jewish religious institutions and on the ritualistic aspect of tradition. There is little evidence of a stress on the ethical and moral ideals of our heritage, in order to challenge the waywardness of our society generally, or of the Jewish constituency particularly.[152]

Rabbi Mordecai Waxman also recognizes the problem and urges that it be given the attention it deserves. He insists that *halachah* "must be weighed in the scale of ethics, with due recognition that ethical standards have changed over the course of time. . . . The central issue . . . must be not whether a law is ancient or modern but whether it is ethical or unethical."[153]

Another problem that Conservative Judaism must face is the transformation of the synagogue from a house of prayer and a house of study into a "service center," providing religious rites of passage and ecclesiastical functionaries to perform them. Rabbi Stanley Rabinowitz is completely on the mark when he notes that the "suburban synagogue is not a *shul*, and it has become a service center for its affiliated members rather than a communal center."[154] This, of course, is true not only of the Conservative synagogue but of the Reform synagogue and, to a lesser extent, of the Orthodox as well. But synagogues as service centers, I am persuaded, cannot in the long run endure. Perhaps one of the basic reasons for the degeneration of the synagogue is the total and unrestricted freedom of each congregation to run its affairs just as its membership (more precisely, its frequently nondemocratically chosen and self-perpetuating board of directors) pleases. I tend to agree with Arthur Levine, the current president of the United Synagogue, who remarks that the "concept of the autonomous synagogue is, I believe, an anachronism, and a new relationship has to be created."[155]

Finally, Conservative Judaism, as well as Orthodoxy and Reform, will have to confront realistically the demographic factors currently operative that seem likely to alter the face of American Jewry. Zero population growth in American society at large and "negative population growth" in the Jewish community, if present trends continue, will entail radical changes. The Conservative synagogue, as well as all others, will have to deal with an aging Jewish population, a smaller number of children of school age, and a diminishing reservoir for the recruitment of membership. The growth in the number of the aged and the retired will place upon all synagogues the obligation to deal constructively with the problem of increased leisure time. Conservative and other synagogues will also have to deal with the problem of intermarriage. The rate of intermarriage in the relatively open society of the United States will probably continue to rise. This will not necessarily mean total assimilation within a few generations, but new and effective methods will have to be devised to bring the non-Jewish marriage partner into the Jewish community and to create families with children who will identify with the Jewish community and wish to perpetuate its religious heritage.

Judaism as a whole somehow has managed to survive the corrosive acids of modernity. American Judaism has also succeeded in overcoming the assimilatory trends that have prevailed on this continent throughout the more than three centuries of the existence of the Jewish community. If Conservative Judaism, as well as the other branches of Judaism, deal thoughtfully, honestly, and soberly with their problems, I, for one, am persuaded that all of them, though perhaps numerically diminished, will remain vital and dynamic religious movements, enriching both the Jewish and the larger American world.

NOTES

1. Morris Axelrod, Floyd J. Fowler, and Arnold Gurin, *A Community Survey for Long Range Planning* (Boston: The Combined Jewish Philanthropies of Greater Boston, 1967), p. 119.

2. Sidney Goldstein and Calvin Goldscheider, *Jewish Americans* (Englewood Cliffs, New Jersey: Prentice-Hall, 1968), p. 177.

3. Albert J. Mayer, *Milwaukee Jewish Population Study* (Milwaukee: Jewish Welfare Fund, 1965), p. 48.

4. Marshall Sklare, *Conservative Judaism: An American Religious Movement*, new, augmented edition (New York: Schocken Books, 1972), p. 256. The first edition of this work was published in 1955.

5. Charles S. Liebman, *The Ambivalent American Jew: Politics, Religion, and Family in American Jewish Life* (Philadelphia: The Jewish Publication Society of America, 1973), p. 63.

6. For a discussion of folk, as distinguished from universal, religion, see Gustav Mensching, "Folk and Universal Religion," in Louis Schneider, ed., *Religion, Culture and Society* (New York: John Wiley and Sons, 1964). See also E. Wilbur Bock, "Symbols in Conflict: Official Versus Folk Religion," *Journal for the Scientific Study of Religion* 5 (Spring 1966), pp. 204-12.

7. Liebman, *Ambivalent Jew*, p. 46.

8. *Ibid.*

9. *Ibid.*, p. 147.

10. *Ibid.*

11. *Ibid.*

12. By which Liebman here appears specifically to mean "pristine" or "unadulterated" Orthodoxy.

13. Liebman, *Ambivalent Jew*, pp. 47-48.

14. *Ibid.*, p. 48.

15. For a biography of this important figure who played a certain role in the establishment of the seminary, later served for a long time as its president, and also took a leading part in the founding of many other significant Jewish institutions in the United States in the last decades of the nineteenth century and the first decades of the twentieth, see A. A. Neuman, *Cyrus Adler—A Biographical Sketch* (Philadelphia: The Jewish Publication Society, 1942). See also Adler's autobiography, *I Have Considered the Days* (Philadelphia: Jewish Publication Society, 1941).

16. The term Historical School was replaced by Conservative Judaism only after the beginning of the twentieth century.

17. On Schiff, see Cyrus Adler, ed., *Jacob H. Schiff: His Life and Letters*, 2 vols. (Garden City, New York: Doubleday, Doran & Co., 1929), especially vol. II, pp. 53-58.

18. For detailed accounts of the reorganization, see Jewish Theological Seminary Association, *Proceedings of the Eighth Biennial Convention* (New York: Jewish Theological Seminary, 1904), and *Biennial Report*, 1902-04 (New York: Jewish Theological Seminary, 1906). On Schechter's role, see also Norman Bentwich, *Solomon Schechter* (Philadelphia: Jewish Publication Society of America, 1938), pp. 169-71.

19. Sklare, *Conservative Judaism*, p. 165.

20. Schechter, *Studies in Judaism*, First Series (Philadelphia: The Jewish Publication Society, 1896), pp. xvii-xix.

21. *The United Synagogue of America, Fourth Annual Report* (New York: The United Synagogue of America, 1917), pp. 9-10.

22. Adler, *Lectures, Selected Papers, Addresses* (privately printed, 1933), p. 251.

23. For some comments on Finkelstein's career and achievements, see Herbert Parzen, *Architects of Conservative Judaism* (New York: Jonathan David Co., 1964), pp. 207ff.

24. A second edition was published in 1964.

25. The work was reprinted in 1969.

26. Among Finkelstein's major later works are *Akiba: Scholar, Saint, Martyr* (1936); *The Pharisees*, 2 vols. (1938), in which he stresses the social and economic foundations of the conflict between the Pharisaic and Sadducean sects in the period of the Second Temple; the Hebrew *Ha-Perushim Ve-Anshei Keneset Ha-Gedolah* (The Pharisees and the Men of the Great Synagogue, 1950); and *New Light From the Prophets* (1969), a volume that claims to find in the biblical prophets the origin of some Pharisaic teachings contained in the early rabbinic Midrashim. Finkelstein also edited the well-known collection of articles, *The Jews: Their*

History, Culture and Religion, 2 vols. (1949; 2d ed., 1955; 3d ed., 1960) and many of the works emanating from the seminary's Institute of Religious and Social Studies and its Conference on Science, Philosophy and Religion.

27. On Ginzberg, see David Druck, *Rav Levi Ginzberg* (1934), in Yiddish, which contains a bibliography of the great academician's work and was translated into Hebrew (1960); *The Louis Ginzberg Jubilee Volume* (New York: American Academy for Jewish Research, 1945), also with a bibliography by Boaz Cohen; Louis Finkelstein, "Louis Ginzberg," *Proceedings of the American Academy of Jewish Research,* 23 (1954), xliv-liii; a biography by his son Eli Ginzberg with the instructive title *Keeper of the Law: Louis Ginzberg* (Philadelphia: The Jewish Publication Society of America, 1966); and Herbert Parzen, *Architects of Conservative Judaism,* pp. 128-54.

28. Ginzberg's scholarly interests were concentrated on the *aggadah,* the *halachah,* and the writings of the post-Talmudic Geonim. Among his most important works are *Die Haggadah bei den Kirchenvaetern* (The Haggadah Among the Fathers of the Church, 1899-1900); *The Legends of the Jews,* 7 vols. (1909-1938), in which he brought enormous numbers of legends, sayings, and parables from the whole of Midrashic literature together into a continuous narrative, tracing the development of the legends from the rabbinic texts, the Apocrypha and Pseudepigrapha, Hellenistic literature, early Christian writings, and the Kabbalah, connecting them with the legendry of other peoples and cultures, and attempting to distinguish the creations of the masses from those of the scholars; *Geonica,* 2 vols. (1909); *Studies in the Origin of the Mishnah* (1920); *Eine Unbekannte juedische Sekte* (An Unknown Jewish Sect, 1922); *Students, Scholars, and Saints* (1928); *The Significance of the Halachah for Jewish History* (1929); *Genizah Studies,* 2 vols. (1928-29); and *Commentary on the Palestinian Talmud,* 3 vols. (1941).

29. There his most important teacher was the great German Christian Semitist, Theodor Noeldeke, who took a liking to the brilliant young Lithuanian-born Jew and gave him private instruction.

30. Eli Ginzberg, *Keeper of the Law,* p. 237.

31. *Ibid.,* p. 226.

32. *Ibid.,* p. 144.

33. Jules Harlow, ed., *Mahzor for Rosh Hashanah and Yom Kippur* (New York: The Rabbinical Assembly, 1972). Oddly enough, despite the magnificence of this *Mahzor,* the United Synagogue has not pressed its member congregations to adopt it for High Holy Day worship. Most Conservative congregations still use the "Silverman *Mahzor*" which, at least in its Hebrew part, is quite Orthodox.

34. For a detailed account of the origin and activities of the United Synagogue, see Abraham J. Karp, *A History of the United Synagogue of America, 1913-1963* (New York: United Synagogue of America, 1964).

35. The organization was given the title The Rabbinical Assembly of America some time before 1920 and was legally incorporated under that name in 1929. In 1962 it was renamed The Rabbinical Assembly, the International Association of Conservative Rabbis.

36. Under the *halachah,* such a husband could never be legally presumed dead, even after the lapse of many years, and his wife, therefore, could not remarry.

37. This is the accepted custom in Israel, even among Orthodox congregations.

38. The *minyan* is the minimum quorum of ten adult (defined as age thirteen or

over) persons (males, of course, according to tradition) required by the *halachah* for the holding of a public worship service.

39. According to a Jewish Telegraphic Agency dispatch reported in the *Cleveland Jewish News*, 24 June 1977, p. 2, a survey conducted by Rabbi Morton J. Waldman (the survey questionnaire was alleged to have been returned by 570 members, well over 50 percent of the total membership, of the Rabbinical Assembly) found that 53 percent of American Conservative rabbis favored the admission of women into the Rabbinical Assembly. A considerable number of the respondents qualified their approval by stating that it is contingent on whether and when the seminary agrees to ordain women.

40. Hertzberg, "Conservative Judaism," *Encyclopedia Judaica* (Jerusalem: Keter Publishing House Ltd., 1972), vol. 5, col. 906.

41. Agus, *Guideposts in Modern Judaism* (New York: Bloch Publishing Co., 1954), pp. 87-88.

42. *Ibid.*, p. 101.

43. Waxman, ed., *Tradition and Change: The Development of Conservative Judaism* (New York: The Burning Bush Press, 1958), p. 14.

44. *Ibid.*, p. 20.

45. *Ibid.*, p. 21.

46. *Conservative Judaism*, vol. 20 (Summer 1966), pp. 1-19.

47. *Ibid.*, pp. 1-2.

48. *Ibid.*, p. 15.

49. *Ibid.*, p. 6.

50. *Ibid.*, p. 12.

51. *Ibid.*

52. *Ibid.*, p. 8.

53. Waxman, *Tradition and Change*, p. 22.

54. Neusner, "Conservative Judaism in a Divided Community," pp. 17-18.

55. *Ibid.*, p. 14.

56. Sklare, *Conservative Judaism*, p. 114. Cf. Eugene Kohn, "Conservative Judaism—A Review," *Conservative Judaism*, II, 4 (June 1946), p. 12.

57. Sklare, *Conservative Judaism*, pp. 35ff.

58. *Ibid.*, p. 134.

59. Italics mine—B. M.

60. Kaplan, "The Way I Have Come," in *Mordecai M. Kaplan: An Evaluation*, Ira Eisenstein and Eugene Kohn, eds. (New York: Jewish Reconstructionist Foundation, 1952), p. 311.

61. *United Synagogue Recorder* VI, 4 (October 1936), p. 19.

62. Sklare, *Conservative Judaism*, pp. 122-23.

63. *Ibid.*, p. 270.

64. Goldstein and Goldscheider, *Jewish Americans*, p. 194.

65. *Ibid.*, p. 203.

66. Sklare, *Conservative Judaism*, p. 274.

67. *Judaism*, vol. 26, no. 3 (Summer 1977), p. 287.

68. Sklare, *Conservative Judaism*, p. 275.

69. This, it seems to me, is particularly true of the final chapter of the augmented version of his book, published in 1972.

70. Sklare, *Conservative Judaism*, p. 269.

71. *Ibid.*

72. *Ibid.*

73. Agus, *Guideposts,* p. 89.

74. *Ibid.,* p. 90.

75. *Ibid.,* p. 91.

76. *Ibid.,* p. 92.

77. *Ibid.*

78. *Ibid.,* pp. 92-93.

79. Neusner, "Conservative Judaism in a Divided Community," p. 7.

80. *Ibid.,* pp. 8-9.

81. A notable exception was the long-time president of the Jewish Theological Seminary, Dr. Cyrus Adler, who was adamantly opposed to Herzlian political Zionism and, it would seem, had no overweening affection for Zionism in general (see Herbert Parzen, *Architects,* pp. 87ff).

82. Cf. Robert Gordis, *The Jew Faces a New World* (New York: Behrman's Jewish Book House, 1941), pp. 206-08. Although Professor Mordecai Kaplan has written much over the years in support of what is essentially the program of Cultural Zionism, it was another member of the Jewish Theological Seminary faculty, Professor Israel Friedlander, who must be given credit for first introducing the ideas of Ahad Ha-Am into the seminary community and the Conservative movement.

83. See Robert Gordis, in Rabbinical Assembly of America, *Proceedings,* X (1947), p. 73; Ralph Simon in *ibid.,* XII (1949), p. 244; and Norman Shapiro in *ibid.,* XII (1949), pp. 248-49.

84. United Synagogue, *National Board Minutes,* 19 January 1947, pp. 209-16 (quoted in Sklare, *Conservative Judaism,* pp. 218-19).

85. *Proceedings of the 1948 Biennial Convention* (New York: The United Synagogue of America, 1949), pp. 26-27.

86. William Greenfield, in Rabbinical Assembly of America, *Proceedings,* XII (1949), p. 138.

87. An exception for Conservatism, I believe, should be made in the case of Rabbi David Novak, an alumnus of the Jewish Theological Seminary, who demonstrates in his two recently published volumes, *Law and Theology in Judaism,* First Series (New York: Ktav Publishing House, 1974) and *Law and Theology in Judaism,* Second Series (New York: Ktav Publishing House, Inc., 1976) promise of developing into a first-rate theologian. Novak's essay "Theory of Revelation" in the second of these volumes (pp. 1-27) is an admirable piece of philosophical-theological analysis.

88. Sklare, *Conservative Judaism,* p. 212.

89. *Proceedings of the 1948 Biennial Convention* (New York: The United Synagogue, 1949), pp. 128-29.

90. Neusner, "Conservative Judaism in a Divided Community," p. 16. I am in agreement with the basic thrust of Neusner's statement, but I am not altogether happy with the "religious imperialism" implied in his suggestion that "the whole Jewish community in its various organizations and institutions" is to be reconstructed "by the Conservative design."

91. Sklare, *Conservative Judaism,* pp. 261-82.

92. Routtenberg, in Rabbinical Assembly of America, *Proceedings*, XXIX (1965), p. 23.

93. *Ibid.*

94. Sklare, *Conservative Judaism*, p. 264.

95. *Ibid.*, p. 266.

96. *Ibid.*, p. 267.

97. *Ibid*, pp. 278-79.

98. *Ibid.*, p. 279.

99. *Ibid.*, p. 280.

100. Rabbinical Assembly of America, *Proceedings*, XXXIV (1970), pp. 90-91.

101. Probably the most important of Kaplan's works are the following: *Judaism as a Civilization: Toward a Reconstruction of American Jewish Life* (New York: Macmillan, 1934; reprinted by Schocken Books, 1967); *The Meaning of God in Modern Jewish Religion* (New York: Behrman House, 1937; republished by the Reconstructionist Press, New York, 1962); *The Future of the American Jew* (New York: Macmillan, 1948; republished by the Reconstructionist Press, New York, 1967); and *The Greater Judaism in the Making* (New York: Reconstructionist Press, 1960).

102. The reader who has time to peruse only one of Kaplan's works would, I think, obtain the most adequate idea of his theology from *The Meaning of God in Modern Jewish Religion.*

103. "Reconstructionism and the Naturalistic Tradition in America," *Reconstructionist*, 18 February 1955, pp. 33-42.

104. To whom, incidentally, Kaplan has never, to my knowledge, sufficiently admitted his indebtedness.

105. Morgenbesser and Sidorsky, "Reconstructionism and the Naturalistic Tradition in America," p. 33.

106. *What Can A Modern Jew Believe?* (New York: Reconstructionist Press, n.d.), p. 10. This is a Reconstructionist pamphlet.

107. See Joseph Blau, "The Jewish Day School," *Reconstructionist*, 14 November 1958, pp. 29-32, and Jack Cohen, "The Jewish Day School," *Reconstructionist*, 26 December 1958, pp. 27-28.

108. See Kaplan, *Judaism Without Supernaturalism* (New York: Reconstructionist Press, 1958), p. 99.

109. Kaplan, *Judaism as a Civilization*, p. 216.

110. *Ibid.*, p. 419.

111. Kaplan, *The Meaning of God in Modern Jewish Religion*, p. 96.

112. Kaplan, *The Future of the American Jew*, p. xvii.

113. For a brilliant critique of the Kaplanian brand of humanism and a cogent defense of Jewish supernaturalism, see Emil Fackenheim, *Quest for Past and Future: Essays in Jewish Theology* (Bloomington: Indiana University Press, 1968), "Self-Realization and the Search for God," pp. 27-51.

114. The phrase, of course, is Matthew Arnold's.

115. Kaplan, *Judaism as a Civilization*, p. 317.

116. See Eugene Borowitz, *A New Jewish Theology In the Making* (Philadelphia: Westminster Press, 1968), pp. 110-11.

117. See Bernard Martin, "The God We Worship," *Reconstructionist*, 3 February 1967, pp. 14-17, and Kaplan's response, *ibid.*, pp. 18ff.

118. Kaplan, *Judaism as a Civilization*, p. 515.

119. Kaplan, *The Future of the American Jew*, p. 242.

120. See Kaplan, ed., *Jewish Reconstructionist Papers* (New York: Society for the Advancement of Judaism, 1936).

121. Which was promptly put under a religious ban and publicly burned at the McAlpin Hotel in New York City by a group of ultra-Orthodox rabbis.

122. Mordecai M. Kaplan, Eugene Kohn and Ira Eisenstein, eds., *The New Haggadah* (New York: The Jewish Reconstructionist Foundation, rev. ed., 1942), p. 12.

123. *Ibid.*, p. 14.

124. Kaplan, *Judaism as a Civilization*, p. 347.

125. *Ibid.*, p. 348.

126. Eugene Kohn, ed. (New York: The Reconstructionist Press, 1962 edition).

127. Kohn, "The Reconstructionist—A Magazine with a Mission," *Reconstructionist*, 18 February 1955, p. 19. Kaplan says virtually the same thing in some of his own books and essays.

128. *Ibid.*, p. 5.

129. *Ibid.*, p. 6.

130. *Ibid.*, p. 16.

131. *Ibid.*, pp. 17-18.

132. Kaplan, *Judaism as a Civilization*, p. 439.

133. Steinberg, *Anatomy of a Faith*, ed. with an introduction by Arthur A. Cohen (New York: Harcourt, Brace and Company, 1960), p. 247.

134. *The Society for the Advancement of Judaism* (New York: The Society for the Advancement of Judaism, 1923), p. 11.

135. Liebman, "Reconstructionism in American Jewish Life," *American Jewish Year Book*, 70 (New York: The American Jewish Committee, and Philadelphia: The Jewish Publication Society of America, 1970), p. 19.

136. *Ibid.*, p. 93.

137. *Ibid.*, pp. 93-94.

138. *Ibid.*, pp. 94-95.

139. *Ibid.*, pp. 96-97.

140. Cohen, "The Present State of Conservative Judaism," *Judaism*, 26 (Summer 1977), p. 273.

141. Novak, "The Distinctiveness of Conservative Judaism," in *ibid.*, p. 306.

142. Cohen, "Present State of Conservative Judaism," in *ibid.*, p. 271.

143. Rabinowitz, "Where Do We Stand Now?" in *ibid.*, p. 278.

144. Lookstein, "A Critique and a Plea," in *ibid.*, p. 328.

145. Cohen, "Present State of Conservative Judaism," in *ibid.*, p. 271.

146. Petuchowski, "Conservatism—Its Contribution to Judaism," in *ibid.*, pp. 353-54.

147. Waxman, "The Basic Issues—An Analysis," in *ibid.*, p. 284.

148. *Ibid.*

149. Stein, "Promise, Performance and Problems," in *ibid.*, p. 298.

150. Published by the United Synagogue Commission on Jewish Education, New York, n.d.

151. "Statement of the New Curriculum Design for the Communal Religious School," pp. 8-9.

152. Bokser, "The Interaction of History and Theology," *Judaism* 26 (Summer 1977), p. 324.

153. Waxman, "Basic Issues," in *ibid.*, p. 282.

154. Rabinowitz, "Where Do We Stand Now?" in *ibid.*, p. 276.

155. Levine, "Needed—A Definition," *Judaism* 26 (Summer 1977), p. 295.

Michael A. Meyer ⸻

REFORM JUDAISM

The origins of today's American Reform Judaism lie in the social, political, and intellectual transformation undergone by Central European Jewry when it began the process of acculturation and emancipation. A segment of the Jewish community during the first decades of the nineteenth century sought to reform Judaism in such a way as to adapt it to the new situation of an entity no longer physically and intellectually isolated from its environment. The early reformers did not seek to establish a separate denomination; they were concerned rather to influence the religious life of all Jews. They wanted to make worship services aesthetically satisfying; they sought to render theology and ritual more compatible with philosophical principles, moral sensibilities, and political loyalties. However, only a portion of European Jewry, mainly in Germany, was won over to the ideas of the reformers, so that by midcentury the larger German communities were split into traditional and liberal factions.

During the 1840s congregations subscribing to the European modifications in theory and practice were established in the United States. By 1873, Rabbi Isaac Mayer Wise was able to bring together a nucleus of liberally oriented synagogues in a Union of American Hebrew Congregations (UAHC). Both the UAHC and the Hebrew Union College (HUC), the rabbinical seminary established by Wise in Cincinnati two years later, were intended to encompass and serve the broadest spectrum of American Jewry. But the influx into the United States of traditionally inclined East European Jews, on the one hand, and the pressure of more radical reformers, on the other, soon drove both of these institutions into a more separatist and more narrowly defined position. By the end of the century, the UAHC, the HUC, and the Central Conference of American Rabbis (CCAR, established in 1889) had become the institutions of but a single branch of American Jewry, the Reform Jews.

Until the 1930s, and to some extent thereafter, Reform Judaism, as expressed in the Pittsburgh Platform of 1885, focused upon "ethical monotheism." Positively, it stressed the universal ideals of Judaism and the mission of Israel to bring these tenets and values to all of mankind. Negatively, it sought to dissociate itself from what it regarded as no longer viable theological doctrines, from excessive ritualism, and from any expression of Jewish nationalism. Its social composition consisted almost exclusively of Jews from Germany whose economic standing was well above the mean of American Jewry.

With the cessation of massive Jewish immigration to the United States after World War I, resulting in a greater amalgamation of American Jewry, and with the rise of Hitler in Germany, the character of Reform Judaism began to change. The Columbus Platform of 1937 reflected a considerably more positive attitude to ritual and Sabbath and festival celebration, and it affirmed the obligation of all Jewry to aid in building a Jewish homeland in the Land of Israel.[1]

The destruction of the major part of European Jewry in the Nazi Holocaust left American Reform Judaism in the position of undisputed leadership of liberal Jewry. During succeeding years it would increasingly dominate the World Union for Progressive Judaism, the international body of liberal Jewry that had been established in 1926. However, as it emerged into the postwar world, American Reform Judaism was modest, at best, in size and influence. The UAHC consisted of slightly more than 300 congregations with which about 75,000 families were affiliated. The Hebrew Union College was ordaining about a dozen Reform rabbis per year, and the CCAR had a total membership of little more than 500.

What must first be noted about Reform Judaism in the last thirty years is its remarkable growth. By 1975 the number of UAHC congregations had reached more than 700, with family membership more than tripling to about 250,000; the Reform leadership could claim it represented one million American Jews, a third of the total number affiliated with any synagogue. The UAHC headquarters, having been moved from Cincinnati in 1951, consisted of an entire building in New York City, the population center of American Jewry. By 1975 the Union had thirteen regional offices in all parts of the country and was administering a network of eight summer camps. The Hebrew Union College had merged in 1950 with the nondenominational Jewish Institute of Religion (JIR), founded in New York by Stephen S. Wise in 1922. Four years later a branch was added in Los Angeles, and in 1963 a campus in Jerusalem. In addition to the rabbinical school, the HUC-JIR developed a graduate studies program in Judaica, and schools of education, archaeology, cantorial training, and Jewish communal service. By 1975 it was ordaining as many as fifty rabbis a year, and the membership of the CCAR had climbed to the one thousand mark.

This growth is explicable by reference to a number of factors. The postwar period was generally one of expansion for American Jewish institutions. The wealth of American Jewry increased rapidly following the depression and war years, making possible a higher level of support for Jewish causes. Movement to the suburbs brought with it synagogue affiliation as an expected propriety. The Christian religious revival of the 1950s also influenced renewed interest in the Jewish religion. In addition, Reform Jewry during this period possessed in Rabbi Maurice Eisendrath, president of the UAHC from 1943 to 1973, and biblical archaeologist Nelson Glueck, president of the HUC-JIR from 1947 to 1971, two particularly dynamic and ambitious leaders, each intent on expanding his own institution while vying for the position of undisputed head of the movement. The most dramatic growth came in the fifties and sixties; by 1975 the upward curve had begun to level off.

In some respects Reform Judaism of the first postwar generation represented a continuation and expansion of interests and concerns which had characterized the American movement nearly since its inception. The Pittsburgh Platform had already deemed it a Jewish obligation "to participate in the great task of modern times, to solve on the basis of justice and righteousness the problems presented by the contrasts and evils of the present organization of society." In succeeding decades individual rabbis spoke out on public issues from their pulpits and the CCAR passed resolutions condemning war and social injustices, but the Reform movement as a whole was only minimally involved. That was to change once Eisendrath became president of the UAHC. A new, vigorous staff encouraged formation of social-action committees in Reform temples and published books attempting to relate Jewish moral values to major political, economic, and social problems afflicting American society.

Despite considerable internal opposition, especially from congregations in the South, the movement as a whole—as well as individual Reform rabbis—actively supported the drive for racial desegration. By the second half of the sixties, American Reform had expressed its unequivocal opposition to the war in Vietnam, the CCAR in 1965 declaring that there can be no "military solution to the fundamental social and economic problems of the Vietnamese" and calling for an immediate beginning to a gradual withdrawal of American forces.[2] Reform leaders joined in protests and demonstrations, often at the expense of personal abuse. The abiding commitment of the movement to presenting its moral and religious perspective on public issues was institutionalized in 1961 when the UAHC established its Religious Action Center in Washington, D.C. The center has since served the purpose of making possible a direct influence on significant legislation while at the same time educating the Reform constituency to issues under current consideration.

The ecumenical movement emanating from Vatican II led to the expansion of interfaith activities, which had long been fostered by American Reform Judaism. Clergy institutes were held in various congregations, and dialogues among scholars were initiated by the UAHC. The Jewish

Chatauqua Society of the National Federation of Temple Brotherhoods continued and expanded its project of bringing lecturers on Judaism to college campuses around the country. And the HUC-JIR, which had opened its graduate program to Christian students as early as the 1940s, awarded to an ever greater number of non-Jews the doctor of philosophy degree in Jewish Studies.

Reform interest in Jewish theology grew significantly in the postwar period. A number of Reform rabbis articulated their views in individual writings,[3] and the CCAR established a Commission (currently a Committee) on Theology, composed of members especially drawn to the subject.

However, there has not been theological agreement. A portion of the Reform rabbinate has continued to favor the rationalism which dominated the earlier period of the movement. Although the ebullient faith in moral progress voiced by previous generations of Reform Jews was sobered first by the Holocaust and then by the racial and international conflicts of the postwar period, the notion of progressive revelation, meaning that each succeeding age advances in its understanding of the divine, has been maintained by members of this group. Nor was the notion of the mission of Israel entirely forsaken, though it was usually expressed more modestly, less presumptuously, than in the past. However, this universalistic, rationalistic theism, which posits a providential God who is the source of order and moral action in the universe, became in the last generation an intermediate position increasingly abandoned as the result of a decided polar movement that led away from it in opposite directions.

While humanistic and naturalistic positions had been held by some Reform rabbis earlier, the postwar period witnessed their open emergence. A recent study showed that 28 percent of Reform rabbis regard their theological stance as either nontraditionalist, agnostic, or atheistic. The percentage among the adult laity was similar, nearly 50 percent among young people, and possibly still higher among rabbinical students.[4] Two factors seem most responsible for this growth of non-theistic, nonsupernaturalistic positions. Biblical criticism and psychoanalytic reductionism have continued to provide severe challenges to the traditional doctrine of revelation even after theologians attempted to defend or modify it. In addition, the Holocaust has seemed to some so irreconcilable with any comprehensible notion of divine providence as to render theism untenable. What sets this theologically more radical wing of Reform Judaism apart from a purely secular Jewish identity is the desire to participate in the life of a synagogue and to give ceremonial expression to moral aspirations.

At the same time, however, there has emerged from the Reform rabbinate a group of theologians propounding a far more traditional and particularistic theology then had been characteristic of the movement heretofore. Influenced by Christian existentialism, but even more by the European Jewish thinkers Franz Rosenzweig and Martin Buber, its members have sought to create a specifically Jewish theology born out of a new confrontation with the classical texts of Judaism. They have viewed these texts, not merely as inspired human documents linked to a particular period of spiritual development, but as the vehicle of a divine revelation directly addressing the present generation of Jews. The central concept of this circle has been the covenant between God and the Jewish people, originating in biblical times but renewed and freshly understood in each generation. They maintain that God cannot be defined by human reason or His existence proven; He can only be encountered. Though allowing for biblical criticism, the approach is frankly supernaturalistic, affirming a personal God who can and does speak to the modern Jew even as He spoke to his biblical ancestors—provided only that he will listen and study the texts. Prayer retains its traditional significance: a dialogue between God and the worshiper, removing the necessity of altering or radically reinterpreting the theistic cast of the traditional prayerbook.

Early in the history of the Reform movement, when its first advocates sought to win over a Jewish community firmly rooted in Jewish tradition, arguments for individual reforms in liturgy or practice were justified by detailed reference to the *halachah*, the system of Jewish law. In the course of time, however, an increasing number of Jews lost their attachment to the legal tradition and cared little whether the use of an organ at services or the vernacular in prayers, for example, could be justified by reference to biblical or talmudic precedent. The Orthodox, for their part, were reluctant to accept any departure from current practice even if a basis could be found for it in some earlier layer of Jewish law.

The last decades have witnessed a remarkable renewal of interest in *halachah* on the part of many Reform rabbis and also a segment of the laity. In 1944 Solomon Freehof, who in recent years has served as chairman of the CCAR Responsa Committee, published the first volume of his *Reform Jewish Practice* in which he attempted to elucidate the relationship between Reform observance and the prescriptions of Jewish law. A second volume followed and then a series of five collections of Reform responsa dealing with scores of questions concerning aspects of synagogue worship and individual observance. Some of these responsa sought precedent in the *halachah* for existing practices among Reform Jews; others simply enlightened the questioner regarding the position of traditional Judaism on an issue that needed decision. Often Freehof's own view diverged—sometimes sharply—from the authoritative Orthodox position.

Unlike traditional responsa, these of a Reform variety were not intended to possess binding force. Freehof intended to supply only "guidance, not governance." However, the desire on the part of Reform Jews to relate their practices to those of traditional Judaism—wherever their own religious, moral, and aesthetic sensibilities allowed—indicates a new stage in the history of Reform Judaism. A generation no longer in revolt against the *halachah* and no longer satisfied with determining practice on the basis of personal preference alone was seeking to establish a new relationship to the vast corpus of Jewish law. It would not allow the *halachah* to be determinative—and therefore Reform Judaism could not be considered halachic—but it listened respectfully to what the legal decisors had to say and weighed carefully their arguments and conclusions.

Closely related to the desire to seek moorings in the legal tradition has been the wish for a Reform "guide." The question of such an authoritative compendium of Reform observance has been one of the most explosive issues facing the Reform rabbinate in recent years. Its opponents have argued that any guide would detract from the individual's freedom in religious matters that they consider the hallmark of Reform. They also regarded such a project as a step in the direction of Orthodoxy, which continued to be bound by a sixteenth-century code, the *Shulhan Arukh*. Proponents of a guide have felt that at least a portion of the laity desires to know what is expected of a Reform Jew and that without such a guide the movement is excessively amorphous, lacking in clear definition. Moreover, they have stressed, a guide is not at all the same as a code.

Until the present time the CCAR has not produced a comprehensive guide for Reform Jews. Instead, individual rabbis have undertaken the task on their own, their works accepted and distributed by that portion of their colleagues which shares their views.[5] However, in 1972, the CCAR did publish *Tadrikh le-Shabbat, A Shabbat Manual,* a guide for Sabbath observance composed by its Sabbath Committee. In addition to historical background, purposes of Sabbath observance, home services, and Sabbath hymns, the *Tadrikh* includes a listing of *mitzvot:* Sabbath prescriptions and proscriptions for Reform Jews. While the authors thus sought to salvage the traditional term *mitzvah,* theological differences did not allow them to call *mitzvot* "divine commandments." They spoke of them instead as "options and opportunities" to enrich celebration and observance of the Sabbath, leaving open their relationship to the will of God.

The desire for a guide arose within the context of a marked increase of traditional ceremonials in Reform congregations. Half a century ago, most Reform synagogues prided themselves on the decorum of their religious services, their abandonment of rituals that originated in folk superstitions, and the ethereal atmosphere of a worshipful, largely passive congregation stirred by the preachments of its rabbi and exalted by the contrapuntal singing of its professional choir. Today this situation has changed, at least somewhat, for nearly all Reform congregations. A majority of Reform rabbis now favor incorporating more traditions; some even advocate merger with Conservative Judaism.[6] Services today are likely to include a generous quantity of Hebrew and have the musical portion conducted by a cantor with or without the assistance of a choir. Rather than the "cathedrals" of an earlier period, congregations have built more intimate sanctuaries (expandable for the High Holy Days) out of a desire to stress intimacy rather than awe in worship. More commonly today rabbis, cantors, and in some cases laymen wear a prayer shawl and/or a head covering. Often the rabbi will substitute a discussion with congregants for the usual sermon, enabling a dialogue to take the place of the exhortatory sermon.

The *bar mitzvah* ceremony, once rejected by Reform in favor of confirmation, has made its way into the Reform temple along with *bat mitzvah*, the equivalent for girls. Many Reform Jews have found a deep significance in these personal ceremonies, though some have treated the religious and educational aspects as secondary to the celebration. A number of congregations have introduced the traditional penitential service of *Selihot*, while a very few Reform homes—but all youth camps—mark the Sabbath not only by the blessings said at its beginning but also by the intimate and symbolic ceremony of *Havdalah* at its conclusion. The wedding canopy and even the breaking of the glass during the wedding service, once almost universally abandoned, have been generally reintroduced, though the latter ceremony is purely superstitious in origin. While Reform services continue generally to be more formal than those of the Orthodox, a definite trend toward freer self-expression by the congregation and a more favorable attitude to ritual seems apparent.

The religious education of their children was long regarded by Reform parents as a minimal project. Sunday schools held classes for two hours per week and conveyed little more than a sense of Jewishness, some knowledge of Bible stories and holidays, and a cursory familiarity with Jewish beliefs. The last thirty years have witnessed considerable intensification of Jewish education in the Reform movement. Many Reform religious schools now provide children with weekday as well as weekend classes; most require—or at least provide the opportunity for—Hebrew instruction, and they acquaint the students directly with Jewish customs and ceremonies through weekend sessions at a camp. Perhaps the most startling development has been the very recent creation of five Reform Jewish day schools in Beverly Hills, Toronto, New York, Phoenix, and Miami. While such schools serve only a miniscule percentage of Reform pupils, they offer the opportunity of far more intensive Jewish education for those parents dissatisfied with what even an expanded supplementary religious school program can provide.

The National Federation of Temple Youth in the last decades has likewise enlarged its educational program. While some young people have engaged in social-action projects through a "Mitzvah Corps," others have participated in a yearly "Torah Corps," consisting of concentrated study and discussion of Jewish sources in the setting of a summer camp. The study aspects of the regular camp programs have likewise expanded as classes in Hebrew and Jewish subjects have become a fixed part of the schedule.

No transformation within Reform Judaism has been as dramatic and complete as its sharp reversal on Zionism. Gathered in Richmond, Virginia, in 1898, a UAHC national council declared: "America is our Zion. . . . The mission of Judaism is spiritual, not political. Its aim is not to establish a state, but to spread the truths of religion and humanity throughout the world."[7] The same sentiment echoed from congregational pulpits and from the classrooms of the Hebrew Union College. There were, indeed, some Zionists in the Reform movement even in the first decades of this century—including such prominent figures as Rabbis Stephen S. Wise and Abba Hillel Silver—but they represented a small minority. Most Reform Jews rejected any expression of Jewish nationalism as contradictory to the universal mission of Israel among the nations. This attitude began to change notably during the 1930s with the influx of more ethnically oriented East European Jews into the movement and the obvious need of Jews in Germany, persecuted by the Nazis with ever greater severity, to obtain a secure refuge. In 1937 the UAHC declared the need for all Jews, regardless of ideological differences, to unite in furthering the establishment of a Jewish homeland in Palestine. By 1942 the CCAR was sufficiently Zionist in composition to pass a resolution favoring the creation of a Palestinian Jewish army. The persistent anti-Zionists in the Reform rabbinate now formed their own organization, the American Council for Judaism, but nearly all soon abandoned it to a group of diehard laymen.

The establishment of the State of Israel in 1948 was welcomed by virtually all Reform Jews. Its impact on the Reform movement, still limited in the fifties, grew gradually until it became a major force in the last decade. One after another, Reform congregations began to change their pronunciation of Hebrew to that used in Israel, often first in the religious school, then in the regular worship services. Israeli synagogue melodies slowly replaced those inherited from Central Europe, and English hymns of an earlier age gave way to popular modern Hebrew songs. Study of Israeli society was integrated into the religious school curriculum, while Israeli dances and tunes—and often Israeli counselors—became standard at NFTY camps. The CCAR paid tribute to the influence of the new state by making a religious festival of Israeli Independence Day and holding some of its annual conferences in the Holy Land. Beginning in 1970, the HUC-JIR required of its entering rabbinical students that they spend their initial year of study at its Jerusalem School. The World Union for Progressive Judaism not only decided to become a constituent of the World Zionist Organization but also moved its headquarters to Israel. The most remarkable steps of all were taken recently by the UAHC in sponsoring a Reform Jewish *Kibbutz* in Israel and affirming "the value of *aliyah* (immigration to Israel) as a valid option for contemporary Liberal Jewish commitment and self-fulfillment."[8] These actions of American Reform institutions reflect the sentiment of a constituency which, while for the most part not perceiving the Diaspora as peripheral to the life of the Jewish people, today regards support of Israel as essential to being a good Jew.[9] By 1975 there were scarcely any Reform Jews who would still define Jewish identity in exclusively religious terms.

In its revaluation of tradition and ceremony, in the emphasis which it placed on survival of the Jewish people, and in its support of Israel, the Reform movement was drawing into an ever closer relationship with Jews not of the Reform persuasion. In the mid-seventies Alfred Gottschalk, president of the HUC-JIR, was a regular participant in conferences held in Jerusalem that discussed issues of concern for all of Jewry; Alexander Schindler, president of the UAHC, served concurrently as chairman of the Conference of Presidents of Major American Jewish Organizations. One troublesome issue, however, was forcing Reform Judaism to move in the opposite direction: the problem of mixed marriages. The last decade in particular has been characterized by a steeply rising incidence of Jews marrying outside their community. No Orthodox or Conservative rabbi will perform a Jewish wedding ceremony for such a couple; Israelis tend to regard such marriages as necessarily diminishing the strength of the Jewish people. Most Reform congregants also believe mixed marriages are bad for the Jewish people and would prefer that their children marry within the faith. But the majority of the young people do not regard them as any great disaster either for the Jews or for themselves personally.[10] And even about two-thirds of the adults condone, if not actually encourage, their rabbi's officiating at mixed weddings.[11] Reform rabbis have come under considerable pressure from their congregants to sanctify such unions, and often they have believed themselves justified by the hope or promise that in specific instances the non-Jewish partner will gradually be brought into Judaism or at least the children be raised as Jews. By the mid-seventies the number of Reform rabbis who perform mixed marriages, at least under special circumstances, was approaching half of the membership of the CCAR.[12]

This explosive and divisive issue was brought to the rabbinical conference held at Atlanta in 1973.[13] After lengthy and rancorous debate, a resolution was passed declaring the CCAR's "opposition to participation by its members in any ceremony which solemnized a mixed marriage." There was no reference to the invocation of sanctions nor to the exclusion of mixed couples from participation in the synagogue. But the stand of the CCAR was now stronger than it had been heretofore. The minority was deeply dissatisfied with the resolution. A number of them formed the Association for a Progressive Reform Judaism, which stood opposed to what was regarded as making "second class citizens within the Reform rabbinate of those who believe they serve Judaism best through officiating at religious intermarriages while maintaining their own norms and standards in those cases." The same organization, though its few score members chose to remain within the CCAR, likewise set itself in opposition to those trends, championed by the majority, which seemed a betrayal of Reform Judaism's earlier positions. Specifically, it criticized the tendency to make concessions to Orthodoxy for the sake of Jewish unity, the trend toward regarding the State of Israel as the center of Jewish life, and the pronounced shift in emphasis from universalistic human aspirations to particular Jewish concerns.[14] The formation of the APRJ was symptomatic of a condition which seemed increasingly to characterize Reform Judaism in recent years: the lack of consensus.

Divergence in theology, differences over the role of authority, the question of mixed marriage—these issues have deeply split Reform Judaism to the point that it appears today more a loosely knit "organization" than a "movement" in the proper sense. Two recent events, one a failure, the other a success, are indicative. In 1971 representatives of the UAHC, CCAR, and HUC-JIR began to work on what it was hoped would be a new platform for American Reform Judaism. It was to be completed in time for the centennial celebration of the UAHC in 1973.[15] A series of meetings produced position papers and a great deal of discussion, but the promised "new document for a new age" was not forthcoming. The differences among the committee members on basic issues were simply too wide to be easily bridged. Only in 1976 was a CCAR committee able to formulate a centennial document which reflected on the accomplishments and failures of the past and roughly defined the parameters of Reform in the present. It was adopted by the CCAR.[16]

A year earlier, in 1975, the CCAR published its first new prayerbook for weekdays, Sabbaths, and festivals since the most recent revision of the *Union Prayerbook* in 1940. It represented a sharp departure from its predecessor. The new volume bore a Hebrew title, *Sha'are Tefilla* ("Gates of Prayer") and could be purchased in an edition that opened Hebraically from the right side. It was larger in length and breadth than the *Union Prayerbook* and was almost 400 pages longer than its predecessor. But the difference in bulk was not the most significant point of comparison. Whereas the earlier prayerbook had reflected a more or less uniform theology and practice, the new *Gates of Prayer* unabashedly revealed the marked disagreements within the Reform community. No less than ten services were included for Sabbath evening, ranging from the severely traditional to the explicitly humanist. As in the Orthodox *siddur,* there were prayers for putting on the *tallit* (the prayer shawl) and even the *tefillin,* the phylacteries worn in daily prayer by very few Reform Jews. The new prayerbook was in fact an anthology, a reflection of the variety of religious expression that was required to serve the needs of so diverse a constituency. At best it was a tribute to the ideal of relgious choice—to be traditional or innovative—that Reform Judaism continued to prize.[17]

Coping adequately with internal dissension was only one of the problems faced by Reform Jewry in the mid-seventies. The period of rapid growth in membership had come to an end, religious school enrollments dropped with the demographic decline of appropriately aged Jewish children. While in the fifties and sixties religion had been central to the Jewish identity of most Reform Jews, by 1975 ethnicism, focused especially on activity in support of Israel, drew the energies of many Reform Jews away from the synagogue. In the new scale of priorities the institutions of Reform Judaism ranked far behind the local Jewish community's Federation. For most, the impact of the Holocaust and the State of Israel had gradually weakened the sense of specifically Reform identity, and they now regarded religious distinctions among Jews as of relatively minor significance. Especially was this true among a portion of the youth who in some cases espoused more traditional practices than their parents and in others dissociated themselves entirely from religious Judaism. This generation gap was paralleled by a similar gulf between rabbi and layman. Younger rabbis, in particular, were increasingly much more observant than their synagogue membership, a considerable number adhering to the dietary laws. Not surprisingly, a recent survey found that 71 percent of Reform rabbis perceived a "Jewish distance" between themselves and their congregants.[18]

The most severe problem was not at all new. It had plagued Reform Judaism all along. From its very beginnings the Reform movement had drawn a great many Jews for whom religion, and in some cases Jewishness, was distinctly peripheral to their lives. They attended synagogue rarely, having joined for reasons of respectability and their children's Jewish identity. Many, especially in the larger cities, were not desirous of deeper involvement. They were content to come to the temple for the High Holy Days or for the celebration of life-cycle events. At present this segment tends to see the rabbi as more of a priest who officiates on special occasions than a spiritual or moral guide, while, for their part, the rabbinical and lay leaders are now rarely imbued with that effervescent self-confidence which had done battle with apathy in an earlier age. A few have become discouraged or themselves indifferent.

Yet there is another side to the picture which is not as bleak. In 1975 each synagogue contained a larger or smaller core of laity sincerely devoted to Reform Judaism. Among the younger rabbis were men—and since 1971, women—who possessed a richer Jewish knowledge and a deeper Jewish commitment than many of their older colleagues. Reform Jewish education was continually being improved and expanded, teachers were more adequately trained, better textbooks were being published. In Israel a beachhead of a dozen congregations was established. In America, despite the mixed marriage question, Reform Judaism seemed more integrally a part of the total Jewish community than ever before. A nucleus of members in nearly every congregation sought a sense of genuine community within the temple.[19] Above all, there remained a large portion of the one million Jews calling themselves Reform who continued to believe seriously in a liberal approach to the religious tradition. For them Reform Judaism steered a path between authoritarian religion on the one hand and idolatrous secularism on the other. With all of its diversity, it alone offered a religious expression of Judaism both intellectually attractive and emotionally satisfying. Or, put differently, Reform Judaism remained for many Reform Jews an indispensable sanctifying element in the ceaseless flux of human life.

NOTES

1. The Pittsburgh and Columbus Platforms are reproduced in Sylvan D. Schwartzman, *Reform Judaism Then and Now* (New York: Union of American Hebrew Congregations, 1971), pp. 214-18, 243-56.

2. *CCAR Yearbook*, LXXV (1965), p. 67.

3. See the following works: Eugene Borowitz, *A New Jewish Theology in the Making* (Philadelphia: The Westminster Press, 1968); Samuel S. Cohon, *Judaism—A Way of Life* (Cincinnati: Union of American Hebrew Congregations, 1948); Emil L. Fackenheim, *Quest for Past and Future: Essays in Jewish Theology* (Bloomington: Indiana University Press, 1968); Roland B. Gittelsohn, *Man's Best*

Hope (New York: Random House, 1961); and Arthur J. Lelyveld, *Atheism Is Dead: A Jewish Response to Radical Theology* (Cleveland: World Publishing Company, 1968). See also the essays in Bernard Martin, ed., *Contemporary Reform Jewish Thought* (Chicago: Quadrangle Books, 1968), and the symposium in *Dimensions,* Fall 1967.

4. Theodore I. Lenn and Associates, *Rabbi and Synagogue in Reform Judaism* (New York: Central Conference of American Rabbis, 1972), pp. 98-101, 253, 355. The seminarian figures (p. 323) are based on a very small sample and exclude the New York campus.

5. See the following works: Morrison David Bial, *Liberal Judaism at Home: The Practices of Modern Reform Judaism* (Summit, New Jersey: Temple Sinai, 1967); Frederic A. Doppelt and David Polish, *A Guide for Reform Jews* (New York: Bloch Publishing Company, 1957); and Abraham J. Feldman, *Reform Judaism: A Guide for Reform Jews* (New York: Behrman House, 1956).

6. Lenn, *Rabbi and Synagogue,* p. 187.

7. *Proceedings of the Union of American Hebrew Congregations* V (1898-1903), p. 4002.

8. Statement of the Israel Commission of the UAHC, approved by the UAHC board, May 1976.

9. Leonard J. Fein et al., *Reform Is a Verb: Notes on Reform and Reforming Jews* (New York: Union of American Hebrew Congregations, 1972), pp. 37, 120.

10. *Ibid.,* pp. 57-58.

11. Lenn, *Rabbi and Synagogue,* p. 134.

12. *Ibid.,* p. 128.

13. *CCAR Yearbook,* LXXXIII (1973), pp. 59-97.

14. Jack Bemporad, "Issues Confronting the Association for a Progressive Reform Judaism" (mimeographed, n.d.3).

15. *Dimensions,* May 1972.

16. *CCAR Yearbook,* LXXXVI (1976), pp. 174-78.

17. See the critical review by Jakob J. Petuchowski in *Conservative Judaism,* Fall 1975, pp. 7-15. The new *Passover Haggadah* published by the CCAR in 1974 likewise allows considerable variation, but it is kept within a single framework. The new edition is considerably closer to the traditional *Haggadah* than its predecessor.

18. Lenn, *Rabbi and Synagogue,* p. 138.

19. Fein, *Reform Is a Verb,* p. 140.

David Polish _____

ISRAEL AND DIASPORA JEWRY: AN AMERICAN PERSPECTIVE

The paramount reality of modern Jewish life is the State of Israel. Before its birth, not all Jews aspired to it, but those who did succeeded in bringing virtually all of World Jewry into its orbit. During the past thirty years Diaspora Jews have been motivated primarily by the existence, the achievements, the perils, the inspiration of Israel—so much so, that the first generation to live contemporaneously with this unprecedented reality is impatient with criticism or disaffection concerning Israel. It is assumed that Israel, under the pressure of threat and adversity, cannot help being flawed, but this is counterbalanced by the wonder that this beleaguered state has managed to achieve as much as it has in only thirty years.

Diaspora Jews exist as proud and Jewishly conscious communities by virtue of Israel. Had Israel not emerged in the wake of the Holocaust, it is quite possible that many Jews throughout the world would have been engulfed by either despair or embittered alienation. Israel came into being at a time of mourning and desolation for the Jewish people, and no other factor in its history gave it the same courage and sense of Jewish worth and purpose. For vast numbers of Jews, Israel is the people's shrine; its political leaders are the Jewish people's heroes; its triumphs reverberate in remote settlements; its traumas pain Jews in distant places. More than anything else, Israel has awakened within the awareness of Jews the sense that, through its existence, they are no longer impotent instruments of history but have the capability of confronting and even sharing it. This is the general perception, and most Jews consider it valid.

Yet increasingly Israel and World Jewry recognize that statehood has generated not only compelling political and military problems bearing on the state's existence, but issues which touch on the nature and purpose of the state itself. Alternating euphoria and anguish cannot defer consideration of moral and existential questions. In fact, those questions become increasingly urgent as Israel's struggle continues. They are not, however, the product of statehood alone. Although statehood has informed them with special intensity they agitated Jewish thought long before the state. Central to these was the issue about the nature of the Jewish people.

Until the Emancipation Jews perceived themselves and were generally perceived by others as a people in exile, retaining strong national characteristics hallowed by religious disciplines and beliefs that were fixed in covenant consciousness and messianic expectation. With the Emancipation, changes in Jewish self-perception began in response to non-Jewish conditions laid down as a prerequisite for admitting Jews into the new age. Those conditions called for the abandonment of the Jewish national-collective character and the adoption, instead, of a confessional-ecclesiastical status. Early Reform Judaism was receptive to this definition; it developed a theology which demonstrated that, with the destruction of Jewish political sovereignty, national attributes became obsolete and were replaced by a higher form of existence—the purely religious unity of Jews committed to ethical monotheism. This understanding was challenged by pre-Zionist Jews and, with the rise of modern Zionism, the national essence of the Jewish people was proclaimed in opposition to Reform. Until the early 1930s Reform and Zionism stood in confrontation over this issue. It was resolved in a synthesis on two levels; first, when Reform Jews increasingly entered the ranks of the Zionist movement as workers and leaders, and second, when Reform Judaism appropriated the concepts of Jewish peoplehood and Jewish national striving as legitimate aspects of Jewish existence.

Even before the State of Israel came into being, there was a division within Zionist thought as to the nature of the Jewish people. Theodor Herzl saw Zionism as a political movement for bringing as many Jews as possible to Palestine, with the consequent withering away of the Diaspora. Jews choosing to remain behind would become absorbed among the nations. The Jewish people and the Jewish state would become one. What Herzl regarded as an historical inevitability became for Jacob Klatzkin an historical imperative; the Diaspora has no validity, and a conscious effort should be made to dissolve it in the wake of the creation of a Jewish state. Challenging this position was Ahad Ha-Am who argued that a vast Diaspora would continue to exist for an indeterminate time and that it would be a major task of a Jewish state to serve as a "spiritual center," nourishing the Diaspora.

The realization of Jewish statehood has raised the issue to a far greater and more practical dimension than in pre-state times. No sooner did Israel come into being than the argument broke out again, this time with implications that could bear on the future of the state and the people. While the immediate importance of the Diaspora as a source of support and *aliyah* was not questioned, the ultimate viability of the Diaspora was challenged by many Israelis and Zionists. The Herzlian theory appeared to be validated by the very existence of Israel. The Ahad Ha-Am theory seemed to be weakened by the Nazi Holocaust which had destroyed virtually all of East European Jewry outside of Russia, whose Jews were apparently doomed to a creeping spiritual and political Holocaust.

Conversely and unexpectedly, the psychological trauma preceding the Six-Day War in 1967, and the shattering consequences of the Yom Kippur War in 1973, reversed the deprecation of the Diaspora. Israelis who had paid little heed to the Diaspora and, indeed, had been its severe detractors discovered in moments of peril that Diaspora Jewry was Israel's greatest moral and political resource. A generation of sabras had grown up, contemptuous of *Galut* (the Exile) and especially of what was deemed its craven submission to the Nazis. Only the apprehension of Adolph Eichmann, one of Hitler's most destructive agents, and his ensuing trial in Jerusalem awakened young Israelis to the realization of European Jewry's ordeal.

But it was through the isolation which suddenly engulfed Israel in May 1967 and in October 1973 that the sense of identity with World Jewry was endowed with the greatest intensity. Israelis became existentially aware that they were Jews. Diaspora Jews became existentially committed to the survival of Israel, not only out of profound kinship but out of awareness of the interdependence of both segments of the Jewish people. In June 1967 the Central Conference of American Rabbis declared, "their ordeal is our ordeal, their fate is our fate." The identity of all Jews with the Jewish people was irrevocably established. The dichotomy between Israelis and Jews, significant as it is in establishing political distinctions, was minimized.

This is no way dispelled the dispute, generated by the Emancipation, over nationhood and religion. To be sure, the ideological struggle over the understanding of Judaism as an ecclesia had long since spent itself; it had now been replaced by the equally untenable dogma that Judaism and nationhood were coequal. In Israel nonreligious circles may pragmatically recognize the claim of Jewish religion, in its diversity, as an expression of Jewishness, particularly in the Diaspora, but at the same time they do not take this claim seriously. In the Diaspora even synagogue-oriented Jews think in ethnic structures and identify with the Jewish people and with Israel chiefly in secular terms. While a good case can be made for the mutuality of some forms of secularism with religion—for example, financial support for Israel, *aliyah*, political action in behalf of Israel—many Zionists reject efforts to associate such acts with deeds of piety. Thus, whereas, in pre-Emancipation times, Jewish identity and unity were predicated on religion rooted in peoplehood, today's Jewish configuration is expressed in nationhood-peoplehood with religion as ancillary.

While the importance of the Diaspora has been established for a beleaguered State of Israel, the singular nature of the Jewish people as part state, part Diaspora is still in the process of gestation. The radical transformation of the Jewish people since 1948 is more clearly recognized as a historical and social phenomenon than as a conceptual mutation. From the year 70, when the Jewish state was destroyed, until almost nineteen centuries later, World Jewry was a people in *Galut*, literally so in lands of oppression, theoretically so in free lands. Jews in Eastern Europe were clearly under the double banishment of expulsion from their ancestral home and the political, social, economic, and religious disabilities imposed by nations which treated them as aliens. In more benign and enlightened countries, Jews who may have considered returning to a sovereign Jewish nation were denied that right, both because that nation did not exist and because access even to Palestine was restricted. Hence, they, too, endured a kind of exile.

The creation of the State of Israel has demolished the principle of *Galut* for all Jews who are free to make *aliyah*. (For some, even freedom in democratic lands is perceived as contingent, and *Galut* is therefore not annihilated.)

Statehood has created an additional new factor in Jewish peoplehood. While Jewry was a unicum during the period of *Galut*, there being no other people living in exile, today's Jewry is a unicum of another sort, occupying both its own state and the territory of its host nations. It is singular in a number of characteristics. Unlike any other people, its majority lives outside the homeland; a substantial element, almost equal to the Jewish population of Israel, continues to live in *Galut* (the Soviet Union); its Diaspora in the free world is more intimately bound to the homeland than is any other ethnic Diaspora. As a nation, Israel shares certain common characteristics with other states, although even as a state it is denied the recognition and the system of national alliances that other states enjoy as a matter of right. But as a people of which the Jewish state is an inseparable part, World Jewry is distinguished by its universal, yet particular nature; by nationhood which is both paramount and subordinate to peoplehood; by existence both in the space of its own territory and in timeless, ever-shifting expanses of a world-Diaspora.

It was inevitable that, as a consequence of this unique condition, the Jewish people should now find itself engaged in seeking ways to define the relationship between Israel and the Diaspora. In the aftermath of the Holocaust, and in the wake of recurrent crises faced by Israel, Jews are not nearly as concerned with this apparently theoretical issue as they are with the problems of Israel's protection and survival. For most Jews, ideology is superseded by pragmatic considerations. The primary relationship with Israel is one of wholehearted commitment and zealous response to encroaching danger. Yet, there are signs that a Diaspora generation which has been conditioned to respond fervently to Israel's needs, largely out of personal involvement in or witness to the Holocaust and the struggle to create the Jewish state, is being followed by a new generation which does not react with the same visceral intensity. There is the possibility that time may create a growing distance between Israel and the Diaspora, and a considerable segment of Jewry in America already attests to that. Professor Daniel Elazar has pointed out that while the pro-Israel forces in Jewish life are more articulate and better organized, as well as deeply committed to Jewish survival, there is another component that is passive, indifferent, alienated. This polarity is not likely to dissolve but rather to become more pronounced, with each category becoming increasingly rooted in its position. Recruits for the alienated will be coming increasingly from the ranks of those to whom Jewish survival is not a primary value and who, with accelerating momentum, are increasing the intermarriage statistics. It is questionable whether this trend can be arrested, and this places upon Israel and Diaspora leadership the added responsibility of seeking new directions instead of trusting in questionable premises whose power is slipping.

One of these premises is that Israel and the Diaspora, especially Western Jewry, while bound together for the sake of Israel's preservation, are essentially separate, totally autonomous entities. The second premise is a corollary: that even while they are separate and distinct, one is subordinate to the other. Some Israelis see the Diaspora as Jewishly inadequate but essential to Israel's survival, while some Diaspora Jews see Israel as dependent upon World Jewry for its existence. These premises stem from a perception which, while recognizing the interrelationship of all Jews, considers the Jewish people as the instrument of the State of Israel. This perception, which cannot be lightly dismissed, does not entertain a hopeful view of the Diaspora's future. It sees Soviet Jewry as doomed to disintegration, with only those who make *aliyah* capable of being saved as Jews. It sees South American Jewry as caught in the vise of political unrest, with its toll of anti-Semitism on the one hand and widespread defection of the young to radical movements on the other. It sees American Jewry as jeopardized by an abnormally low birth rate, a mounting intermarriage rate, and growing assimilation, all tending to create the prospect of a loyal but numerically diminished Jewish community with declining influence in America. This perception insists that for Israel to survive, it must assume primacy in the Jewish world, attract the greatest possible number of young Jews from the Diaspora, and aspire to contain a majority of World Jewry within its borders.

An alternate position is taken by some Diaspora and Israeli Jews. They argue that a fatalistic view of the Diaspora can become a self-fulfilling prophecy, and that while no one can predict what will ultimately transpire, a despairing outlook on the Diaspora will most certainly hasten its doom. Instead, to the extent that it is possible, and for the sake of Israel as well as of the Diaspora, measures should be taken to preserve the Diaspora and to help make it viable as a spiritual and political entity. Two requirements are called for, one theoretical, the other pragmatic. First, in order to try to stem disintegration, Israel and World Jewry must recognize not only the reality but the desirability of the preservation of the Diaspora. Wherever it is a free Diaspora, it has shown remarkable creativity and exercised noteworthy influence on its host societies. In addition, the degree of its viability is a measure of its capacity and will to support Israel. A dessicated Diaspora cannot but weaken Israel and rob it of its only fully dependable ally. Therefore it is necessary for Jews to accept the principle that, while all Jews must steadfastly stand by Israel, the Jewish people does not exist for the Jewish state, but rather, the Jewish state exists for the Jewish people. This represents a radical political assessment whereby the Jewish unicum chooses to identify itself as a worldwide entity with a national base in Israel. Although it may now appear quixotic, Mordecai Kaplan's proposal that the Jewish people certify its national-diasporal character in a covenantal declaration has great validity, especially since the paradigm already exists and needs only to be proclaimed.

It is also argued that in a world where nationalism as an ultimate value is being challenged, a more desirable alternative can be offered by the Jewish model of a synthesis of national devotion and global existence. This view has certain consequences. If, indeed, the entire world Jewish community, with an axis radiating to and from Israel, is the primary polity, then its relationship with Israel requires a far greater degree of participation than present conditions permit. It is true that a number of instruments exist by which Diaspora Jews are permitted to share in certain aspects of Israel's life, but they function primarily within the premise of "Diaspora in the service of Israel." As long as this premise remains dominant World Jewry will not be able to share more fully in Israel's struggles and achievements. The sharing will be more vicarious then existential.

Ever since the Six-Day War, increasing attention has been given to how Diaspora Jewry can more effectively enter the counsels of Israel and participate in some of the decisions which must affect the Diaspora as well as Israel. It must be understood that, in seeking an adequate formula to encompass such an idea, Israel will continue to bear the brunt of jeopardy, sacrifice, and possible loss of life. Therefore, there must be great circumspection and sensitivity both in addressing the issue and in resolving it. Yet, as has been indicated, in the volatility of our world, the Diaspora is not immune to the consequences of decisions which may be made unilaterally in Israel. It is first necessary to overcome resistance to the idea of greater collaboration and participation. Some proposals have already been made. One calls for establishing a Diaspora-Israel instrument for the purpose of discussing many issues currently within the province of Israel alone. It is not suggested that this be a legislative body, but neither is it contemplated that it be an academic assembly alone. What is proposed is that Diaspora Jews be selected by their own territorial agencies to meet with Israelis, in and out of government, for the purpose of joint examination of political and social problems in a manner that would affect official decision-making. Such a process need not be determinative, but it should be influential.

In addition to the intrinsic merit of the proposal, such an instrument would encourage a greater degree of responsible discourse on matters affecting Israel and World Jewry. It would intensify a sense of greater sharing in Jewish life; it would quicken a sense of accountability; it would generate a stronger desire for service to the Jewish people; and it would help cultivate a new and sorely needed generation of Jewish leaders. Above all, it would transform the aspiration for Jewish unity into a palpable reality.

In constructing such an instrument, two prerequisites must be noted. First, the methods of asserting the Diaspora's involvement in Israel's affairs, and vice versa, must be defined. Second, the categories to be discussed must also be defined. In the first area, it ought to be understood that the purpose of dialogue is not confrontation but the exchange of concern. It would serve no purpose if the Diaspora and Israel were consistently to line up on opposing sides. The test of true dialogue would come if differences of opinion were to transcend territorial identities. Early in 1976 an unofficial gathering of this kind took place in Israel, and one of its significant byproducts was the absence of geographical distinctions.

All matters affecting life in Israel would be susceptible to consideration as legitimate items of concern for World Jewry. Clearly, all issues, particularly those of defense and security, would be subject to ultimate decision by Israel alone, but they would not be out of bounds for Diaspora consideration. Out of this would emerge areas of joint endeavor in which the Diaspora would invest not only its financial resources but its work and its people. It has been suggested, for example, that jointly sponsored programs be developed not only to encourage *aliyah* but to make Diaspora Jews available for systematic tours of duty in Israel to supplement their fellow Jews who are subject to long periods of reserve service in the armed forces. Supplementary work in hospitals, social services, and agriculture readily suggests itself. This program of service to Israel not only has intrinsic merit but may come to be regarded as the "dues" by which Diaspora Jews can justify their demands for fuller participation in Israeli affairs. Without an intensive development of such a program as a minimal act of commitment to Israel, it is questionable whether Diaspora Jews could justifiably call for mutuality with Israel. It is noteworthy that, while antagonism to joint consultation existed before the Yom Kippur War, there is growing receptivity to it now. Thus, a leading Israeli writes: "It is therefore proposed to set up a permanent *coordinating body* to deal with the relations between Israel and the Diaspora, in order to tighten and institutionalize the links between the two sides." (Yitzchak Korn, General Secretary, Labor Zionist Movement, *Forum*, no. 24, pp. 116-17.) While the writer limits the range of discussion to "only those questions that are of interest to the whole Jewish nation," his position indicates a measure of openness.

Concurrent with the need for an adequate means of dialogue with Israel is the need for a restructured American Jewish community. In its internal affairs American Jewry is a reflection of the inadequacies of its own relationships with Israel. There is no adequate forum for the discussion of issues. Decisions are made within small groups. The democratic process in which communities have full opportunity to share in discussion and decision is wanting. The involvement of the academic community in the affairs of Jewish life is minimal. Although there is widespread alienation on college and university campuses for reasons other than failures by the Jewish community, that alienation is intensified because some of our richest human resources are kept at arm's length.

History has demonstrated that, on those rare occasions when the American Jewish community united for a common cause, significant results ensued. In 1917 the American Jewish Congress, originally called into being as the inclusive agency of American Jewry, united the Jewish community in behalf of the postwar reconstruction of East European Jewry and gave a powerful impetus to the Zionist goals of the Jewish people. In 1943 the American Jewish Conference rallied American Jewry to a vigorous campaign in behalf of the creation of a Jewish state. Neither of these bodies endured beyond the achievement of their goals. Yet, today American Jewry confronts not only an immediate situation but a challenge to Israel's survival which could continue beyond at least the present generation. American Jewry has no adequate agency to involve large masses of Jews not only for crisis situations but for a continuous struggle. Neither has it developed a democratic process out of which popular decisions could be reached, untapped human resources cultivated, and accountability to the people made possible. All this would require either a new body or the expansion of some existing body, preferably the latter. Together with the maturing of American Jewry as a polity, a responsible vehicle of discourse with Israel could then emerge. Opponents of this proposal contend that the concept is unworkable, that it is unrealistic to call for a "one person, one vote" structure. It is, indeed, premature to think along such lines. Even in an ideal Jewish community it is questionable whether people who do not belong to survivalist organizations and do not contribute to at least the United Jewish Appeal should have a voice in Jewish policy. But there are steps antecedent to universal participation, such as the designation by large communities or regions of representatives to a national deliberative body, or the co-opting of academic people to such a body.

Concomitant with this, and in all likelihood because of the tightly structured nature of organizational life in American Jewry, the issue of dissent became increasingly pronounced after the Yom Kippur War. Wherever, for whatever motives, however lofty, policy is determined without adequate public discussion, dissent will take strong and often irresponsible forms. If it cannot be channeled into established structures, it will erupt into unconventional and destructive forms. It is inevitable that the issues plaguing Israeli society will reverberate in American Jewry, and it is illusory to believe that somehow neither Israel's devoted friends nor her enemies, who monitor her as carefully as they are monitored, would be sheltered from the realities of Israeli existence. Support for Israel among survivalist American Jews is virtually unanimous. But opinion about various aspects of Israeli policy is not. American Jewish leadership has been so constituted as to try to reduce controversy to imperceptible levels. The results were at times detrimental.

One example was the spontaneous reaction by many American Jews against the Mexican government's support of the United Nations resolution in 1975 condemning Zionism as racist. American Jewish leaders, without consulting the Jewish communities, quickly met with the president of Mexico for purposes of mollifying him. Assurances were made by the leaders to American Jewry that they had succeeded in convincing the Mexican government that it had made a mistake. But a few months later Mexico gratuitously intruded itself into a Security Council debate and attacked Israel for infringing on the sovereignty of Uganda. It is conceivable that a more democratic process might have come to the same decision originally reached by the Jewish leaders. But the unilateral action of bypassing American Jewry created confusion among many Jews who had spontaneously acted against the Mexican government.

Furthermore, during the Israeli, American, and Egyptian negotiations on the Sinai disengagement plan after the Yom Kippur War of 1973, the United States secretary of state persuaded members of the Conference of Presidents of Major American Jewish Organizations to call upon American Jewry to lobby in behalf of placing United States personnel in the buffer zone between Israel and Egypt. Without reference to the merits of the plan, the action by the conference on so important an issue illustrated how major policy is made by Jewish leaders in behalf of the Jewish community which has little opportunity for sharing in decision-making. Although this issue could have far-reaching effects on American Jewry, the conference acted both unilaterally and in response to external pressure.

The issue is no longer whether dissent is permissible. Rather it is how dissent can best be given expression. Discussions within major national Jewish bodies have indicated that ways must be found to legitimize authentic differences of opinion. It has been suggested that such differences should be expressed within existing Jewish structures and that they should then be conveyed to appropriate agencies in Israel. Issues affecting the social and economic life of Israel, and in the judgment of some, the issue of peace with the Arabs, are considered valid areas for concern and intervention by organized American Jewry. These proposals come as a result of debates and dissenting views that spilled over into the general press. Some felt that the spectacle of Jewish divisiveness could prove harmful to Jewish interests, but at the same time others recognized that divisiveness could widen unless means for adequate internal discussion could be developed. The controversy in 1976 over a public protest against unauthorized settlement in Israel's West Bank helped bring the issue to a head. Debates over this appeared to recognize that the issue was a legitimate one but that dissenters should not have "gone public." Regardless of the merits of this position, responsible Zionist bodies were alerted to the implications of this problem and were urged to address themselves to the need for an authentic forum where political diversity could be expressed.

Yet, in the wake of increased pressures upon Israel by the new American administration, internal controversy subsided. The Jewish community closed ranks, dissenting groups became less strident and less public, and suffered defections as well. By general assent, the Presidents' Conference came to be acknowledged as the central Jewish seat of authority in matters relating to Israel.

This new development was preceded by a development within world Zionism that reflects an awareness that traditional Zionist principles need to be reexamined. The World Zionist Organization has created a Commission on Zionist Ideology, with active counterparts in Israel and in the United States. Various historical circumstances have compelled the reassessment. For one, the universal rallying of Jews to the support of Israel has blurred distinctions between Zionism and non-Zionism. Does this mean that virtually all Jews have become Zionists, or rather that the principles of Zionism have become diluted? Ever since the creation of the Jewish state, Zionism has borne a name it cannot adequately define.

Second, the inner condition of the Zionist movement reflects disorientation and a sense of malaise.

Until 1967, and in Israel especially, Zionism came to be regarded with derision as a vestigial appendage of a state which had already realized the goals of political Zionism and in which spiritual Zionism was a quaint reminder of a naive past. Third, as a consequence of the Yom Kippur War, we confront efforts by hostile sectors of the world to impose their own definitions of Judaism and Zionism upon us. The "racist" resolution by the United Nations should demonstrate that even the basic position of political Zionism remains unfulfilled—universal recognition of the Jewish state. Thus even the Basel Platform, the Zionist Declaration of Independence, is challenged. In addition, the Emancipation doctrine that Jews are members of a cult alone, that Jewish nationalism is alien to true Judaism, has been reinvoked. Jews do not have to be reminded that Judaism and Zionism are not synonymous, but they must nevertheless insist that Zionism as the impulse for restoration is an indispensable component of Judaism, and that prior efforts to extirpate that component have failed.

Among the questions which the proposed new formulation of Zionism asks are: What are the differences and similarities between Zionism, Judaism, and the State of Israel? What should be the relations between Israel and the Diaspora? What should the Jewish people expect of the State of Israel? What are the responsibilities of Jews toward Israel? What is meant by the "centrality of Israel"? Out of the debates that are being engendered by these issues it is hoped that a consensus might be achieved which will clearly characterize Zionism.

Perhaps the most controversial question is concerned with the "centrality" of Israel. The present Zionist platform is deliberately vague on this question. However, historical developments have forced a confrontation with more precise alternatives. One is that Israel is the political center of the Jewish people, speaking for it, making certain critical political decisions in its behalf, existing as the dominant polity in Jewish life. There is much to commend this position. Israel emerged as the magnet which drew the survivors of the Holocaust and as the instrument for organizing the vast operation of rescue and rehabilitation. The campaign to save Soviet Jews and the awakening of the Jewish consciousness of many of them emanate primarily from Israel. The rescue of Jewish hostages by Israeli commandos in Uganda in 1976 symbolized for Jews everywhere the active intervention by Israel in behalf of both Israelis and Jews in general. Certainly, many feel, Israel has earned the right to represent Jews everywhere. Others take a divergent position—that Israel alone could not long act in behalf of World Jewry, that it is the

Jewish people acting in concert with Israel that makes Israeli intervention possible. Among the most striking examples of this are the vast fundraising arms of the Jewish people which serve as arteries of supply and development for Israel. On a political level, the World Jewish Congress, which includes representatives from Israel, maintains contact with Jewish communities throughout the world, engages in diplomatic intercession in behalf of Soviet and other Jewries, and mounts intensive political campaigns in Israel's behalf. Leaders of the Congress and others would contend that the concept of centrality cannot—in political terms—be limited to Israel, and that, in fact as well as in theory, World Jewry stands in a relationship of mutuality or bilateralism with Israel. This issue is being debated vigorously, and while we cannot project the results, it is fair to speculate that, as Israel continues to find itself embattled, it will not only accept but invite increased sharing in its problems while simultaneously insisting upon its centrality.

At the same time it is acknowledged by the Diaspora that, whatever political and ideological differences may exist, Israel is existentially the center of Jewish life. It is the dominant reality. It is the most significant focus of loyalty and response in Jewish life. It is the most compelling source of Jewish aspiration, the most rewarding wellspring of Jewish consolation. With all its acknowledged social problems, Israel is a source of pride to Diaspora Jews because it is building a viable nation. For all its imperfect culture, it has done most to inspire Jewish cultural and spiritual creativity in the Diaspora. Nothing has so aroused historical consciousness, and hence the potentiality for covenant consciousness, as Zionism. The transformation of awareness of our past from an attenuated textbook tie with our history to a living reunion is a precondition for the rebirth of the people's spirit. For American Jewry, Israel has reestablished the awareness of the people's proximity to its history and civilization. Jewish worship in America has been given vitality by Israeli culture, which affects our religious life from both religious and so-called secular sources. Summers and years of study in Israel prove more effective than our own formal educational efforts. A comparison of the state of our culture before and after the creation of Israel would be embarrassingly instructive. To assign total spiritual autonomy to American Jewry would only hasten the de-Judaizing process. The Holocaust has undoubtedly played a major part in the awakening, but the Holocaust alone, without the redemptive birth of the State of Israel, might have given us nothing but despair.

Israel has given *Galut* Jews an existential response to the land, a response which perceives Israel and its spirit more authentically than may be reflected by the externals of Israel's culture and our own. It has given us cultural, psychological, and moral strength. It has reinforced our will to live and to labor on behalf of our fellow Jews. It has helped make us Jews again. It has galvanized us in the struggle to survive. In its ordeal, it consumes virtually all our concern and possesses our beings.

The political confrontations in which Israel is embroiled bear upon the future of the Jewish people. The issues which have been discussed here bear upon the future of Judaism.

Walter I. Ackerman _____

JEWISH EDUCATION

THE CENTRAL PROBLEMS

A report on the state of Jewish education in the United States published shortly after the end of World War II noted the outstanding problems confronting the field at that time: a shortage of adequately trained teachers; a disproportionately large number of school units whose smallness precluded effective programming; inadequate financing; a general indifference to Jewish education on the part of parents and community leaders; the absence of clearly defined standards of achievement; the lack of sophisticated curriculum planning; and a high dropout rate following *bar mitzvah* and confirmation.[1]

Almost thirty years later an examination of Jewish education in the United States disclosed that the majority of Jewish children who attend Jewish schools do not remain in school long enough for any significant learning to take place; that Jewish schools have not succeeded in attracting and holding competent teachers; that school budgets are increasingly hard pressed to meet the demands of spiraling costs; that curriculum design is by and large an uncoordinated piecemeal effort; and that the climate in which Jewish education functions remains essentially unsupportive.[2]

Did nothing happen in between?

In the years immediately following World War II Jewish education in the United States was faced with the task of responding to three complementary phenomena which had deeply influenced the character and consciousness of American Jewry—the Holocaust, the establishment of the State of Israel, and the final stage in the process of acculturation to America of what was already the largest and most affluent Jewish community in the world.

The Americanization of the immigrant Jew and of his children had, of course, begun many years before. The immediate effects of that process were surely apparent by the middle of the present century; the long-range implications for Jews and Judaism remain among the imponderables of our time. By the end of World War II the average Jew in the United States probably had more in common with his fellow Americans of similar socio-economic status than with Jews in other parts of the world. Whatever the vestiges of other times and places still discernible in their elders, the majority of the children attending Jewish schools in the 1950s were the offspring of native-born parents[3] and Americans in every sense. With the onset of the decade of the seventies, Jewish schools in the United States were already addressing themselves to third-generation American Jews.

The statistics of demography are but the external sign of changes in the thought and behavior of American Jews which profoundly affected the form, organization, and content of Jewish schools. The last quarter of a century has confirmed the supplementary nature of Jewish education and given added witness to the ineluctable dilemma which arises when there is so much to learn and so little time in which to learn it. Despite the impressive growth of the day school, afternoon schools which meet for four to six hours a week and one-day-a-week schools which offer two to three hours of instruction weekly are the dominant forms of Jewish schooling in the United States and account for some 80 percent of pupil enrollment.[4] The inherent limitations of a system of supplementary education are further underscored by the fact that a large majority of the children who enter a Jewish school do not continue their studies beyond the elementary school level.[5] These data force the conclusion that with the exception of a small, although growing, minority, most parents are unwilling to allot more than a minimal amount of time to the Jewish education of their children—which is to say that the learned and erudite Jew of the tradition is no longer an effective model.

Even though the schools of limited attendance referred to above are of the synagogue—by the middle of the 1960s more than 90 percent of the Jewish schools in the United States were sponsored and maintained by congregations affiliated with one or another of the three major religious groupings[6]—it is erroneous to believe, as some observers do, that the limited amount of time available for Jewish education is somehow the fault of the synagogue and a consequence of its policies. The truth of the matter is that Jewish educators in America have always been hard pressed in their attempts to stake a sizable claim in the territory of pupil time. Schools which required more than ten hours a week of attendance were largely an exception even before the rise of the synagogue to its present position of dominance among Jewish institutions. Even the staunchest supporters of the community school, an institution which was ideologically nonsynagogal and considered by many the paradigm of intensive supplementary education, doubted the power of that school to attract and hold more than a small minority of Jewish children of school age.[7]

It would appear closer to the mark to view the synagogue and its school—of both the afternoon and the one-day-a-week types—not as cause and effect but rather as two parallel strands of the same cloth. If, as most commentators agree, membership in a synagogue is less a matter of religious belief and impulse and more a means of Jewish identification compatible with American mores, it seems reasonable to view the congregational school as another point on the same continuum. Large numbers of Jewish parents clearly want their children to retain and maintain some measure of identification with Jews and Judaism; they look to the Jewish school to provide the stuff of which Jews are made. At the same time they are unwilling to support educational settings which cut into the time available for activities considered more central to the development and future of their children and whose teachings are perceived as conflicting with the norms of the majority culture.

Jewish schools, like schools of all kinds in most times and places, reflect the attitudes of the public they serve. Jewish educators, like their fellows in other educational frameworks, are not always free to do what they would like and are often constrained within the parameters set by circumstances beyond their control. Because the congregational school which would remain true to the imperatives of the religious tradition is faced with the extraordinarily difficult, if not impossible, task of educating children for a life-style which their parents have rejected, it is not altogether surprising that Jewish educators should have drawn a slow line of retreat away from the standards of intellectual achievement which are the hallmark of normative Judaism. Whereas Jewish schools in the past, including those in the United States, have always operated on the assumption that knowledge is the key to proper conduct, one may discern a noticeable trend in current practice which eschews the intellect in favor of an emphasis on the affective.[8] The distressing fact that most Jewish schools in this country have neither succeeded in imparting any kind of real Jewish knowledge to their students nor been able to develop even the minimum of intellectual competencies required of the literate Jew, coupled with developments in general education which are drawn from the rhetoric of the "counter-culture" and the findings of the "human potential" movement in the behavioral sciences, has resulted in a shift of focus in which the idea of *being* supersedes that of *knowing*. A concomitant of this approach is the distinction drawn between the "educated" Jew and the "identified" Jew—"What the child should know about Judaism is not so important as that he should want to be a Jew"[9]—and the conviction that the techniques of informal education are more effective than the methods of the classroom in the formation of identity.

It is not at all difficult to cite other examples of the pervasive influence on Jewish schools of American educational thought and practice. An examination of a recent issue of *The Pedagogic Reporter*, a quarterly which reports on trends and developments in Jewish education around the country, reveals the extent to which innovations in American education—both those which have been proven effective and those which border on fad—have been translated for use in the Jewish school.[10] The fact is that the Jewish school in the United States has modeled itself after the public school in almost every respect—organizational patterns, administrative techniques, means of pupil control and discipline, and methods of instruction.

The Americanization of the Jewish school, a process whose beginnings are rooted in the work of Jewish educators who were addressing themselves to a community of immigrants,[11] is surely understandable and perhaps unavoidable. There is room, however, to question its desirability. What a child learns in school derives as much from his experiences in that setting as from the specific content of instruction. The structure of the school, the methods of instruction it employs, the sanctions it invokes, and the relationships it fosters all denote a particular view of man and the world and are vital to the internalization of the values which the school holds. When Jewish schools adopt the models and manners of American schools they all too often neglect the relationship between method and principle and deny the practical educational implications of the tradition they teach. There is much to consider in the observation that "We have not looked at our own tradition for the kinds of directions we can find for developing our own response to the need for self-direction and the striving to integrate the roles of emotion and intellect to which the open and affective education movements have been the responses in the general field. . . . The best thought of general education is certainly necessary . . . *but it is not sufficient without the Jewish core*"[12] (italics mine).

In its classical formulation Jewish education is nothing less than a religious imperative. Traditional Judaism required no justification for the education of children other than that contained in the divine command: "Take to heart these words with which I charge you this day. Impress them upon your children." (Deut. 6:6,7). The study of the sacred texts is a form of worship and the acquisition of knowledge the key to human perfectibility. The vicissitudes of Jewish life and the secularization of Western culture have contributed noteworthy permutations of the original concept. Zionist thought viewed education as the means of fostering national pride and will. The Jewish socialist movement and its network of Yiddish schools stressed the importance of education in the development of class consciousness and its contribution to the achievement of an egalitarian society. Jewish education in pre-World War II America, heavily influenced by the work of Kurt Lewin and the mental hygiene movement, was regarded as a means of avoiding social marginality and an important line of defense in the struggle against anti-Semitism.

Jewish education in the United States following World War II has not been informed by an overarching view which gives clear purpose and direction to the day-to-day work of the schools. The authority of the divinely ordained principles which guide Orthodox Jewish educators has no counterpart in other quarters. Objectives, therefore, tend to be couched in quasi-behavioral terms which are grounded in a concern for group survival rather than in a vigorous philosophical conception. Most schools would probably subscribe to the following statement of goals: (1) to provide knowledge of the classical Jewish texts and the tradition embodied therein; (2) to foster a lifelong commitment to the study of Torah; (3) to develop some pattern of personal observance; (4) to develop a facility in the Hebrew language and a familiarity with its literature; (5) to nurture an identification with the Jewish people through a knowledge of its past and to encourage a concern for its survival and welfare the world over; (6) to stimulate a recognition of the unique place of Israel in the Jewish imagination, both past and present, and to foster the acceptance of some sort of personal obligation to participate in its development; (7) to encourage participation in American society, based on a conscious awareness of the relationship between Jewish tradition and democracy; and (8) to inculcate faith in God and trust in His beneficence.[13]

TEACHING THE HOLOCAUST

The above description serves as both background and condition for a discussion of the attempts of the Jewish school to deal with the Holocaust. The growing sense of security which characterized a generation of American Jews born to affluence and seemingly limitless opportunity lent support to the view that "America is different" and surely complicated the search for an approach to a theme whose details are witness to the fragility of Jewish existence. It was not until well into the decade of the fifties that Jewish educators began to grapple with the educational problems posed by the Shoah (Holocaust). This delayed reaction is wholly understandable—the enormity of the events themselves and the time required for some comprehension of their meaning; the absence in those years immediately after the war of a body of scholarly research which is the precondition of appropriate instructional material; and not the least, the deterring influence which stemmed from the fact that most of the children in Jewish schools were of elementary school age. The central issue, of course, was and still remains the purpose of teaching the Holocaust.

While some Jewish educators might cautiously question the wisdom of dealing with the subject at all on the elementary school level, most shy away from such a suggestion even as they remain uncertain in their approach. Proposals such as "The Shoah should become part of our tradition . . . a day of remembrance in the calender";[14] the teaching of the Holocaust should ". . . evoke sentiment for the 'world that is no more' " and provide "the link that the American Jewish child needs in order to identify with that which we wish him to identify with in his own heritage";[15] ". . . the facts of Jewish history may perhaps succeed in inspiring strength, . . . security and a sense of inner purpose";[16] and "the teaching of the historical facts of intergroup conflict and of persecution and discrimination [should include] some elementary information on the findings of the social sciences [on] the psychological structure of prejudiced people and the social and political structures under which prejudice and group hostility manifest themselves"[17]—all these seem to suffer from a prosaism which denies the cataclysmic nature of the events they seek to recount. Moreover, adult needs are rarely translated into educational experiences which are meaningful to children.

A far more powerfully generative approach is to be found in the position of those who would teach the Shoah as a subset of an embracive theory of Jewish life and experience. It is difficult to cavil with those who hold that "To teach the Shoah in isolation . . . will not suffice. Instead, the 'Shoah' must be treated within the framework of our essential theological concepts, the nature of Jewish existence, and a critical approach to Western civilization . . . only after the student is exposed to the major issues in Jewish history and thought can he be ready to grasp some of the awesome and mystical implications of the 'Shoah'."[18] Without such a context for guide the tragedy which befell the Jews of Europe is inevitably reduced to an indifferent recitation of meaningless facts and figures. Within such a context the telling acquires purpose—". . . neither to sadden, nor frighten, nor embitter the young, but to strengthen them with mature understanding. . . ."[19]

The gradual inclusion of the Holocaust as a regular feature of the curriculum of the Jewish school has not quieted debate. The fear of that deadening trivialization which hovers over every subject which is turned into a course of study has impelled educators to look for new and unusual ways of insuring that children will come to know and feel the events which changed the physiognomy of their people. Techniques of simulation, role-playing, and group dynamics have been employed to create empathy, shock, and even fear. In some instances there is a blurring of that which is specifically Jewish in the Holocaust in favor of a more generalized approach in which the Shoah, American involvement in Vietnam, and discrimination against blacks and other minority groups are all presented as equally relevant examples of man's endemic propensity for evil. Those who would argue that the child should be exposed to the full brunt of the Jewish catastrophe in Europe are firm in their conviction that the ". . . study of the Holocaust must not be wrapped in the gauze of abstractions. If the child is not to be pampered, he cannot be spared learning . . . that Jews are especially vulnerable to the worst excesses of history. He cannot be spared reading about the agony of the boy who dies slowly on the gallows in Elie Wiesel's *Night*. He cannot be spared the photographs in albums on the Holocaust; the frightened little boy who has his hands up in the air . . . the pious-looking, elderly Jew whose beard is being snipped off by an amused German lout. Though such photographs are hardly things of beauty and joy forever . . . they can be an occasion for underscoring the truth that to be human is to be open to the suffering of others; that to be human is to look on the other as a brother and not as a stranger . . . a hard light needs to be kept on the atrocities and suffering."[20]

The patent intractability of that view is countered by those who maintain that a "hard line" is neither good history nor good education. "To see only man's *'yetzer hara,'* or view history's evil acts alone, is to distort both men and history, both our past and more significantly our future." The idea that a relentless recounting of Jewish suffering will somehow result in a heightened identification with Jews and Judaism is a vain and unfounded hope; the denial of the human capacity for compassion as exemplified by the selfless acts of those many Gentiles who risked their lives to save countless numbers of Jews produces an imbalance which enthrones death over life. "The wholesale condemnation of the non-Jewish world blurs all real distinction, blots out the memory of saintliness, records only the acts of infamy and reduces us all to a paralyzing despair."[21]

Despite the wide variety of materials currently available for the teaching of the Holocaust, it is difficult to arrive at a measure of their effectiveness. The absence of data based on carefully controlled research restricts evaluation to information garnered from impressionistic inference. While the testimony of pupil reaction derived from such sources is skewed in the direction of indifference and ignorance of basic facts, it also discloses instances of profound empathy and identification. Unfortunately, we know too little to be able to account sensibly for either type of reaction. Reliable conclusions which can serve as the legitimate ground for future curriculum development will require a more rigorous and detailed analysis of the teaching and learning of the Holocaust than has been the case to date.[22]

TEACHING THE STATE OF ISRAEL

The gloom of the Holocaust was pierced by the establishment of the State of Israel. The wave of enthusiasm which swept American Jewry in 1948 left an indelible imprint on Jewish education. The birth of the new state infused Jews with a pride and purpose which were reflected in increased school enrollments, a renewed interest in the study of Hebrew, a rash of instructional materials, and in countless other ways. Indeed, the fact of the state was a major vindication of half a century of educational effort in the United States, an effort which had drawn its inspiration as much from the aspirations of modern Jewish nationalism as from the mandates of religious tradition.

Over the years Israel as subject matter has permeated the overwhelming majority of Jewish schools in the United States. A study conducted shortly after the Six-Day War in 1967 noted that modern Israel was treated as a distinct and definable topic in more than 50 percent of the 700 responding schools in the sample. In schools where the study of Israel was not an independent element, various aspects of life in that country were integrated into the curriculum through ongoing work in Bible, history, Hebrew language instruction, current events, customs and holidays. In short, there is hardly an area of the curriculum which is without some degree of attention to, and emphasis on, Israel. In addition to formal instruction the relationship of Jews in America to the Jewish state is expressed through special events such as the celebration of Israel Independence Day, bulletin board materials, exhibits and art objects from Israel in the school building, visits by Israelis to the school, music and dance, pen-pals, and numerous other activities.[23]

The school, however, is only one locus of Israel-centered activity. The deep concern of American Jews for the welfare of Israel serves to reinforce the work of the school and very often draws youngsters of school age into the circle of communitywide activity. In addition, and perhaps most important, are the educational programs in Israel developed by American Jewish educators working together with, and sometimes prodded by, agencies and institutions overseas. Over the years thousands of youngsters have been able to spend varying amounts of time in Israel in an almost endless variety of educational settings. A large percentage of these young people has benefited from scholarship programs established by local agencies. Indeed, in a great many Jewish circles a trip to Israel sometime during the years of high school or college has come to be considered an integral part of the Jewish educational experience. That position is mirrored in a statement issued in the aftermath of the Six-Day War by the American Association for Jewish Education, the umbrella organization for Jewish education in the United States: "It should . . . become part of the responsibility of the organized Jewish community to help American Jewish young people enrolled in our high school programs to have at least one summer of personal experience in Israel."[24]

The idea of a learning experience in Israel rests on the same assumption that guides all programs in international education—without a living contact with a land and its people, one's knowledge of a country must remain incomplete. It should be obvious, however, that the use of Israel as an educational resource and the large investments of effort and money involved in sending students there are geared to something more than an opportunity to "get to know the country," as important as that may be. Jewish schools in America look to programs in Israel as a means of strengthening the Jewish identification of their students; as an experience which affirms and strengthens the bond with the Jewish people; as an opportunity to create some sort of relationship with the Jewish state; and as a source of motivation for continued study and activity at home.[25] Israeli educators and agencies involved with American students see the various programs as the first stage of a process which they hope will culminate in *aliyah*.

A number of studies designed to measure the effects of educational programs in Israel for Americans provide some helpful information. Respondents generally report a stronger sense of Jewishness and a heightened identification with Israel, as well as a quickened desire to become more involved in Jewish affairs upon returning home and a readiness to consider the possibility of *aliyah*. Programs whose purpose, among other things, is the development of specific skills, that is, Hebrew language fluency, usually achieve positive results.[26] These findings are not totally unexpected and can be explained without reference to complicated theory. Unfortunately, we do not know whether the enthusiasm inspired by the immediate experience generates any significant longterm change in attitudes and behavior.

The manner in which Israel is treated, in formal and informal settings both here and abroad, has undergone noticeable change over the years. In the period immediately following the establishment of the state, the dominant tendency was to picture a utopia inhabited by fearless pioneers concerned only with the future of their people. (Ask anyone who attended a Jewish school during the 1950s about the Jewish National Fund and United Jewish Appeal films.) The passage of time, the constant flow of information from Israel, the adaptation of methodological conceptions developed in the public schools and, above all, a deep commitment to Jewish life in America all worked together to force instruction to move closer to the reality of life in the Jewish state. A striving for cogent analysis and balanced criticism replaced the romanticism of an earlier time.

The rhythm of interest in Israel and its manifestation in the work of schools is in no small measure influenced by events there. Periods of crisis evoke heightened activity and are the occasion for new expressions of loyalty and support. The Six-Day War, for instance, led to the publication of a statement of objectives for the teaching of Israel which urged schools "to present to the student . . . the very real options which Israel offers to him as a Jew and as a loyal citizen of the land in which he resides. The needs of Israel and the needs of the Jewish people in America require that we explore the critical question of how the individual Jew can best fulfill himself—whether by the enrichment of his Jewish life in America and/or by *aliyah* to Israel.[27] The full implications of that declaration can be comprehended only in the context of the events of June 1967.

Neither the recognition of *aliyah* as a legitimate goal nor the wide range of activities which focus on Israel has substantially affected the basic orientation of Jewish education in America. Despite the valence of Zionism and its offshoots in the curriculum, Jewish schools are concerned primarily with educating their pupils to live as Jews in the United States. Israel is, therefore, most often perceived and used as a means of strengthening Jewish life in America—a posture, incidentally, which permits something less than the fullest utilization of the possibilities for education which are explicit in the most significant achievement of the Jewish national rebirth.

The issues discussed thus far contain within them all the problems and promise of Jewish schools in America. While couched in the language of education, they reflect the interest and concerns of the larger Jewish polity. They bespeak an extraordinary challenge not only to Jews but to all who believe that to create those conditions which permit the full flowering of minority cultures is to enrich the quality of life in America. Fundamental questions of human existence are refracted through the groping for means of translating the past into terms which contribute to self-definition in the present. The sensitive presentation of alternative life-styles can teach that man is, after all, free to choose the principles which guide his everyday life. Questions of philosophy, curriculum design, personnel, communal support and interest, and funding are all related, in one way or another, to the topics presented above. The themes of Americanization, the Holocaust, and Israel are among those subjects whose substance gives meaning to the organization and administration of Jewish education.

STRUCTURE

The structure of Jewish education remains today essentially what it was thirty years ago—a network of autonomous school units maintained by voluntary effort. The vast majority of the more than 2,000 schools in the United States are sponsored by congregations. The final authority for the conduct of the congregational school and its affairs is vested in the congregational board which generally acts through an appointed school committee. Noncongregational schools have their own school boards which are responsible for every aspect of the institution's activities.

In recent years there has been a noticeable trend in the direction of consolidation and merger of small congregational schools, even when of different religious orientation, and the formation of some sort of communal school under community auspices. At first restricted to the high school level, the movement now touches the elementary school as well. The creation of intercongregational, communitywide schools is not, however, the result of a fundamental change in outlook; it is the pragmatic solution to problems of finance and personnel which strain the resources of all but the largest schools.[28]

Bureaus of Jewish Education, the educational arm of the organized Jewish community, provide services beyond the ability of the individual school-supervisory personnel, in-service training for teachers, central audiovisual and pedagogical libraries, testing programs, placement services, publications, and a wide variety of other educational activities. The national educational commissions of the major synagogal organizations develop broad educational policy as part of their continued attempts to set and maintain standards, conduct regional and national conferences, and sponsor extensive publication programs. It would be incorrect, however, to view these communal and national agencies as the upper levels of a hierarchical structure akin to that which characterizes the bureaucratic organization of public school systems. Only where a Bureau or a national agency contributes directly to the funding of a project or program can it exercise meaninfgul control. Otherwise its effectiveness depends in no small measure upon goodwill and a delicate pattern of personal and institutional relationships.

This loose federation of schools, communal agencies, and national commissions clearly safeguards the autonomy of the individual school. Whatever the advantages of this Jewish counterpart of the American passion for "local control," the price is extraordinarily high. The lack of a definitive structure which sets the boundaries of partisan initiative encourages wasteful duplication, underutilization of limited resources, and school units which are too small to be educationally viable. It also prevents rational, long-range, communitywide planning for Jewish education. Patterns of organization are but means to an end; surely the time has come to reexamine the structure of Jewish education in this country and to determine the form which suits the purpose.

SETTINGS

The growth of the day school is clearly the most significant development in Jewish education in the last thirty years. When viewed in historical perspective, that thrust of expansion must be considered one of the major indices of the maturing of American Jewry. The entire process may perhaps best be understood by examining the shift in attitude of one of America's most prominent and influential Jewish educators. Writing in 1918, the late Alexander Dushkin, then a member of the dedicated coterie of young men attracted to the Bureau of Jewish Education in New York by Samson Benderly, expressed his reservations about the day school by noting that Jews "must develop schools which will preserve Jewish life in this country without interfering with America's cherished plan of a system of common schools for all the children of all the people."[29]

That statement was addressed to a community of recently arrived immigrants whose uncertain place in American life was defined by grinding poverty and the travail of adjustment. Fifty years later Dushkin would declare: ". . . There has grown up a third generation of American Jewry whose parents are American born and who . . . feel themselves at peace as citizens of the American democracy . . . the Jewish community is now larger, better organized, more influential, actually and potentially than it was fifty years ago. . . . In the years ahead it will be increasingly *obligatory* [italics mine] for Jewish educators to promote the establishment of day schools as the intensive core of the American Jewish school system . . . to include 25 percent of our children. . . ."[30] The striking rise in day school enrollments, a movement which now embraces Conservative and Reform schools as well as their Orthodox forerunners, is concrete evidence of a telling change in the image Jews have of themselves and of their relationship to American society.

Parents who are concerned about the Jewish education of their children cannot complain about a lack of opportunity. The basic unit of the school—whatever its type—is surrounded today by a network of ancillary settings which extend the range of educational activity beyond the limits of formal schooling.

Youth groups are well within the reach of every youngster. The largest of the youth organizations are those sponsored by the national synagogue bodies. Zionist youth groups can be found in every large metropolitan center. The latter work independently of the school and rarely have any contact with it. The synagogue youth organizations are part of the same congregational framework as the school and provide innumerable possibilities for the integration of formal and informal programs.

One of the more significant developments of this period is the use of camping as an educational tool. Hebrew-speaking camps such as Masad, Yavneh, the Ramah camps sponsored by the Jewish Theological Seminary, and the network of camps affiliated with the Union of American

Hebrew Congregations, all of whom reach their campers through the schools, have had a profound influence on thousands of youngsters who, long after their days in camp, still carry the stamp of an intensive educational experience. There are many who would claim, and not without justice, that the expansion of educational camping ranks alongside the growth of the day school as a major achievement of Jewish education in the past quarter of a century.

The success of summer camping programs has led many schools to utilize camp settings during the school year. Weekend retreats and camp programs conducted during public school vacations, sponsored by individual schools or organized for a group of schools by a Bureau, are now common and considered a necessary part of the school curriculum. In many places monthly weekends in camp combined with guided work at home in-between have replaced the traditional one-day-a-week Sunday school.[31] We do not yet know whether this form of schooling is more effective than the conventional pattern. There can be no doubt, however, that it is beyond the ability of a formal school setting to duplicate the resonance of a shared experience of study, prayer, and play in a camp environment.

ENROLLMENT

The steady rise in enrollment which began its ascent immediately after World War II reached a peak in the early sixties and has been declining ever since. During the ten-year interval between 1946 and 1956 the number of children attending Jewish schools of all kinds more than doubled—from 231,028 to 488,432; in the 1957-58 school year school registers counted 553,600 pupils; a decade later (1966-67) the figure stood at 554,468; data for 1970-1971 disclose a decline of 17.5 percent over the four-year period to a registration of 457,196.[32] While there is some doubt about the validity of the latest estimates, there is no question that most schools have suffered serious decreases in enrollment; informed observers suggest that the downward trend has not yet reached its bottom. The decline in total school enrollment cited here has been accompanied by a parallel increase in the number of Jewish children of school age who receive no Jewish education at all.[33]

Various reasons have been offered in explanation of the drop in enrollment—a decline in the birth rate among Jews, fewer young couples in established Jewish communities, a dwindling of parental interest, population shifts which have taken families with school-age children away from the areas served by existing Jewish schools. The data presently at hand does not permit the identification of the specific weight of each of these factors nor do we know what other elements might be at play.

The decrease in overall enrollment is in some measure mitigated by an examination of pupil distribution among the various types and levels of schools. Day schools continue to grow and today are responsible for some 75,000 pupils, 21 percent of the total, as compared to 47,000 in 1958, then 8 percent of the total.[34] High schools—that is, programs for youngsters above the age of thirteen which meet at least once a week—similarly report increased enrollments. "The proportion of the Jewish school population enrolled on the post-elementary level rose from an estimated 7.7 percent in 1958-59 to a reported 15.6% in 1966-67 . . . figures received from a significant number of communities indicated a continuation of this trend through 1971-72."[35] A survey conducted in May 1973 elicited responses from one-third of the known supplementary high schools and one-fifth of the day schools of record; an extrapolation of the findings of that study suggests that some 65,000 to 75,000 pupils are currently enrolled in secondary school programs.[36] If, as some recent studies suggest,[37] supplementary schooling can be effective when students attend long enough, then the increase in enrollment in the post *bar mitzvah* years is an encouraging sign.

Notice must also be taken of the explosive expansion of Jewish Studies programs in American colleges and universities. Over 300 different institutions of higher learning in this country now offer courses in Jewish Studies; forty universities claim to offer a major and twenty-seven to sponsor graduate programs.[38] This is surely one of the most important developments in Jewish life during the last decade and a half. While little is known about the nature of the students enrolled in these programs—previous attendance in a Jewish school, religious orientation, career plans, and the like—one conclusion is permissible: more students of college age are now involved in Jewish Studies than ever before.

PERSONNEL

The major developments in the area of personnel form a kaleidoscopic pattern of contradictory trends. Upper level administrative posts and positions which demand specialized educational skills go unfilled for lack of qualified personnel. Experienced educational directors in contracting congregational schools face an uncertain future, while properly trained principals for day schools are in short supply. Graduate programs in Jewish education are attracting an increasing number of young men and women at the same time that trained teachers find it all but impossible to find full-time employment except in an exhausting combination of mornings in a day school and afternoons in a congregational school. In this mix of problem and promise the situation of the teacher is clearly the most intractable.

The American Jewish community has never been able to produce a sufficient number of native-born teachers for its schools.[39] The reasons are hardly obscure; the consequences are all too evident. In our time the European-born teacher of an earlier period has been replaced by Israelis. The Israeli teacher is a critical factor in the teaching force in weekday elementary and secondary schools. While there is some doubt about their exact number, there is general agreement that without them "the staffing of weekday schools in America would be impossible . . . their presence makes possible the continuation of the American Jewish educational enterprise as we know it."[40] The penalties of an excess of imports are as severe in education as in economics. A chasm dug by the differences in native cultures separates an Israeli from his American audience. His or her conspicuous presence in the Jewish school pushes that institution into a corner which is isolated from the mainstream of American Jewish life.

The prospects of attracting young, talented, and enthusiastic Americans to careers as teachers in Jewish schools are not encouraging. Afternoon schools, the major source of teaching positions, were barely able to guarantee their teachers a living wage, even during the period of their fullest flowering. The irreversible trend in the direction of a reduction in the hours of instruction in the mid-week congregational school has forced the Jewish teacher into the debilitating confines of a part-time occupation. There is a painful truth in the observation that "If schools now operating only ten to twelve hours a week continue to engage teachers who will teach only ten to twelve hours a week, then no matter how fairly they may pay them per hour, Jewish education has no future."[41]

There has been no dearth of sensible suggestions and practical proposals for securing the economic base of the teacher and providing him with the status and challenge which are the irreducible elements of a profession—consolidating schools in order to increase teaching loads, training teachers who would be able to work in both formal and informal settings, creating specialized roles as additions to classroom duties, and so on. The readiness of the central agencies of the organized Jewish community to act quickly and tellingly to insure the calling of the Jewish teacher is the ultimate test of their commitment to Jewish education.

CURRICULUM

The generally constraining influence of problems of finance, personnel, and structure has happily not prevented a wide variety of efforts in curriculum development. The work of the National Curriculum Institute of the American Association for Jewish Education, the ambitious program of the Melton Research Center of the Jewish Theological Seminary, proposals for curricular reform initiated by the Commission on Jewish Education of the Union of American Hebrew Congregations and its counterpart agency in the United Synagogue of America, the activities sponsored by Torah U'Mesorah, the materials prepared by private commercial firms and the endeavors of individual schools—all attest to an unprecedented level of activity.

An analysis of the various programs discloses the curricular issues which currently concern practicing Jewish educators. The materials prepared by the National Curriculum Research Institute which deal with the American Jewish community, the Holocaust, and Israel speak to those who would shift the focus of the Jewish school from the past to the present.[42] The curriculum development program of the Reform movement reflects the continuing tension that confronts those who seek to find a proper balance between what the child ought to know and what he wants to know. The concern for the student and his interest here finds expression in "a national survey . . . conducted to determine the interests, concerns and problems of students on all age levels. The most prevalent concerns and issues were then tabulated and organized into several broad categories."[43]

Conservative educators, spurred by the initiative of their own national agency, are presently engaged in heated debate over a curriculum whose avowed reach is more modest than previous models which, in attempting to teach something about everything, produced pupils who knew precious little about anything. The proposal suggests a two-year core curriculum: "ability to read Hebrew to follow a sabbath service . . . the facts of the Holocaust . . . the rise of the state of Israel, Bible stories, holidays, observances, etc.," followed by a three-year course of study centered on one of five options—"Modern Hebrew, History and Community, Judaism, Torah Sources, Mitzvot and Tefillah."[44] The goals of the curriculum, stated in the language of behavioral objectives, are to bring approximately three-fourths of the participating pupils, no matter what option they have chosen, to: the ability to converse with reasonable fluency in Hebrew; familiarity with objective historical material from major periods and the ability to relate such objective data to concepts; familiarity with major biblical texts in either Hebrew or English, selections from rabbinical and later post-biblical literature, selections from the Haskalah period and from modern Hebrew literature, and the ability to lead weekday religious services, Kabbalat Shabbat, follow other services passively, read any Haftarah, read Torah portions, and perform home rituals.[45]

Torah U'Mesorah, the National Society for Hebrew Day Schools, building on the knowledge and skills which distinguish the day school

pupil from his peers in other settings, has embarked on a "Moral Sensitivity Training Program." A variety of instructional materials, including specially prepared texts, model lessons in print and on tape, and
teacher's guides, are available to schools interested in "expanding the
moral sensitivity and understanding of their pupils."[46] The teaching and
learning of Hebrew, a major subject in schools of all orientations, has
received the attention of several commercial firms and a number of
programs based on a sophisticated grasp of the principles of second-
language learning are widely used.[47] The most ambitious curriculum
development program currently underway is that of the Melton Research
Center of the Jewish Theological Seminary. Although the materials produced thus far are largely limited to Bible instruction,[48] the total conception of the Melton Center seeks to create a new type of Jewish school. The
hallmark of its approach is an attempt to nurture reverence for the
tradition together with the training of the young student in those
methods of enquiry and reconstruction of meaning which characterize
the work of scholars in their various disciplines. The machinery of the
center, consisting as it does of scholars, curriculum writers, on-going
colloquia, field-testing, and in-service teacher training, is in itself an
important innovation in Jewish education.

Space does not permit a detailed analysis of the logic and consistency
of the programs cited. The lack of relevant data also prevents any estimate of their effectiveness. The very fact that they exist, however, does
admit some pertinent generalizations. They are, first of all, the Jewish
educational establishment's response to the lashing criticism, from both
within and without educational circles, of Jewish schools for their failure
to achieve any appreciable results, either cognitive or affective. As such
they signify a marshaling of resources uncommon for Jewish education.
They reflect a growing sophistication among Jewish educators and a wide
acquaintance with trends in general education. They are, in point of fact,
largely translations of current practice in general education and only
rarely the product of original theoretical constructs whose base is in the
experience of the Jewish people and the system of values which is unique
to Judaism. Their reach underscores the need for well-trained, full-time,
professional teachers and specialists. Curriculum development is a complicated process whose success depends on the ability of the expert to
channel his ideas from the language of speculation to tested materials
and methods of classroom instruction which inspire the willing cooperation of the teacher. Despite these strictures and no matter what their
ultimate effectiveness, the various programs have already achieved
something of incalculable importance. They have created a sense of
movement, a feeling that something, after all, can be done, and a willingness to experiment that are essential to the viability of any enterprise.

FUNDING

The manifest desire of the schools and their supporters to improve the quality of Jewish education is dependent for its realization upon the financial resources at their disposal. Intensive Jewish education is expensive Jewish education; the increase in the number of day schools requires drastically higher expenditures. The recruitment and retention of teachers, curriculum development, ancillary and support services— even for less intensive afternoon and one-day-a-week schools—all require large investments of money. Although the current expenditure for Jewish education in the United States is well over $100 million a year, a sum which is all the more impressive for its voluntary nature, it is clear that the traditional patterns of funding are inadequate to the demands of expanding programs in a period of spiraling inflation.

Variegated patterns of record-keeping, coupled with an apparent reluctance to divulge relevant information, makes it difficult to ascertain the exact amounts contributed by synagogues to the maintenance of their schools. It is reasonable to assume, however, that in a period of decreasing membership and increasing operational costs there will be no significant rise in direct subventions to schools from congregational budgets. The data on tuition fees for three-day-a-week afternoon schools indicates that it bears no relationship to the actual cost of educating a child. Over a twenty-year period, from 1951-1952 to 1969-1970, tuition fees were raised from $50 a year for members and $65 a year for non-members to $85 and $150, respectively.[49] Tuition schedules are obviously conditioned by the fear that an increase in fees will result in a decrease in enrollment.

Federation and Welfare Fund allocations represent the other major source of funding for Jewish education. Day schools are the major beneficiaries of direct allocations to schools. Federation allocations nationwide in 1970-71 came to 13.3 percent of day school budgets, a decrease of .6 percent from the previous year. The growth in the amount of federation allocations has not at all kept pace with the inevitable increase in the size of day school budgets.[50] The recourse of the day schools to higher tuition fees contains the very real danger of moving intensive Jewish education beyond the financial reach of a large number of Jewish families.

Overall Federation allocations to Jewish education doubled in dollar amount during the period from 1966 to 1970 to an aggregate sum of $9,707,881—an increase of 2 percent to a total of 13 percent of the monies allocated by federations for local needs.[51] That figure is less impressive than might appear at first when it is compared with data from an earlier period. In 1947—a year in which there were 234,358 pupils enrolled in afternoon and one-day-a-week schools and 14,835 in day schools[52]—

federation allocations for Jewish education represented 8.7 percent of all funds distributed locally.[53] In other words, over a twenty-five-year period which was witness to a peak increase of 130 percent in supplementary school enrollments, an approximate increase of 500 percent in day school registration, and an unparalleled inflationary cycle, federation allocations to Jewish education increased by less than 50 percent. The glaring discrepancy between fervent declarations of commitment to Jewish education and actual practice hardly requires comment.

The picture I have sketched demands a reassessment of the relative responsibility of each of the three sources of support for Jewish education. Congregations must review their fiscal procedures to determine the obligations that are sensibly within their purview. If tuition is primarily the responsibility of the parent, then steps must be taken to bring tuition into some realistic relationship to the cost of educating a child. The readiness of Jewish parents to shoulder the burden of high tax rates in support of quality public education must find its counterpart in Jewish education, even at the cost of a decrease in enrollment. The stance of Federations must similarly be subjected to searching review. There can be no justification of the continuation of a pattern of allocation which is rooted in long-ago, outdated historical circumstance.

What, then, indeed, has happened in Jewish education over the last three decades? An accurate representation suggests a picture composed of both light and shadow. The increase and subsequent decline in enrollment is offset by the evident fact that more Jewish children than ever before, both absolutely and relatively, are receiving an intensive Jewish education in day schools. While elementary school dropout rates remain at a disturbingly high rate, secondary school registration has risen. Moreover, more college-age students are involved in Jewish studies on an academic level than in any previous period in the history of the American Jewish community. Data indicates that the financing of Jewish education lags woefully behind the needs. The same data, however, reveals some increase in Federation support; statistical averages obscure substantial increases in allocations in communities across the country. Equally important is the knowledge that Jewish education now receives the sort of attention in Federation circles for which there was no match thirty years ago. We are a long way from solving the critical problem of teacher supply and retention, but we can point to the growth of a corps of professional educational administrators whose academic qualifications are the equal of those required for comparable positions in public education. Achievement levels in the supplementary schools remain at a low level. At the same time current curriculum projects point to a stubborn and persistent search for a means of raising standards and intensifying the effects of Jewish education.

The record certainly is no call for celebration, but neither is it a signal for frustrating retreat. Our sages understood the problem all too well—"The day is short, the task is great. . . . It is not up to you to complete the work, yet you are not free to desist from it."

NOTES

1. Uriah Z. Engelman, "Jewish Education," *American Jewish Year Book* (New York and Philadelphia: The American Jewish Committee and the Jewish Publication Society of America) 49 (1947-1948), p. 167.

2. Harold S. Himmelfarb, "Jewish Education for Naught: Educating the Culturally Deprived Jewish Child," *Analysis* (Washington, D.C.: Institute for Jewish Policy Planning and Research of the Synagogue Council of America), no. 51, September 1975.

3. Alexander Dushkin and Uriah Z. Engelman, *Jewish Education in the United States* (New York: American Association for Jewish Education, 1959), p. 87.

4. *National Census of Jewish Education* (New York: American Association for Jewish Education), Information Bulletin no. 28, December 1967. Since the time of this census, day school enrollment has risen from 13.4% to about 21% of the total number of children attending Jewish schools.

5. *Ibid.* See also Hillel Hochberg, "Trends and Developments in Jewish Education," *American Jewish Year Book* 73 (1972); Hillel Hochberg and Gerhard Lang, "The Jewish High School in 1972-73: Status and Trends," *American Jewish Year Book* 75 (1974-1975).

6. *Ibid.*

7. I. B. Berkson, *Theories of Americanization* (New York: Teachers College Press, Columbia University, 1920), pp. 104-105, 116-117.

8. I have discussed this development in "The Present Moment in Jewish Education," *Midstream*, vol. XVIII, no. 10, December 1972, pp. 3-24.

9. As quoted in Eugene B. Borowitz, "Problems Facing Jewish Educational Philosophy in the Sixties," *American Jewish Year Book* 62 (1961), p. 149.

10. "1974-1975 Program Roundup," *The Pedagogic Reporter*, vol. 27, no. 2, Winter 1976, pp. 3-33.

11. For an elaboration of this idea, see my "The Americanization of Jewish Education," *Judaism*, vol. 24, no. 4, Fall 1975, pp. 416-435.

12. Joseph Lukinsky, "The Education Program of the Jewish Theological Seminary—Distinctive Assumptions," in "New Models in Preparing Personnel for Jewish Education," *Jewish Education*, vol. 43, no. 3, Fall 1974, p. 11.

13. The statement of goals given here is adapted from Alexander M. Dushkin, "Common Elements in American Jewish Teaching," *Jewish Education*, November 1945, pp. 5-12. For statements of the educational aims and objectives of each of the major religious groupings, see Alexander M. Dushkin and Uriah Z. Engelman, *Jewish Education in the United States*, pp. 35-38. While these statements of curricular aims and objectives date from the 1950s, I doubt that a reformulation today would result in any substantial change.

14. Judah Pilch, in "The Shoah and the Jewish School," *Jewish Education*, vol. 34, no. 3, Spring 1964, p. 164.

15. Sara Feinstein, *ibid.*, p. 168.

16. Isaac Frank, in "Teaching the Tragic Events of Jewish History," *Jewish Education*, vol. 34, no. 3, Spring 1964, p. 178.

17. *Ibid.*, p. 179.

18. Zalman F. Ury, in "The Shoah and the Jewish School," *Jewish Education*, vol. 34, no. 3, Spring 1964, p. 169.

19. Harold Schulweis, in "Teaching the Tragic Events of Jewish History," *Jewish Education*, vol. 34, no. 3, Spring 1964, p. 184.

20. The material here draws on Schulweis's article mentioned above, his more recent statement "The Holocaust Dybbuk," *Moment*, February 1976, and the subsequent correspondence in *Moment*, May-June 1976.

21. *Ibid.*

22. A promising start in this direction may be found in Diane K. Roskies, *Teaching the Holocaust to Children: A Review and Bibliography* (New York: Ktav Publishing House, 1975).

23. Alvin Schiff, "Israel in American Jewish Schools," *Jewish Education*, vol. 30, no. 4, October 1968, pp. 6-24.

24. *Israel and the Jewish School in America: A Statement of Objectives*, The Commission on Teaching About Israel in America, American Association for Jewish Education, 18 May 1969.

25. Dov Shefatyah, *Ha'bikur B'Yisroel K'hailek Min Ha'hinuch Hayehudi B'Arzot Ha'Brit* (Jerusalem: Jewish Agency, Department for Education and Culture in the Diaspora, 1974), pp. 27-34.

26. Dov Shefatyah, *Hashpa'at Ha'bikur B'Yisroel al Hesaigim Limudiim V'al Shinuim B'Amadot* (Jerusalem: Jewish Agency, Department for Education and Culture in the Diaspora, 1974); Dan Ronen, "The Effects of a Summer in Israel on American-Jewish Youth," *In the Dispersion*, 5/6, Spring 1966, pp. 210-280.

27. *Israel and the Jewish School in America: A Statement of Objectives*.

28. George Pollak and Benjamin Efron, "Current Trends in Jewish Communal Education," *The Pedagogic Reporter*, vol. XXVII, no. 3, Spring 1976, pp. 2-9.

29. Alexander Dushkin, *Jewish Education in New York City* (New York: Bureau of Jewish Education, 1918), pp. 21, 137-138.

30. Alexander Dushkin, "Fifty Years of American Jewish Education: Retrospect and Prospects," *Jewish Education*, vol. 37, nos. 1-2, Winter 1967, pp. 44, 48.

31. B. Lipnick, "An Organic Peer Community: An Experiment in Jewish Teen-Age Education," *Jewish Education*, vol. 43, no. 4, Summer 1975, pp. 38-41.

32. Hillel Hochberg, "Trends and Developments in Jewish Education," *American Jewish Year Book* 73 (1972), p. 199.

33. *Ibid.*, p. 198.

34. *Ibid.*, pp. 201-203.

35. Hillel Hochberg and Gerhard Lang, "The Jewish High School in 1972-73; Status and Trends," *American Jewish Year Book* 73 (1972), p. 199.

36. *Ibid.*, p. 237.

37. Harold S. Himmelfarb, *The Impact of Religious Schooling: The Effect of Jewish Education Upon Adult Religious Involvement* (unpublished Ph.D. disserta-

tion, the University of Chicago, 1974).

38. Will Maslow, *The Structure and Functioning of the American Jewish Community* (New York: American Jewish Congress, 1974).

39. For a full treatment of the Jewish teacher, see Oscar Janowsky, ed., *The Education of American Jewish Teachers* (Boston: Beacon Press, 1967).

40. Hyman Chanover, "Israelis Teaching in American Jewish Schools: Findings of an Exploratory Survey," in Janowsky, *Education of American Jewish Teachers*, p. 233.

41. Leo Honor, "The Teacher's Calling," *Jewish Education*, vol. 28, no. 3, Spring 1958, pp. 54-55.

42. Reference is to the following publications: *Meet Your Jewish Community; Dilemma; Multi-Media Resources on the Jewish Community; Viewpoints* (Instructional Units on Controversial Issues Affecting the State of Israel); *The Jewish Catastrophe in Europe; The Holocaust: A Case Study of Genocide*. These and other materials are available from the American Association for Jewish Education.

43. Jack Spiro, "Toward a Conceptual Framework for Reform Jewish Education," *Compass*, Commission on Jewish Education, CCAR-UAHC, no. 13, January-February 1971.

44. *Basic Premises Upon Which the New Curricular Program is Based* (mimeographed), September 1975. For an example of reactions to this proposal, see discussions at the annual fall Principals' Conference (1975) of the New England Region of the Educators' Assembly.

45. *Ibid.*

46. See materials listed in *Publications Catalogue*, Torah U'Mesorah, 1975-76.

47. The reference is to *Habet U'Shma*, produced by the Chilton Publishing Co., and *B'Yad Halashon* of the Educational Materials Corp.

48. The materials for the teaching of Genesis are illustrative of the Melton approach.

49. Hillel Hochberg, "Trends and Developments in Jewish Education," *American Jewish Year Book* 73 (1972), p. 221.

50. *Ibid.*, p. 209.

51. *Ibid.*, p. 225.

52. Uriah Z. Engelman, "Education," *American Jewish Year Book* 49 (1947-48), p. 161.

53. Uriah Z. Engelman, "Jewish Education," *American Jewish Year Book* 51 (1950), p. 164.

Daniel Jeremy Silver _____

HIGHER JEWISH LEARNING

The American university inherited from its European parent a classic curriculum which defined civilization as that culture which was European and Christian. Other cultures were studied not for their intrinsic merit but for tangential reasons—to provide missionaries and diplomats with language or social skills needed for work in the field, or to provide scholars with linguistic and historical background for their studies. Old Testament studies and Hebrew were pursued for their value in New Testament interpretation and for the light they cast on early church history. Philo and Maimonides were useful to flesh out studies in medieval religious philosophy, but there was no interest in the Talmud or *The Guide to the Perplexed* as literary and religious classics in their own right. The history of modern Europe was taught without reference to the presence of Jewish communities of size and cultural consequence.

Over the centuries the institutions concerned with Christian letters developed naturally from cathedral school to a university based on a classic curriculum in Western civilization—from Canterbury to Cambridge. Jewish learning entered the modern world in the nineteenth century as Jews entered the larger world with their political emancipation. By this time the academy was fully formed around a series of parochial assumptions which effectively blinded its scholars to the value of the Jewish literary deposit and to the pursuit of Jewish learning for its own sake.

As a Christian place, the European university not only operated with a narrow definition of civilization but with a social posture dependent on conventional anti-Semitism. Quotas on enrollment and faculty appointment were the rule, if matriculation was even allowed. The American university system is the child of Europe's, and in the beginning assumed the form of its parent. Harvard and Yale had Jewish quotas. Jews were not made welcome, but America's Jews were unwilling to give the university a wide berth. A university degree was perceived as the ticket of admission to the larger community and its beckoning opportunity.

Respect for the scholar, an almost pathetic eagerness to be American, and a hard-headed judgment that control of some professional skill was the way to mine the American lode led great numbers of young Jews to enroll. They were so eager for what they conceived as the main chance that they asked no questions about the *tref* in the curriculum, and hopeful parents silenced their fears about assimilation and apostasy. In this respect Jews differed significantly from Roman Catholic immigrants who, generally, were willing to support the plans of their bishops to establish colleges where their children could be educated in a spiritually supportive atmosphere, even though remaining among their own might deny them some useful contacts.

In their eagerness to take a degree bright young Jews abandoned the myths and pieties which for centuries had supported the rabbinic curriculum and accepted a set of new pieties: the university as a society of reasonable men pursuing their studies without bias of any kind. The univiersities spoke boldly of scholarly independence and, in fact, in the late nineteenth century the elite universities began to cut their official ties with denominational sponsors. The university saw itself as a sanctuary of reason, and there were many who accepted the "scientific" assumption that religious interests were outdated and unworthy. Caught up in the great hopes of the age, few Jews paused to consider the reality of the Protestant chapel whose spire rose above the campus and whose services were attended by the president and the board of trustees, or to evaluate the limitations of the curriculum.

For many bright young Jews the late nineteenth century was not only an age of political and social emancipation, but an age of intoxicating cultural emancipation. The university represented the community of reason, what the world would soon be. College was the new Jerusalem from which a new Torah of universalist humanist teachings would shine forth and enlighten the world. Once his degree was in hand, the Jewish undergraduate went back to the rough-and-tumble world where the executive suite and the better suburbs were closed to him; but those who remained in this new Jerusalem became devoted citizens, academicians of Jewish descent who consciously and deliberately put as much distance as they could between themselves and the "unenlightened" and "parochial" community of their fathers.

Most of the Jews who poured into America's universities in the early decades of the century sought to become technically or professionally competent and did not ask too many questions about the liberal arts curriculum. It was enough that the courses they took prepared them to dig in the American mother lode. Jews came, but Jewish learning did not follow. Jewish learning was outside looking in and had no alternative but to depend on those professional institutions which were organized by the Jewish community to train rabbis who could provide the synagogues with an inspiring pulpit, an effective religious school, and liturgical guidance, as well as advice in the reformulation of Jewish practice in line with the ever-changing realities of the American situation.

The first seminaries were established in the last quarter of the nineteenth century: the Hebrew Union College (Cincinnati-1875); the Jewish Theological Seminary of America (New York City-1886); the

Jewish Institute of Religion (New York City-1922, merged with the Hebrew Union College-1954). Those who founded these institutions took as their models the rabbinical colleges which had been established in the previous generation by the recently emancipated communities of Central Europe, particularly the Jewish Theological Seminary (Breslau-1854) and the Hochschule für Die Wissenschaft des Judenthums (Berlin-1872), schools whose curriculum and approach were radically different from that of the traditional *yeshivah*. Instruction was in German, not Yiddish. The library included general historical and philosophic works and not simply *sefarim*. Talmud was displaced as *the* curriculum in favor of a number of departments permitting specialization in Bible, Semitic languages, Hellenistic studies, rabbinics, Jewish history, theology, and comparative religions.

These schools approached Jewish learning in what was for Jewish learning a new way, the so-called Science of Judaism *(die Wissenschaft des Judenthums)*. At base *Wissenschaft* was no more than Jewish scholarship carried out on the assumption that the critical approach developed for philological and literary investigations in the national universities was equally applicable to the Jewish literary deposit. Where the traditional student of Torah had sought God in his texts, the *Wissenschaft* scholar sought the original meaning of the text, its literary history, its place in the history of ideas, and so forth. The Science of Judaism turned the Jewish scholar into a co-worker with Herr Professor, even though they did not work as faculty colleagues. It also brought into question the key traditional piety that Judaism had been a consistent, single, and unitary instruction and duty since Moses had received the written and oral Torah on Mt. Sinai.

The new breed of Jewish scholar, early twentieth-century model, was one of a small band of men (women had not found their place in the world of Jewish letters) who controlled the traditional sources and knew something about the analytic methods favored in his particular specialty. Generally, he had earned a traditional *semichah* (ordination) and subsequently had qualified himself in linguistics, Semitics, philosophy, or folklore at a major university. The rabbi had been the learned man. A rabbi now was simply a rabbi; the rabbi with a Ph.D. was on his way to being a recognized scholar. The Ph.D. certified that his scholarship was modern and, in approach, distinct from the Talmudic accomplishment and dialectic.

The rabbinical colleges of America built their faculties around such men.[1] Their erudition and interests led the seminaries to develop extensive library collections and to publish scholarly monographs, and their intellectual presence inspired an occasional student to start on the road to scholarship. But there were problems. The *Wissenschaft* scholar was committed to a critical approach which inevitably questioned denominational pieties. In the event, the seminaries proved remarkably open-minded and tolerant, but it was clear that cool academic research was not their major focus. They had been organized to produce synagogue professionals, not research scholars. The rabbi received a certificate which attested to his capacity to serve. Those who wanted to teach at the seminary generally had to leave and take advanced academic courses elsewhere. For the first time since rabbinic Judaism had become normative, the title "rabbi" was no longer synonymous with the highest degree of scholarly attainment.

During these years the *Wissenschaft* spirit was instrumental in the founding of one unique institution, the Dropsie College for Hebrew and Cognate Studies (Philadelphia-1909). This graduate academy was the result of the happy existence of a large and unspecific bequest for Jewish learning and the presence in America of a number of first-rate Science of Judaism scholars (Cyrus Adler, Max Margolis, Henry Malter) who were unhappy with seminary employment and eager for a freer, less vocationally oriented, setting. Dropsie's student body was drawn largely from *maskilim*, immigrant and first-generation Hebraists who loved Jewish literature, and from rabbis who still held sacred the transitional commitment of the rabbinate to scholarship and wanted to pursue advanced textual studies. In 1910 Dropsie undertook to publish what had been a distinguished English scholarly journal, *The Jewish Quarterly Review*. The JQR, whose long-time editors, Abraham Neuman and Solomon Zeitlin, were scholars of eminence, regularly published articles in Bible, Hebrew and cognate studies, apocryphal literature, rabbinics, linguistics, Jewish philosophy, and Jewish history. Until this generation what the JQR published defined, in effect, the parameters of Jewish studies.

With their extensive libraries and sizable faculty, the Hebrew Union College-Jewish Institute of Religion and the Jewish Theological Seminary came to accept themselves as *the* centers of Jewish scholarship. In time both joined Dropsie in developing Ph.D. programs, but research and original scholarship were never the focus of their energies. Their funding constituencies were more concerned with their effectiveness as service institutions than as research centers. Soon, beside students preparing for the rabbinate, their halls were filled with school administrators and religious school teachers mastering classroom skills; cantors and music directors studying liturgy and choir management; laymen pursuing adult education interests and, latterly, social workers preparing themselves for Jewish institutional settings.[2] Much was accomplished, but the seminaries faced not only a basic question of purpose but a number of practical problems. By tradition, women were excluded from seminary classrooms. Seminary faculties were sometimes forced to toe a sectarian line. Purely academic standards were sometimes lowered, even sacrificed, so that a rapidly expanding community would be provided with the needed number of congregational rabbis. A seminary graduate was not yet a full-fledged scholar, often not even a half-fledged one—a fact underscored throughout the early decades of the century by the continuing enrollment of future seminary faculty in European graduate schools (Julian Morgenstern, Nelson Glueck, Jacob R. Marcus).

The wave of East European immigrants to America (1880-1924) inevitably catalyzed the replication here of a number of *yeshivot* of the East European type. Yiddish was the language of instruction; the curriculum was limited to Talmud and *musar*. Some *yeshivot* remained in this mold, but within a decade of its establishment Yeshivat Rabbenu Yitzchak Elchanan (New York City-1897) granted its students permission to take courses at local universities and to have some of their classes in English. Under the leadership of a Dropsie graduate, Bernard Revel, this *yeshivah* transformed itself into the Rabbi Isaac Elchanan Theological Seminary "to prepare students of the Hebrew faith for the Hebrew ministry." The seminary went on to become a many-sided university, Yeshiva University (New York-1928), which offered a full range of undergraduate, graduate, and professional studies within a traditional environment.[3]

In Europe, *yeshivah* education involved the training of male adolescents. Training was stiff, focused and unremitting, so that by the age of seventeen or eighteen the best minds were qualified as masters of the tradition. American law required that all preparatory students be trained in science, civics, and English, and there was less time for Talmud and much to master besides. By and large, American *yeshivot*[4] have remained places for the education of high school and college-age youth, and their graduates are looked on more as narrow-gauged Talmudists than masters of Jewish Studies, a field which is now both much broader and committed to other analytic approaches. *Yeshivah* graduates who wish to qualify as scholars go on to graduate studies at some university.

In the nineteenth century the American university system, reflecting America's democratic ethos, broke loose from the European model of a single track elitist curriculum and began to spawn a variety of institutions, all called colleges, each with its special curricula and clientele. Jewish Studies followed this lead. The Jewish Studies equivalent of the community college is a training center for religious school teachers become College of Jewish Studies. Gratz College (Philadelphia-1897) was the first such community college. Similar schools opened shortly in other major cities.[5] Though such schools bear the title "college," have sought accreditation, and take inordinate delight in academic gowns and degrees, they are not research institutions and their teaching is at an undergraduate level.

There were fine scholars in America before World War II. Most were located in the seminaries, some were on the faculty of Dropsie College, some were in the pulpit (Solomon Freehof, Abba Hillel Silver, Leo Jung, Milton Steinberg, Robert Gordis). A rarer bird was the scholar who found his way on to a university faculty (Harry A. Wolfson, Salo Baron). In 1920 an American Academy for Jewish Research was established with an invited membership. The AAJR published an annual, *Proceedings*, which was broadly distributed, but its membership was limited to a baker's dozen. In 1935 its thirteen fellows included only five who had completed their advanced studies in the United States (Israel Davidson, Louis Finkelstein, Isaac Husik, Ralph Marcus, Harry A. Wolfson), an indication that America still did not provide the necessary research and graduate training institutions to be self-supporting. The field was small. The JQR's subscription list numbered less than one thousand. Dropsie and the seminary faculties continued to depend upon European immigrants (Joseph Dov Soloveitchik, Leo Baeck, Abraham J. Heschel).

The first Jews to teach Bible or Hebrew in American colleges had done so in what was, in effect, a Protestant seminary setting, and some were apostates (for example, Judah Monis). Toward the end of the nineteenth century a few departments of religion and Oriental languages evidenced interest in Jewish faculty, preferably those trained in the renowned German academic tradition and particularly men who could teach biblical criticism without being cowed by pressures from denominational councils and who could broaden New Testament studies with rabbinic parallels. Nordheimer, Gottheil, and Jastrow were acceptable colleagues because they had been trained in *Wissenschaft* norms—trained, that is, to teach Judaism with critical dispassion. As members of a university faculty, they might have a subject that was particular but their perspective would be universal.

During the first half of this century Jewish Studies, that is, conscious and critical interest in Jews, Jewish institutions, and the Jewish tradition as a subject area, developed slowly as established faculties in the "better" universities became dissatisfied with the traditional boundaries of the received curriculum. Hellenistic Judaism and the Pharisees clearly had had an impact on the emerging Christian tradition; the Harvard of George Foot Moore needed a Harry Wolfson. Jews had played a significant economic role in medieval Europe, and the Columbia History Department needed a Salo Baron. It did not hurt that Nathan Littauer and Nathan Miller were able to provide the wherewithal; but the impetus for the study of Jews and Judaism came from faculties, not from the development office—a fact of no small consequence, as the funding of Jewish Studies has required, and continues to require, a large and continuing outlay of university cash for scholars and books.

America's emergence as a world power after World War II catalyzed an intellectual revolution on the American campus. The insularity of the earlier curriculum was no longer seriously defended. A wide range of area studies developed to complement the Western Civilization praxis. Religion departments began to include courses in Catholic, Buddhist, and Jewish thought, as well as the standard New Testament and Church history offerings. The monopoly of senior positions in Bible, long maintained by Protestant scholars, was broken. Semitic language departments began to list conversational Hebrew as well as Biblical grammar. The social sciences offered courses in the history of the Jews as well as the history of Southeast Asia. Near Eastern studies began to include seminars on Zionism and on the social and political institutions of Israel.

"Jewish Studies" had come into being; but it was rarely, and never easily, defined. To some it meant the classic disciplines of *Tanakh*, Hellenistic literature and rabbinics, Hebrew, and Jewish theology. Others were interested in Yiddish literature, *kahal* structures, Ladino, the demography of the modern community, and the like. The term was as broad as the historic Jewish experience, and definition was pleasantly complicated as a number of scholars in various disciplines (by this time Jews provided a significant proportion of the faculty of many universities) found that they were moved by emotions that they had only partially acknowledged, particularly deriving from the Holocaust and the establishment of the State of Israel, and were eager to explore the Jewish component in their studies of Persian literature or the Gregorian chant or Renaissance art.

The postwar generation of Jewish undergraduates began to ask for Jewish learning as part of their general education. They no longer looked to college to provide them with a passport into American opportunity; they belonged. What they wanted was "an education," and that meant exploring themselves and their roots as well as their world. Other students had more practical motivations (preparation in Hebrew for a junior-year program in Israel, content preparation for a social-work career in a Jewish institutional setting). Still others were caught up in the ethnicity fad or wanted a Jewish parallel to Black Studies. The combined surge of faculty and student interest resulted in two remarkable decades of growth during which Jewish learning became firmly established in America's universities (1955-1975).

Before World War II, less than a dozen scholars taught Judaica on a full-time basis in American universities; perhaps an equal number of Jews taught Hebrew. By 1975, some 300 colleges were offering one or more undergraduate courses in Jewish Studies; nearly 250 faculty had appointments in the field, and perhaps another 400 persons taught on a part-time basis. Some estimates suggest that as many as 50,000 undergraduates took courses in Jewish Studies during the 1973-74 academic year. That same year 125 applications for predoctoral grants from candidates for the Ph.D. in an area of Jewish Studies were received by the National Foundation for Jewish Culture.

The colleges which now offer courses in Jewish Studies began to do so for varying reasons and continue to do so with varying emphases. Sometimes a religion department wanted to be ecumenical. Particularly after the Six-Day War, some schools found it prudent to respond to student pressure for a Hebrew House or for a course on the Holocaust. In many cases there was no clear academic rationale for the offerings. It was the case of an idea whose time had come and of a program that was "up for grabs" by anyone who expressed any interest. In at least one instance a Jewish Studies program emerged out of a Jew in the English department whose interest was radical literature, a Jew in anthropology whose interest was in the *shtetl*, and a Jew in history who was a specialist in labor organizations.

Jewish Studies programs have grown from above and below, out of faculty interest in Jewish data and undergraduate interest in Jewish values. Given this wide diversity of interest and the large number of specializations possible (after all, Jewish Studies encompasses nearly four millenia and all the continents), it is no wonder that vice presidents for academic affairs have had a difficult time deciding where a chair of Jewish Studies should be placed and what capacities the incumbent should possess. Single scholars are usually placed in a Semitic language department, in Near Eastern studies, or in Religion, with the promise that a cross-departmental offering would be developed.

The breadth of the field suggests that any Jewish Studies department which wants to offer courses leading to a graduate degree must have a sizable faculty: someone must know the Bible and related literature, another rabbinics, another contemporary Jewish thought, still another the sociological and demographic components of modern Jewish life; and, since there is no scholarship without language competence, courses in Hebrew and Yiddish and perhaps Aramaic should be available, in addition to all the languages in which Jews have written and in which scholars have written about Jews. A good case can be made that no one person can be expected to be competent within such obviously broad categories. Medieval Jewish philosophy is quite a different area from *Midrash* or the legal codes. Can a single historian master a history which reaches from the Bronze Age in West Asia to the Space Age in America? No single scholar can teach all of the courses required for an undergraduate major, much less for a graduate degree. Add to the cost of faculty the cost of maintaining extensive library holdings and it is clear why a certain amount of makeshift exists even at facilities like the Phillip W. Lown Institute of Advanced Judaic Studies at Brandeis University, where a considerable Jewish Studies faculty is in place. If a school can hire only a single person, he will have to spend much of his time teaching basic surveys of Judaica and finding people who can be borrowed from elsewhere on the faculty—sociologists who can contribute a course on the *shtetl* or the *kibbutz*, classicists or philosophers who can offer a course in Alexandrian Jewish literature or medieval Jewish philosophy, or community rabbis and Hebraists from local Colleges of Jewish Studies who can be responsible for language courses or some specialty. The use of local rabbis and teachers will continue to be a debated issue; some have denominational biases, some are not scholars, and academic types are not immune to the usual disdain of the professional for the amateur, however competent.

The situation is dramatically different at a few universities where the faculty is deeper, the academic tradition older, and where Jewish Studies has emerged less in response to undergraduate soul-searching than out of the felt needs of the scholarly enterprise. These schools have supportive courses in language, history, religion, the classics, Islamic studies, and the Middle East, which make it possible for well-conceived programs of undergraduate concentration and graduate studies to develop. In such schools, where the faculty often shares research interest in a broad range of topics—from the phenomenology of religion to patterns of cultural interaction, from the nature of religious leadership to the forms of mystical experience—a vigorous and significant scholarly exchange has developed.

American Jewish scholarship is no longer dependent on a brain drain from abroad. Jewish Studies involves a number of disciplines, and students follow many paths and go to many places to gain competence. Graduate training in the core disciplines of Jewish Studies is available at Brandeis, Harvard, Brown, Columbia, and Yeshiva universities, as well as at the seminaries. Centers exist for research and training in specific areas. Yiddish language and literature is the focus of a joint program of the Max Weinreich Center of the YIVO Institute of Jewish Research and Columbia University's Department of Linguistics. There are special reference libraries such as that of the American Jewish Historical Society at Waltham, Massachusetts, and the Leo Baeck Institute of New York City (German-Jewish culture in Europe and America).

A corporation of men and women who share a common interest in Jewish learning, each with a specialty within the larger field, has come into being. Ten years ago the dozen scholars who participated in the first meeting of the Academic Advisory Council of the National Foundation for Jewish Culture were strangers to each other. The sociologists around the table had never met the historians, and the men who taught in the seminaries did not know each other or, except by reputation, those who taught in a secular setting. Over the past decade an intellectual community has emerged. The Association for Jewish Studies was founded in 1968 to provide a forum for professional interests and a focus for the Jewish Studies enterprise. The AJS has published several books and the first two volumes of a scholarly journal, *The AJS Review*. Slowly, but perceptibly, a sense of order and articulated purpose has emerged and standards are being set. I suspect that for some time Jewish Studies will be defined as those studies which the members of the Association pursue.

The current membership of the AJS is comprised largely of postwar graduates of American and Canadian universities, with a small sprinkling of graduates of the Hebrew University and Bar Ilan. Its 1975 conference included papers in a variety of areas: American Jewish History, Medieval Biblical Exegesis, Bible, Emancipation and Enlightenment, Renaissance Jewish History, Medieval Hebrew Poetry, Midrash, and Jewish Historiography and Historical Consciousness. The public interest issues of contemporary Jewish life were conspicuously absent, suggesting that, although a number of significant social science scholars are AJS members, the Jewish Studies field has not bridged the distance which separates the liberal arts from the social sciences in most academic settings.

Jewish Studies is no longer carried on in isolation. Methodologies and concept structures common in the university necessarily will be appropriated for, and by, Jewish Studies. The special American interest in sociology and social analysis already has provided a set of methodological and analytic tools which the Marshall Sklares and Daniel Elazars have applied with skill in their studies of the contemporary Jewish community and its institutions.

Most researchers now recognize the advantage of integrating Jewish data into their ongoing research. S. D. Goitein's use of *Genizah* material to provide further understanding of the economics and the demography of the Mediterranean basin during the Middle Ages is a magnificent case in point. In return, Jewish scholars have available to them all the research and conceptual tools developed in this century.

There is no doubt that this two-way process is well advanced, nor that a practical problem has emerged which is yet to be faced, much less surmounted. The age of the Renaissance man is over. Each discipline, indeed, each subdiscipline, has its own language, set of conceptual tools and methodologies; and no scholar can be expert in many. In most colleges, the Jewish Studies person will have to be something of a generalist. The Jewish experience is so long and its geography so scattered that even a competent survey course should require five or six professors; yet, usually, only one is available. The Jewish Studies field wrestles here with a problem not uncommon in the academic enterprise. Should the field organize itself for the pursuit of knowledge and to permit research by scholars, or to provide insight and sensitivity to undergraduates? The answer is, of course, both/and; but it is not yet clear how the Jewish Studies field will adjust to this two-sided need.

Seminary faculties have been encouraged by their colleagues in the universities to use the new methodologies. The old anhistorical way is still the only way in some traditional schools, but no work of competence can long be denied if only because the traditionalists must refute "heretical ideas." There is already a good deal of movement between seminary and secular faculties, and common membership in the AJS certainly will benefit studies in both types of institutions.

The field of Jewish Studies has made, and continues to make, significant contributions to the critical understanding of the Jewish experience, but it is not Jewish learning in the traditional, value-laden *talmud torah* sense. Jewish Studies refines a perception of Torah which binds the dimension of time and the study of mankind into the received tradition. Its results present a stimulating challenge to the faith and the faithful. It is the responsibility of the seminary and the rabbinate to blend the new insights with the old. Whether such a Torah can inspire and bind men to it remains an open question, one which, in the final analysis, the field of Jewish Studies is not compelled to answer.

NOTES

1. The following partial list of major figures on the early faculties of the Hebrew Union College and the Jewish Theological Seminary indicates the European university where they received their advanced degree: Moses Buttenwieser (Heidelberg); Kaufman Kohler (Erlangen); Jacob Lauterbach (Göttingen); Henry Malter (Heidelberg); Jacob Mann (Jews' College); Alexander Marx (Königsberg); David Neumark (Berlin); Solomon Schechter (Cambridge).

2. The Hebrew Union College-Jewish Institute of Religion complex now includes two schools of education, a School of Sacred Music, the Edgar Magnin School of Graduate Studies, the Jacob Loucheim School of Judaic Studies, and the California School of Jewish Communal Service. The Jewish Theological Seminary administers a Seminary College of Jewish Studies, Teachers Institute; the Cantors Institute, Seminary College of Jewish Music; an Institute for Advanced Studies in the Humanities; the Abbell Institute in Rabbinics; the Melton Research Center (Education); the University of Judaism; and the Jewish Museum.

3. Its schools include Yeshiva College for Men, Stern College for Women, the Bernard Revel Graduate School for Jewish and Semitic Studies, the Ferkauf Graduate School of Humanities and Social Sciences, the Belfer Graduate School of Science, the Wurzweiler School of Social Work, and the Albert Einstein College of Medicine.

4. A list of *yeshivot* can be found in *The American Jewish Organizational Directory*, 9th ed., Margaret F. Goldstein, ed., Frankel Mailing Service, New York, 1975, pp. 116-117.

5. Hebrew Teachers College of Boston (1921); Herzliah-Hebrew Teachers Institute of New York City (1921); Spertus College of Chicago (1924); Baltimore Hebrew College and Teacher Training School (1902, 1919); Bureau of Jewish Education-College of Jewish Studies of Cleveland (1924, 1952); Midrasha College of Jewish Studies of Detroit (1926).

Eric L. Friedland _____

THE SYNAGOGUE AND
LITURGICAL DEVELOPMENTS

The storm and controversy in the Jewish liturgical sphere was over a long time ago. The furor that greeted early nineteenth-century prayerbook revision has since substantially abated, if it has not actually spent itself. The clashes between the traditionalist and Reform parties limned by Jakob J. Petuchowski in his *Prayerbook Reform in Europe*[1] revolved around issues raised by the civic emancipation of the Jews that came on the heels of the French Revolution and by the Jews' gradual and unsteady entry into Western European society. Hence, understandably, these disputes no longer possess any of the same urgency in this fourth quarter of the twentieth century.

Echoes of that fierce war of texts gained in volume a century later for a mercifully brief period only months after World War II ended, when the *Sabbath Prayer Book*[2] that had recently been issued by the Jewish Reconstructionist Foundation was publicly banned by some two hundred Orthodox rabbis meeting at New York's Hotel McAlpin. For many sadly reminiscent of the Nazis' revival and reenactment of the odious medieval practice of burning books and human lives, the ban, or *herem*, elicited a shudder and outcry among all sectors of the Jewish community, transcending denominational lines.[3] In this day and age controversies *cum studio et ira* over matters liturgical have made way for others of greater moment. This is not to say that liturgical activity came to an irreversible halt, that prayerbooks are no longer being written or compiled, or that prayer itself has been renounced or everywhere ceased to be a topic of discussion. Undeniably modernity and secularity have exacted their heavy toll; yet religion courses in colleges and universities across the nation continue to enjoy a vogue that shows few signs of diminishing, and many new sects and denominations clamor for their place. Statistically, regular synagogue attendance and the devotional life may be at a low ebb in many places; but experimentation with old and new forms of worship seems to have gained an unprecedented momentum in settings as diverse as Chabad Houses, Hillel Foundations, and *havurot*. A wrangle over the wording of a given prayer is hardly our style at this stage; broader concerns evoke the passions and commitments of the contemporary Jew. Nevertheless, the prayerful expression is still pretty much in demand.

The change in attitude and mood outlined above rose out of the profound transformation affecting the American Jewish community within the last two or three decades. A dual movement can be discerned as currently taking place. On the one hand, the Jews in the United States have been undergoing a qualified homogenizing process— socioeconomically, educationally, professionally, and religiously. The regional differences that divided the immigrant generation (1881-1924) of East European Jews into *Landsmannschaften* have dwindled into fast-fading memories. Intermarriages between the descendants of the German Jews (and others who came over in the 1840s and later) and the offspring of refugees from Eastern Europe beginning at the end of the last century have all but effaced what was once a sharply separative factor. The distinctions between the Yiddishist and the Hebraist, the Zionist and the Bundist, the believer and the atheist, the socialist and the advocate of free enterprise, and so forth that were so clear-cut and well defined fifty years ago have just about disappeared. Even the boundary lines between Conservative and Reform Judaism are nowhere nearly as explicit or definitive as they may have been three generations ago.

Prominent members of New York's famed Reform Congregation Emanu-El, men such as Jacob Schiff and Louis Marshall, were not being all that selflessly and unreservedly ecumenical toward *kelal yisrael* or hospitable to views or life-styles dissimilar to their own when, at the turn of the century, they supported the Jewish Theological Seminary of America and brought Solomon Schechter from England to head the Conservative rabbinical school then experiencing severe growing pains. They were interested chiefly in weaning the newly arrived Russian Jews from the brand of Orthodoxy the latter were accustomed to, in rendering them socially and culturally acceptable, and in making them over into "complete" Americans. Nowadays interaction between Conservatism and Reform occurs on an entirely different plane. The immigrant past recedes, while the socioeconomic and geographical gap that underlies the ritual and doctrinal divergencies between Conservatism and Reform narrows. Wolfe Kelman reports of synagogue mergers that have recently come to pass:

As already noted, there has been an increase in mergers between congregations of similar orientation. But mergers have also taken place between congregations of different denominational affiliation. The trend began in the smaller communities and is now apparent in larger centers of Jewish population as well. For instance, the Orthodox, Conservative, and Reform congregations in Duluth, Minnesota, with separate buildings but some overlapping membership, have merged into one congregation with a new rabbi of Conservative background. In San Francisco, an aging Conservative congregation in an older part of the city merged with a struggling new Reform suburban congregation whose rabbi now heads the new congregation. (There has been an intrasynagogue merger development as well. For example, in Philadelphia eight Conservative congregations have merged to form four. The partners in these mergers consisted in most instances of an urban congregation and a younger suburban one with the former selling its property to join the latter.)[4]

This intramural "ingathering of the exiles" is being shored up by accumulating shared values and experiences. There is scarcely a Jew who does not feel some sort of emotional tie to Israel. The mode of expression or the degree may vary; the tie itself is indubitably constant. Adversities, such as the fate of punitive discrimination and persecution throwing the lives of Soviet and Argentine Jews into confusion or the present runaway rate of assimilation and intermarriage in its own ranks, cement a bond among the several segments of American Jewry.

On the other hand, despite growing signs of unification, there is little chance of any monolith arising. New alignments are taking place, however transient or durable they ultimately prove to be. Often enough the older nineteenth-century-derived divisions barely satisfy the yearnings and discontents of inquiring young Jews. On the contrary, these divisions may stifle or discourage, often quite unintentionally, their groping expressions. The upsurge of traditionalism, whether of the Lubavitcher Hasidic variety or any other, and the attraction of the *havurah* movement for many, within or outside the synagogal context, serve as a partial index of the adequacy or inadequacy of the familiar institutional structures for the inner needs of Jews.

Certain segments of Orthodoxy do not find it necessary to cooperate with non-Orthodox groups, as, for instance, under the aegis of the Synagogue Council of America. From their point of view, such collaborative enterprises necessitate compromise and recognition of others' legitimacy. Out of unity a new polarization has occurred. A comparative complacency resulting from the melting-pot principle in the American Jewish milieu has lent courage to these "nonconformist" traditionalists in asserting their own position and in standing up for convictions that are not aimed to please or flatter. This assertiveness is less a defensive tactic of a beleaguered minority vis-à-vis the other branches of Judaism than the outcome of a newly acquired self-assurance. Analogously, the Zion-centered activities of the American Jewish community are not without their critics, carping or sympathetic. What had become an unshakable tenet for the Jewish religionist and secularist alike, undeviating support of Israel, is more and more subject to probing reexamination. Children of the "homogenizing" generation question its middle-class assumptions, priorities, and sensibilities, and listen to and try out alternative social and political theories, frequently at drastic variance with their parents'. In all the foregoing the drive for independence is concurrently a *recherche du temps perdu*. For instance, a cursory glance at such Jewish student publications as *genesis 2* and *Chutzpah* will uncover a renewal of interest on the part of college youth in the likes of Ber Borochov (1881-1917), a Marxist Zionist, and his less radical contemporaries who have long since fallen into neglect.

How are all these aforementioned developments reflected in the prayerbooks that have been issued in the last generation? What light do present-day liturgical creations cast on the inner life of Jewry today? What, at any rate, are the rabbinical composers, translators, and commentators of the *siddurim* in use in the modern synagogue striving for? How do they respond to the conflicting demands of an age-old tradition with its well-defined architectonic of teaching and practice, on the one hand, and of a faddist, kinetic, helter-skelter secular society in which we have our being?

This is not the place to go into the history of the Jewish liturgy after the Emancipation.[5] Perhaps the single most important and influential prayerbook to be produced a little over thirty years ago was the Reconstructionist *Sabbath Prayer Book*. The textual revisions are interesting enough in and of themselves; they are slightly bolder than, but in the main along the lines of, the European Liberal prayerbooks up to the eve of the Holocaust, that is, those rites on the Continent that are subsumed under the category of what Petuchowski aptly labels "Reform from within." Comparatively speaking, the most far-reaching changes lie in the omission of the *birkhot ha-shaḥar*, the preliminary benedictions, which were originally to be recited in the privacy of one's home anyway,[6] the rigorous curtailment of the *Musaf*, and the erasure of the "chosen people" idea from the pages of the prayerbook. The most fecund and enlivening part of that prayerbook is the supplement, which contains an overwhelming abundance of biblical, rabbinic, medieval, and modern material, with practically every prayer reproduced in both Hebrew and English.

Issued a year later (1946) by the Rabbinical Assembly and the United Synagogue of America, the Conservative *Sabbath and Festival Prayer Book* was also graced with a supplement, and, like its Reconstructionist counterpart, divided its readings according to theme. Both prayerbooks indent verses for responsive readings. A few of the themes, such as Zion, America, God, Torah, and justice, are similar. The Reconstructionist supplement contains by far the richer selection, including, for example, some seventeen poetic outpourings from the bards of Spanish Jewry's Golden Age. Moreover, it embraces a wider range of newly composed pieces in Hebrew and in English.

Under a kind of mandate given by the crucial Columbus Platform adopted in 1937 by the Reform Central Conference of American Rabbis, with its positive reappraisal of Catholic Israel "in all lands and in all ages," the Conference began fleshing out the lean frame of its *Union Prayer Book* (I, rev. ed., 1918; II, rev. ed., 1922) with materials of medieval provenance, whether or not they had ever found their way into the classical *Siddur*, and prayers recruited from the old prayerbook (such as *yismeḥu, hashkivenu,* and *magen avot*). Hence, the newly revised editions of the *Union Prayer Book* I and II (1940 and 1945, respectively) made freer and ampler use of an extended range of literary ingredients covering a longer and less discontinuous span from Israel's varied peregrinations in time and space. The style of the *Union Prayer Book* of the 1940s in the reclamation of older religious writings, liturgical and otherwise, was in large part congruent with the Reconstructionist and Conservative prayerbooks in the second half of the same decade, though nowhere on the same scale. It took another twenty years before Rabbi Bernard Bamberger notified the Central Conference of American Rabbis that an anthology, to go hand in hand with the *Union Prayer Book,* was on the verge of completion.[7] Four years later it was announced that agreement had been reached that the anthology was (1) to supplement the *Union Prayer Book,* (2) to comprise material devotional and inspirational in character, (3) to embrace the entire sweep of Jewish literature, (4) to be postbiblical, (5) to include non-Jewish scholars, and (6) to be of the same size as the *Union Prayer Book.*[8] The project was never carried through;[9] soon thereafter plans were underway to revamp the *Union Prayer Book.* The outcome was, of course, the recently published *Gates of Prayer: The New Union Prayer Book.*[10]

It was the Reconstructionist *Sabbath Prayer Book,* not to mention the succeeding Reconstructionist liturgies,[11] that clung most faithfully to the principle of an anthological supplement. This principle would be adhered to with every regard for, and scarcely any disruption of, the Mishnaic *matbe'a shel tefillah.* An additional prayer, poem, or responsive reading from the supplement would be positioned before, after, or in the middle of a statutory prayer, always with a corresponding theme. As an example, the first benediction before the *Shema,* or the benediction concerning the luminaries *(yotzer),* has after the opening sentences the rubric: "For other readings on 'God in Nature,' see Supplement, pages 360-391." The editors were set on allowing for flexibility, choice, and variety, while conserving the time-honored and familiar fabric of the Jewish liturgy as sketched out and executed by the tannaitic sages.[12] The compilers have sound precedent for their procedure, particularly in those occasional inserts or liturgical interpolations called the *qerovot.*[13] In spite of the traditional allowance for introducing such supernumerary pieces in the case of the *Amidah,* the Reconstructionist liturgists deemed it advisable to leave the *Shema* and the *Amidah* uninterrupted and intact.[14]

This simultaneous deference to classical form and recognition of the need for diversity and novelty are what Joseph Heinemann tellingly describes as the "dialectics of conformity and spontaneity in Jewish liturgy." Given special emphasis by the Reconstructionists, it became in effect an implied axiom in a good deal of subsequent prayerbook revision. A weighty case in point is the Reform *Gates of Prayer* which, with all its verbal and theological departures from the traditional norm, hews doggedly to the *matbe'a shel tefillah*.[15]

The Reconstructionists' energetic espousal of textual variations in a basically Ashkenazic-rite service—a carryover and extension of the nineteenth-century European and American Liberal prayerbooks' partiality for the Sephardic liturgical variant or hymn, such as the lilting and beguiling *el nora 'alilah* by the Spanish Moses ibn Ezra (c. 1055-post 1135) for the fifth and last service on Yom Kippur—was to be taken up by non-Reconstructionist prayerbooks. To illustrate further, the Reconstructionists' utilization of the Palestinian-based pre-*Shema* evening benedictions as found in Sa'adiah Gaon's rite[16] was to be repeated in *Gates of Prayer* in the special service for Yom Ha-Atzmaut.[17]

There is something which has seen some ups and downs in American prayerbooks in the past seventy-five years: private, personal devotions. It took some time before the ancient rabbis' individual and intimate prayerful compositions[18] were to be emulated. Some of the early free-form, virtually all-English Reform prayerbooks that antedate the *Union Prayer Book* and that were in varying degrees Protestant-inspired[19] made ample provision for such spiritual, contemplative exercises. When the *Union Prayer Book* eventually superseded these nonconformist productions, it squeezed out for a while private prayer, except for *elohay netzor*, the silent prayer at the conclusion of the *Amidah*, and for five uninspired pieces in a sort of catchall appendix toward the end of the book.[20] There is also a long silent prayer immediately prior to the climactic confessional *(vidduy)* during the morning service of Yom Kippur.[21] The late teens and the twenties of the present century saw an outburst of English devotional creativity on both sides of the Atlantic with the appearance of the revised edition of the *Union Prayer Book* and Israel I. Mattuck's three volumes of the vagarious but enormously fertile and often inspired British *Liberal Jewish Prayer Book* (1924, 1926). The last-named edition of the *Union Prayer Book* not only contains at the end of the volume before the lectionary a whole section titled "Prayers for Private Devotion,"[22] but also meditations leading into each of the Sabbath and festival services that manifest a profound religious inwardness.

Inward turning shows up preeminently in the unjustifiably ignored, exquisite though unpretentious *Blessing and Praise: A Book of Meditations and Prayers for Individual and Home Devotion*.[23] In England this same propensity for the contemplative was to assert itself with the 1931 edition of the West London Synagogue's *Forms of Prayer*, where a highly structured, moderately traditional service is made to yield room for six new introductory prayers and others for "Silent Devotion," the latter as an alternative to the last two paragraphs of the *Shema*. Every one of these engaging and heartfelt meditations comes up again in the American Reconstructionist prayerbooks for use either at the outset of the service or during the return of the scroll to the ark.[24]

The trailblazing Reconstructionist *Sabbath Prayer Book* pressed into service not only ancient and medieval religious poems and gleanings that had all but sunk into centuries-long oblivion, but searching latter-day lyrical verses such as those by the contemporary Hebrew poet Ya'akov Cahan (1881-1960)[25] and David Frischmann (1859-1922). Frischmann, a talented literary man and major influence in modern Hebrew literature, was responsible for the auspicious Hebrew translation of the deeply religious poem *Gitanjali* by the Indian pacifist and internationalist author, mystic, and guru, Rabindranath Tagore (1861-1941). Some original compositions intended specifically for the *Sabbath Prayer Book* compare favorably with these pieces. The ever vigorous Mordecai M. Kaplan himself wrote an exalted orison of sorts, an eloquent expression in verse of man's apprehension of God.

GOD THE LIFE OF NATURE

Our fathers acclaimed the God
Whose handiwork they read
In the mysterious heavens above
And in the varied scene of earth below,

In the orderly march of days and nights,
Of seasons and years,
And in the checkered fate of man.

Meantime have the vaulting skies dissolved;
Night reveals the limitless caverns of space,
Hidden by the light of day,
And unfolds horizonless vistas
Far beyond imagination's ken.
The mind is staggered,
Yet soon regains its poise,
And peering through the boundless dark,
Orients itself anew
By the light of distant suns
Shrunk to glittering sparks.

The soul is faint,
Yet soon revives,
And learns to spell once more the name of God
Across the newly visioned firmament.

Lift your eyes, look up;
Who made these stars?
He who marshals them in order,
Summoning each one by name.

God is the oneness
That spans the fathomless deeps of space
And the measureless eons of time,
Binding them together in act,
As we do in thought.

He is the sameness
In the elemental substance of stars and planets,
Of this our earthly abode
And of all that it holds.

He is the unity
Of all that is,
The uniformity of all that moves,
The rhythm of all things
And the nature of their interaction.

He binds up the Pleiades in a cluster
And loosens the chains of Orion;
He directs the signs of the Zodiac
And guides the constellations of the Bear.

God is the mystery of life,
Enkindling inert matter
With inner drive and purpose.
He is the creative flame
That transfigures lifeless substance,
Leaping into ever higher realms of being,
Brightening into the radiant glow of feeling,
Till it turns into the white fire of thought.

And though no sign of living thing
Break the eternal silence of the spheres,
We cannot deem this earth,
This tiny speck in the infinitude,
Alone instinct with God.

By that token
Which unites the worlds in bonds of matter
Are all the worlds bound
In the bond of Life.

It is He who forms the mountains
And creates the wind,
And reveals His inner mind to man;
He who makes the dawn and darkness,
Who marches over the heights of earth;
The Lord, God of hosts, is His name.

God is in the faith
By which we overcome
The fear of loneliness, of helplessness,
Of failure and of death.

God is in the hope
Which, like a shaft of light,
Cleaves the dark abysms
Of sin, of suffering, and of despair.

God is in the love
Which creates, protects, forgives.
His is the spirit
Which broods upon the chaos men have wrought,
Disturbing its static wrongs,
And stirring into life the formless beginnings
Of the new and better world.

Thou art my portion,
O Eternal;
Thou art my share.
Thou wilt show me the path of life;
Fullness of joy is in Thy presence;
Everlasting happiness dost Thou provide.[26]

The Reconstructionist prayerbooks have had many imitators, particularly in the Conservative and Reform camps, both in the United States
and abroad. It is the scheme of an anthology, as embodied in the supplement, that has exercised an all but universal appeal. Private congregational creations—mimeographed, Xeroxed or printed—exploit this
scheme without always acknowledging the source. The anthologizing
tendency has been reinforced and enriched by Nahum N. Glatzer's
Language of Faith,[27] a sheaf of sensitively garnered prayers of Jewish
authorship from everywhere.

Among the rare exceptions to this anthologizing tendency in prayer-books are, for American Orthodox rites, David de Sola Pool's *Book of Prayer* (Sephardic)[28] and Philip Birnbaum's *Daily Prayer Book: Ha-Siddur ha-Shalem*,[29] and, from the Conservative side, Ben Zion Bokser's *Ha-Siddur* and *Ha-Mahzor*[30] and Max D. Klein's two volumes of *Seder Avodah*.[31] What sets these books apart is that they are all-purpose comprehensive manuals of prayer, each a *vade mecum* designed for all occasions of life, private and public, domestic and communal, ordinary weekday and the day of "solemn assembly"—a totality the newer liturgies have a hard time recovering. The fragmentation of the traditional prayerbook's unity, a unity which an Isaac M. Wise and a David Einhorn were able to recapture liturgically, is, in a manner of speaking, a mutation peculiar to the present stage of the twentieth century.

A word might be said about the latest of the official prayerbooks to be published, namely, the teeming and energetic Reform *Gates of Prayer*. The components that went into the making of this new rite are of remarkably diverse origins. Religious pluralism is the fundamental working principle in what is in a sense a composite rite intended to satisfy a whole gamut of theological dispositions and outlooks. The countless *cahier*-type of innovative services that came for scrutiny before the prayerbook committee, a proportion of these mildly avant-garde or even blatantly *outré*, were tamed, fortunately without necessarily being chloroformed, and dovetailed into the *Union Prayer Book* version of the *matbe'a shel tefillah*. A comparison of Arthur Waskow's radical and unconventional *Freedom Seder*[32] with the *New Union Haggadah*,[33] the latter preceding *Gates of Prayer* by a year, or of the polydox, nontheistic *Book of Common Service*[34] with the sparely domesticated version in the new prayerbook's Sabbath Eve Service VI will bear this out. The creative attempts of the various Hillel Foundations are represented, as in Service VIII (pp. 244-259);[35] and there are, of course, the old *Union Prayer Book* services retained (for example, Sabbath Morning Service III), containing a minimum of change. In this last instance, the editors are obviously anticipating the wishes and needs of the Jewish counterparts of those Catholics who, in defiance of the liturgical reforms set in motion by Vatican II, insist on hearing the Tridentine Latin mass or of those Episcopalians who have no use for tampering with the stately language of the Elizabethan *Book of Common Prayer*.

It is clear that fresh concerns loom large in the prayerbooks that have come out in the last thirty years, cares and preoccupations that did not exercise the minds of former compilers or that the editors themselves had not yet mustered up the courage to confront. Shifting social mores and evolving theological concepts are leaving their distinct imprint on the liturgy. *Gates of Prayer* bends every effort to be rid of as much of the habitual sexism in our language and imagery as possible, and every so often takes pains to correct a historical injustice by underscoring the positive role women have played in the Jewish past, as in the following highly significant loose paraphrase of the prefatory paragraph of the *Amidah*, known as *Avot* ("[God of the] Fathers"):

> Our God and God of our fathers, God of Abraham, Isaac, and Jacob, Amos, Isaiah, and Micah, a heritage has come down to us along all the painful paths our people has travelled.
>
> *Our God and God of our mothers, God of Sarah, Rebekah, Leah, and Rachel, Deborah, Hannah, and Ruth, a heritage has come down to us.*
>
> When others worshipped gods indifferent to goodness, our mothers and fathers found the One whose law unites all people in justice and love.
>
> *A heritage of faith has come down to us out of the life of our people.*
>
> When knowledge was the secret lore of princes and priests, our sages opened their doors to all who sought understanding.
>
> *A heritage of learning has come down to us out of the life of our people.*[36]

So far no authoritative ritual or printed prayerbook embraces a service specifically designed for women, for example, one for the birth of a daughter or for celebrating Rosh Ḥodesh, the New Moon, as a women's holiday.[37] It is undoubtedly only a matter of time before these and similar feminist ceremonies occupy their rightful place in Jewish public worship, however grindingly slow progress is made.

Another topic that has been receiving no more than passing attention is the vexatious subject of Arab-Jewish relations. At least a couple of rites make use of an extract from Martin Buber's writings touching on this question.[38] As clouds continue to hover over the political horizon in the Middle East in our time, the relationship between the two kindred peoples, tortured as it has been for so long, has not as yet come to any intense, sustained liturgical expression.

Indeed, it is fairly clear that the present prayerbooks are essentially apolitical, or perhaps even depoliticized.[39] The patriotic fervor of the 1940s is mellowed to the degree that Robert N. Bellah's concept of "civil religion" no longer quite suits the Jewish community in the United States the way it once might have. Although strengthened ties with Israel are reflected liturgically, there is nothing in the American prayerbooks parallel to the "National Service" in the British *Service of the Heart* culminating in "God Save the Queen." As a matter of fact, none of the current manuals provide a service for the Fourth of July, Thanksgiving Day, or Labor Day.[40] The prayer for the government in *Gates of Prayer* sounds noticeably neutral in comparison to its counterpart in the old *Union Prayer Book*. It probably goes without saying that the aftermath of the fiasco in Vietnam and the atrocities committed there, as well as the disgrace of Watergate, have qualified American Jewry's uncritical national zeal and semi-idolatrous love of America—liberal, radical, conservative, or otherwise. Disenchantment with the United States' messianic pretensions has not led to licking our *galut* wounds or, for that matter, to joining *en masse* the company of the liberation theologians. Is *Gates of Prayer* succumbing to a this-worldly, deferred eschatological hope in devoting so much space to "special themes," most of them incidentally from the *Service of the Heart*, such as humanity, justice, unity, peace, Israel's mission, and redemption?

Doubt is no longer subject to taboo or ban in the context of congregational worship (not that it ever really was systematically barred from Jewish prayer). At least some contributors to the synagogue liturgy have assimilated the talmudic dictum: "Since we know that the Holy One Blessed be He is truthful, we do not prevaricate before Him."[41] The Reconstructionist *Sabbath Prayer Book* duplicates the prayer on doubt (pp. 251-253) in the English Reform *Forms of Prayer*, but almost as if to immunize the worshiper against doubt by mentioning its name and by asking divine pardon for one's presumptuousness. By contrast, the non-Orthodox prayerbooks that have been published within the last decade are far less given to hedging and do recognize doubt's legitimate polar function alongside its antithesis, faith. The dialectic is valued for the part it carries out in begetting a stronger, subtler, and more mature religious understanding. Thus the theme of honest doubt is accorded a respectful niche in the "Special Themes" section of *Gates of Prayer*.[42]

There is little question that at the moment things are in a state of considerable religious ferment. American Jewish life seems astir with spiritual vitality, if we are to take the plethora of present-day liturgical productions as any indication. However, serious questions remain. We may be witnessing a steady proliferation of worship publications of various kinds, but how many of these can we frankly say enjoy an originality on the order of the works of David Einhorn, Isaac M. Wise, Benjamin Szold, and Marcus Jastrow of yesterday? To be sure, these nineteenth-century compilers drew upon the preparatory labors of previous liturgists, but they themselves had at their command an unfailing instinct for textual symmetry and harmony of parts and for theologically "sound doctrine" (of course, in light of their *Zeitgeist*) which seems, in equivalent current-day terms, temporarily in short supply. Instead we have a profusion of patchwork mélanges, verbal collages as it were, that are in many instances jejune and hit-or-miss in character. There is no gainsaying the merits of the supplement, or the anthological principle, in a prayerbook, especially if it means exposing the contemporary worshiper to the many-sided richness of the Jewish religious tradition and if it proves conducive to the devotional life. There is warrant for asking, however, whether the age of the supplement is not also the age of the epigone, when a potpourri eclecticism is in the ascendancy.

On the one hand, *Gates of Prayer*, as a notable example, represents the ripest achievement in prayerbook development; on the other, only a fraction of that book can truly be called indigenous, native-grown, or original. It is a well-known fact that the classical *Siddur* was never simply the summary result of any single age or clime; it has been unceasingly susceptible to enhancement, enlargement, and embellishment. This is surely all to the good. The question that persists is: What are we seeing today? The feeling for the transcendent has been blunted; immanentism is in, but no less difficult to pinpoint. Many a modern worshiper is beset by the problem of "identity diffusion," to use Erik Erikson's phrase, in which a uniform style, in life or liturgy, does not register very well. The spate of liturgical productions irrepressibly reminds one of the oft-quoted witticism attributed to Solomon Schechter that at a time when every Jew prayed, one prayerbook was enough, but now when few Jews pray, we need a hundred different ones.

Perhaps we are traversing a spiritual interregnum and journeying on a well-lit path, the strength of whose light, like the rising sun before it reaches its zenith, casts too much shade. That independent Orthodox Jewish thinker, Eliezer Berkovits, puts it well in postulating a never-ending task:

The task is always the same—to set the Eternal One always before oneself; in Jewish living, to transform the confrontation with the world into a confrontation with God; in Jewish praying, to move from the island of self-confrontation into the living presence of God.[43]

NOTES

1. Jakob J. Petuchowski, *Prayerbook Reform in Europe* (New York: World Union for Progressive Judaism, 1968). See especially ch. 5, "Battle of the Proof Texts," pp. 84-104.

2. *Sabbath Prayer Book* (New York: The Jewish Reconstructionist Foundation, 1945).

3. Eric L. Friedland, *The Historical and Theological Development of Non-*

Orthodox Jewish Prayerbooks in the United States (Ann Arbor, Michigan: University Microfilms, 1967), pp. 170-171.

4. "The Synagogue in America," in *The Future of the Jewish Community in America*, David Sidorsky, ed. (Philadelphia: The Jewish Publication Society of America, in collaboration with the Institute of Human Relations Press, 1973), p. 169.

5. On this history, see Ismar Elbogen, *Der jüdische Gottesdienst in seiner geschichtlichen Entwicklung* (Frankfurt am Main: J. Kaufmann Verlag, 1931), pp. 394-443; Friedland, *Development of Non-Orthodox Prayerbooks;* Abraham Millgram, *Jewish Worship* (Philadelphia: The Jewish Publication Society of America, 1971), pp. 569-99; and Petuchowski, *Prayerbook Reform*.

6. Solomon B. Freehof, "The Structure of the Birchos Hashachar," *Hebrew Union College Annual*, XXIII, Part Two (1950-1951), pp. 339-354. *Cf.* Leo Merzbacher's omission of the same in his *Order of Prayer* (2d ed., New York, 1860), and utilization of two of these benedictions in his morning service for personal use in the home, *elohay neshamah, yehi ratzon . . . she-targilenu*, and the *Shema* form the entire individualized domestic service.

7. *Central Conference of American Rabbis Yearbook*, LXIX (1960), p. 97.

8. *Ibid.*, LXXIII (1964), p. 71.

9. For their part, however, the British Reformers did come out with an anthology of their own, according to a different concept, expressly for the High Holy Days. The variegated, subtle, intensely spiritual, and urbane assemblage is called *Returning: Exercises in Repentance*, Jonathan Magonet, ed. (London: Reform Synagogues of Great Britain, 1975).

10. *Gates of Prayer* (New York: Central Conference of American Rabbis, 1975).

11. Other prayerbooks bearing the imprint of the Jewish Reconstructionist Foundation are the *High Holiday Prayer Book: Prayers for Rosh Hashanah*, vol. I (New York, 1948); *High Holiday Prayer Book: Prayers for Yom Kippur*, vol. II (New York, 1948); *Festival Prayer Book* (New York, 1958); and *Daily Prayer Book* (New York, 1963).

12. *Berakhot*, pp. 28b ff.

13. See Joseph Heinemann, with Jakob J. Petuchowski, *Literature of the Synagogue* (New York: Behrman House, Inc., 1975), p. 210.

14. Latter-day imitators have overlooked this reservation and exercise in caution. See Sidney Greenberg and Jonathan Levine, *Likrat Shabbat* (Bridgeport, Connecticut: The Prayer Book Press of Media Judaica, Inc., 1973); Sidney Greenberg and S. Allan Sugarman, *A Contemporary High Holiday Service* (Bridgeport, Connecticut: The Prayer Book Press of Media Judaica, Inc., 1971).

15. The doctrinally radical Sabbath Evening Service VI serves as a strong example corroborating this point.

16. See Israel Davidson, Simḥah Asaf, Yissakhar Joel, eds., *Siddur Rav Sa'adiah Gaon*, 2d ed. (Jerusalem: Meqitzey Nirdamim Society, 1963), p. 110. *Cf.* Jakob J. Petuchowski, ed., *Tefillat Shaḥarit le-Shabbat* (Cincinnati: Hebrew Union College, 1970), p. 6; Jakob J. Petuchowski, ed., *Shaḥar Avakeshkha: A Weekday Morning Service Based on the Traditional Birkhoth Hashachar* (Cincinnati: Hebrew Union College, n. d.), p. 5; Eugen J. Messinger and Lothar Rothschild, eds., *Tefillat 'Arvit le-Shabbat; Gebetbuch für den Freitagabend* (Vereinigung für religiös-liberales Judentum in der Schweiz, 1965), p. 13.

17. *Gates of Prayer*, p. 595, bottom; *cf.* pp. 599-600 and 602, top, all of which are of the old Palestinian rite.

18. See C. G. Montefiore and H. Loewe, *A Rabbinic Anthology* (New York and Philadelphia: Meridian Books and the Jewish Publication Society of America, 1963), pp. 361-364. *Cf.* the rubric at the conclusion of most every silent *Amidah* in Jules Harlow, ed., *Mahzor for Rosh Hashanah and Yom Kippur* (New York: The Rabbinical Assembly, 1972) and *The Bond of Life: A Book for Mourners* (New York: The Rabbinical Assembly, 1975), especially p. 163, where the private meditation of the talmudic sage, R. Elazar, is furnished as an alternative to the customary *elohay netzor*, also supplied.

19. For example, Gustav Cottheil, *Morning Prayers* (New York: Temple Emanu-El, 1889); Joseph Krauskopf, *The Service Manual*, 2d ed. (Philadelphia: Edward Stern & Co., 1892); Harry Levi, *Sunday Service* (Boston: Temple Israel, 1919); and Joseph Leonard Levy, *A Book of Prayer* (Pittsburgh: Publicity Press, 1902).

20. *Union Prayer Book*, I, 1895, pp. 93, 195, 276, and 278-282.

21. *Union Prayer Book*, II, 1894, pp. 173-178.

22. These ultimately formed part of the contents of the *Union Home Prayer Book* (Philadelphia: Central Conference of American Rabbis, 1951).

23. *Blessing and Praise* (Cincinnati: Central Conference of American Rabbis, 1923).

24. It is to be observed that in *Forms of Prayer* the preceding set of prayers in English, the ones right after *mah tovu*, are all accompanied by a Hebrew translation that is, as ill luck would have it, afflicted by an awkward and forced style. The linguistic stiltedness was done over and replaced with smooth and comely renditions by Joseph Marcus (1897-1975), a scholar in Genizah and payyetanic literature, in the *Sabbath Prayer Book*. Marcus also provided new Hebrew translations for the remaining meditations and for other pieces in subsequent Reconstructionist prayerbooks.

25. *Sabbath Prayer Book*, pp. 352-353, 356-359. *Cf.* Bernard Martin, *Prayer in Judaism* (New York and London: Basic Books, Inc., 1968), pp. 244-246; *Service of the Heart*, pp. 225-227; and *Gates of Prayer*, p. 664.

26. *Sabbath Prayer Book*, pp. 382-391. Both Morris Silverman's *High Holiday Prayer Book* (Hartford: Prayer Book Press, 1951), p. 5, and *Likrat Shabbat* (pp. 56-57) reproduce it in part.

27. Nahum N. Glatzer, *Language of Faith* (New York: Schocken Books, 1967).

28. David de Sola Pool, *Book of Prayer* (New York: Union of Sephardic Congregations, 1941).

29. Philip Birnbaum, *Daily Prayer Book* (New York: Hebrew Publishing Company, 1949).

30. Ben Zion Bokser, *Ha-Siddur* and *Ha-Mahzor* (New York: Hebrew Publishing Company, 1957 and 1959, respectively).

31. Max D. Klein, *Seder Avodah*, I and II (Philadelphia: Maurice Jacobs, Inc., 1951 and 1960, respectively).

32. Arthur Waskow, *Freedom Seder* (New York, Chicago, San Francisco: Holt, Rinehart and Winston, 1970).

33. *New Union Haggadah* (New York: Central Conference of American Rabbis, 1974).

34. *Book of Common Service,* Experimental edition (Cincinnati: Institute of Creative Judaism, 1976).

35. *Cf.* Richard N. Levy, *New Windows on an Ancient Day, An Experimental Sabbath Evening Service* (Central Conference of American Rabbis, 1970); Richard N. Levy, *Service for the New Year: Rosh Hashanah and Yom Kippur* (Los Angeles Hillel Council, 1969, 1970).

36. *Gates of Prayer,* pp. 229-230; *cf.* pp. 254-255.

37. Arlene Agus, "This Month Is for You: Observing Rosh Hodesh as a Woman's Holiday," in *The Jewish Woman: New Perspectives,* Elizabeth Koltun, ed. (New York: Schocken Books, 1976), pp. 84-93; Daniel I. Leifer and Myra Leifer, "On the Birth of a Daughter," *ibid.,* pp. 21-30; Aviva Cantor Zuckoff, "Jewish Women's Haggadah," *ibid.,* pp. 94-102.

38. Richard N. Levy, *Service for the New Year,* 1969, p. 6; *cf.* Nahum Waldman's poem, "To Touch Hands in Peace," in *Likrat Shabbat,* p. 60.

39. Arthur Waskow's *Freedom Seder* seems to be an exception proving the rule.

40. In contrast, for example, to the Reconstructionist *Sabbath Prayer Book,* pp. 538-561. The new *Book of Common Service* has "A Thanksgiving Service" (pp. 69-74) which appears somewhat contrary to the major trend.

41. *Yoma* 79b.

42. *Cf.* Jules Harlow, *Maḥzor,* pp. 18-19; and quotations in *A Book of Common Service* such as "Faith and doubt are twin offsprings of mystery" and "There is no certainty without some doubt" (pp. 10 and 13).

43. "Prayer," in *Studies in Torah Judaism,* Leon D. Stitskin, ed. (New York: Yeshiva University Press-Ktav Publishing House, 1969), p. 95.

Arnold Forster

ANTI-SEMITISM

Anti-Semitism in the United States came to a unique and critical juncture in 1945, with the end of a war which changed the course of the world and of many fundamental popular perceptions and attitudes as well. From then on, the ancient curse of overt prejudice against Jews, along with so much else in human affairs, assumed a number of new aspects and eventually followed new directions.

When the Allied armed forces opened the Nazi concentration camps and death factories in that last year of the war, the world suddenly recognized the enormity of the crimes committed by a "civilized" state. Anti-Semitism—the defamation, subjugation, or persecution of Jews as Jews—was thereupon swiftly condemned almost everywhere it appeared, as were the ideas which generated it. "Thereafter," Oscar Handlin has written, "it was impossible to consider such ideas simply as speculative theories, rationally to be argued about. Rather, it became clear that anti-Semitism was a kind of blind hatred that had doomed six million Jews to the extermination chambers. Everywhere there was an instinctive revulsion against ideas that had had such horrible consequences."[1] Further, scholars and psychologists had begun to cut the underpinnings of Jew-baiting, demonstrating the fallacy of the racist view of man and exposing the real nature of prejudice.

Such developments not only seemed to preclude a repetition of the more overt and vicious forms of anti-Semitism among all except the lunatic hate fringe, but helped to open certain doors long closed to Jews. Though never experiencing *de jure* discrimination in America, Jews had frequently been victims of social, academic, and economic deprivations. The new beneficence opened up the great universities and graduate schools which had long imposed quotas, and new careers beckoned in an expanding civil service and in other areas where merit and talent were the criteria for admission and promotion. Jews achieved a greater degree of economic and political security and social acceptance than they had enjoyed anywhere since the Dispersion.

While those gains achieved in the framework of law were solid and (given the nature of American society) most likely irreversible, certain negative undercurrents still flowed. Old prejudices and fears remained, and in measurable degree. A 1945 survey by the American Jewish Committee revealed that 56 percent of Americans thought that "Jews have too much power in the United States" and that 19 percent—almost one in every five—considered Jews "a threat to America." An Anti-Defamation League study in 1949 indicated that 65 percent of non-Jews thought Jews to be less fair in business dealings, that 50 percent would have objected to working for a Jewish employer, and that 33 percent thought it proper to bar Jews from certain neighborhoods.[2] America's confrontation in Europe with the ultimate racist society apparently had erased the more vicious and violent aspects of bigotry. The untamed emotions and public callousness which had marshaled such broad anti-Semitic views into organized, nationwide crusades in the 1920s and 1930s seemed no longer to be part of the American psyche, and the surviving Gerald L. K. Smiths were shunned and isolated. Unhappily, the problem became subtler. The dangerous flowerings of hate had been recognized for what they were and had been cut down, although obviously the roots remained and the soil was unlikely to lose its fertility completely.

The vulgar anti-Semitism that remained in the 1950s and the early 1960s was symbolized by the strutting Nazi, George Lincoln Rockwell, or by the exclusionary membership policies of the world-famous West Side Tennis Club in Forest Hills. But neither of these carried noticeable effects to the overall Jewish community; both tended to embarrass the American public when placed in the spotlight of publicity.

The rise of the radical Right in the 1960s presented special problems of anti-Semitism. For a time many of the old-style anti-Semites found new and interested audiences in large, extremist membership organizations such as the John Birch Society. Most of these carried on "anti-Communist" crusades, and their leaders were all too anxious to enlist the aid of any dedicated "patriots." Hungry for success, they were able to overlook such nonessential or tolerable personal quirks as anti-Semitism. Their generally narrow-minded minions across the country were not troubled by the injection of prejudice; in the main, they could not distinguish between political negativism and the negativism of bigotry. The anti-Semitic quotient in the John Birch Society, at first denied or gingerly opposed by its leadership, was found to be reflected (if not pervasive) in Birch policies and publications by the early 1970s. By then, however, the radical Right was in decline and the problems it presented to Jews—as well as those it presented to society in general—became academic.

Through the first twenty years of the postwar era, then, anti-Semitism had been unable to reestablish its pre-Auschwitz foothold on the public scene. Intolerance had lost out to *tolerance*, although it is quite significant that we were calling so positive a phenomenon by so negative a term not too many years ago, and it is possible that we were doing so because we sensed more than a few contradictions in the apparent progress. Christian and Jewish religious leaders, for example, hailed the arrival of a post-Nazism era of goodwill between their faiths, urging a new understanding and even cooperation. Nevertheless, traditional concepts of Jewish "guilt" were still widely taught in the churches.

In 1966 Charles Y. Glock and Rodney Stark, survey researchers at the University of California at Berkeley, demonstrated the relationship between deep religious belief-and-content to anti-Semitism in what they termed a sequence of "belief→feelings→actions."[3] These social scientists found that the Christian particularist's belief that "the Jews *remain* guilty" of the Crucifixion, that they continue to reject Christ and that they "have suffered under divine judgment ever since,"[4] tends to lead to human judgments of an anti-Semitic nature and, potentially, to open hostility. The Glock-Stark sequence actually erupted in concrete form during the 1950s and 1960s: *belief* (guilt in "deicide")→*feelings* (resentment against Jews)→and, in a period of about two months early in 1960, *actions*—643 incidents across the country of synagogue and Jewish cemetery desecrations, the vandalizing of Jewish homes, and the beating of Jews.[5]

Such incidents, of course, were juvenile, at least in form, and it is certain that they shocked adult sensibilities which, on their darker side, were not unstained by the root cause. In a later project of the University of California study cited above, researchers Gertrude J. Selznick and Stephen Steinberg found anti-Semitism in America "widespread and pervasive, but not in a dangerous form." They showed that while only 5 percent to 10 percent of the population could be considered "rabid" anti-Semites, social club discrimination was "widely accepted, even among the least prejudiced third of the population," and that "while only a handful said they would be inclined to vote for an anti-Semitic candidate, over a third indicated that his anti-Semitism would make no difference to them."[6] The study indicated, indeed, that *indifference* to anti-Semitism seemed to be the growing problem.

This was 1969, and the Selznick-Steinberg findings documented a change that Jews had sensed in the previous two or three years—the arrival of new attitudes, new forms of the ancient curse. The initial outrage produced by the Holocaust had begun to fade, and a second turning point had been reached.

Two thousand years of history have produced in Jews sensitive antennae, genuine survival mechanisms that warn of danger. Their experience has taught them that anti-Semitic disaster can follow periods of great stability and prosperity for the Jews—as was the case with both the Inquisition and the Holocaust. This is not to say that any comparable tragedy was now being foreseen (that, surely, is out of the question), but the new and hard-won status of American Jewry began to show unmistakable signs of deterioration by the end of the 1960s and Jews began to sense a profound uneasiness. Sympathy for Jews and antipathy toward anti-Semitism have certain limits; these limits are exceeded when the Jew is no longer perceived as a victim, whether or not that perception is accurate. At this point, the non-Jewish world apparently automatically undertakes to make him a victim anew.

"JEWS CONTROL CRIME IN THE UNITED STATES," stated a facsimile newspaper headline in a quarter-page advertisement for a book about gangland's Meyer Lansky in June 1971. The newspaper in the mock-up was as totally fictitious as the anti-Semitic allegation (which was not made in the book itself) was totally false. In 1959 this could have been the work of a George Lincoln Rockwell, but in 1971 it was an advertisement placed by one of America's most prestigious publishers on the book page of the *New York Times.*

There were few expressions of protest, and the president of the publishing house expressed astonishment and resentment that there had been any criticism at all of his advertisement, designed, perhaps unwittingly, to exploit the appeal of latent bigotry.[7] Similarly, relative silence followed a series of allegations (ironic in view of the above) by the popular author Truman Capote that the publishing business in America is "Jewish-controlled," "Jewish-oriented," and run by a "very powerful, very parochial Jewish clique" which can "make or break writers" and which, in so doing, has frozen out a number of non-Jewish writers except for an occasional "goy Yid" approved by this "god-damned Jewish Mafia." These were not the words of a professional hate-monger but of one of the most honored literary figures in America, and they were stated in two mass-circulation magazines and on one of the country's most popular television shows. Capote's sentiments have been echoed elsewhere; a liberal Vermont newspaper carried a column in May 1972 complaining that "American culture is rapidly becoming Jewish," that "anti-Christ is in the driver's seat and where it will all end up is not pleasant to contemplate."

The Jewish "culture" sometimes offered in the marketplace at the beginning of the permissive 1970s was often neither pleasant to contemplate nor at all comforting to Jews. Consider, for instance, the realm of the motion picture, the makers of which, dedicated as they are to the enrichment of their bank accounts, will go only as "far out" as the traffic will allow. In the summer of 1972 the film version of *Portnoy's Complaint,* eliminating whatever redeeming values the original novel may have had, presented a parade of vulgar anti-Semitic stereotypes described by one New York critic as "screeching impersonations of *Der Stuermer* cartoons" taking part in an orgy that another called "quintessential anti-Semitism." (Extending its impact, an article in a major American newspaper quoted a line of Portnoy's which it termed "prophetic" with respect to Secretary of State Henry Kissinger: "Yes, I was one happy Yiddel down there in Washington. . . .") A year after *Portnoy* the musical film *Jesus Christ Superstar* began its extended runs before more persons than had witnessed the anti-Semitic Oberammergau Passion Play in three centuries—and, as in the German pageant, Jesus was here portrayed as the victim of an evil Jewish conspiracy. When the American Jewish Committee issued a scholarly analysis of the rock opera showing its scriptural distortions and potential for harm, two of America's major drama critics leveled allegations of censorship against the committee for exercising its own critical right to point out that the film was repeating, reinforcing, and rhythmically proclaiming the world's oldest anti-Jewish canard.

A new era in the media and the arts (to focus on only one of many general areas for the purpose of specific examples) had already seen the introduction of an unflattering stereotype, the "Jewish Princess"; noxious cartoon books, one even marked, "Approved by the Elders of Zion"; and "lovable" television bigots—all clearly outdoing the vicious "stage Jew" of yesteryear who had died in his creators' shame when America had first grown up to recognize the heinousness of hate. The new acceptability of ancient prejudices symbolized the turn of events in which Jews began to feel something of a slippage in security, if not an open siege.

They sensed that their concern and the focus of their protective interest in the future would necessarily involve some redefining of traditional notions of anti-Semitism and a serious reorientation of long-held convictions about the nature of its sources. The new definition would have to include an attitude which can properly be described as *insensitivity,* or callous indifference, to Jewish concerns or to Jewish security, evidenced, as touched on above, in expressions or other behavior on the part of respectable institutions or persons who would be shocked to be thought of as anti-Semitic.

The prime manifestation was perhaps an indifference even to the old-style, blatant anti-Semitism itself. It was with near disbelief that the American Jewish community read November 1969 news stories reporting a federal grant for the construction of part of a road leading directly to certain tourist projects—including an anti-Semitic passion play—sponsored by the late Gerald L. K. Smith in Eureka Springs, Arkansas. The issue was not Smith, who had been spurned and ostracized for decades, nor his rabid Jew-baiting, which had ceased to be attention-getting, but rather the fact that Smith was to be the recipient of United States government largesse for his activities. It was almost inconceivable to those who had been watching with growing concern the acceptance of the local Smith "projects" by the good people of Eureka Springs, who appeared able to overlook all but the potential for profit that a Gerald Smith could bring to their town. The callousness extended to Arkansas' governor, to its two rather distinguished senators, and to the secretary of commerce of the United States, all of whom enthusiastically endorsed the government expenditure, albeit with pious disclaimers about the sponsor himself. "While I do not agree with the views expressed over the years by Gerald L. K. Smith," began a plea on behalf of the subsidy written to a constituent by then-Senator J. William Fulbright. In the terminology of an insensitive era, viciously expressed hatreds could be described as "views" and regarded as no obstacle to their author's receiving benefits from the public treasury.

The government's road grant was eventually canceled for reasons unrelated to the issue of bigotry—and Gerald L. K. Smith died in 1976—but both the Smith Foundation's tourist projects and the indifference that had made them successful continued to thrive.

The Brooklyn coordinator of a minority teachers' association in New York, another recipient of federal grants, appearing on a radio discussion program in December 1968, read a poem which began (and continued in the same vein): "Hey, Jew boy, with that yarmulke on your head/You pale-faced Jew boy—I wish you were dead." The president of the poem reader's association stated that he found "no anti-Semitic overtones" in the poem, and shortly thereafter another spokesman of the association, speaking on the same radio station, said of Jews: "As far as I'm concerned, more power to Hitler. He didn't make enough lampshades out of them." The significance of the episode, in terms of what was happening in America, was not the fact that bigots still think and speak evil, but that (in this instance, which tells something of the climate) the federal government was hesitant even to reconsider its grants, and the highly regarded "educational" radio station rationalized the opening of its microphones to the evil by arguing that anti-Semitism exists and that it cannot, through self-censorship, be shut out from our hearing.

In 1948, after history's fiercest fires of anti-Semitism, Jewish hope and health were reborn in the rebirth of the homeland in the State of Israel. In the wake of the Nazi nightmare, the question asked by a whole people, Where are the persecuted to go?, had been answered. In the quarter century thereafter Jews the world over acquired a deep and abiding commitment to the survival of Israel. In America, as throughout the Diaspora, Jews became and remain convinced and resolved that, whatever legitimate controversies may exist in the Middle East, Israel's continued existence as a sovereign Jewish state is non-negotiable. Propaganda manifestos or scholarly disquisitions advocating the dissolution of this sovereignty in any manner, or equating Israeli defense with Arab assault, are seen by American Jews as attacks against themselves and World Jewry. They feel that their own security and their only hope for survival as a people depends in large measure on the survival of Israel; thus they tend to perceive activities supporting those sworn to eradicate the Jewish state as (still another changed aspect of the definition of anti-Jewishness) the *ultimate anti-Semitism.*

This is not to say that such activities developed in America without a linkage to the more traditionally defined forms of anti-Semitism. Early in the Middle East conflict the Arab states acted upon the realization that world support for the State of Israel was centered in this country—both in the commitments of the United States government and in the active will of American Jewry. In the early 1950s the Arab League began building a network of information centers throughout the country. Over the years these centers, and Arab embassies as well, distributed blatant anti-Semitic tracts along with extremist political propaganda, and on a number of occasions worked with gutter-level anti-Semites in "anti-Zionist" activities.[8]

This alliance fed the fires of professional anti-Semitism with international political fuel, and some of those who had been attracted for one reason or another to what may have seemed legitimate political issues were hypnotized by the flames. One can, of course, be unsympathetic to Israel's position on specific matters without being anti-Jewish. But published and spoken anti-Israel sentiments from non-Jewish sources, often the most respectable, all too often also carried an anti-Jewish message.

On Palm Sunday in 1972 one of America's most renowned liberal clergymen, the dean of the National Episcopal Cathedral in Washington, basing his sermon—in the Palm Sunday tradition—on Jerusalem, assailed Israel as its "oppressor" and linked the alleged oppression to the "fatal flaw" in mankind which brought about the Crucifixion. Politicizing the "deicide" canard, the dean declared: "Now the Jews have it all [Jerusalem]. But even as they praise their God for the smile of fortune, they begin almost simultaneously to put Him to death."

Many church groups which had been notoriously silent throughout Jordan's twenty-year illegal occupation of Jerusalem's Old City, during which the sacred Western Wall and other holy places were barred to all Jews (and to Christians in Israel), now revived the notion that Jerusalem should be internationalized—as though there was something odious about Jewish sovereignty over Judaism's holiest city, a city in which Jews had always maintained a presence and in which they had constituted the majority of the population for more than a century. A noted liberal church organization published an "even-handed" document dividing the blame for the Middle East conflict between the Jews and Arabs equally, but burdening Israel with the entire responsibility for making peace.[9] A Jesuit priest prominent in the American anti-war movement described Israel to his audiences as "a criminal Jewish community."

Biased slurs against Israel on a political level, however painful to Jews, were none the less political, but slurs against Jews *as Jews* had to be (but so often were not) recognized for what they were. Allegations of American Jewish "dual loyalty" (suggesting disloyalty) were freely aired over the nationwide CBS radio network in September 1973 by a commentator who termed the question he raised "a touchy issue that American Jews don't like to talk about. . . . The issue is whether you are an American first and a Jew second and, if forced to choose, which commands your loyalty first." (No one, of course, thought to ask just when, or by whom, American Jews are going to be *"forced* to choose.") The commentator also told his network audience that when someone suggested that the United States change its policy in the Middle East, "the pro-Israeli propaganda machine in America *crucifies* him in public" (emphasis mine).

The same implications became slightly more notorious when expressed some years later by Spiro Agnew, once vice president of the United States, who stated that American policy in the Middle East was "less than even-handed" because "as you look around in the big-news business, you see a heavy concentration of Jewish people." The notoriety, however, was due to the fact that the media had opened their microphones to the former vice president only when they scented sensationalism in such tasty fodder for controversy. At about the same time there surfaced a complaint from the chairman of the Joint Chiefs of Staff of the United States that the Jews "own, you know, the banks in this country, the newspapers," and that there was too much pro-Israel influence on Congress. The significant thing to note in this case, with respect to influence and power, was that the officer in question, General George Brown, was subsequently reconfirmed for the highest military post in America for an additional two-year term after these remarks had been made public.

An example of the change in perception of the Jew was seen in the heavy component of pro-Arab propaganda specifically denigrating American Jews which began to emanate from political extremists, particularly those of the totalitarian Left (traditionally the self-proclaimed advocates of the abused and persecuted), appealing to large segments of America's youth in the early 1970s. At the 1971 national convention of the spearhead group of the radical Left in America, the Trotskyist Socialist Workers Party, a Middle East resolution was introduced via a report which stated that "the major task confronting American revolutionists remains that of educating and radicalizing youth about the real history of the Zionist movement and the revolutionary character of the Palestinian and Arab struggle for *destruction of the State of Israel*" (emphasis mine). The party's newspaper in 1970 had published an official al-Fatah document calling for the dismantling of Israel and adding: "Jews contributed men, money and influence to make Israel a reality and to perpetuate the crimes committed against Palestinians. The People of the Book . . . changed roles from oppressed to oppressor."

Indeed, when the Jew was no longer perceived as a victim, however false the perception might have been, all hell could break loose.

Historically, the United States provided that society in which Jews received acceptance and opportunity to a degree without parallel in any other. And while the ancient disease of prejudice was met by no demonstrable cure in the decades following World War II, as indicated earlier, the organized and violent forms of anti-Semitism were condemned and ostracized by the public will and conscience. But clearly the things that hurt, the things that endanger, are not always either organized or violent. A redefinition of the problem is necessitated by the realization that the public conscience might have been subsequently dulled by the very gains made by the Jewish people, by the winning style of the Jewish state, and by the receding of the Holocaust into history. In 1974, I tried to create a new definition of the term in a joint effort with Benjamin R. Epstein, *The New Anti-Semitism.*

We were not, we reported, concerned with the Gerald Smiths and the hooded Klansmen of the world. Our concern was twofold: (1) harmful anti-Jewish fallout from actions or positions of otherwise responsible people, predicated upon their insensitivity or indifference to the rights and security of Jews; and (2) actions or positions which, if sustained or implemented, would result in the destruction of Israel as a Jewish state. These were the elements which constituted a new definition. These are what anti-Semitism clearly would be in the years to come.

A need for a reexamination by Jews of their own position may also be indicated—if only by the sharing of the new indifference and insensitivity among some Jewish commentators who, in an often chic escape from Jewish identity, would see any danger to Jewish peoplehood as no danger at all.

An old Hasidic story may serve as an epiphany of understanding—that of the student who says to his rabbi: "O master, I love you."

The rabbi responds with a question: "Tell me, do you know what hurts me?"

The young man, bewildered, says: "Why do you ask me such a confusing question when I have just told you I love you?"

The rabbi shakes his head. "Because, my friend, if you do not know what hurts me, then how can you truly love me?"

Anti-Semitism in America, no longer a Hitlerian reversion to medieval nightmare, was still perhaps, in the third quarter of the twentieth century, a lack of understanding of the hurt for not being able to feel it.

NOTES

1. Oscar Handlin, *American Jews: Their Story* (New York: Anti-Defamation League, 1976), p. 38.

2. Raymond Franzen and Louisa Franzen, *Studies of Anti-Semitic Prejudice*, unpublished mss., June 1949. Tables and summaries of the Franzen and American Jewish Committee studies were published in the present author's *A Measure of Freedom* (Garden City, N.Y.: Doubleday, 1950).

3. Charles Y. Glock and Rodney Stark, *Christian Beliefs and Anti-Semitism* (New York: Harper and Row, 1966), p. 103.

4. *Ibid.*, p. 208.

5. *Ibid.*, p. xi.

6. Gertrude J. Selznick and Stephen Steinberg, *The Tenacity of Prejudice: Anti-Semitism in Contemporary America* (New York: Harper and Row, 1969), pp. 184, 185.

7. This and other illustrative examples presented here are documented in Arnold Forster and Benjamin R. Epstein, *The New Anti-Semitism* (New York: McGraw-Hill Book Co., 1974).

8. The Anti-Defamation League maintained ongoing research into Arab anti-Semitic activities in the U.S. See ADL *Facts*, vol. viii, no. 4, April 1953; vol. 14, no. 2, February 1961; vol. 16, no. 4, July 1965; unnumbered, August 1967.

9. *Search for Peace in the Middle East* (Philadelphia: American Friends Service Committee, 1970). For a refutation, see Arnold M. Soloway with Edwin Weiss and Gerald Caplan, *Truth and Peace in the Middle East—A Critical Analysis of the Quaker Report* (New York: Friendly House Publishers, for the American Jewish Congress and the Anti-Defamation League of B'nai B'rith, 1971).

S. Andhil Fineberg ─────

JEWISH-CHRISTIAN RELATIONS

This discussion will examine the developments in relations between American Christians and Jews that have occurred since World War II. It will not be essentially concerned with anti-Semitism (the subject of the previous chapter), for fears for the future of the Jewish community in the postwar period did not spring primarily from anti-Semitism. Jewish survival was instead threatened by alienation from Judaism, a declining birthrate, and the frequency of intermarriage in a highly assimilative environment. In 1968 a conference of the National Community Relations Advisory Council declared that anti-Semitism "is not at present a principal source of danger to the welfare of the Jewish community nor that of individuals."[1] Surveys likewise found anti-Semitism at a low ebb after a decade of fear aroused by anti-Semitic agitators.[2] Though anti-Semites could not be eradicated, American Jews believed, as Elisha did in his day, that "they that are with us are more than they that are with them."

If American Jews had become outcasts, the disaster would have been glibly explained by historians as the inevitable consequence of the importation of Nazi anti-Semitism, the tensions of the civil rights struggle, the turmoil of the 1960s, the frustrating war in Vietnam, Communist, Arab, and Third World propaganda, the two economic recessions after World War II, and other catastrophes. Explanations of Christian-Jewish relations usually disregard the wise or unwise efforts that were deliberately made to maintain or to alter these relations.

That at various times and places Jews were totally helpless is true. But although some cried *Tut nichts, der Jude wird verbrannt*[3] and were certain that if Jews were doomed they could not save themselves, American Jews and their Christian friends in recent decades have made unprecedented efforts to thwart anti-Semites by building good relations between their respective groups. Religious institutions took part in this multifaceted endeavor, but the major role was played by secular and nonsectarian organizations, including Jewish community relations organizations.

"Good relations" between two groups does not imply that the members of one harbor no prejudices against the members of the other. Good relations exist when, in the main, both groups are respected and when their members do not suffer unfair discrimination in dealing with each other. Judging by the extent to which Jews achieved economic, academic, artistic, and political success, were welcomed in nonsectarian organizations, lived in neighborhoods of their choice, and enjoyed equality in other ways, we may conclude that Jews and Christians accepted each other freely as fellow citizens. By 1945 American Jews had the economic means to improve their relations with non-Jews. They had direct access to highly influential Christians. This was true in religion, education, publishing, film-making, and other areas of endeavor whose output affects public opinion. Jews did not own or control a large share of the communications industry. But the Jewish community included many prominent individuals who were, or knew, the "right people" to deal with Jewish issues. Though "court Jews" are now scorned along with "Uncle Toms," they secured many rights and privileges for their fellow Jews, such as permission to build synagogues, acquire cemeteries, and slaughter animals according to Jewish ritual.[4]

The American Jewish Committee, as its name suggests, was composed originally of the most elite Jews. The Committee, which was the first "civic protective" organization and, in fact, the first human relations organization formed in the United States, consisted for many years of a few hundred influential Jews. The fact that in the 1940s its membership increased twenty times while other "defense" organizations also acquired enormous followings, manifested the demand of the Jewish rank and file to participate in making decisions affecting their relationship to Christians.

A lasting effect of the fear aroused in American Jews in the 1930s by what was happening to German Jewry and by domestic anti-Semitic agitators was the expansion and strengthening of the American Jewish Committee (founded in 1906), the Anti-Defamation League of B'nai B'rith (1913), the American Jewish Congress (1917), and the Jewish Labor Committee (1933), known at the time as "the Big Four."[5] These "defense" agencies were the keystone of the National Community Relations Advisory Council (1944) which in 1975 included nine national and one hundred local organizations, all of which had become known as community relations organizations.

That American Jews considered these organizations effective is indicated by the increase of their annual income from $4.5 million in 1945 to more than $19 million thirty years later.[6] By 1975 the number of national organizations that the *American Jewish Year Book* classified as "community relations organizations" had increased to twenty-two.

The change of terminology from "defense" and "civic protective" to "community relations" was significant.[7] Like the name "Anti-Defamation League," "defense" and "protective" suggested combatting enemies; "community relations" implied cultivating friends. The difference in these approaches was crucial. For centuries Jews seriously misunderstood the nature of prejudice. Consequently, the "disproof" method was considered indispensable. It was esteemed as the most effective way to prevent the deterioration of Christian attitudes toward Jews. To "answer the charges" by providing refutation for every canard was the chief defense. [8] A series of leaflets, "Anti-Semitic Lies Exposed," published in the late 1930s by the Woburn Press of London, included such titles as *The White Slave Traffic, The Kol Nidre,* and *International Finance.* In 1944 the president of the ADL published a book whose purpose was indicated in these lines: "The forgeries, libels and calumnies used by anti-Semites to engender hatred against the Jews must be denounced and stigmatized whenever and wherever they rear their ugly heads." Although the author complained that "libels and fictions that support hatred against Jews refuse to die though exposed time and time again," he republished many of them with refutations. [9] The urge to answer every anti-Jewish allegation has persisted, but in the past thirty years no community relations organization has published a compendium of such scurrilities.

American Jewish tactics in combatting enemies and cultivating friends among Christians were influenced by the disastrous *Selbstverteidigung* of German Jewry. The Central-Verein Deutscher Staatsbürger Jüdischen Glaubens, German Jewry's sole defense organization, from its inception until its dissolution, clung to a naive faith in answering "charges" against Jews and libel suits as instruments for silencing hostile Christians.

The effect of winning libel suits against defamers was exemplified by the case of Julius Streicher and Karl Holz, who were tried for alleging that "Judaism encouraged deception, sexual abuse and ritual murder of non-Jews." They were found guilty and sentenced. "And yet," wrote the author of a well-documented study of over three hundred suits by Jews against their detractors in the Weimar Republic, "as they emerged from the courtroom they were greeted by a great throng of tearful sympathizers shouting, 'Heil!,' singing racist songs and carrying on so passionately that observers could only wonder whether the trial had not won new converts to the Nazi cause." [10]

The American Jewish organizations decided that Christians could be immunized against hate-mongers' harangues if the Jews allowed them free speech but made bigotry unpopular. Although the Jewish War Veterans of the United States continued to urge the adoption of group libel legislation, all the other Jewish organizations gauged Christian reaction correctly. They avoided the backfire of libel suits and the pitfalls of group libel legislation. [11]

Another error that American Jews avoided was recognition of the so-called Jewish problem. Having accepted George Washington's assurance that they were not living in the United States by toleration or indulgence but by right equal to that of any others, they dealt with problems and issues resulting from the needs of a minority religious group but never as though the Jews were a "problem." *Kashrut*, observing the Sabbath on a day other than the Christian Sunday, religious exercises in the public schools, ritual slaughter, and the like, presented problems that would not have arisen without Jews, but these problems did not present themselves in the framework suggested by "the Jewish problem" or "the Jewish question." Louis Marshall, a founder and president of the American Jewish Committee, declared: "We do not recognize the existence of a Jewish question in the United States."[12] It is a short step from "the Jewish problem" to "the Jews are our problem." Apparently Germany's Jews and others, for whom these were and still are favored topics for learned discussion, did not perceive the semantic implications.

Customarily *Deutschen* and *Juden* were put into juxtaposition by Jews as well as by Christians, as though they were mutually exclusive terms. Jews who proudly claimed that they were devoutly German used terminology that made "Jew" and "German" antithetical.[13] In the United States the comparable terms were always American Christians and American Jews. Indeed, Jews fiercely rejected the idea that the United States is a Christian country.[14] Increasingly in the past thirty years the nation's heritage, culture, and tradition have been called "Judeo-Christian."

The organization that propagated the term Judeo-Christian was born in 1929. The National Conference of Christians and Jews expressed its purpose in this statement:

Believing in a spiritual interpretation of the universe and deriving its inspiration therefrom, the National Conference exists to promote justice, amity, understanding and cooperation among Protestants, Catholics and Jews and to analyze, moderate and finally eliminate intergroup prejudices which disfigure and distort religious, business, social and political relations, with a view to the establishment of a social order in which the ideals of brotherhood and justice shall become the standards of human relations.[15]

Although the National Conference of Christians and Jews (NCCJ) was formed by the Federal Council of Churches, a Protestant organization, to dispel the miasma of anti-Catholic bigotry that shrouded the presidential candidacy of Alfred E. Smith, it quickly acquired the support of eminent Jews. Before long there were "round tables" of the three faiths in most large urban centers and in many small cities and towns. Liberal and Conservative rabbis and Protestant clergymen participated in dialogues, and some exchanged pulpits. For many years Catholic participation was limited to the laity, but a few Catholic priests were in the forefront of the goodwill movement from its inception. Orthodox rabbis and Catholic clergy were generally skeptical, fearing that intermingling would contribute to conversion and intermarriage.

The NCCJ scrupulously avoided religious conversion. In its policy, programming, and activities, no religion was ever considered superior to another, since such thinking would be an ingredient of prejudice. The keynote of NCCJ's appeal has always been that the brotherhood of man under the Fatherhood of God cannot become a reality without goodwill and understanding across religious lines.

The brotherhood movement, sustained by the NCCJ, presumed that attitudes could be changed by bringing people into friendly association in which they would learn to appreciate each other despite religious differences. To reduce prejudice, knowledge was supplied about the beliefs, practices, and aspirations of other groups. "One God: the Ways We Worship Him" was a typical theme of the quest for brotherhood.[16] In February 1943 and annually thereafter Brotherhood Week was observed as a period for consecration to the ideals of brotherhood and as a time for appropriate programs.

A fundamental technique pioneered by the NCCJ was "dialogue." In a statement of the National Association of Intergroup Officials, dialogue was described as "the effort of clergy and laymen of the various faiths to explore mutually positions and attitudes that are at variance, eliminating unreal differences, and understanding those undergirded by religious convention and conscience; to clarify issues and to search for workable modes of accommodation, all in the atmosphere of respect and confidence." Altogether unlike the medieval disputations in which rabbis were required to debate in forums where Judaism was certain to be declared inferior to Christianity, the modern dialogue brought mutual respect.

Dialogue brought such statements as this from Christians:

The hostility based on religious differences has been replaced among liberal Christians and Jews by a recognition of the two religions as supplementary. Both are needed. If we are to take a stand against all the powers of the human underworld, the New Testament message of love and the moral realism of the Old Testament with all the greatness of its religious certitude, must be brought to bear against them together.[17]

The idea that "it is God's manifest intent that the Jews and the Christians be inextricably interlocked in the historical process . . . that neither can be saved without the other"[18] was too radical a change in Christian theology to prevail in one generation. To couple Christianity and post-Biblical Judaism as divinely ordained partners ran contrary to Christianity's missionary tradition. A few missions to the Jews continued to operate in the United States. But there were almost no converts. In America there was no such pressure on Jews to become Christians as Jews elsewhere experienced.

Throughout Christian history Jews had been accused of maintaining different standards of conduct for transactions involving Christians and for those with other Jews. The presumption that, if Jews abided by the mandates of their religion, they would deal ethically with Christians was essential for the new relationship. Dispelling xenophobia was necessary. It was accomplished by bringing knowledge of Jews and Judaism to Christians. The need had been apparent for many generations. It led Moses Mendelssohn to write his *Rituellgesetze der Juden* in 1778 to convey a basic knowledge of Jewish law to non-Jews.[19] The Fischer Verlag in Germany and the Woburn Press in Britain published information about Judaism for Christians. But the tone of these publications was defensive; the writers assumed that the readers were prejudiced.

The literature promoted by the NCCJ and the American Jewish organizations about Jews and Judaism was not apologetic. The authors assumed that the readers had a friendly interest. The books, pamphlets, and magazine articles were fitted to a variety of audiences, ranging from elementary school children to mature scholars. *What is a Jew?*, *What Do You Know About the Jews?*, *Jewish Religious Life in the United States*, and *Jews in American Life* were typical titles.[20]

On Jewish holidays explanations of the observance appeared in the mass media, along with messages of goodwill from prominent Jews and Christians. Christians learned the awesome significance of Rosh Hashanah and Yom Kippur and about the *seder* at Passover. Hannukah became a companion to Christmas in the mass media.

The ecumenicism that sought to remove the rough edges of Jewish-Christian relations was welcomed by liberal Christians and among Reform and Conservative Jews. Orthodox Jews were timorous. It is not surprising that refugees were skeptical. They assumed that any indication of anti-Semitic feeling, such as the desecration of a cemetery, proved that the floor under Jewish-Christian relations was collapsing. But all the while anti-Semitism was becoming so unfashionable that those who harbored it denied their anti-Jewish bias. This was especially true among clergymen. Anti-Semitism was branded un-Christian. In keeping with the spirit of interreligious brotherhood, a study of Protestant textbooks was made with the cooperation of their publishers to ferret out and discard aspersions on Jews and Judaism and to present both in a favorable light. Much less ambitious studies were made of Catholic textbooks.[21]

In both Protestantism and Catholicism something occurred after World War II that had never happened before. The image of the Jew as worthy of respect replaced the image of the contemptible Jew. It has often been said that the horror of the Holocaust aroused such great compassion that it changed the non-Jew's attitude toward Jews. Yet previous massacres had no such effect. The historical record would suggest that slaughter aroused sadism rather than pity; otherwise, Jewish history would not have been a chronicle of repeated martyrdom. The terrified Jew with the Torah clasped to his bosom, fleeing from a demolished village, had traditionally been considered a sinner, punished for having rejected and crucified Jesus and for crimes of more recent invention, including alleged ritual murder.

Statements emanating from the Roman Catholic Church's Vatican Council II deplored persecution of Jews but did not mention the Holocaust. Bishops at the council who had participated in interfaith dialogue worked vigorously, against strong opposition, for the adoption of the Declaration on the Relation of the Church to Non-Christian Religions, which included a statement on the Jews. The Declaration was proclaimed by Pope Paul VI on October 28, 1965. Although the reaction of American Jews ranged from qualified enthusiasm to bitter disappointment, the declaration decried anti-Semitism and proclaimed that what happened to Christ cannot be charged against all the Jews then alive nor against the Jews of today. "Although the Church is the new people of God, the Jews should not be presented as rejected or accursed by God, as if this followed from the Holy Scriptures." This statement, finally adopted by a vote of 1,770 to 185, was the result of determined pleading by American and other liberal bishops against opponents who preferred no statement or one that did less to remove the stigma of deicide from the Jews.[22]

The results of the declaration will appear only in the course of generations, but that doors were opened between American Jews and Catholics soon became evident. In 1966 the National Conference of Catholic Bishops in the United States created a Secretariat for Catholic-Jewish Relations, not to win Jewish converts to Catholicism but to eliminate prejudice between Catholics and Jews. Many friendly exchanges followed. An instance was the decision of the congregations of St. Patrick's Cathedral and Temple Emanu-El in New York to conduct a year of dialogue. The rabbi and the archbishop spoke from each other's pulpits.[23] Protestants were not expected to issue documents resembling the Catholic statement on the Jews and the Catholic Guidelines for Relations to Jews. American Jewish clergymen and scholars met in many more sessions and for lengthier discussion with their Protestant counterparts than with Catholics. Occasionally members of the three faiths gathered to discuss mutual concerns. But no source similar to the Vatican and to the National Conference of Bishops existed that could speak for all of the

Protestant denominations. The largest American Protestant body, the National Council of Churches, composed of thirty communions and over forty million members, took prominent positions on social issues and became deeply involved in the civil rights movement. The statements of the Council on these issues were liberal and generally similar to those issued by Jewish organizations, but in regard to the State of Israel the Council disappointed its Jewish friends.

The National Council of Churches and other Protestant authorities insisted that all nations should accept Israel's right to exist, but the Council declared in a statement issued on May 2, 1969: "Equally indispensable is the recognition of Palestinian Arabs to a home acceptable to them which must now be a matter of negotiation." The same support for the Palestinian Arabs was given in a statement issued on October 18, 1973. In deploring the outbreak of renewed hostilities in the Middle East in 1973, the Council assessed blame on neither Israel nor the Arabs. Its divided sympathy between Israel and its Arab enemies evoked alarm in Jewish circles. Again the worth of dialogue was questioned.

In regard to the Jews of the Soviet Union, the position of the Council was more satisfactory. A resolution of February 14, 1972, condemned the harassment and persecution of Soviet Jews and Christians and of intellectual, political, and ethnic dissenters. No mention was made of the right to emigrate, but there was ample evidence on various occasions that American Protestants fully sympathized with the efforts of American Jews on behalf of Russian Jewry.[24]

To maintain good relations with Jews, the National Council of Churches ultimately took a step similar to that of the Catholic bishops. In 1973 the Office of Christian-Jewish Relations was created as one of its ministries, "as an arm of the member communities of the Council." Here the effect of earlier dialogue can be traced. The first director of the new office, an Episcopalian priest, had earned his Doctor of Philosophy degree at the Hebrew Union College-Jewish Institute of Religion.

Another indication of improved interreligious relations at the national level was the formation of the Interreligious Committee of General Secretaries. Since 1970 the secretaries of the National Council of Churches, the National Conference of Catholic Bishops, and the Synagogue Council of America have met several times each year. The gains in the interreligious field were clearly a matter of dialogue, discussion, and education. The changes cannot be ascribed to social action.

At the 1947 plenary session of the National Community Relations Advisory Council (NCRAC) the educational approach to better group relations was defined by the director of the Anti-Defamation League of B'nai B'rith as "the use of all available teaching and community relations techniques to do two things: (1) to create a climate of opinion favorable to the American Creed and unfavorable to prejudice, and (2) to form those basic attitudes on which good human relations are built." Benjamin R. Epstein continued: "In our contemporary society, the individual's opinions and attitudes are formed and hammered into line by the converging forces represented by the newspapers he reads, the radio he listens to, the films he sees, the speeches he hears, and those community institutions with which he comes into contact and of which he is a part."[25]

The educational approach was criticized as altogether ineffective by the director of the American Jewish Congress, who urged that prejudice arises out of discrimination rather than vice versa. David Petegorsky located the problem of all group relations in the failure of American society to achieve complete democracy. The chief fault was racism. Petegorsky called for social action, and the use of "the weapons available to the citizens of a democracy, the ballot box, legislation, judicial enforcement and precedent, administrative regulation, petition, the powers of municipal and state governments, test cases to establish basic principles, pressure on political parties."[26]

In *Action for Unity* Goodwin Watson lauded social action and discounted the educational methods, as Petegorsky did at the NCRAC. Dr. Watson wrote: "Most agencies would be well advised to decrease the amount of time and effort now spent on periodicals, posters, pamphlets, films, radio programs and public meetings devoted to expressions of the idea of good will."[27] A typical attack on efforts to further brotherhood by educational means declared: "The important task of creating and maintaining a productive social atmosphere is not to be accomplished by denying the efficacy of conflict in the advancement of human progress. Nor is it to be achieved through such verbal nostrums as 'unity,' 'harmony,' and 'brotherhood.' "[28] A highly esteemed professor of psychology at Harvard University, Gordon W. Allport, wrote: "Those who wish to improve group relations would do well to engage in a many-pronged attack."[29] But he also wrote in the same chapter that "it is wiser to attack segregation than to attack prejudice directly."[30]

In the two decades after 1947 educational work continued. As has been noted, Jews and Christians continued to deal with attitudes of Christians toward Jews that were not based on discrimination but on misconceptions and hatreds. By dealing with prejudice as an attitude due to religious rivalry and misunderstanding, Jews and Christians had made remarkable progress in what they were saying and thinking about each other's religions and their adherents. Slighting the American Jew as an alien was another matter of thought and emotion, rather than deliberate discrimination. In 1954-55, taking advantage of the tercentenary of Jewish settlement in America, Jews made American Christians aware that, far from being newcomers to these shores, Jews were among the

early settlers and pioneers. The national tercentenary dinner was attended by some 1,800 religious, communal, and civic leaders, with President Eisenhower as guest of honor. Over 400 cities held local observances.[31]

Though the brotherhood movement continued, it received less support after World War II. The theory prevailed that discrimination, rather
than prejudice, should be attacked. Moreover, the focus on intergroup
relations turned from interreligious to race relations. Jews became active
and highly prominent in a coalition of Negro, labor, and religious organizations that supported the civil rights movement and sought to
improve the condition of Negroes, among whom "blacks" became the
preferred designation. The Jewish contribution in funds, personal activity, and expertise was extraordinary. It created some difficulty for Jews in
the South when rabbis from the North marched with Martin Luther King
from Montgomery to Selma, Alabama. Self-protection necessitated more
veiled assistance to the civil rights movement by southern Jews than by
northern Jews, but they made an appreciable contribution. That the
synagogue and home of Rabbi Perry E. Nusbaum in Jackson, Mississippi, were bombed is significant.[32]

The relationship of Jews to blacks in the United States has been unlike
that of any other white group in several respects. The merchants and
landlords in poor black districts were usually Jews and became objects of
harsh criticism that was often unfair and smeared all Jews. The Jews were
the "soft underbelly of the establishment." They occupied positions
most accessible to black aspirants. Yet, more than any other white group,
Jews accepted the responsibility of assisting blacks. Jewish memories of
oppression and their passionate determination to secure justice for all
made most Jews eager to secure dignity and equality for blacks. But
others, and especially blacks, saw it differently. They argued that those
who had suffered oppression owed more to victims of oppression than
others did. Ultra-liberal Jews thought so also. It was equivalent to demanding more assistance for victims of a flood from those who had
emerged from it penniless than from the affluent.[33]

From 1954 to 1968, while barriers of segregation were falling, Jews
enjoyed a gratifying rapport with blacks appreciative of their cooperation in working for racial equality. But when black expectations were
unfulfilled and the civil rights coalition fell apart, the relationship of
Jews and blacks deteriorated. Jews became the targets of militant blacks.
The situation worsened when Jews found it necessary to attack some affirmative action measures which they believed discriminated unfairly
against them.[34]

Having acquired high visibility and leadership roles in the struggle for
black advancement, Jews set far higher standards for themselves than

groups which had not supported the blacks' struggle. Tensions grew with the rapid movement of impoverished blacks from the South into Jewish districts of cities and nearer suburbs, especially in the Northeast.[35] The deterioration of those areas and attendant crime were due to poverty, but the misery in neighborhoods that became "unlivable" caused racial antagonism against blacks. The situation was not altogether bleak. Jews retained some loyal black friends, especially in the National Association for the Advancement of Colored People and the National Urban League. Moreover, the Jewish-black symbiosis, with its mixed emotions, began in the 1970s to melt into the broad white-black relationship.

The struggle for civil rights and liberties that extended through the 1960s and early 1970s was waged for the benefit of "minorities." Blacks were the chief beneficiary until women gained recognition as a minority, while Jews who, prior to World War II, were regularly called a minority group were now excluded from that classification. The loss of minority status deprived Jews of the special protection which, in the view of liberal Christians, minorities deserved. The remarkable change in the meaning of "minority" is best explained by applying this definition, given by John P. Dean: "When the majority group (that is, the dominant group controlling the major sources of wealth and power) considers an out-group to be inferior in status, and manifests this attitude by some kind of differential treatment, a minority group may be said to exist."[36] Dean decided that the Jews were a minority, but that was in 1955. Since then legislatures and courts have accorded benefits to "minority group" members, without granting those benefits to Jews. "Affirmative action" created increasingly divisive situations, although Jewish agencies fully supported measures to overcome blacks' disadvantages, except those that involved quotas.

Numerically the Jewish group was small when compared to the black, and tiny in contrast to the number of women. But Jews were not treated differently from white Christians, although many elite social clubs excluded Jews, as well as blacks, from membership. While individual Jews encountered occasional prejudice and discrimination, Christians assumed that Jews enjoyed the rights, opportunities, and comforts enjoyed by prosperous white Christians. That hundreds of thousands of American Jews, mainly the elderly, had become impoverished did not become public knowledge before 1972. How increasing Christian awareness of poverty among Jews will affect their image of the Jewish group is not yet predictable.

Another development that might have impaired Christian attitudes toward Jews was the mass media's frequent reference to "the Jewish vote." This phrase suggested that Jews voted according to selfish group interests rather than for the good of all the members of the national or local community. The existence of a Jewish vote was denied for generations by perspicacious Jews. Jewish leaders insisted that Jews did not vote as a bloc but cast their ballots as individuals for candidates they believed would best serve the entire electorate. There was a lurking fear that Jewish candidates would suffer if Christians believed they would deal with political issues as Jews, rather than as good citizens.

Jewish attitudes in regard to "the Jewish vote" have changed radically in recent years. Political analysts, journalists, and social commentators made it common practice to determine with more or less accuracy how members of various groups intended to vote or did vote and, in nearly all instances, included the Jewish group in their surveys.[37] Had the Jewish vote alone been publicized or cited as an indication that Jews acted differently than Christians in the electoral process, serious injury to Christian-Jewish relations might well have resulted. But the opinion-molders had abandoned the melting-pot theory and popularized the idea of a pluralistic American culture. The Protestant establishment and the Puritan tradition had few defenders against those who insisted that it would be better for the nation if ethnic groups retained their cultural ties to the lands of their origin.[38]

The right of labor, farmers, veterans, women, older citizens, and other groups to vote each according to its interest was not questioned. A similar privilege was extended to the various ethnic groups in respect to the lands of their origin. It was evidently expected that Jews would consider their interest as Jews, as well as their responsibility as citizens. Candidates sought the favor of many groups and courted the Jewish vote. Predicting how Jews would vote and reporting how they did vote became normal practice. The chief concerns of Jews in the most recent national election were presumed to be Israel and Soviet Jewry. Political parties and candidates were swayed accordingly.

In the 1960s, when the peril of Israel and of Soviet Jewry necessitated strong support on the part of the United States, the need of Jews in foreign lands altered Jewish-Christian relations. It was no longer enough that American Christians regard American Jews as equals, fully entitled to share in all of the nation's benefits. Something more was required by American Jews of American Christians: that they give moral and diplomatic support to Soviet Jews and Israel, as well as approve governmental financial assistance to Israel.

Jewish community relations moved to new ground. All the issues discussed at NCRAC meetings in the 1940s were domestic. The 1974-75 Program Plan presented five domestic and seven international issues. Israel, Soviety Jewry, and the Jews of Syria and of Latin America required diplomatic support. Civil rights and liberties remained on the agenda, along with church and state. Conflict was inescapable if American Jewry refused, as it did, to abandon Jews abroad and the long-range interests of American Jews. The battle in the 1970s was not with domestic anti-Semites; it was with foreign foes, Arabs and Communist nations and their supporters, who took advantage of the fact that, while anti-Semitism was disreputable in the United States, Zionism was a political movement and therefore a legitimate ground for attack. The diaphanous line between Jews and Zionists made it possible to strike at all Jews, while disclaiming anti-Semitism.

The future of Jewish-Christian relations in the United States cannot be wholly determined by Jews. But they can prevent a virulent outbreak of anti-Semitism and retain the advantages of a benevolent atmosphere. To insure the continuance of friendly relations American Jews will need to: (1) avoid the errors of the past; (2) reject prophets of doom; (3) contribute their share to what must be done for the nation's welfare; (4) find allies to deal with each issue; and (5) participate actively in the brotherhood movement.

1. Blunders committed spontaneously by unsophisticated Jews that encourage scapegoating will not be avoided unless Jewish community relations organizations furnish proper instruction. Anyone may debate calumny publicly as though it were honest criticism. Any small group of hysterical Jews may invade an insignificant anti-Semite's meeting and thus bestow publicity and importance on him that he would otherwise never gain.[39] Now that the American Jewish community has acquired expertise in community relations, these skills should be disseminated as well as practiced.

2. All Jews, including Rabbi Meyer Kahane, want Christians to think well of Jews and to respect them. But the founder of the Jewish Defense League can hardly expect Christians to appreciate such sentiments as "So long as one Gentile lives opposite one Jew, the possibilities of a Holocaust remain."[40] That Gentile may be one of the many who are "philo-Semites." Those who destroy their own faith in unoffending Christians and counsel their fellow Jews to trust none should be repudiated. There can be no good relations of any kind—domestic, labor, international, interreligious or interracial—without some faith in the fundamental decency of the other party. For good Jewish-Christian relations, Jews must reject the advice of those who expect Christians to supply all of the good will; it must be reciprocal or it will wither and perish.

3. Even if healing the sick, caring for the needy, and uplifting the fallen, without regard to race, creed, or color, had no effect on others' opinion of Jews, Jews would not fulfill the commandments of their

religion *(mitzvot)* unless they did their share to promote the general welfare of the nation as a whole. That such activity is essential to combat anti-Semitism is generally considered a truism.[41] Jews as individuals will continue to participate in the work of nonsectarian organizations to abolish racism and unemployment, to obtain decent housing and education for everyone, and to defend the rights of all who are deprived. It has been argued that the Jewish community relations organizations should now abandon all their other programs and become "community service" organizations, devoted solely to improving the economic, educational, and social condition of the entire nation.[42] These theoreticians overlook the glaring fact that, in every stage of national development in the United States, some groups have been treated much better than others by their fellowcitizens and that, even if it were true that in a materialistically utopian state prejudice and discrimination would vanish—a debatable theory—that ideal state could not be attained in even three or four more generations. Meanwhile, developments in Jewish-Christian relations could become disastrous.

In the past decade on some occasions lower-middle-class Jews have lamented that the "Jewish establishment" has cultivated the entire national field for the sake of others but neglected its own garden. It is not the duty of Jewish organizations to do all that needs to be done for the entire nation on any score. Neither, however, should they desist from laboring for the common good. Jewish resources are limited. They should not be used selfishly, but crucial Jewish interests should not be slighted.

4. Needless heartache has already been caused, and more will come, unless Jews realize that no allies will always agree on everything. Angry, militant blacks lost many friends for their people when they denounced the liberals who had been the blacks' best friends because they would not support all black demands. It is not advisable to turn scornfully upon those who have been helpful to some extent, and may again become helpful, when they walk only part of the way. It is better to part with respect and find others who will go the rest of the journey.

Blacks, Jews, and other religious groups were allies in the civil rights movement, but blacks did not agree with Jews completely on affirmative action. Nor did Catholics and the major Jewish organizations agree on abortion or on use of public funds for private schools. Most Jews and most Protestants have not seen eye to eye on religious observances in the schools. Nevertheless, there are issues on which Protestants, Catholics, and Jews can and will combine their forces in a joint effort.

The National Conference of Christians and Jews, which is nonsectarian, has supported Israel's claims without reservation. The World Council of Churches and the National Council of Churches, as well as the

Vatican, have denounced anti-Semitism. They defend Israel's right to exist as a nation, but their views on Israel will not satisfy Jewish wishes unless they retract statements already made on behalf of the Palestinians. Secular allies must be found when the religious part company.

5. All Americans became aware of the civil rights movement. How many were aware of the brotherhood movement can only be conjectured. But nearly all felt its influence. Born before the NCCJ, which proclaimed the brotherhood of all people as its goal, the movement was supported by thousands of organizations and institutions and by millions of people who brought education to bear against group prejudices of all kinds.

Brotherhood can easily be eroded by cynicism and skepticism. The brotherhood movement will always need encouragement and renewal. In every program and project, each individual was identified as Protestant, Catholic, or Jew and encouraged to respect all members of all groups and to treat them without bias or discrimination. The elimination of group differences was not sought; what was asked was that these differences be recognized and rendered benign.

The brotherhood movement has brought rabbis and Jewish scholars to countless Christian audiences. Under its influence courses in Jewish studies have been established in many universities and colleges. The catalog of accomplishments is too long for recital. American Jews need protection against prejudice rather than against discrimination. The attempt of Jews to seek enactment of civil rights laws on their own behalf has been negligible. When Jews sought entrance into medical schools and the executive suite they used the method of persuasion. The friends and allies Jews will need in dealing with current issues will be men and women who have felt the influence of the brotherhood movement directly or indirectly.

The developments of the past thirty years have shown American Jews that harmonious relations between Christians and Jews in the United States can be modified by deliberate efforts for good, as they have always been deliberately manipulated for evil. Jewish-Christian relations should never hereafter be left to happenstance.

NOTES

1. *Combatting Anti-Semitism Today,* A report of a conference under the auspices of the National Community Relations Advisory Council, New York, 1968, p. 8.

2. Charles Herbert Stember and others, *Jews in the Mind of America* (New York: Basic Books, Inc., 1966), p. 208. The findings of the authors are based on surveys.

3. From *Nathan the Wise,* by Gotthold Ephraim Lessing.

4. *Universal Jewish Encyclopedia,* vol. 3, p. 385.

5. The staffs of the four "defense agencies" were very small before 1938 and

were expanded greatly in the subsequent five years, as much as tenfold in one instance.

6. The exact figures are in the 1945 report of the Council of Jewish Federations and Welfare Funds and the report of the Large City Budgeting Conference of March 1976.

7. *American Jewish Year Book* 54, 1953, p. 162, note 2.

8. *Universal Jewish Encyclopedia*, vol. 1, p. 406: "The most immediate task of ['the modern defense against anti-Semitism'] is the refutation of the many canards issued by the anti-Semites." Vol. 3, pp. 3-10, supplies canards and "facts," many of which furnish cross-references to other works. For opposition to "refutation," see S. Andhil Fineberg, "Strategy of Error," *Contemporary Jewish Record*, vol. 8, no. 5, February 1945, pp. 25-30.

9. Sigmund Livingston, *Must Men Hate?* (New York: Harper & Brothers, 1944), pp. XIII and XIV.

10. Donald L. Niewyk, "Jews and the Courts in the Weimar Republic," *Jewish Social Studies*, Spring 1975.

11. The fallacies of group libel legislation were exposed in S. Andhil Fineberg, "Can Anti-Semitism be Outlawed?" *Contemporary Jewish Record*, vol. 6, December 1943, pp. 619-631.

12. Quoted by Gerald S. Strober, *American Jews—Community in Crisis* (Garden City, New York: Doubleday and Co., 1974), p. 119.

13. Adolf Leschnitzer, *The Magic Background of Modern Anti-Semitism* (New York: International Universities Press, Inc., 1956).

14. A surprising exception is a book by a rabbi who served as a community relations worker: Arthur Gilbert, *A Jew in Christian America* (New York: Sheed and Ward, 1966).

15. James E. Pitt, *Adventures in Brotherhood* (New York: Farrar, Straus and Company, 1955), p. 37.

16. Florence Mary Fitch, *One God: The Way We Worship Him* (New York: Lothrop, Lee & Shephard Co., 1944).

17. F. W. Foerster, *The Jew—A Christian View* (New York: Farrar, Straus and Cudahy, 1961), p. 153.

18. James E. Wood, Jr., ed., *Jewish-Christian Relations in Today's World* (Waco: Baylor University Press, 1971), p. 139.

19. *Universal Jewish Encyclopedia*, vol. 7, p. 473.

20. The American Jewish Committee and the Anti-Defamation League issued annual catalogs of books and pamphlets they distributed. Films were also made for the educational program.

21. Bernhard E. Olson, *Faith and Prejudice—Intergroup Problems in Protestant Curricula* (New Haven: Yale University Press, 1963).

22. Judith Herschkopf, "The Church and the Jews: The Struggle at Vatican II," *American Jewish Year Book* 67, 1966, pp. 45-77.

23. *New York Times*, 12 February 1975.

24. National Council of Churches of Christ in the United States of America, "Resolution on Violation of Religious Freedom and Human Rights," adopted by the general board on 14 February 1972.

25. Report of the 1947 plenary session of the National Community Relations Advisory Council, pp. 27-31.

26. *Ibid.*, pp. 32-46.

27. Goodwin Watson, *Action for Unity* (New York: Harper & Brothers, 1947).

28. Don Hager, "Blindspots and Brotherhood," *Jewish Congress Weekly*, 24 January 1955, p. 5.

29. Gordon Allport, *The Nature of Prejudice* (Cambridge, Massachusetts: Addison-Wesley Publishing Co., Inc.), p. 514.

30. *Ibid.*, p. 509.

31. David Bernstein, "The American Tercentennary," *American Jewish Year Book* 57, 1956, pp. 101-118.

32. Perry E. Nussbaum, "Mississippi Rabbi Under Fire," *Reconstructionist*, vol. 35, 12 December 1969, pp. 21-24.

33. In the magazine of the National Association for the Advancement of Colored People, this writer held that white Christians were no less duty-bound than Jews to help blacks. See S. Andhil Fineberg, *The Crisis*, February 1969.

34. Nathan B. Jones, "The Future of Black-Jewish Relations," *The Crisis*, January 1975, pp. 18-27.

35. An example of what has happened to many Jewish communities was described by Yona Ginsburg, *Jews in a Changing Neighborhood: The Study of Mattapan* (New York: Free Press, 1975).

36. John P. Dean, "Patterns of Socialization and Association Between Jews and Non-Jews," *Jewish Social Studies*, vol. 17, July 1953.

37. Samuel Lubell, *The Future While It Happened* (New York: W. W. Norton & Co., 1973).

38. Irving M. Levine and Judith B. Herman, *The New Pluralism in Overcoming Middle Class Rage*, Murray Friedman, ed. (Philadelphia: Westminster Press, 1971).

39. The quarantine treatment for deflating anti-Semitic agitators was first described as "the silent treatment." See S. Andhil Fineberg, "Checkmate for Rabble-Rousers," *Commentary*, vol. 2, September 1946, pp. 220-26. This treatment was endorsed by the NCRAC on 17 December 1947.

40. Meyer Kahane, *The Jewish Defense League* (Radnor, Pennsylvania: Chilton Book Co., 1975).

41. A notable statement of this frequently spoken and written concept is to be found in *Bigotry in Action* (an American Jewish Committee pamphlet, 1966).

42. Ann G. Wolfe, ed., *A Reader in Jewish Community Relations* (New York: Ktav Publishing House, Inc., 1975), pp. 275-278.

Erich Rosenthal _____

INTERMARRIAGE AMONG JEWRY: A FUNCTION OF ACCULTURATION, COMMUNITY ORGANIZATION, AND FAMILY STRUCTURE

INTRODUCTION

Fifteen years have passed since I addressed myself to the task of studying the extent of Jewish intermarriage in Washington, D.C., and in Iowa; nearly ten years since a similar report was issued for the state of Indiana.[1] While the findings of these surveys were never questioned, it was observed that they were not representative of the levels of Jewish intermarriage in large Jewish communities. However, subsequent surveys revealed that the earlier findings were indicative of a new trend toward higher levels of intermarriage. At the same time there is some indication that earlier studies had not been designed to catch the full extent of intermarriage. My purpose here is to relate the earlier findings in a more systematic way to social structure and social theory. While the phenomenon of intermarriage has previously been related to the process of acculturation and community organization, the relationship between three types of families—the preindustrial or rural, the companionship or tempered romantic love, and the personality growth—has to the best of my knowledge not been explored.

The Type II family, the companionship family, is the major focus of attention in this essay. There are good reasons for this. In the preindustrial or rural family (which, in the present context, translates into the Orthodox Jewish family) intermarriage is no real issue because of its rare occurrence. Again, in the Type III family, personality growth, intermarriage is no issue because religious background is excluded from consideration in mate selection. Since, in addition, Type III is a quite recent phenomenon, it has not received much scientific study. As the majority of American Jews gave up European patterns of marriage and family and adapted to a highly urbanized environment, the companionship family became the dominant form among them. Since the Type II family was the focus of most family research between 1930 and 1960 there is a great deal of material to which we can relate the phenomenon of Jewish intermarriage.

How do we define intermarriage? In a way, this definition depends on the definition of who is a Jew. If a Jew is considered a member of a religious group, then intermarriage can be defined as a marriage where one partner professes a religion different from that of his spouse. In this case, marriages in which a partner has converted to the faith of the other cannot be considered religious intermarriages. Quantitatively, this definition yields a lower number of intermarriages than if a Jew is considered a member of an ethnic group and intermarriage is defined "as a marriage in which one or the other partner was identified with a non-Jewish religious-cultural viewpoint at the time that he/she met his/her future spouse."[2] Students and functionaries of organized religion may have a greater interest in those intermarriages where a conversion has not taken place, while sociologists and anthropologists are interested in all cases in which cultural and social boundaries have been crossed or disregarded. Since this discussion is designed to incorporate the findings of a variety of empirical studies into a sociological frame of analysis, we will have to accept the various definitions the investigators utilized in their surveys. The terms intermarriage, mixed marriage, and exogamy will be used interchangeably.

THE PROCESS OF ACCULTURATION

As immigrants, Jews encountered economic, cultural, and social barriers. However, in a democratic society where equalizing processes between immigrants and older settlers and between different racial, ethnic, and religious groups are at least not discouraged and at best consciously fostered, these barriers will be lowered with increasing length of settlement. Over time, then, Jews will become "acculturated," that is, less distinguishable from older settlers and other immigrant groups.

Sociologists call this process the "race-relations cycle" to which all immigrant groups have been exposed. Intermarriage is the final stage in this process, which starts with competition and conflict among groups upon initial contact and which ends, after an intermediate phase of accommodation, in assimilation and amalgamation.[3] This process occurs on three levels: (1) acculturation—shedding foreign language, customs, work and leisure-time habits, and adopting new cultural traits; (2) a decrease in social distance between the immigrant group and other groups, and (3) changing feelings of belongingness and group identification.

The most significant phase in acculturation is the birth of each new generation—so that it can be said that each successive generation lives in a culture uniquely its own. The dimensions of these separate worlds have been systematically outlined by Warner and Srole:

The ethnic generation born abroad and migrant to this country (the parental or the P generation) is the one attached most strongly to the ancestral social system and its derivative, the ethnic community in Yankee City, and least to the Yankee City social system.

The offspring of these immigrants, the filial first or the F¹ generation, having been born, reared, and schooled in the United States, know nothing of the ancestral society of their parents except as it is partially represented in the ethnic group's community organization. The members of the F¹ generation acquire wider external relations with the Yankee City society than their parents and bring more elements of American culture into their internal group relations. The children of the F¹ generation, whom we label F², and the children of the F² generation, whom we label F³, exhibit similar progressive shifts in social personality.[4]

These generational differences were confirmed by the results of Bigman's Greater Washington Jewish population survey which found that intermarried families increased from 1.4 percent among the foreign-born, the first generation, to 10.2 percent among the native-born of foreign parentage, the second generation, to 17.9 percent among the native-born of native parentage, the third and subsequent generations.[5] While the cessation of large-scale Jewish immigration to the United States hastened the process of acculturation and accelerated the tendency toward intermarriage, the arrival of European refugees in the 1930s and of Hasidic groups and displaced persons after World War II may have helped to moderate the trend to exogamy.

JEWISH COMMUNITY ORGANIZATION, SIZE, AND DENSITY

If residences of American Jews were evenly distributed over the United States and if mate selection would occur at random—that is, regardless of religious background—the intermarriage *status* rate for Jewish couples would be 98 percent.[6] To stem the familial and social integration or absorption of Jews into the larger community, an elaborate apparatus called "community organization" has been developed which is designed to maintain social and cultural boundaries. Recently, historian Irving A. Agus has made the claim not only that the Jews owed their continuous existence in Europe to the development of community organization but also that the Jews pioneered the art of local self-government before the onset of the Middle Ages. Agus states that merchants assembled "at an important fair. . . would automatically be the most authoritative ruling body known to Jewish law."[7] I was able to catch a last glimpse of the organizing functions of these fairs when I observed the monthly cattle markets in Hesse, Germany, in the 1930s.[8]

In the United States at the present time Jewish community organization involves the employment of specialists such as rabbis, teachers, fund-raisers, and social workers. Within the context of the discussion of intermarriage it appears that community organization has a direct effect on the level of endogamy/exogamy: a well-organized community creates a fairly well-functioning marriage market. I was able to demonstrate this relationship in considerable detail when I systematically compared two small Jewish communities in two small Louisiana towns. One made every effort to utilize community organization while the other showed very little interest. In the latter the marriage rate was very low at the same time that intermarriages were very frequent. By contrast, the former community was much more successful in organizing its religious, cultural, and social life with a high rate of marriages, most of them endogamous.[9]

It will be recalled that during World War II American soldiers who were stationed overseas married foreign women who became known as war brides. It is my opinion that the war brought about a rise in the formation of Jewish intermarriages as men and women were torn from their home communities. It should also be recalled that local Jewish communities made a tremendous effort to organize local USO clubs in order to create an atmosphere of "a home away from home." This effort at community organization—Sabbath meals, dances, Sunday morning breakfasts—may have contributed to keeping the level of exogamy lower than it might otherwise have been.

When lay persons discuss the causes of Jewish intermarriage they often attribute a high level of exogamy to the small size of the Jewish population or to "density," the proportion that a subgroup constitutes of the total population in a given locality. However, size and density become relevant only when the effort to organize the community and the will for group survival have been weakened or abandoned, as was the experience of the Louisiana town mentioned above. That density alone is not sufficient was demonstrated a long time ago in Germany, where the Jewish intermarriage rate was highest in large cities, despite their relatively high density of Jews, and lowest in the hinterland, where a strict Orthodoxy served the thinly distributed Jewish families as a strong barrier against intermarriage.

Once group cohesion is weakened, however, the factor of density operates in the expected manner: the smaller the proportion that Jews constitute of the total population in a given locality, the larger the intermarriage rate becomes. For example, in Indiana between 1960 and 1963 the intermarriage formation rate was 38.6 percent for the five large Jewish settlements and 63.5 percent for those counties where there was only a scattering of Jewish families.[10]

TYPES OF FAMILIES AND INTERMARRIAGE

In the United States we can distinguish between three types of families, each with a specific level of Jewish intermarriage. In this context Type I is the observant Orthodox family with intermarriage virtually near zero. Type II is the companionship family, a category into which most Jewish families—and, for that matter, most American families of all faiths—belong. Jewish families are subjected to the crosspressure between group loyalty which discourages and romantic love which encourages intermarriage. In Type III religious and cultural background factors are disregarded in favor of personality growth, and intermarriage is no longer considered to be a problem. The differences between the three types are outlined in Table 1. I would prefer to speak of three stages of family development, the first leading to the second, and the second to the third. However, since at this time all three stages are extant it is safer to speak of types. Each type is related to a specific stage of scientific and technological development and to a particular phase of capitalism. (For example, totally effective birth-control methods and the welfare state have facilitated the third family type of personality growth and self-fulfillment.)

Table 1. Types of Families

Type I: Preindustrial and Rural Families*

FUNCTION:	Production, consumption, and child rearing
BASIC VALUE:	Economic survival, dowry arrangements
STRUCTURE:	Institution based on mores, law and public opinion: external social pressure
DOMINANCE:	Patriarchal, authoritarian
MATE SELECTION:	Arranged marriages, matchmaking
ELOPEMENTS:	Rare
RELIGIOUS INTERMARRIAGE:	Very rare
DURATION:	Infrequent divorce
MOTTO:	"Matchmaker, Matchmaker, Make Me a Match" *(Fiddler on the Roof)*

Type II: Tempered Romantic Love*

FUNCTION:	Limited consumption, limited child rearing

Table 1 (continued)

BASIC VALUE:	Togetherness supported by homogamy: common *back*ground in terms of race, religion, ethnicity, class, and education
STRUCTURE:	Companionship based on affection, consensus, and common interests: internal social-psychological pressure
DOMINANCE:	Moderately democratic
MATE SELECTION:	Courtship and dating
ELOPEMENTS:	From 10 to 20 percent
RELIGIOUS INTERMARRIAGE:	Occasional to frequent
DURATION:	Frequent divorce
MOTTO:	"My Heart Cries for You!"

Type III: Personality Growth†

FUNCTION:	Further erosion of housekeeping and child rearing
BASIC VALUES:	Personality growth and fulfillment ("To do one's thing"). *Fore*ground is most important; economic equality of women
STRUCTURE:	Unmarried couples, one-parent "families," commune as quasi-consanguine household
DOMINANCE:	Radically egalitarian
MATE SELECTION:	Encounter
ELOPEMENTS:	Rare
RELIGIOUS INTERMARRIAGE:	Very frequent
DURATION:	Temporary alliance
MOTTO:	"Why Can't a Woman Be More Like a Man?" *(My Fair Lady)*

*After W. F. Ogburn, "The Changing Functions of the Family," in R. Winch, *Selected Studies in Marriage and the Family* (Holt, 1968), pp. 58-63, and E. W. Burgess and H. J. Locke, *The Family* (American Book Co., any edition).

†After Paul C. Glick, *Some Recent Changes in American Families*, U.S. Bureau of the Census, Current Population Reports: Special Studies: Series P-23, no. 52 (Washington: U.S. Government Printing Office, 1975).

TYPE I: PREINDUSTRIAL FAMILY

The Type I family was and is prevalent in a large number of rural and preindustrial societies where the transfer of property is needed to furnish the base for a new family unit. In other words, the dowry system and arranged marriages go hand in hand. In the United States, among Jews, the Type I family is still found among Orthodox Jews. According to a recent newspaper report matchmaking "survives in such Old World enclaves as Borough Park, where Hasidic and other Orthodox Jews from communities across the country often seek the services of the Brooklyn matchmaker."[11] The significance of the economic factor in this Type I family is substantiated by these comments: "The girls, they are looking for a *yeshiva* boy, someone who is smart and will make a lot of money and have a good position" . . . "The boys, they are looking for a beauty. Sometimes money helps." This, of course, refers to the dowry. This type of Orthodox family, then, is formed without the presence of romantic love: "You don't have to be madly in love to get married. That comes later." It goes without saying that the matchmaker arranges marriages between Jewish men and women, so that the intermarriage formation rate is zero. It appears, however, that the winds of modernity are beginning to blow into these enclaves and bring about divorces: "Today, the young girls, if they're unhappy, they want a divorce. . . . They don't want to suffer. I tell them women suffer, but they say, 'No, no more.'"

TYPE II: COMPANIONSHIP FAMILY

As mentioned before, the Type II family, the companionship family or "tempered romantic love" is the prevalent family form among the larger (non-Orthodox) sector of the Jewish population in the United States.

The tempered romantic love ideal is a compromise between the excitement of pure romance and the desire for happiness and group survival. The pure romantic love ideal tends to subordinate considerations of race, religion, ethnic origin, or class. In an urban milieu romantic love serves as a basis for mate selection because it facilitates and reinforces the immediate attraction of two comparative strangers. However, the desire for a successful marriage, that is, one which will not terminate in divorce, and for group survival demand that one marry a member of one's own race, religion, or cultural group. Hence the term "tempered romantic love" for the Type II family. The late Ernest W. Burgess, who was the most intense student of the Type II family, formulated it as follows:

"Falling in love" in our society typically takes one of two forms. The more romantic of these is infatuation, or "love at first sight," which is generally associated with notions of one's affinity, of supreme happiness in marriage, and of passionate love overcoming all barriers of culture, class, and prudence. The more prosaic conception is that of love which gradually develops out of companionship and friendship. Here the emphasis is not upon personal beauty, sex appeal, or other external characteristics, but upon congeniality, mutual interests, and comradeship.[12]

To limit the power of pure romance and to increase the likelihood of in-marriage, Jewish communities in large cities in the United States have utilized two major devices and one minor one, namely, the Jewish neighborhood, Jewish education, and organized social activities.

The Jewish Neighborhood

It has been estimated that about 80 percent of all American Jews live in the ten largest metropolitan centers in the country. Within these metropolitan areas, however, the Jewish population is not randomly distributed. On the contrary, at any given time the Jewish population is concentrated in a few specific neighborhoods. A set of institutions to meet the special needs of the group gives these neighborhoods the quality of self-conscious communities.[13] While discriminatory housing patterns contributed their share to enforced segregation of the Jewish population, there is empirical evidence that, in the 1950s at least, the desire for voluntary self-segregation on the part of the Jews was at least as strong. The chief motivation for building a separate neighborhood was fear of intermarriage. As one informant put it, "Parents fear more than anything else and fear more than at any other time in history . . . the marriage of their children to outsiders."[14] The intense drive to settle in a high status area arose from the wish to impress upon the children the *voluntary* nature of the settlement in contrast to the area of first settlement, the "ghetto."

Jews are well aware of the fact that dispersal over a rural—and, for that matter, urban—area increases the likelihood of intermarriage. There are many cases on record where Jews established their residence in a Jewish neighborhood within an urban area although a residence outside the Jewish neighborhood or in the rural area would have been a more efficient or profitable location. There is no way to determine whether the strategy was successful or counterproductive, as in the cases where young people joined the youth rebellion of the 1960s. However, it is likely that any gains from self-segregation were offset by college attendance away from home.

Jewish Education

Exposure to Jewish education is considered to be the second device to help prevent intermarriage. It is believed that young men especially can be kept from marrying outside the group if they have been exposed to a Jewish education, including a *bar mitzvah* ceremony.

In the Washington study, it was found that the relationship between Jewish education and intermarriage differed significantly between the foreign-born and native-born men of foreign parentage, on the one hand, and native-born men of native parentage on the other. Among the foreign-born men the absence or presence of religious education was not, apparently, a significant factor in intermarriage.

Among the native-born men of foreign parentage, those who were exposed to religious education were more likely to intermarry than those who were not. Only further research can reveal the reasons why, for the second generation, Jewish education appears to have had negative results.

For the third generation, however, Jewish education was apparently significant. Of the native-born men of native parentage who had had some religious education, 16.4 percent were intermarried. By contrast, the intermarriage rate was nearly twice as high, 30.3 percent, among men without religious education.[15]

The unexpected finding that in the second generation those who had been exposed to religious schooling had a higher intermarriage rate than those who were not is supported, if only indirectly, by a recent study which investigated the strength of the religious bond on intermarriage. The tentative conclusion was that, in the case of the Jews, it may be the ethnic rather than the religious bond which prevents intermarriage in the second generation.

It appears that ethnic, cultural, and social bonds—expressed in a common language and through voluntary organizations rooted in the "old country" and dedicated to common values and ideals—are much stronger and broader than purely religious ones. Since the ethnic ties of the third generation have been virtually destroyed, a religious bond alone holds the members of the group together. This may help to explain why, in the third generation, exposure to religious education cut the intermarriage rate in half.

The Washington data thus confirms the popular belief that religious education—in the third generation, at least—does serve to check intermarriage.

Organized Jewish Activities

Again, tempered romantic love means to select one's mate freely and spontaneously but within a staged homogamous framework. Numerous profit and nonprofit agencies are involved in arranging the staging. There are "lecture dances" at which enterprising professional or self-styled psychologists give pep talks to the singles and reassure them that when the dance begins they will meet their future mate "tonight."[16] There are dances under the auspices of temples and synagogues, social activities in Jewish community centers, "Singles' Weekends" in Catskill resorts, tennis matches and cruises designed to organize the marriage market for special groups such as Jewish college graduates, young single people, and divorced and widowed men and women within a specified age range.[17]

The Threat of Divorce

There was and may still be a widespread belief that religious intermarriage is bound to lead to failure, that is, divorce. A more scientific formulation would be that religious intermarriages yield significantly larger proportions of divorce than do in-marriages. This common-sense "sociology" is not supported by scientific evidence. Despite the gravity of the issue, very few studies have attempted to find an answer, and these few were designed too poorly to warrant serious attention. Nevertheless, tracts issued by various denominations and advice given by clergymen to their young parishioners warned of the danger of intermarriage. "Marriage between partners of similar backgrounds is difficult enough," so the argument ran.

Sociologists do not agree with this statement. To the question, "How great are the chances for *success*?" (italics theirs), sociologists Bossard and Boll replied: "That is the most difficult question of all to answer, for no one knows."[18]

Burgess, as a professional sociologist, knows that it is wrong to state categorically that religious and cultural differences between bride and groom *must* lead to marital failure:

Religion may be either a highly integrating, or a neutral or a disintegrating influence. It is generally highly integrating where religious values are of predominant importance to both members of the couple. Conflict over religion appears to be equally as disintegrating in its effects.

Cultural backgrounds may be either an integrating, neutral or disintegrating factor in marriage. Wide differences in cultural backgrounds are generally disintegrating, sometimes neutral; but for those who place a high value on individualization and variety they may be an integrating influence.[19]

While there is, then, no empirical data to support the widely held belief that religious intermarriage leads to frequent divorce, there is considerable, though not perfect, evidence that the opposite relationship holds true, namely, that previous divorce leads to subsequent intermarriage. My analysis of marriage licenses in Indiana shows that in cases where one or both partners had previously been divorced the intermarriage rate was 67.7 percent, that for both partners "first married" it was 39.6 percent, and for partners one or both previously widowed it was 18.8 percent.[20]

Several, but by no means exhaustive explanations are suggested for the tendency of previously divorced persons to intermarry subsequently: there are individuals whose first marriage was an intermarriage which terminated in divorce and who subsequently entered a second intermarriage. It would appear that for them religious boundaries had a low value. It is safe to assume that in the marriage and divorce data analyzed there are a number of such cases. Their precise number cannot be determined since the marriage license form does not give any information on the endogamous/exogamous nature of the first marriage.

Then there are individuals whose first marriage was endogamous. It is safe to assume that in many cases family and community pressure contributed to the choice of a mate who belonged to the same religious group. However, differential social mobility among such couples led to a divorce and subsequent intermarriage for the more mobile spouse. The perusal of wedding notices and obituaries suggests such a pattern among highly upwardly mobile individuals. For some persons involved in an endogamous first marriage religious homogamy did not compensate for other cultural differences or personality conflict. A subsequent intermarriage may be entered into in the hope that greater compatibility, personal satisfaction and happiness will be achieved.

At one time it had been assumed that the relatively high frequency of intermarriages among remarriages was the result of the limited supply of eligible mates. In the light of the current findings such an explanation is too simple. Just what the role of supply and demand does play in the formation of intermarriages and whether the explanations presented above do hold can only be ascertained by future research.[21]

Secular Education

It may bear repeating that American Jews have attempted to insure group survival through voluntary segregation in a high status area with a modicum of Jewish education and heightened self-consciousness. At the same time American Jews have a penchant for exposing their children to a long period of secular education beyond the high school level.[22] These demands are met by the institution of the college which, in its classic form, attempts to free the young adult from the ties of his immediate family and community in order to foster the full development of mind and personality. The young student is expected to respond to the exposure to new ideas and contact with people of different races, cultures, and religions with a loss of intellectual rigidity, parochialism, and ethnocentrism and, therefore, with a greater readiness for intermarriage. It might, accordingly, be expected that the level of intermarriage is likely to rise with increasing length of secular schooling.

An analysis of the Greater Washington, D.C., data revealed that this expectation held true only for the foreign-born. Among the native-born (of both foreign and native parentage) a different pattern is obtained. Jewish men who had only attended or graduated from college had a higher intermarriage rate than those with graduate training. Among the native-born of foreign parentage 15.6 percent of husbands who had not gone beyond college intermarried, compared with 11.4 percent of those with graduate education. Among the third generation the differential effect of length of education was considerably larger: 37 percent of the men with only undergraduate training were intermarried, compared with 14.9 percent of those with graduate education.[23]

The findings that graduate study lowers the intermarriage rate among the native-born is rather unexpected. In my opinion, the most likely explanations are as follows: Young men who pursue postgraduate training in those professions often characterized as "Jewish" professions (for example, medicine, dentistry, pharmacy, and law) may come from families that are strongly identified with Jewish life. Or, those young men may define their college years as a preprofessional training ground in which exposure to the "liberal arts" is minimal and commitment to preprofessional courses is maximal.

American Jews are not the only group that has experienced the weakening effect of secular education upon group cohesion. A study of a Ukranian-Canadian community which is now in its fourth generation revealed that higher formal education was the "single, most powerful" factor which led to "decreasing ethnic loyalties and involvement."[24]

Exchange of Cultural Backgrounds

To strengthen morale on "the home front" during World War II programs were developed in which Americans of different religious and ethnic backgrounds were brought into prolonged intimate contact. In one such program weekend visits were arranged between Protestant and Jewish college students. The Jewish girl arrived at her friend's home Friday afternoon, sat down to a quiet supper after which everybody retreated to his/her room behind closed doors. The Jewish girl was not upset. On the contrary, she welcomed the cool atmosphere. Two weeks later the Protestant girl came to the Jewish girl's home. The father asked the visitor whether the temperature of the house was comfortable and showed his concern for her welfare during her whole stay. In the same vein, the mother was anxious to anticipate and fulfill the visitor's needs. The Protestant girls loved this warm atmosphere.[25] Now substitute a Jewish man for the Jewish girl and you have the makings of an intermarriage as the following case history will demonstrate.

I am visiting a large typing pool in order to check on an interview schedule I designed. I say to the secretary who is doing the graphic work, "I wish I knew how to transliterate Shavu t." Thereupon somebody says, "Why don't you ask the *shikse?*" I look up and around and notice that the lady at the next desk refers to herself as the *"shikse."* She was born in a small town in Minnesota and brought up in the Lutheran faith. In accordance with Lutheran practice she participated in Confirmation exercises at the usual age of fourteen years. One of the questions she will be asked is, "Will you ever marry a Catholic?" to which she is to reply with a resounding "No." She does not want to commit herself and say no. After consultation with her girlfriend the two decided to resolve the dilemma by keeping quiet when the question is asked. As a young adult this young lady came to New York City and married a Jewish man by whom she had three children, but from whom she has been divorced for a number of years. She loves Jews and all things Jewish. Above all she loves the freedom with which Jews express their feelings. Her Jewish in-laws love her. I ask her whether she has converted to Judaism. "What for?" she asks, "to be indoctrinated again? Once was enough, too much, in fact!"

This case shows that a person may prefer to exchange one's own background for another atmosphere, and that in a multi-ethnic or -religious society the different social climates which distinguish so-called subcultures can and do compete with each other.[26] This devaluation of one's own background foreshadows the Type III family organization in which background factors are considered to be insignificant in a marriage.

Sex Differentials

The substitution of a Jewish man for a Jewish woman was deliberate since, in the Type II family (tempered romantic love), Jewish men marry out of their faith much more frequently than do Jewish women. In Iowa during the 1950s, of all Jews who were intermarrying, 75 percent were men; in Indiana, in the early 1960s, 66 percent were men. There is some evidence that, in the Type II family, Jewish women are more conservative than Jewish men and submit in their attitudes and practices to the pressure for homogamy more readily than men do. While conservative women may resign themselves to spinsterhood, the more adventurous may find a partner across religious and sometimes racial lines.[27] As the Type III family becomes more frequent, Jewish women may feel less pressure to limit themselves to a homogamous marriage.

Elopements

However, even when tempered romantic love is the norm, there are individuals who become involved in pure romance and passion, with the result that concern for similarity of background is defied and family, friends, and neighbors express their disapproval of the match. Such couples overcome these obstacles through elopement, "running away with the unannounced intention of getting married." It was found that elopements accounted for about 13 percent of all marriage licenses in Indiana involving at least one Jewish partner for the years 1960-1963.[28] Among the elopements the intermarriage formation rate was 77 percent, approaching the level one could expect if Jews would select their mates at random.

It still remains to be explained why about one-fourth of those who elope marry within their religious faith. Parents may, of course, object to the prospective son- or daughter-in-law on grounds other than religion. Some elopements may also be spurious: the couple "elopes" with the parents' knowledge and consent in order to escape a formal wedding.[29]

By contrast, the intermarriage formation rate for arranged mar- riages—as measured by interstate marriages with one spouse from Indiana and one from out-of-state—was only 30 percent.

Residential Preferences of the Intermarried

It is an established sociological fact that families and households are never randomly distributed within an urban area. Space allocation can be enforced, as it was in the racial ghetto, or it can be determined by cost of housing, religion, life cycle, and life-style. For example, members of the counterculture would not feel at home and would not be welcome in a middle-class area—such as, say, Bayside, Queens County, New York. The few surveys that have analyzed the residential pattern of the intermarried couples where the non-Jewish partner has not converted to Judaism reveal that such couples prefer some neighborhoods over others. The Washington survey revealed a preference for the Virginia suburbs and Prince Georges County.[30] It is my hypothesis that, in intermarried households with children, it is the husband who deter- mines where the family will settle. If the husband is Jewish, his house- hold will settle in a neighborhood where there is a sizable group of Jewish families, perhaps even a majority. If the husband is Gentile, the mixed family will settle in an area that is predominantly Gentile. Let us first consider the case of the Jewish husband. The Jewish neighborhood offers the children of mixed parentage the greatest amount of protection. If these children are not in church on Sunday, they will not be conspicu- ous; Jewish children do not go to church, either. If they are not at synagogue or temple services on the Sabbath, they share this absence with many Jewish youngsters, thus again avoiding conspicuousness. In public school these children will not be taunted for being half-Jewish. In a Jewish neighborhood the child of mixed parentage is also protected from picking up anti-Jewish attitudes. A few years ago an elementary school boy whose parents—father Jewish, mother Roman-Catholic— had settled in a neighborhood where Jews were in the minority came home spouting anti-Jewish slogans. His parents were very upset and decided to enroll the youngster in a Jewish religious school. When they were told that the boy was welcome at a tuition fee of $300, the parents felt that this was too high a price to pay for this inoculation.

In the case where the non-Jewish husband settles in a Gentile neighborhood, the wife most likely has to conceal her Jewish background in the interest of her children and will have to let the children become integrated in the neighborhood and school life.[31] This differential distribution affects the validity of surveys which try to measure the extent of intermarriage. In Jewish neighborhoods it is assumed that Mrs. Cohen and Mrs. Shapiro "must" be Jewish. In Gentile neighborhoods Mrs. McDougall may find it much safer not to reveal her Jewish background.

TYPE III: PERSONALITY GROWTH

What is personality development in marriage? Burgess, the protagonist of tempered romantic love, recognized the conflict and seemed himself to be torn between a relatively stable family and the fulfillment of personality growth. He conceded that personality development "may be the best criterion of marital success" but that this criterion disregards not only the happiness and stability of the marriage but also the "judgment of society," that is, external social pressure toward conformity. At the same time, he allows that personality growth may be reserved for "exceptional cases," such as great artists and persons of eminence who were either "the products of unhappy homes" or partners to "unhappy marital unions."[32]

Yesterday's artists' colony becomes today's middle-class suburb. Similarly, personality development as a basic value is no longer restricted to the artist or other "outsider." Rather, it has become democratized, that is, widely accepted. The Women's Liberation movement played a major role in spreading and extending the quest for personality growth and self-fulfillment on the American scene. A recent survey of American parents with children under the age of thirteen gives us an opportunity to assess the extent of this striving toward self-fulfillment. It was found that 43 percent of these young families consider self and self-fulfillment top priorities. At the same time, "they deemphasize money, work, family and marriage." The surveyors claim that this "New Breed," better educated and more affluent, has adapted "the new values, born on college campuses in the sixties, to their lives as parents."[33] Unless it can be claimed that specific Jewish values countervail, it is likely that the proportion of Jewish households with children under thirteen years of age is not lower than 43 percent. This likelihood is based on the fact that college attendance has been practically universal for Jewish youth during the past twenty years. It appears likely, then, that as the value of self-fulfillment prevails, Jewish intermarriage is bound to increase.

The increased emphasis on individual self-fulfillment, then, is the first cause of an increased rate of intermarriage. The second cause is that "the judgment of society," to use Burgess' term, has been drastically and forcibly altered. No longer does the romantic impulse have to be restrained within the boundaries of race, religion, class, and ethnicity (in this descending order).

With the outbreak of World War II, many barriers were lowered, if not entirely removed, with the result that all types of intermarriages began to increase. A major factor in lowering the barriers and equalizing the status of Jews, Catholics, and Protestants was the military chaplain. The official code made him responsible for the spiritual welfare of all the men to whom he was assigned, regardless of religion. Thus Christian chaplains would assist Jewish soldiers in organizing Jewish religious services and Jewish chaplains would do the same for Protestants and Roman Catholics.[34] Former chaplains strongly believe that these arrangements helped to lower religious barriers considerably and to engender better interreligious feelings after the war.[35] Another factor that contributed to better Jewish-Christian relations was and is the ecumenical movement, which "emphasizes the spiritual bond linking Christians and Jews, while deploring all persecutions and displays of anti-Semitism."[36] The result is that the representatives of organized religion—rabbis, priests, and ministers—no longer protect the institutional walls as zealously as before and occasionally cooperate in officiating together at a mixed marriage.

The more positive interaction between members of different religions was paralleled and perhaps supported by a simultaneous decline in racial separatism and racism. Again, World War II has had a major effect. Not only did it bring about closer contact between American black soldiers and white women, but it also brought white men into contact with nonwhite women, especially Oriental war brides. Black soldiers were torn from their local communities, where residential and social segregation had been enforced, and spent the war years in areas where such controls were either weak or totally unknown.[37] After the war, efforts were made, through the ecumenical movement, to overcome racial segregation within the churches. At least as significant were school desegregation and the civil rights movement in the early 1960s, which through demonstrations and freedom rides broke down segregation laws. Long-standing laws prohibiting marriage between a white and a black person began to be rescinded in 1948. All such laws were declared invalid by the United States Supreme Court in 1967.[38]

By now the impact of these social forces upon the marital status and living arrangements of the American people can be assessed in quantitative terms. The Type III family has been carefully analyzed by Paul C. Glick, the family specialist of the U.S. Bureau of the Census, in two articles.[39] In addition, the Census Bureau recently published a separate Bulletin on *Marital Status and Living Arrangements* which received considerable attention in the New York and Chicago press.[40] According to

Glick, American family life has experienced two distinct cycles since the end of World War II. Between 1945 and 1960 the institution of the family was held in high esteem with the result that "all but 4 percent of those at the height of the childbearing period eventually married" and that American society experienced a baby boom, a high level of fertility that peaked around 1958. This familistic period was followed by a lowering of the marriage rate and the fertility rate and a sharp increase of the divorce rate, as well as an increase in the number of adults sharing their living quarters with an unrelated adult of the opposite sex, an antifamilistic cycle. According to Glick, these demographic changes reflect changes in "basic underlying attitudes toward conformity with traditional behavior, especially as such conformity comes in conflict with the development of the full potentiality of each member of the family."[41] This antifamilistic era is further characterized by the virtual disappearance of elopements and a sharp rise in illegitimacy, especially among teenagers.[42]

Within the context of this chapter, there arises the question how these antifamilistic tendencies affect Jewish endogamy/exogamy. First, let us consider the effect of the decline in the formation of first marriages (both bride and groom previously single) upon intermarriage. Between 1960 and 1974 the rate of single women, fourteen to forty-four years old, entering a first marriage declined from 112 per 1,000 to 103.[43] This decline of or delay in first marriages was accompanied by an increase in the number and percentage of unmarried couples living together. Between 1970 and 1976 "the number of . . . individuals who shared their living quarters with a person of the opposite sex approximately doubled."[44] It seems reasonable to assume that considerations of cultural and family background are less important for such liaisons than they would be for a proper marriage. To the extent that such liaisons turn into legal marriages, they contribute to a higher level of exogamy. However, one does hear of cases where the liaison is dissolved in favor of a Jewish marriage partner.

Second, attention must be focused on the effect of remarriage upon intermarriage. Between 1960 and 1974 the rate of widowed and divorced women, fourteen to fifty-four years old, entering a remarriage increased from 129 per 1,000 to 151.[45] It will be recalled that the analysis of the Indiana marriage license data revealed a considerable tendency on the part of previously divorced persons to subsequently intermarry. It is safe to assume, therefore, that the recent rise in divorces has contributed to a significant rise in Jewish intermarriages. Of course, there are cases where the divorcée, in order to continue receiving alimony, prefers to live with a man without entering the married state.

During the periods when Type I and Type II families were the only forms of family organization, opposition to religious intermarriage was mild compared to the taboo on racial intermarriages. However, at the same time that the Type III family has been in the ascendance, "there has been a trend . . . toward an increasing tolerance of racially mixed marriages; . . . married couples with the husband's first marriage dating back before 1940 have the highest rate of racial endogamy and those dating back only to the 1950s have the lowest."[46] It appears that the weakening of the taboo on racial intermarriages has softened the opposition of white parents toward religious intermarriage. The film *Guess Who's Coming to Dinner* was released in 1967. It underscored the parental sentiment, "Let's be grateful she is bringing home a *white* man!"

The growth of the Type III family also coincides with the Women's Liberation movement. The quest for self-fulfillment, antifamilistic attitudes and behavior are basic values. The question arises whether these values contribute to the formation of intermarriages. It appears that the leadership of this movement includes many Jewish women. Their participation can be explained by the fact or the feeling that they have experienced discrimination both as members of the Jewish group and as members of the female sex. Their quest for self-fulfillment stresses foreground rather than background, growth potential rather than rootedness, and it stands to reason that adherents to the movement will disregard background factors such as religion, ethnicity, and class and be inclined toward intermarriage.

The reader will recall that in the old-fashioned family structure (Types I and II) elopement was used to deal with matches that were disapproved of by family and friends. At the current stage of family development there is no longer any need to elope. A recent article in the *New York Times* recounts the experiences of judges and justices of the peace during the last several decades. Decades ago it was necessary to elope, to run across state lines to Gretna Greens where one was able to get married instantly without a blood test, waiting period, or other obstacles. The judges recall that couples came to get married in a hurry because of pregnancy, or to give the baby a name, or out of a sense of propriety, "a conviction that unlicensed sex or uncertified cohabitation carried moral and societal stigmas."[47]

While it has no direct bearing on the issue of Jewish exogamy, in order to stress—if such emphasis is needed—how far our society has traveled from Type I and Type II families, the increase in illegitimacy should be recorded here. Although access to birth control devices and abortions have become more readily available between 1960 and 1968, the illegitimate ratio per 1,000 births rose from 53.4 to 97.8 for white women.[48] While the increased occurrence of illegitimacy is unsettling to members of the older generation, they appear to be even more disturbed that it is no longer shameful to bear a child out of wedlock. A woman who lives in a small town in Missouri with a population of 2,658 expressed it as follows:

. . . the poor girls just go ahead and have their illegitimate babies. And they're only children themselves—fifteen or sixteen years old. Even fourteen! Half the time, they don't even know who the father is. But the strange thing—the thing that is so hard for my generation to understand—is this: It's no disgrace. They're not ostracized. Nobody even seems to mind. Not even when the baby turns out to be half black. Or half white. Or whatever.[49]

An examination of the Type III family structure leads to the conclusion that the decline of, or delay in, first marriages, the upsurge of divorces, and subsequent remarriage of divorcés, the relaxation of the taboo on racial intermarriage, and the quest for self-fulfillment are contributing to the rise of Jewish intermarriage.

At its extreme, the Type III family denies the fact that the family is a group and a most important one at that, a group that sociologists have labeled a primary group. Within this frame of mind, religious or class homogamy matters little, if at all.

CONCLUSION

In societies where individualism and democracy are dominant values intermarriage is bound to occur. To minimize the frequency of intermarriage Jewish communities have been trying to keep the frequency low with the help of a "survival" formula consisting of voluntary segregation, residence in a high status area, a modicum of Jewish education, and Jewish group consciousness in the form of Zionism (which is defined as supporting the State of Israel). The evidence presented earlier revealed that secular education, especially a college education with a strong liberal arts orientation, interfered to some extent with the success of this formula that was designed to support the Type II family (tempered romantic love) which emphasized common background factors.

For this type of family the survival formula was probably the best line of defense. However, when the Type III family became dominant in the 1960s, the old formula lost its strength. So far no one seems to have come up with a device that would contain pure romantic love, the stress on foreground factors, sexual freedom, and the devaluation of the family as a primary group. For people who abrogate the institution of marriage and the family, intermarriage is no longer an issue at all.

Historically, American Jewry has experienced three waves of immigration, Sephardic, German, and East European. Genealogical research has come to the conclusion that the earliest group, the Sephardim, had experienced considerable losses by 1840 through intermarriage with Ashkenazic Jews and with Gentiles and through celibacy.[50] Strangely enough, there appears to have been no follow-up on Stern's most important genealogical research. It would be very important to know what has become of the German-Jewish families who settled in the United States before the Civil War. It has been suggested that about half of them are no longer identifiable as Jews today. What we may be witnessing today is the beginning of the social integration of the third and largest wave of Jewish immigrants who arrived after 1880.

APPENDIX

PROBLEMS OF MEASUREMENT

This appendix is offered to show that the measurement of inter-marriage is by no means a simple matter. To count identical objects we must have an operational definition. When it comes to intermarriage two different definitions can be applied. One is as follows: A person is considered and counted as intermarried if he professes a religion differ-ent from that of his fiancée or spouse. Persons who converted to the religion of the spouse in order to create a homogamous marriage are ex-cluded from this definition. Marriage license data procured from local registrars or a state department of vital statistics are of this kind. When people can be interviewed or asked to fill out a schedule, it is possible to define a couple as intermarried if one of the partners was born into another faith. Each research report and—even more so—a discussion of research findings should specify which operational definition was employed.

The extent of religious intermarriage can be measured in two different ways. One is based on the information furnished by marriage licenses which require the bride and groom to state their religions. Such data reveals the *formation* of intermarriages. The other measurement is based on censuses, whether complete enumerations, sample surveys, or com-munity studies. Such data informs us about the *status* of families and reveals the ratio of religiously mixed families to the total number of families.

It is of the utmost importance to distinguish between the formation of intermarried families and the ratio of such families to a total population. Let us assume the existence of a Jewish community of 100 families, each one composed of a Jewish husband and Jewish wife. Each family has two children who marry other Jews. Not only is the formation of intermar-riage zero, but also the proportion of intermarried households enumer-ated in a survey would be zero. Now let us assume that all of the 200 children intermarry, that is, that intermarriage is 100 percent. The number of intermarried households enumerated in a survey will be only 200 out of 300, or 67 percent. Of course, a generation later, when the parents of the intermarried couples have died, the proportion of inter-married households will rise from 67 to 100 percent. As can be seen from this example, any analysis of intermarriage data must make clear whether it deals with marriage formation or family status.

The intermarriage rate is computed by determining the ratio of inter-married families to the total number of families in which one or both partners to the marriage are Jewish. This was the procedure used by the United States Bureau of the Census. It differs from the Canadian practice, which defines the rate as the ratio of intermarried individuals to all Jews who marry.

Since the U.S. Bureau of the Census does not enumerate the religious composition of the population (partially in response to objections raised by Jewish organizations), the organized Jewish community has de-veloped a genre called "the local Jewish population survey" which tries to determine the size of the local Jewish population and the shifts of this population within the area in order to determine new sites for religious and communal institutions. The survey also investigates social charac-teristics in order to align educational, social, and recreational needs. Since most of these surveys were and still are based on lists furnished by Jewish organizations, it stands to reason that such a procedure will yield only a minimum of intermarried households. When Stanley Bigman designed the Greater Washington Jewish population survey in such a manner that each resident in the area had a chance to be included, the intermarriage rate came to about 12 percent rather than the 5 or 6 percent that had been traditional for this type of survey for the last forty years. In other words, a survey which is limited to membership lists does not and should not be expected to yield accurate data about the extent of inter-marriage in a local community.

NOTES

1. Erich Rosenthal, "Studies of Jewish Intermarriage in the United States," *American Jewish Year Book* 64 (New York, 1963), pp. 3-53.
   Erich Rosenthal, "Jewish Intermarriage in Indiana," *American Jewish Year Book* 68 (New York, 1967), pp. 243-264; reprinted in *The Blending American* (Patterns of Intermarriage), Milton I. Barron, ed. (Chicago, 1972), pp. 222-242; partially re-printed in *Eugenics Quarterly* 15 (December 1968), pp. 277-87.
2. Fred Massarik and Alvin Chenkin, "United States National Jewish Popula-tion Study: A First Report," *American Jewish Year Book* 74 (1973), p. 292.
3. Robert E. Park and Ernest W. Burgess, *Introduction to the Science of Society* (Chicago, 1924), p. 736.

4. W. Lloyd Warner and Leo Srole, *The Social Systems of American Ethnic Groups* (New Haven, 1945), p. 30.

5. Erich Rosenthal, "Studies of Jewish Intermarriage in the United States," *American Jewish Year Book* 64 (New York, 1963), pp. 18-19.

6. Paul C. Glick, "Intermarriage and Fertility Patterns Among Persons in Major Religious Groups," *Eugenics Quarterly* 7 (March 1960), p. 35.

7. Irving A. Agus, *The Heroic Age of Franco-German Jewry* (New York, 1969), p. 215.

8. Erich Rosenthal, "Der Viehmarkt," *Der Morgen* 10 (March 1934), pp. 556-59.

9. Erich Rosenthal, "Studies of Jewish Intermarriage. . . ." *Year Book* 64 (1963), pp. 12-14. In a similar vein, a recent analysis of intermarriage data for Canada attempts to relate variations in Jewish exogamy to variations in levels of anomie (lack of social solidarity): Werner Cohn, "Jewish Outmarriage and Anomie: A Study of the Canadian Syndrome of Polarities," *The Canadian Review of Sociology and Anthropology* 13 (February 1976), pp. 90-105.

10. Erich Rosenthal, "Jewish Intermarriage in Indiana," *American Jewish Year Book* 68 (New York, 1967), Table 8, p. 253.

11. Marcia Chambers, "Finding a Find, Catching a Catch for Brooklyn's Orthodox Jews," *New York Times*, 31 January 1977, p. 23.

12. Ernest W. Burgess, *The Family: From Institution to Companionship* (New York, 1945), p. 469.

13. Erich Rosenthal, "This Was North Lawndale," *Jewish Social Studies* 22 (April 1960), pp. 67-76.

14. Erich Rosenthal, "Acculturation Without Assimilation? The Jewish Community of Chicago, Illinois," *American Journal of Sociology* 66 (November 1960), p. 285.

15. Erich Rosenthal, "Studies of Jewish Intermarriage in the United States," *American Jewish Year Book* 64 (New York, 1963), pp. 29-30.

16. For an early detailed description of a "lecture dance," see Walter Bernstein, "Mingle," *New Yorker*, 24 June 1950, pp. 52-61.

17. The afternoon newspaper, the *New York Post*, carries a full tabloid page of advertisements for these activities in its Friday edition.

18. James H.S. Bossard and Eleanor S. Boll, *One Marriage, Two Faiths* (New York, 1957), p. 119.

19. Ernest W. Burgess and Harvey J. Locke, *The Family*, 2d ed. (New York, 1953), pp. 441-442.

20. The evidence is marred by the fact that the marriage licenses do not reveal whether the first marriage was an endogamous one. Erich Rosenthal, "Divorce and Religious Intermarriage: . . .," p. 436.

21. Erich Rosenthal, "Divorce and Religious Intermarriage: . . .," p. 439.

22. Erich Rosenthal, "The Jewish Population of the United States," this book, pp. 25-62.

23. Erich Rosenthal, "Studies of Jewish Intermarriage . . .," *American Jewish Year Book* 64 (1963), pp. 21-24.

24. J. T. Borhek, "Ethnic Group Cohesion," *The American Journal of Sociology* 76 (July 1970), p. 44.

25. The author is not so naive as to believe that every intergroup contact leads to peace and harmony.

26. In some Jewish circles it is assumed that the rejection of one's background is always a result of self-hatred. The case history reported here should remind us that this is not necessarily so.

27. In the thirties native-born women had a "second chance" with the arrival of European refugees. There is some slight evidence that Jewish women are married to black artists, intellectuals, and musicians. This last situation, but perhaps both situations, can be considered cases of "marrying down."

28. A couple was considered to have "eloped if the following conditions were present: (1) the usual residence of both groom and bride is outside Indiana; (2) the birthplace of both groom and bride is outside Indiana; (3) the marriage license is issued in a border county of Indiana; (4) groom and bride are married in a civil ceremony." Erich Rosenthal, "Jewish Intermarriage in Indiana," *American Jewish Year Book* 68 (New York, 1967), p. 248.

29. *Ibid.*, p. 249.

30. Stanley K. Bigman, *The Jewish Population of Greater Washington in 1956* (Washington: The Jewish Community Council, 1957), pp. 124, 126.

31. My hypothesis is not confirmed by the Washington study. Bigman found that the largest proportion of intermarried households with husband Jewish as well as with wife Jewish settled in the same area, namely, the Virginia suburbs. (Source identical with note 30.)

32. Ernest W. Burgess and Harvey J. Locke, *The Family*, p. 436.

33. The General Mills American Family Report, 1976-77, *Raising Children in a Changing Society* (Minneapolis, 1977), pp. 72-74.

34. Samuel M. Silver, *Mixed Marriage Between Jew and Christian* (New York, 1977), pp. 47-48.

35. Although this thesis does not seem to have been tested by scientific means, it appears to be very reasonable. Altogether, the study of the role the military chaplain and the often-related USO operation played in intergroup relations during the war and in the postwar world has been severely neglected.

36. *New Catholic Encyclopedia*, vol. 16, supplement 1967-74 (1974), p. 143.

37. Grace Halsell, *Black/White Sex* (New York, 1972), pp. 135-163.

38. Constance Baker Motley, "The Legal Status of the Black American," *The Black American Reference Book*, Mabel M. Smythe, ed. (1976), pp. 119-121.

39. Paul C. Glick, *Some Recent Changes in American Families*, U.S. Bureau of the Census, Current Population Reports, Special Studies, Series P-23 no. 52 (Washington, D.C., 1975), and Hugh Carter and Paul C. Glick, *Marriage and Divorce*, rev. ed. (Cambridge, 1976).

40. U.S. Bureau of the Census, Current Population Reports, "Marital Status and Living Arrangements: March 1976," Series P-20, no. 306 (Washington: Government Printing Office, 1977). *The New York Times* summarized this report on 20 March 1977, on p. 1 and p. 59; the *Chicago Tribune* featured an article titled "The Changing American Family" by Philip M. Hauser, professor of sociology and director of the Population Research Center at the University of Chicago in its Sunday Supplement of 27 March 1977.

41. Paul C. Glick, *Some Recent Changes . . .*, pp. 1-2.

42. "Times Are Hard for That Old-Time Marrying Judge Waiting for Elopers," *New York Times*, 14 February 1977, p. 32.

Phillips Cutright, "Illegitimacy in the United States: 1920-1968," U.S. Commission on Population Growth and the American Future, *Demographic and Social Aspects of Population Growth*, Charles F. Westoff and Robert Parke, Jr., eds. Volume I of Commission Research Reports (Washington, D.C., 1972), p. 383.

43. Hugh Carter and Paul C. Glick, *Marriage and Divorce*, rev. ed., (Cambridge, 1976), p. 395.

44. U.S. Bureau of the Census, "Marital Status and Living Arrangements . . .," p. 4.

45. Carter and Glick, *Marriage and Divorce*, rev. ed., p. 395.

46. *Ibid.*, p. 125.

47. "Times Are Hard for That Old-Time Marrying Judge Waiting for Elopers," *New York Times*, 14 February 1977, p. 32.

48. Cutright, "Illegitimacy in the United States," p. 383.

49. Berton Roueché, "Profiles: Hermann, Missouri," *New Yorker*, 28 February 1977, p. 50.

50. Malcolm H. Stern, *Americans of Jewish Descent* (Cincinnati: Hebrew Union College Press, 1961).

W. Gunther Plaut _____

CANADIAN EXPERIENCE: THE DYNAMICS OF JEWISH LIFE SINCE 1945

In many ways Canadian Jewry can be understood only in its relationship to the presence of the six million Jews in the United States, even as Canada itself cannot be discussed without constant reference to its southern neighbor. The United States and its history may be described intelligibly without constant reference to Mexico, the Caribbean, or Canada, for its existence is only marginally affected by its smaller neighbors. But for Canada it is the overwhelming presence of the United States, along the three and a half thousand miles at its southern border, which determines a good deal of its economy and psychology. Even its immigration patterns have been influenced, for many people unable to go directly to the United States (after 1924, when American immigration laws severely restricted access) have in the past thirty years first gone to Canada, especially in the decades before and after World War II. While the land mass of Canada is larger than that of the United States, its population—which has for the last generation been holding at about 10 percent of its neighbor's—is concentrated in a narrow one-hundred-mile strip north of the border, and in some ways the north-south bonds are stronger than those that tie east to west.

This very fact has also had other correlates. After World War II and well into the 1950s a sense of Canadian (as distinguished from French-Canadian) identity was at a low ebb, and many predicted once again the amalgamation of Canada and the United States. But in the wake of the disillusionment which swept over the United States in the latter stages of the Vietnam War, the rise of French-Canadian sentiment for secession and a series of new Federal protectionist economic measures combined to raise the level of Canadian nationalism to a new postwar high. While such favorite U.S. terms as "Americanism" and "un-American" did not have their parallels north of the border, Canadians increasingly began to define themselves less by their own character than by their desire not to be Americans—the more so since giant U.S.-controlled corporations and the all-pervasive American media, especially the electronic networks and such magazines as *Life, Time,* and *Reader's Digest* choked off indigenous Canadian self-expression. Even certain forms of vocal anti-Americanism could increasingly be heard, though on the whole they did not express any deep-seated popular sentiment.

In most respects the two nations remained what they had been: political and military allies, with an undefended border separating them for political and economic purposes; both subject to the same cultural pressures, so that the casual visitor might be hard put to explain in just what way the two countries were distinguished from each other. First and foremost, there was the French factor, with Francophones facing special problems of cultural attrition and isolation. But there were distinctions in the English sector as well, and they expressed themselves no less in the Jewish community. In many respects Canadian Jews were, indeed, much like their American counterparts, but on closer investigation they exhibited important differences and formed a community that had its own characteristics and played its own separate role on the stage of world Jewish life.

In 1945 there were about twelve million people living in Canada, of whom about 180,000 were considered or considered themselves Jewish. [1] The vast majority were located in Montreal and Toronto (about four-fifths of the total) while the rest were found mainly in a few urban centers such as Winnipeg, Vancouver, Calgary, Edmonton, Saskatoon, Regina, Windsor, Hamilton, and Ottawa. Most of these Jews were of East European background who had come after the turn of the century. A small number had settled much earlier, the original community in Montreal going back to the middle of the eighteenth century and in Toronto to the middle of the nineteenth. Montreal's Jewry had large components from Russia and Rumania, Toronto's from Poland, and Winnipeg's from Rumania. In 1945 a significant segment of Canadian Jewry was still foreign-born and, in acculturation, at least one generation behind its counterpart in the United States. Since immigrants from Germany were at a minimum (they had come primarily in the nineteenth century and had settled in the United States), the development of Reform Judaism so prominent in the United States was severely retarded. In addition, British conservatism hardly encouraged radical religious experimentation of the American kind. On the other hand, the Jews who had settled in Canada were not subject to the same assimilatory pressures as were their brothers to the south. There, the melting-pot philosophy became national policy (or at least was understood to be national policy), while the fact that Canada was the result of the coexistence, juxtaposition, and sometimes confrontation of two cultures — French and British — prevented so simplistic a pattern from developing. The very constitution of the country allowed for two distinct cultures and, by this duality, maintained the durability of ethnic differences.

There were other reasons, too. In French Canadian cities like Montreal, Quebec City, and Sherbrooke, Jews tended to identify with the English minority and were therefore doubly isolated.[2] Further, East European Jews had come to Canada generally several decades later than they did to the United States. This delay had exposed them to the sharpened political ideologies which had come to dominate the European Jewish communities, such as Bundism and the varieties of Zionism. The Canadian Jewish immigrant tended to hold on to these ideologies much more than had been the case with immigrants who had come in earlier periods of weaker partisan commitment. Finally, in those areas of English Canada where British influence dominated the social structure (as in Toronto, London, and Vancouver), the old-country class and group distinctions persisted for a long time. This tended to "keep Jews in their place"— which, in turn, encouraged protective self-isolation on the part of Jews.

Thus there was relatively little direct pressure on Jews to abandon their folkways, and especially their Yiddish language. The Jewish community of Winnipeg was a prime example of this temper of Canadian life which gave emphasis to ethnicity rather than religion *qua* faith. Even though the two founding cultures were distinguished both by linguistic differences and by the fact that the French were largely Roman Catholic and the British Protestant, the faith elements themselves were first and foremost defined in ethnic terms. By 1945 the Jews in the United States had developed into a distinct *religious* group, on a theoretical par with Protestants and Catholics (regardless of their own practice or nonpractice of religion), while in Canada the emergence of the Jew as a religious third of the Judeo-Christian complex had not yet occurred in 1945. In the United States the separation of church and state had been built into its Constitution; in Canada such a separation was slow to emerge. In Quebec the Roman Catholic Church had a dominant position which was both cultural and political; in some cities in English Canada, such as Toronto, the Anglican Church over which the king or queen presided held a position of power; and in much of the countryside the amalgamated United Church was dominant. Thus the ethnic identity of the Jewish community was fairly secure, but its religious identity had a relatively low status, which as late as 1944 was expressed in Ontario by a provincial law making the teaching of Christianity in the public schools a matter of curricular obligation.

The ethnic identity of non-British and non-French minorities also made it easier to preserve existing power structures. At the end of World War II these structures clearly excluded Jews almost completely and often restricted their access to business and professional opportunities, to desirable living accommodations, and vacation resorts. Though anti-Semitism was no longer semiofficially countenanced (as it had been in Quebec and tolerated in the Social Credit Party in Alberta in the decades preceding), Jews found themselves clearly set apart in terms of people-hood and not, as in America, as members of a religious faith. Their own internal organization thus favored a comprehensive approach and made possible the effective reestablishment of the Canadian Jewish Congress as the single spokesman of Canadian Jewry—for this Jewry felt as one group, one people, a distinct minority in the world surrounding them. This became especially true after the rise of Adolf Hitler which galvanized the community into a farily collective response.[3] In contrast, in the United States the synagogue was conceived to be the linchpin of Jewry; therefore no single comprehensive organizational structure was possible because the differences between synagogues and between religious and nonreligious institutions stood in the way. The American Jewish Conference, created to meet the war emergency, dissolved once its immediate aims had been met.

There had been notable attempts at Canadian interreligious and intercultural fraternization, but on the whole they remained marginal, so that at the end of the war the Jewish community, while living in legal freedom and with unlimited economic opportunities before it, felt itself still socially and politically isolated—a minority privileged to live in the ambience of Canadian freedom, but a minority nonetheless. It was a group which defined itself largely in terms of its ability to resist the negative impact of the outside world; consequently, it was habituated to looking over its shoulder for the approval of the Gentile or, at worst, for the effects of his disapproval. Young Jews were just beginning to graduate in larger numbers from universities and were entering the professions after their return from the war, and no one could at that time predict the phenomenal economic expansion which would benefit them in the next generation. In 1945 Canadian Jewry was emerging from its cocoon, unsure of its future but sure of its identity, experiencing a sense of continued pressure from the environment and looking for ways of dealing with it effectively. The full internal emancipation of Canadian Jewry had not as yet been completed when the war came to an end.

A number of factors combined to give postwar Canada a new look. One was the new global responsibility which the United States assumed and which perforce drew Canada into the vortex of international concerns. The formation of the United Nations was cordially endorsed by the Federal government, and in time support for the world organization became a cornerstone of its policy. Lester B. Pearson, career diplomat and later to be prime minister of the country, received the Nobel Prize for his success in stabilizing international tensions in the wake of the Sinai Campaign of 1956. During the 1950s until the end of the 1960s Canada moved from being a dependency of the British Empire with narrow parochial interests to a position as a medium and mediating power on the world scene. At the same time it opened its borders to new immigrants (four million in the next three decades, increasing its population by nearly 25 percent), pursuing a policy which recognized that a sparsely populated country could not expect to reach the acme of productivity and wealth and that, as long as the population of the nation was limited, its relatively small market would keep prices relatively high. In the years following 1945 the living standard of Canadians rose appreciably and dramatically, but it still lagged 10-20 percent behind that of the United States—a lag which expressed itself in high Canadian prices and lower Canadian wages.

For the new immigrants who came from southern and eastern Europe and included a sizable number of Jews liberated from concentration camps, Canada was a most desirable destination. While the United States had severely limited new immigration, Canada in comparison was wide open. It was at this point that Canadian and American and Jewish history began to diverge once again. In the U.S. new blood was relatively rare and in the total American Jewish population almost invisible, but on the Canadian scene the new Jewish immigrant was much in evidence. In a population of some 75,000 Jews in Toronto in 1945, thousands of arrivals with KZ numbers on their arms made an appreciable difference. In the 1950s French-speaking Jews came in large numbers from North Africa to Montreal, and Czech and Hungarian Jews fleeing Communist oppression migrated to Toronto. Some ten thousand American war resisters, among them a number of Jews, came to live permanently in Canada, and during the 1970s immigration of Soviet Jews began to increase. All the while there was migration or reimmigration from Israel, until the two largest communities in Montreal and Toronto had thousands of *Yordim* (settlers from Israel) in their midst. Not all of these would admit that they desired to make Canada their permanent home, and only a portion of them were native Israelis. But their arrival made an important difference in that it added to the number of Canadian Jews who were familiar with Hebrew, even as the large-scale postwar immigration from Central Europe had greatly increased the use of Yiddish. (In the mid-fifties Melech Ravitch was writing in Montreal, and Toronto still had a Yiddish daily newspaper, but no English-language weekly—suggesting that the Yiddish-speaking minority had an important stake in their cultural past, while the English-speaking majority had not as yet acquired a compelling need for even a weekly Jewish perspective.)

The new immigrants fulfilled one other function both on the general and the Jewish scene. By the early sixties, when they had taken root, their very presence broke through the more rigid patterns of the established community and gave it once again a multifaced aspect; they revitalized among the immigrants of former decades the emotional patterns of their European upbringing. More Jews now felt that they themselves had been liberated from the horrors of Nazism, that they themselves were in a real way survivors of the Holocaust. Knowledge and discussion of the Holocaust became an increasingly important subject of Canadian Jewish life. Added to this was, of course, the most important ingredient of postwar Jewish history, the establishment of the State of Israel. While it took a few years for Israel to make its full impact on the Diaspora, Canada, because of its ethnic orientation, was among the first to experience it fully, and its more recent European antecedents prevented problems of dual loyalty from emerging seriously. Love of Israel and Zionism were the accepted mode of Jewish life. Perhaps only with the exception of South African Jewry (whose agenda was somewhat different from that of Canadian Jewry) there was no country in the world in which Zionism was embraced with greater enthusiasm and Israel more deeply loved and defended than in Canada.

Most important, the new immigrants brought with them a self-assertiveness which had been largely lacking from the more staid expressions of Jewish life in the past. The war and its aftermath were thus a true watershed for Canadian Jews. In earlier immigrant phases the newcomer had tried to fit himself into an established pattern, especially into its economic traditions. The Canadian Jew himself now became an important fashioner of new social patterns and was able to participate in the enormous economic advance the country was about to experience. Frontier societies meant the opening of new and uncharted enterprises and the wide use of risk capital. The older families, whose fathers and mothers had worked assiduously at establishing a good business and had looked after fairly successful stores, were hesitant to risk the savings of one or two lifetimes in these beckoning ventures. The newcomers, on the other hand, had no such hesitation and to a significant degree it was they who, in relatively short order, anticipated the great prizes which the booming Canadian economy in the first postwar years was about to bestow. They were all desperately poor at first and many of them remained at the bottom of the social ladder, but there were others who grasped the great opportunities and participated in the nation's unprecedented growth. Their success rather rapidly broke down the old social structures. *Yichus* (family connection and background), which once had been the most important accreditation of persons, now took second place to wealth and success. In the generation after the war the Jewish community moved from a moderately situated class of citizens to a distinct middle-class and often upper-middle-class status, headed by a few barons of economic power. This was most evident in Montreal and Toronto, which was emerging as the new financial center of Canada. It was somewhat less spectacular in other communities where immigration and economic expansion were slower, but it held true also for the West which exhibited significant repetitions of the eastern models. The numbers were smaller, but the patterns persisted.

Although the previously established structures in the Jewish community maintained their identity, there were now significant shifts within the community. This became most obvious in Toronto, which began the period as a distinct second to Montreal (where most of the national Jewish organizations were headquartered) and which in 1975 was equaling it and giving promise of surpassing it as the leading Jewish community in the country.

One effect of the new immigration was a reemphasis on the religious aspects of Jewish life. As they did in Israel, the immigrants greatly enhanced the power of Orthodoxy which (in contrast to the situation in the United States) had a position of established strength in Canadian Jewry. Not only was this position now strengthened by immigration; it also led to the sharpening of ideological differences. While a similar development was to be experienced in some American communities (notably in New York), intrareligious cooperation there had been generally accepted as a pragmatic procedure. In Canada, however, a process of religious polarization took place. It was emphasized by the power of Israel's rabbinic establishment which exerted its influence far beyond Israel's borders. The repeated attempt to give the National Religious Affairs Committee of the Canadian Jewish Congress a format which would approximate that of the Synagogue Council in the United States met with failure because of the principled rejection of the traditionalists. They felt that their cooperation in such a venture would appear to signify implicit recognition of Conservative and Reform Jews.

Although in most Canadian communities this was not a major problem, it became one in Toronto in the 1960s because of the presence and strength of recently arrived ultra-Orthodox groups and ideologies whose persistence moved the moderate traditionalists appreciably to the right. It was a development not unlike that experienced in Israel where pressure from the Neturei Karta was felt in the Agudah, which in turn would pressure the Mizrachi, which in turn would pressure its coalition partner in the government—leading to the popular saying current in the 1960s that when the Rebbitzin Blau (wife of the Neturei Karta leader) raised her voice, Golda Meir (then prime minister) would begin to worry. In similar fashion Hungarian Hasidim (even though they themselves hardly participated in communal life) had their point of view expressed in forums far removed from their own spiritual habitat. The domino effect of international politics was operative in Jewish religious life in Canada as it was in Israel.

In fact, all religious life stood to the right of its U.S. counterpart. The Reform movement had briefly attempted a radical position when, in the 1930s, Toronto's Holy Blossom Temple had established Sunday services, buttressed by an anti-Zionist ideology. But at the conclusion of the war these ventures to the left were quickly reversed and Canadian Reform was in many ways more like American Conservatism than American Reform. Canadian Conservative Jews experienced an unprecedented growth in the postwar years and became an influential factor in the Jewish religious life of the country. They, too, moved at first to the right—but this movement was halted by the polarization which took place in the face of strengthened Orthodox ideology. Now suddenly the Conservatives were classified (by the traditionalists) with the Reformers, and a brief attempt to distance themselves from the latter was firmly rejected by the Orthodox leadership to whom they remained dissidents whose degree of dissent did not matter. In consequence, the Conservatives now made a turn to the left and liberalized their attitudes vis-à-vis the Reformers and in many instances began to stand with them. Meanwhile Conservative day schools (at first the sole domain of the Orthodox) grew apace and obtained community funding or, as in Quebec, government funding.

In 1974 Reform Jewry, too, established its first day school when the rabbis of the five Reform synagogues in Toronto helped to found the Leo Baeck Day School. Not that this pathbreaking venture signified the complete erosion of an earlier liberal position which considered day schools regressive, divisive, exclusivist, and inimical to the general path of Canadian Jewish life. There were still enough people left (and not only in the Reform sector) to whom day schools were anathema. But while the Orthodox and Conservatives quickly overcame this ideological negation, this was not the case in the Reform movement where, by a long tradition and American precedent, day schools (also called parochial schools, with all the pejorative implications of that term) were nonexistent. At the present time, it may be predicted that Reform congregations as congregations will support the new school, which, however, had great difficulty in securing communal support. The reasons for this development exceed the limits of this discussion, but it could not be overlooked that the prejudices against Reform as a religious group (not aga2int Reform Jews as communal leaders both politically and economically) were hard to eradicate. Holy Blossom Temple, long known as one of North America's prestigious synagogues, was commonly referred to as "the Church on the Hill." It was an expression which portrayed the old rejectionist attitude of much of the community toward the Liberal Jewish life-style and ideology. That attitude had not disappeared by the late 1970s.

Nonetheless, Reform synagogues of which there were only three in 1945—in Montreal, Toronto, and Hamilton—now spread throughout most Canadian cities, but in all instances they remained in the minority. The general public and the Jewish community frequently turned to them for communal leadership, but the bulk of Jewry belonged either to Conservative and Orthodox or to no religious institutions. It was a development not likely to alter perceptibly in the immediate future.

Increased immigration and the general expansion of the Canadian economy after 1945 favored the entrepreneurial class in which Jews, by long tradition, were prominent. In the larger urban centers they now moved from the edge of poverty which they had occupied in the 1920s and 1930s into the middle class and upper-middle class, many of them becoming well-to-do in the process, especially those connected with land development and building trades. The drive for higher education proceeded apace, and soon it was an accepted fact that Jewish children, if reasonably endowed, would finish high school and go to university. However, the American hope of sending children to prestigious universities in the East or West, away from home, found no parallel in Canada. On the whole, local universities became the place where one went to school, and although McGill and the University of Toronto had a superior scholastic rating, going to university was in itself a badge of distinction and opened the way to professional advancement; one did not have to go away to become accredited at home. Only in advanced degrees was a foreign address of some significance, but this, too, was slow in coming.

This rootedness in the home base was in part a reflection of an absence of mobility. Certainly there was nothing that approached the internal postwar American migration to the West and Southwest of the United States, nor did major Canadian cities develop suburban sprawl with its dislocation of community patterns. True, Vancouver became the target of general as well as Jewish migration and its wealth rose dramatically. True also that young people increasingly left the small communities where but a few Jewish families had resided for a generation or more and went to the large city. And finally, in response to renewed nationalism in Quebec, a steady migration of Montreal Jews to Toronto and farther west decreased the Jewish base in Montreal in the 1970s. But none of this fundamentally affected the pervasive psychological status of Canadian Jews who generally were content to stay where they were and moved only because of marriage or particular business and professional interests   and in such cases the United States was usually the goal, with physicians a particularly mobile group.

On the whole, the migration to the United States was steady but minor, with a brief period of notable exception in the 1960s when people with secondary degrees were attracted to American universities and other funded institutions and organizations and left Canada permanently. Subsequently, this "brain drain," as it became known, caused Canadian universities to spend a great deal of money to reverse the trend. Their effort became successful toward the end of the 1960s when at the height of the Vietnam disillusionment and racial tensions, as well as of the increase of big-city crime in the United States, many Canadian professionals began to return. American professionals joined them and assumed significant business and university posts. By 1970 many American professors (and a goodly number of Jews among them) were found in the expanding network of Canadian universities, a fact which caused a great deal of public discussion in the face of the increasingly nationalistic temper of the country. It was not directed at Jews *qua* Jews but against Americans, and it became a facet of the trend which saw Canadians define their Canadianism to a significant degree in terms of anti- or non-Americanism. Toward the middle of the 1970s unemployment had caused sufficient concern in the country to restrict immigration in general and to restrain the free interplay of professional appointments. This brought American migration to Canada to a near halt. Moreover, reduced public funding and a government-enforced anti-inflation program caused Canadian earning power to lag behind its American counterpart. By 1978 the flow was once again from Canada to the United States, albeit at a lower rate than fifteen years before.

The most important single development in the demographic area was doubtlessly the rise of Quebec nationalsim. Fanned by a sense of general economic frustration, an intellectual elite who found themselves disadvantaged by the power barons of Anglo-Saxon origin surged to new political heights in the 1960s, and there was a distinct possibility that the Parti Quebecois might in fact assume power. But the victory of Robert Bourassa in the provincial elections of 1973, on a nonsecessionist platform, halted this trend at least temporarily. Yet by the mid 1970s it was rising again, and the province instituted a series of measures designed to make Quebec a predominantly French-speaking province by law, with English relegated to a distinctly second-class position. This policy was concretized in the highly controversial "Bill 22" and caused the Anglophone minority to reassess its status.

At this writing a new election in Quebec in November 1976 has in fact brought the separatist Parti Quebecois to power. Its leader, René Lévesque, campaigned on the promise that he would hold a province-wide referendum on Quebec's independence within two years of election. The result, though it did not make Quebec's separation from

Canada a certainty, created great unrest in the Jewish community. There was serious doubt among its members about a Jewish future in the province; they wondered how well Jews could integrate themselves into a society which was avowedly French and Catholic.*

Their memories of the 1930s, when the Duplessis government had not discouraged anti-Semitic expressions in the province and especially not in the countryside, were now revived once again. Heretofore Jews had largely identified with the Anglophone minority and chosen English as their primary language, a fact which was not substantially altered by the influx of French-speaking North African Jews. Jews felt that they would be the first targets of a successful Quebec separation, and significant numbers of them began to look westward to reestablish a more secure future. In many ways they came to feel that even in the freedom of Canada they were still strangers in a strange land.

But even before 1976 it had become evident that Montreal had lost its two hundred years of preeminence in Canadian Jewish life to Toronto.[4] National institutions were still headquartered in the Quebec metropolis, but much of the de facto leadership had moved to Toronto. That in time the national organizations would have to follow suit appeared likely, though the traditionally slow pace of change in institutional life would prevent any sudden dramatic shift. The Canadian Jewish Congress was still housed in the splendid facility named after Samuel Bronfman, its long-time president, the founder of the Seagram empire and a commanding figure in Jewish life for a generation. With his passing Montreal's hegemony also began to fade, and Congress leadership was now shared with other communities. Similarly the Canada-Israel Committee, established after years of intraorganizational rivalries, still had its headquarters in Montreal. However, in 1976 this key institution of Canadian Jewry, which represented the total community vis-à-vis the public and the government in all matters relating to Israel, was headed by two cochairmen residing in Toronto.[5]

Jewish patterns began to loosen and change, along with the structure of Canadian society at large. Where formerly Jews were rigorously excluded from sensitive posts and key positions in government and in

---

*By mid-1976 the Lévesque government had introduced an even more far-reaching language bill (known as "Bill 1" and later as "Bill 101"), the implications of which were perceived by many Jews to undermine their future in Quebec. As a result of spreading uncertainty, young Jewish professionals and others with economic mobility began to leave the province in increasing numbers. There was no question that the face of the Jewish community of Montreal would be permanently altered, but the full extent of these changes could not be predicted at this writing.

universities, by the seventies they had reached many positions of eminence. David Lewis became leader of the New Democratic Party (the third of the three major Federal parties); social worker David Barrett became premier of British Columbia; a number of provinces included Jews in their cabinets, or had Jews as leaders of opposition or third parties. Thus in 1976, with the Conservatives in power in Ontario, the opposition New Democrats were headed by Stephen Lewis (David's son) and the Liberals by Dr. Stuart Smith, the former a Toronto lawyer and the latter a Hamilton psychiatrist. David Croll, once mayor of Windsor, Lazarus Phillips, and Carl Goldenberg were members of the senate, and Windsor M. P. Herbert Gray had been the first Jew to join the Federal cabinet (the second, Barnett Danson, Minister of Defense, had been the founder of a Toronto synagogue). In 1961 Louis Rasminsky was appointed head of the Bank of Canada (similar in function to the Federal Reserve Bank in the United States). The judiciary also included Jews in increasing numbers on every level, culminating in the elevation of Samuel Freedman as chief justice of Manitoba and in 1974 in the appointment of Bora Laskin as chief justice of the Supreme Court of Canada.

The smaller communities had frequently seen Jewish mayors, such as in Thunder Bay (where Justice Laskin's brother was mayor for many years), in Saskatoon, and later in Ottawa itself. Eventually even in traditionally "WASP" Toronto the old pattern was finally broken when Nathan Phillips acceded to the mayor's chair and held it for four consecutive terms. After his departure from office, the city bestowed on him the unusual honor of naming its principal square after him. Nathan Phillips Square in front of the famed city hall he had helped bring into being is a vivid reminder both of a man and of a new era in the acceptance of Jews in public life. Not much later, Philip Givens, prominent Zionist activist, became the city's mayor, graduating later to Federal and Provincial politics and all the while remaining a vigorous spokesman of the Jewish community—a combination which would have been thought unlikely, if not impossible, only a generation before.

While all of this heralded a significant leveling of traditional differences, it did not mean a fundamental rearrangement of the power bases of Canadian life. Heavy industry and the large corporations, as well as the chartered banks, remained essentially outside the realm of Jewish influence. There was no Jewish-owned equivalent of the *New York Times* in Canada, nor was there an independent entertainment industry of sufficient impact which could dominate public taste in the manner of Hollywood. In any case, private influence in the arts was limited because of the public ownership of the Canadian Broadcasting Corporation, which itself was remarkably free of top Jewish personnel. But Jews participated freely and contributed outstandingly to science, art, and literature. Leonard Cohen and Irving Layton were Canada's best-read poets, and the stature of Abraham Klein as a major literary figure was being recognized slowly yet surely by the mid 1970s. Mordecai Richler was one of Canada's most popular novelists and certainly the one most widely read abroad; Sigmund Samuel and Sam and Ayala Zacks became Canada's foremost private art collectors and donors; and on stage such names as John Hirsch, Maureen Forrester (who had been converted to Judaism), Johnny Wayne and Frank Schuster, and theatrical entrepreneur Ed Mirvish became household words.

In the postwar years Canadian Jewry had advanced from a small and largely parochial community into a vigorous and vibrant society of Canadian citizens who were taking their place in the larger environment with great zest, and who, while making advances in the economic and public arenas, nonetheless maintained a remarkable identity as an ethno-religious unit in the Canadian fabric.

After World War II the inner structure of Canadian Jewry did not so much alter as it came to intensify its potential. The impact of the State of Israel was, of course, a prime factor. In 1945 many Canadian Jews still saw themselves in their traditional *Galut* role—legally free, but emotionally and practically circumscribed by the surrounding Gentile environment. This produced a relative political quiescence on their part, and when this was disturbed it occasionally tended to cause widespread unease among the Jews. Thus, the often vigorous critique of the establishment by Abraham L. Feinberg, rabbi of Holy Blossom in Toronto, was material both for newspaper headlines and for a rise in Jewish insecurity. But such misgivings yielded to increasing self-assertion, especially after the Six-Day War in 1967, when proud identification with the valor and courage of the Israelis gave the Jews a new image, not the least in their own eyes.

Visits to Israel, increasing *aliyah,* and vigorous fund-raising became a part and soon the very center of Jewish life, and in time a new apparatus was developed by the three major Canadian organizations—the Canadian Jewish Congress, B'nai B'rith, and the Canadian Zionist Federation (comprising all Zionist parties and groupings)—to represent the Jewish cause to the public, and particularly to the government. They established the Canada-Israel Committee (CIC) as the chief spokesman and agency of Canadian Jewry in all matters touching on Israel. Its most dramatic impact came in 1975 when it dealt with a proposed United Nations Conference on Crime Prevention which was to be held in Toronto in the spring of that year. The Palestinian Liberation Organization (PLO), recently given observer status at the United Nations, was slated to attend the conference, and this announcement elicited an enormous amount of reaction and resentment. A nationwide campaign, spearheaded by the Canada-Israel Committee, in time involved the premiers of various provinces, engendered wide newspaper support, and showed a countrywide aversion to the proposed participation by the PLO in the conference. After much hesitation the government withdrew the invitation to the United Nations, and the conference was moved to Switzerland. There was little question that the open and strong stance taken by the Jewish community was an important factor in this development.

Yet as late as 1976 the battle for complete self-assertion had not been won entirely. When, prior to the Olympic Games, it was proposed to hold a public Jewish memorial service for the eleven martyrs who had been slain at the Munich Olympics four years before, there was significant resistance on the part of members of the Jewish establishment in Montreal who proposed to soft-pedal the issue. In time their objections were overcome and, when the prime minister participated in a moving service which attracted 5,000 persons and worldwide media coverage, another significant step toward the formation of a firmer Jewish self-image had been taken.

A good deal of the credit for this spirit of self-assertiveness must be given to the new immigrants, and especially to the survivors of the Holocaust. They reacted quickly and vigorously (some critics claimed, too quickly and too vigorously) to any attack on Israel or on Jews in general. Thus high emotion characterized the Jewish community in its long controversy with the United Church of Canada, whose principal publication took a strong editorial stance against Israel's policies after 1967. The newcomers also reacted vociferously and strongly against outcroppings of anti-Semitism. The most famous incident in the 1960s which brought these sentiments into visible relief occurred in Toronto when a neo-Nazi party staged a public demonstration in a downtown park. Toronto Jews led by survivor groups came out physically to prevent such gatherings from taking place, a change from previously accepted reactions which had confined themselves primarily to briefs and presentations but had eschewed physical confrontations. The hesitant policy of the local Canadian Jewish Congress in the Allan Gardens matter brought it to its nadir of effectiveness and caused it to lose much of the internal credit it had built up in previous decades. Though the Congress would take some time recovering, the result was, in the long run, positive. Not only were the established ways of the official community infused with new vigor and pride but the more recently arrived elements in the Jewish community were given a larger voice in the formation of Congress policy.

A somewhat different controversy surrounded the proposed Federal legislation which was to cope with certain public expressions of group hatred and especially with anti-Semitism. The so-called Hate Bill was helped through Parliament upon the advice of a Congress committee under the leadership of Professor (later Dean) Maxwell Cohen. But the act remained controversial. It had been opposed by civil libertarians—Jews among them—who claimed that it encroached on free speech. In the middle 1970s it was again in the limelight when it was to be applied to telephoned hate messages. The act became once more the target of newspaper editorials which raised the old arguments and, in addition, stressed that a law that had hardly been applied was useless and in fact counterproductive. It was a foregone conclusion, however, that the majority of the Jewish community would remain strongly in favor of the maintenance of such a law and be outspoken in its defense.

Related to this spirit were increasing demands for demonstrations in public places, preferably under the glare of television lights and media coverage. Nowhere did this bear greater fruits than in the events surrounding the visit of Soviet Premier Alexei Kosygin to Canada. In every community where he appeared thousands of Jews marched through the streets. In Toronto, under his window on the twenty-seventh floor at the Inn on the Park, ten thousand Jews assembled to listen to Elie Wiesel, who some years ago had first stirred the conscience of world Jewry and urged it to labor for the liberation of Russian Jews. "One, two, three, set my people free!," the marchers sang. In a memorable demonstration in the nation's capital traffic was brought to a standstill when many thousands of Jews who had come from various parts of the country by plane, train, and bus reiterated their unshakable support of Soviet Jewry. They held midnight prayer services in front of Parliament and beleaguered Kosygin's car as it drove by. What impact this unified expression of Jewish will had on the emigration of Russian Jews, which began shortly thereafter, will not be known until the Kremlin's files are opened to future historians. But Canadian Jews felt that they had contributed to this historic turn of events and had, indeed, helped to swing open the iron gates that had imprisoned their brethren for so long. (It might be added that when, later on, increasing numbers of Soviet Jews arrived in Canada for permanent settlement, there developed a gap between the ideal and the real. As happened in Israel, the absorption of the newcomers was not easy, and but a fraction of the attention that had been focused on them while they were still in Soviet Russia was now given them upon their arrival in freedom.)

Fund-raising for Israel became a major preoccupation of the Canadian Jewish community. It was said that, except for South Africa, Canadian Jewry raised a larger per capita share in behalf of Israel than any other national group in the world. Every Israeli university, many *yeshivot*, and other institutions had branches in the country which helped them raise capital and operating funds. It was inevitable that this outflow would sooner or later collide with the needs of the Canadian Jewish community itself, especially when federations began to replace the synagogue as the center of power and controlled the purse strings of Jewish education, whose costs were spiraling along with expanded programs and galloping inflation. In 1975 these tensions were becoming greater rather than smaller, for the traditional emphasis on ethnicity had favored the primacy of fund-raising for Israel proper, while the cultural and social institutions of the community had a harder time gaining their due and frequently obtained their funds through being tacked on to campaigns in behalf of Israel. The satisfaction of these dual needs was still in the future and its outcome, at best, uncertain.

As late as 1957 an interdenominational commission sponsored by the Canadian Council of Churches proposed that the Protestant denominations in Canada should tackle seriously the problem of Christianizing the Jews. "We must look upon the Jewish people [it said] as individuals. They carry their burden of sin and frustrations even as the rest of us. The Jew is a person. We must treat him as such. Wherever we find him, consider him, as all others, as a potential child of God." Fewer than twenty years later such efforts at conversion were abandoned by the official churches, although small "Jews for Jesus" groups had made their appearance and briefly moved the Jewish communities to putative countermeasures.

But while conversion posed no serious threat to Jewish identity, mixed marriage did; it was steeply on the rise in smaller communities and less so in larger ones. By 1975 it was said to have reached 18 percent on a national basis, but these statistics were not conclusive. Some of the Gentile mates converted to Judaism; in Toronto alone each year some seventy-five or more non-Jews were admitted to Judaism, after passing through Conservative and Reform instructional courses. The Orthodox sidestepped the problem and referred potential converts either to New York or to Israel. The rise of out-marriages was, of course, the direct correlate of Jews moving into an open society where religious and ethnic affiliations counted for less and less. Mixed marriage was especially high in British Columbia, but no community was exempt from its increased occurrence.

In fact, the differences between Eastern and Western Canada began to level off as internal migration increased, and with the rise of Canadian nationalism and protectionism the North-South interfaces with the United States remained at their previous levels. Because of its immigration patterns Canada had not experienced the "lost generation" of the American 1920s and 1930s; instead, Canadian Jewry had progressed directly from an immigrant to a self-assertive, middle-class community. It was, in the mid-1970s, an intensely Israel-oriented and self-identified community, with larger numbers of students going to Jewish day schools, with Judaic university programs increasing, and with a few scholars like philosopher Emil Fackenheim and halachist Gedaliah Felder acquiring worldwide reputations. But the process of general assimilation went forward nonetheless, though its negative aspects were as yet less evident in Canada than in the United States. Ben Kayfetz categorized Canadian Jewry in the mid-1950s as "a community with an interest in Judaism much more self-conscious and articulate than that of 20 or 25 years ago, though not as confident and as assured of its goals." Twenty years later Saul Hayes, retiring after a distinguished career of more than thirty years as the executive director of the Canadian Jewish Congress, posed the problem facing Canadian Jewry in this fashion: "The final question is: In our post-Christian, post-Jewish society where humanism, doctrines of equality, real concern for identity and rights characterize our world, is Canadian Jewry endangered or is it strengthened as a vibrant and viable group in our present secular society? As usual, history as it unfolds alone will provide the answer."

NOTES

1. Canadian census figures are obtained at the beginning of each decade, and therefore mid-decade statistics are only approximate. These figures must further be interpreted in the light of the custom distinguishing, in the census, between religion and ethnic origin.

2. The influx of Jews from North Africa, which peaked in the 1960s, did not alter this substantially. Even though most of them were French-speaking, they identified first and foremost with the Jews already settled and, therefore, with a community that had culturally stood with the Anglophones.

3. The Jewish business establishment, however, soon moved away from political action and possible confrontation to the more acceptable realm of charities. Canadian Jews did not develop a counterpart to either the American Jewish Committee or the American Council for Judaism.

4. It was estimated that of the 300,000 Jews in Canada at this time (about 1.4% of the total population), Montreal and Toronto had about 120,000 each, with the former losing and the latter gaining in numbers.

5. Norman May and the writer. For further discussion of the Committee (generally called CIC), see pp. 296-297.

Selected Bibliography ————

Compiled By BERNARD MARTIN

AMERICAN JEWRY SINCE 1945: AN HISTORICAL OVERVIEW

The *American Jewish Year Book,* prepared annually by the staff of the American Jewish Committee and published by the American Jewish Committee and The Jewish Publication Society of America of Philadelphia is an invaluable resource for contemporary American Jewish history. Its articles and essays deal with virtually all the themes discussed in the present work. An index to volumes 1-50 of the *American Jewish Year Book* was prepared by Elfrida C. Solis-Cohen and published by Ktav Publishing House, Inc. (New York: 1967).

Arkin, Marcus. *Aspects of Jewish Economic History.* Philadelphia: Jewish Publication Society of America, 1975.

Baum, Charlotte, Hyman, Paula, and Michel, Sonya. *The Jewish Woman in America.* New York: Dial Press, 1976.

Ben-Sasson, H. H., and Ettinger, S., eds. *Jewish Society Through the Ages.* New York: Schocken Books, 1971.

Blau, Joseph. *Judaism in America: From Curiosity to Third Faith.* Chicago and London: University of Chicago Press, 1976.

Blau, Joseph. *Modern Varieties of Judaism.* New York: Columbia University Press, 1966.

Glazer, Nathan. *American Judaism,* 2d ed., rev. Chicago: University of Chicago Press, 1972.

Glazer, Nathan, and Moynihan, Daniel P., *Beyond the Melting Pot: The Negroes, Puerto Ricans, Jews, Italians, and Irish of New York City*, 2d ed. Cambridge, Massachusetts: MIT Press, 1970.

Howe, Irving. *World of Our Fathers.* New York: Harcourt Brace Jovanovich, 1976.

Janowski, Oscar I., ed. *The American Jew: A Reappraisal.* Philadelphia: The Jewish Publication Society of America, 1964.

Katz, Jacob, ed. *The Role of Religion in Modern Jewish History.* Cambridge, Massachusetts: Association for Jewish Studies, 1975.

Kramer, Judith R., and Leventman, Seymour. *Children of the Gilded Ghetto: Conflict Resolutions of Three Generations of American Jews.* New Haven: Yale University Press, 1961.

Learsi, Rufus. *The Jews in America: A History*, with epilogue by Abraham J. Karp. New York: Ktav Publishing House, Inc., 1972.

Note: The compiler acknowledges his indebtedness to various contributors to this volume for a considerable number of the items and annotations here given.

Liebman, Charles S. *The Ambivalent American Jew: Politics, Religion and Family in American Jewish Life*. Philadelphia: The Jewish Publication Society of America, 1973.

Neusner, Jacob. *American Judaism: Adventure in Modernity*. Englewood Cliffs, New Jersey: Prentice-Hall, Inc., 1972.

Neusner, Jacob, ed. *Understanding American Judaism*, 2 vols. New York: Ktav Publishing House, Inc., 1975.

Priesand, Sally. *Judaism and the New Woman*. New York: Behrman House, 1976.

Sidorsky, David, ed. *The Future of the Jewish Community in America*. New York: Basic Books, 1973.

Silver, Daniel J., and Martin, Bernard. *A History of Judaism*, vol. 2. New York: Basic Books, 1974.

Sklare, Marshall. *America's Jews*. New York: Random House, 1971.

Sklare, Marshall, and Greenblum, Joseph. *Jewish Identity on the Suburban Frontier: A Study of Group Survival in the Open Society*. New York: Basic Books, 1967.

Sklare, Marshall, ed. *The Jewish Community in America*. New York: Behrman House, 1974.

Sklare, Marshall, ed. *The Jews: Social Patterns of an American Group*. New York: The Free Press, 1958.

THE JEWISH POPULATION OF THE UNITED STATES: A DEMOGRAPHIC AND SOCIOLOGICAL ANALYSIS

Associated Jewish Charities of Baltimore, *The Jewish Community of Greater Baltimore: A Population Study*. Baltimore: Associated Jewish Charities and Welfare Fund, 1968.

Axelrod, Morris, Fowler, Floyd J., and Gurin, Arnold. *A Community Survey for Long Range Planning: A Study of the Jewish Population of Greater Boston*. Boston: Combined Jewish Philanthropies of Greater Boston, 1967.

Bigman, Stanley K. *The Jewish Population of Greater Washington in 1956*. Washington, D.C.: The Jewish Community Council of Greater Washington, 1957.

Bogue, Donald J. *The Population of the United States*. New York: The Free Press, 1959.

Carlos, Serge. "Religious Participation and the Urban-Suburban Continuum," *American Journal of Sociology*, March 1970, pp. 742-759.

Chenkin, Alvin. "Jewish Population in the United States," *American Jewish Year Book* 71 (1970), pp. 344-347.

Diamond, Jack J. "Jewish Immigration to the United States," *American Jewish Year Book* 70 (1969), pp. 289-294.

Fauman, S. Joseph, and Mayer, Albert J. "Jewish Mortality in the U.S.," *Human Biology*, September 1969, pp. 416-426.

Freedman, Ronald, Whelpton, Pascal K., and Campbell, Arthur A. *Family Planning, Sterility, and Population Growth*. New York: McGraw-Hill Book Co., 1959.

Freedman, Ronald, Whelpton, Pascal K., and Smit, John W. "Socio-Economic Factors in Religious Differentials in Fertility," *American Sociological Review*, August 1961.

Glazer, Nathan. "The American Jew and the Attainment of Middle-Class Rank: Some Trends and Explanations," in Marshall Sklare, ed., *The Jews: Social Patterns of an American Group*. New York: The Free Press, 1958.

Glazer, Nathan, and Moynihan, Daniel P. *Beyond the Melting Pot: The Negroes, Puerto Ricans, Jews, Italians, and Irish of New York City*, 2d ed. Cambridge, Massachusetts: MIT Press, 1970.

Gockel, Galen L. "Income and Religious Affiliation," *American Journal of Sociology*, May 1969, pp. 632-647.

Goldberg, David, and Sharp, Harry. "Some Characteristics of Detroit Area Jews and Non-Jewish Adults," in Marshall Sklare, ed., *The Jews: Social Patterns of an American Group*. New York: The Free Press, 1958.

Goldscheider, Calvin. "Fertility of the Jews," *Demography*, 1967, no. 4, pp. 196-209.

Goldscheider, Calvin. "Trends in Jewish Fertility," *Sociology and Social Research*, 1966, pp. 173-186.

Goldstein, Ronald M. "American Jewish Population Studies Since World War II," *American Jewish Archives* 22 (April 1970), pp. 14-46.

Goldstein, Sidney. "Completed and Expected Fertility in an American Jewish Community," *Jewish Social Studies* 33, nos. 2-3 (April-July 1971), pp. 212-227.

Goldstein, Sidney. *The Greater Providence Jewish Community: A Population Survey*. Providence, Rhode Island: General Jewish Committee, 1964.

Goldstein, Sidney. *A Population Survey of the Greater Springfield Jewish Community*. Springfield, Massachusetts: Jewish Community Council, 1968.

Goldstein, Sidney. "Socioeconomic Differentials among Religious Groups in the United States," *American Journal of Sociology*, May 1969, pp. 612-631.

Goldstein, Sidney, and Goldscheider, Calvin. *Jewish Americans: Three Generations in a Jewish Community*. Englewood Cliffs, New Jersey: Prentice-Hall, Inc., 1968.

Gordon, Milton M. *Assimilation in American Life*. New York: Oxford University Press, 1964.

The Jewish Community of Pittsburgh: A Population Survey. Pittsburgh: United Federation of Pittsburgh, 1963.

The Jewish Population of Rochester, New York (Monroe County), 1961. Rochester: Jewish Community Council, 1961.

Kennedy, Ruby Jo Reeves. "What Has Social Science to Say About Intermarriage?" in Werner J. Cahnman, ed., *Intermarriage and Jewish Life*. New York: Herzl Press, 1963.

Kranzler, George. *Williamsburg: A Jewish Community in Transition*. New York: P. Feldheim, 1961.

Landesman, Alter F. *Brownsville: The Birth, Development and Passing of a Jewish Community*. New York: Bloch Publishing Co., 1969.

Lazerwitz, Bernard. "A Comparison of Major United States Religious Groups," *Journal of the American Statistical Association*, September 1961, pp. 568-579.

Lenski, Gerhard. *The Religious Factor*. Garden City, New York: Doubleday and Company, Inc., 1963.

Massarik, Fred. *The Jewish Population of Los Angeles*. Los Angeles: Jewish Federation-Council of Greater Los Angeles, 1959.

Massarik, Fred. "The National Jewish Population Study: A New United States Estimate," *American Jewish Year Book* 75 (1974-75).

Massarik, Fred, and Chenkin, Alvin. "United States National Jewish Population Study," *American Jewish Year Book* 74 (1973).

Mayer, Albert J. *Columbus Jewish Population Study: 1969.* Columbus, Ohio: Jewish Welfare Federation, 1970.

Mayer, Albert J. *The Detroit Jewish Community: Geographic Mobility, 1963-1965; and Fertility—A Projection of Future Births.* Detroit: Jewish Welfare Federation, 1966.

Mayer, Albert J. *Estimate of the Numbers and Age Distribution of the Detroit Metropolitan Area: 1956.* Detroit: Jewish Welfare Federation, 1959.

Mayer, Albert J. *Income Characteristics of the Jewish Population in the Detroit Metropolitan Area: 1956.* Detroit: Jewish Welfare Federation, 1960.

Mayer, Albert J. *Jewish Population Study, 1963: Number of Persons, Age and Residential Distribution.* Detroit: Jewish Welfare Federation, 1964.

Mayer, Albert J. *Milwaukee Jewish Population Study, 1964-1965.* Milwaukee: Jewish Welfare Fund, 1966.

Mayer, Albert J. *Movement of the Jewish Population in the Detroit Metropolitan Area: 1949-1959.* Detroit: Jewish Welfare Federation, 1964.

Mayer, Albert J. *Social and Economic Characteristics of the Detroit Jewish Community: 1963.* Detroit: Jewish Welfare Federation, 1964.

Poll, Solomon. *The Hasidic Community of Williamsburg.* New York: The Free Press, 1962.

Rose, Peter I., ed. *The Ghetto and Beyond.* New York: Random House, Inc., 1969.

Rosenthal, Erich. "Acculturation Without Assimilation? The Jewish Community of Chicago, Illinois," *American Journal of Sociology* 66 (November 1960), pp. 175-88.

Rosenthal, Erich. "The Current Status of Jewish Social Research," *Midstream* 17, no. 4 (April 1971), pp. 58-62.

Rosenthal, Erich. "Divorce and Religious Intermarriage: The Effect of Previous Marital Status Upon Subsequent Marital Behavior," *Journal of Marriage and the Family* 32, no. 3 (August 1970), pp. 435-440.

Rosenthal, Erich. "The Equivalence of United States Census Data for Persons of Russian Stock or Descent with American Jews: An Evaluation," *Demography* 12, no. 2 (May 1975), pp. 275-290.

Rosenthal, Erich. "Five Million American Jews," *Commentary* 26 (December 1958), pp. 499-507.

Rosenthal, Erich. "Jewish Fertility in the United States," *American Jewish Year Book* 62 (1961), pp. 3-28.

Rosenthal, Erich. "Jewish Intermarriage in Indiana," *American Jewish Year Book* 68 (1967), pp. 243-264.

Rosenthal, Erich. "The Jewish Population of Chicago, Illinois," in *The Chicago Pinkas*, pp. 9-112. Chicago: College of Jewish Studies, 1952.

Rosenthal, Erich. "Jewish Populations in General Decennial Population Censuses, 1955-61: A Bibliography," *The Jewish Journal of Sociology* 11 (June 1969), pp. 31-39.

Rosenthal, Erich. "Studies of Jewish Intermarriage in the United States," *American Jewish Year Book* 64 (1963), pp. 3-53.

Rosenthal, Erich. "This Was North Lawndale: The Transplantation of a Jewish Community," *Jewish Social Studies* 22 (April 1960), pp. 67-82.

Rubin, Israel. *Satmar: An Island in the City.* Chicago: Quadrangle Books, 1972.

Ryder, Norman B., and Westoff, Charles F. *Reproduction in the United States—1965*. Princeton: Princeton University Press, 1971.

Schmelz, U. O., and Glickson, P. *Jewish Population Studies, 1961-1968*. Jerusalem: Hebrew University, Institute of Contemporary Jewry, 1970.

Schwartz, Arnold. "Intermarriage in the United States," *American Jewish Year Book* 71 (1970), pp. 101-121.

Seidman, H., Garfinkel, L., and Craig, L. "Death Rates in New York City by Socio-Economic Class and Religious Group and by Country of Birth, 1949-1951," *Jewish Journal of Sociology*, December 1962, pp. 254-272.

Seligman, Ben B. "Some Aspects of Jewish Demography," in Marshall Sklare, ed., *The Jews: Social Patterns of an American Group*. New York: The Free Press, 1968.

Sherman, C. Bezalel. *The Jew within American Society*. Detroit: Wayne State University Press, 1965.

Sklare, Marshall. "Intermarriage and Jewish Survival," *Commentary* 49 (March 1970), pp. 51-58.

Westoff, Charles F., Potter, Robert G., Jr., Sagi, Philip C., and Mishler, Eliot G. *Family Growth in Metropolitan America*. Princeton: Princeton University Press, 1961.

Whelpton, Pascal K., Campbell, Arthur A., and Patterson, John E. *Fertility and Family Planning in the United States*. Princeton: Princeton University Press, 1966.

U.S. Bureau of the Census, "Religion Reported by the Civilian Population of the United States, March, 1957," *Current Population Reports*, Series P-20, no. 79. Washington, D.C.: U.S. Government Printing Office, 1958.

For a selected bibliography of Jewish community surveys, see the *American Jewish Year Book* 72 (1971), pp. 87-88.

JEWISH COMMUNAL ORGANIZATION AND PHILANTHROPY

Bernstein, Phillip. *Federation-Synagogue Relationships*, New York, Council of Jewish Federations and Welfare Funds, 1976 (unpublished address); idem, *Address to the Annual Meeting of the Washington UJA-Federation*, 29 June 1976. In these two addresses the executive vice president of the Council of Jewish Federations and Welfare Funds outlines his concept of the nature and function of federations and their relationship to another major shaping factor of the American Jewish community, the religious sector.

Cutlip, Scott M. *Fundraising in the United States: Its Role in America's Philanthropy*. New Brunswick, New Jersey: Rutgers University Press, 1965.

Elazar, Daniel J. *Community and Polity: The Organizational Dynamics of American Jewry*. Philadelphia: The Jewish Publication Society of America, 1976. This work probably constitutes the most up-to-date and fullest account of the development of the organized American Jewish community, its function and its structure, its relationship with other power centers, and the problems it is now facing.

Elazar, Daniel J. "Decision-Making in the American Jewish Community," in David Sidorsky, ed., *The Future of the Jewish Community in America*, pp. 271-315. New York: Basic Books, 1974.

Elazar, Daniel J. "The Reconstitution of Jewish Communities in the Post-War Period," *Jewish Journal of Sociology* 11 (December 1969), pp. 187-226.

Epstein, Raymond. *Major Issues Facing Federations and the Council* (paper delivered at the General Assembly of the Council of Jewish Federations and Welfare Funds, 1974). The then president of the Council of Jewish Federations and Welfare Funds summarizes the key questions facing the organized Jewish community and defines the responsibilities of the community in attempting to deal with them.

Freid, Jacob, ed. *Judaism and the Community: New Directions in Jewish Social Work.* New York: Thomas Yoseloff, 1968.

The Future of the Jewish Community in America: A Task Force Report. New York: American Jewish Committee, 1972.

Gartner, Lloyd. "The Contemporary Jewish Community" in *The Study of Judaism: Bibliographical Essays*, pp. 185-206. New York: Ktav Publishing House, Inc., for the Anti-Defamation League of B'nai B'rith, 1972.

Ginzberg, Eli. "Jews in the Changing Urban Environment," *Conservative Judaism* 27 (Summer 1973), pp. 3-12.

Goldberg, S. P. *Jewish Communal Service, Programs and Finances*, 17th ed. New York: Council of Jewish Federations and Welfare Funds, January 1973. The most authoritative statistical information dealing with every aspect of communal budgeting and financing is to be found in these annual reports by Goldberg. In addition, material on any given agency or development in American Jewish life is often best secured through the various budget digests and other summarizing material prepared by the Council of Jewish Federations and Welfare Funds and available at its office.

Gurin, Arnold. *The Functions of a Sectarian Welfare Program in a Multi-Group Society: A Case Study of the Jewish Welfare Federation of Detroit* (dissertation submitted in partial fulfillment of the requirements for the degree of Doctor of Philosophy, University of Michigan, 1965). This is an exhaustive analysis of the Detroit federation, one of the leaders in its field. The study of this outstanding community, its strengths and weaknesses, and its methods of arriving at decisions constitutes a graphic and detailed insight into the actual functioning of the organized Jewish community in America.

Liebman, Charles S. "Dimensions of Authority in the Contemporary Jewish Community," *Jewish Journal of Sociology* 12 (June 1970), pp. 29-37.

Linzer, Norman, ed. *Jewish Communal Services in the United States: 1960-1970, A Selected Bibliography.* New York: Federation of Jewish Philanthropies, 1972.

Lipset, Seymour Martin. "The Study of Jewish Communities in a Comparative Context," *Jewish Journal of Sociology* 5 (December 1963), pp. 157-166.

Lurie, Harry. *A Heritage Affirmed.* Philadelphia: Jewish Publication Society of America, 1961. This work constitutes the most authoritative description of the history of the Council of Jewish Federations and Welfare Funds, the overall coordinating structure of local federations, and also traces in depth the history of the founding of the federation movement and its development until approximately 1960.

Maslow, Will. *The Structure and Functioning of the American Jewish Community.* New York: American Jewish Congress, 1974.

Miller, Charles. *An Introduction to the Jewish Federation*. New York: Council of Jewish Federations and Welfare Funds, 1976. This brief and popularized review of the federation movement presents in compact form the history of federation, defining its purposes and describing how it plans for priorities, financing, and its various activities.

Morris, Robert, and Freund, Michael. *Trends and Issues in Jewish Social Welfare in the United States, 1899-1952*. Philadelphia: The Jewish Publication Society of America, 1966. The volume consists of exerpts of the proceedings and reports of the National Conference of Jewish Communal Service, the overall professional organization in the Jewish communal field. Because the material is firsthand, reflecting the actual issues of the decades covered, it often presents a more graphic picture of the communal field than more coherent and organized historical reviews.

Richards, Bernard G. "Organizing American Jewry" in Jacob Fried, ed., *Jews in the Modern World*, vol. 2, pp. 482-508. New York: Twayne Publishers, 1962.

Roseman, Kenneth D. "Power in a Midwestern Jewish Community," *American Jewish Archives* 21 (1969), pp. 57-83.

Sidorsky, David, ed. *The Future of the Jewish Community in America*. New York: Basic Books, 1973. The volume consists of eleven essays prepared by outstanding scholars as position papers for consideration by the American Jewish Committee on the future of the Jewish community in America. They cover historical background, demography, religious and educational institutions, and issues in current Jewish communal life.

Sklare, Marshall, ed. *The Jew in American Society*. New York: Behrman House, 1974.

Sklare, Marshall, ed. *The Jewish Community in America*. New York: Behrman House, 1974. This is a companion volume to Professor Sklare's compilation, *The Jew in American Society*, which traces the adjustment of Jews as individuals to contemporary society. In this book the various essays define the adjustment in communal terms, dealing generally with religion, Jewish education, the structure of the community, and relationships with the general society.

Vincent, Sidney Z. *The Jewish Federation: Reflections on an American Institution* (Milender Seminar address), publication of Brandeis University, 1976. A long-term practitioner in the field of Jewish community organization presents his views and judgments based on three decades of observation and experience.

Wolfe, Ann G. "The Invisible Jewish Poor," *Journal of Jewish Communal Service*, Spring 1972. This article, plus other publications by Mrs. Wolfe, presents the controversial thesis that there is a substantial body of Jewish poor in the community that is, for the most part, neglected.

ORTHODOX JUDAISM

Agus, Jacob. *Guideposts in Modern Judaism*. New York: Bloch Publishing Company, 1954.

Belkin, Samuel. *Essays in Traditional Jewish Thought.* New York: Philosophical Library, 1956.

Berkovits, Eliezer. "Authentic Judaism and Halakhah," *Judaism* (Winter 1970).

Berkovits, Eliezer. "Conversion 'According to Halakhah'—What Is It?," *Judaism* (Fall 1974).

Berkovits, Eliezer. "An Integrated Jewish World View," *Tradition* 5 (1962).

Berkovits, Eliezer. "Orthodox Judaism in a World of Revolutionary Transformations," *Tradition* (Summer 1965).

Berkovits, Eliezer. "What is Jewish Philosophy?," *Tradition* 3 (1961).

Blau, Joseph L. *Modern Varieties of Judaism.* New York: Columbia University Press, 1966.

Carlebach, Alexander. "Autonomy, Heteronomy, and Theonomy," *Tradition* 6 (1963).

Duker, Abraham G. "On Religious Trends in American Jewish Life," *YIVO Annual* 4 (1949).

Epstein, Isadore. *The Faith of Judaism.* London: The Soncino Press, 1960.

Feldman, Emanuel. "The American and the Jew," *Tradition* 3 (1960).

Glazer, Nathan. *American Judaism,* 2d ed., rev. Chicago: University of Chicago Press, 1972.

Guterman, Simeon. "Separation of Religion and State," *Tradition* 2 (1960).

Heilman, Samuel C. *Synagogue Life: A study in Symbolic Interaction.* Chicago: University of Chicago Press, 1977.

Himmelfarb, Milton, ed. *The Condition of Jewish Belief—A Symposium.* New York: Macmillan, 1966.

Howe, Irving. *World of Our Fathers.* New York: Harcourt Brace Jovanovich, 1976.

Jakobovits, Immanuel. "The Dissection of the Dead in Jewish Law," *Tradition* 1 (1958).

Jakobovits, Immanuel. "Survey of Recent Halakhic Periodical Literature," *Tradition* (Winter 1965-Spring 1966), pp. 95-101.

Jung, Leo. "Bernard Revel," *American Jewish Year Book* 43 (1942).

Kaufman, Michael. "Far Rockaway—Torah-Suburb-by-the-Sea," *Jewish Life* 27 (August 1960).

Kranzler, George. *Williamsburg: A Jewish Community in Transition.* New York: Feldheim Publishers, 1961.

Lamm, Norman. "The Ideology of the Neturai Karta—According to the Satmarer Version," *Tradition* (Fall 1971).

Lamm, Norman. "The Need for Tradition," *Tradition* 1 (1958).

Lamm, Norman. "Separate Pews in the Synagogue," *Tradition* 1 (1959).

Lamm, Norman. "The Unity Theme and Its Implications for Moderns," *Tradition* 4 (1961).

Lamm, Norman, and Wurzburger, Walter S., eds. *A Treasury of Tradition.* New York: Hebrew Publishing Co., 1967.

Levine, Howard I. "The Non-Observant Orthodox," *Tradition* 2 (1959).

Lichtenstein, Aaron. "Joseph Soloveitchik" in Simon Noveck, ed., *Great Jewish Thinkers of the Twentieth Century.* Washington, D.C.: B'nai B'rith, 1963.

Liebman, Charles S. *The Ambivalent American Jew: Politics, Religion and Family in American Jewish Life.* Philadelphia: The Jewish Publication Society of America, 1973.

Liebman, Charles S. "Changing Social Characteristics of Orthodox, Conservative and Reform Jews," *Sociological Analysis* 27 (Winter 1966).

Liebman, Charles S. "Left and Right in American Orthodoxy," *Judaism* 11 (Winter 1966).

Liebman, Charles S. "Orthodoxy in American Jewish Life," *American Jewish Year Book* 66 (1965), pp. 21-92.

Liebman, Charles S. "A Sociological Analysis of Contemporary Orthodoxy," *Judaism* 13 (Summer 1964), pp. 285-304.

Liebman, Charles S. "The Training of American Rabbis," *American Jewish Year Book* 69 (1968), pp. 3-114.

Lookstein, Joseph. "Coalitionism and Separatism in the American Jewish Community," *Tradition* (Spring 1976).

Markovitz, Eugene. "Henry Pereira Mendes: Architect of the Union of Orthodox Jewish Congregations of America," *American Jewish Historical Quarterly* 55 (1966).

Poll, Solomon. *The Hasidic Community of Williamsburg.* New York: The Free Press, 1962.

Porter, Jack. "Differentiating Features of Orthodox, Conservative, and Reform Jewish Groups in Metropolitan Philadelphia," *Jewish Social Studies* 25 (1963), pp. 186-94.

Rackman, Emanuel. "American Orthodoxy—Retrospect and Prospect," *Judaism* 3 (Fall 1954).

Rackman, Emanuel. "A Challenge to Orthodoxy," *Judaism* 18 (1969).

Rackman, Emanuel. "The Dialectic of the Halakhah," *Tradition* 3 (1958).

Rackman, Emanuel. "The Future of Jewish Law," *Tradition* 6 (1964).

Riskin, Shlomo. "Orthodoxy and Her Alleged Heretics," *Tradition* (Spring 1976).

Rubin, Israel. *Satmar, An Island in the City.* Chicago: Quadrangle Books, 1972.

Rudavsky, David. *Emancipation and Adjustment.* New York: Diplomatic Press, Inc., 1967.

Schiff, Alvin. *The Jewish Day School in America.* New York: Jewish Education Committee Press, 1966.

Schmidt, Nancy F. "An Orthodox Jewish Community in the United States: A Minority Within a Minority," *Jewish Social Studies* 27 (1965).

Schwab, Simon. *These and Those.* New York: Feldheim Publishers, 1966.

Silver, Daniel J., and Martin, Bernard. *A History of Judaism,* vol. 2. New York: Basic Books, 1974.

Singer, David. "The Growth of the Day School Movement," *Commentary* (August 1973).

Singer, David. "Voices of Orthodoxy," *Commentary* (July 1974).

Singer, David. "The Yeshiva World," *Commentary* (October 1976).

Singer, Zvi. "Public Services on the Sabbath," *Tradition* 4 (1962).

Sklare, Marshall. "Judaism at the Bicentennial," *Midstream* (November 1975).

Soloveitchik, Joseph B. "Confrontation," *Tradition* 6 (1964).

Spero, Shubert. "The Condition of Jewish Belief—A Review-Article," *Tradition* (Fall 1967).

Spero, Shubert. "Does Participation Imply Recognition?," *Tradition* (Winter 1966).

Spero, Shubert. "Is Judaism an Optimistic Religion?," *Tradition* 4 (1961).

Spero, Shubert. "The Meaning of Existentialism for Orthodoxy," *Perspective* (Winter 1959).

Spero, Shubert. "The Religious Significance of the State of Israel," *Forum* (24), 1976.

Twersky, Isadore. "Some Aspects of the Jewish Attitude Toward the Welfare State," *Tradition* 5 (1963).

Wurzburger, Walter S. "Alienation and Exile," *Tradition* 6 (1964).

CONSERVATIVE JUDAISM AND RECONSTRUCTIONISM

Adler, Cyrus. *I Have Considered the Days*. Philadelphia: Jewish Publication Society, 1941. An autobiographical memoir by a man who served as president of the Jewish Theological Seminary of America for a long time in the period between the two world wars.

Adler, Cyrus. *Lectures, Selected Papers, Addresses* (privately printed, 1933).

Agus, Jacob. *Guideposts in Modern Judaism*. New York: Bloch Publishing Co., 1954.

Bentwich, Norman. *Solomon Schechter*. Philadelphia: Jewish Publication Society, 1938.

Blau, Joseph. "The Jewish Day School," *Reconstructionist*, 14 November 1958, pp. 29-32.

Blau, Joseph. *Modern Varieties of Judaism*. New York: Columbia University Press, 1966.

Bokser, Ben Zion. "Conservative Judaism in America," *Jewish Quarterly Review* 45 (1954).

Bokser, Ben Zion. "The Interaction of History and Theology," *Judaism* 26 (Summer 1977), pp. 321-25.

Carlin, Jerome E., and Mendolovitz, Saul H. "The American Rabbi: A Religious Specialist Responds to Loss of Authority," in *The Jews: Social Structure of an American Group*, edited by Marshall Sklare. New York: The Free Press, 1958.

Cohen, Gerson D. "The Present State of Conservative Judaism," *Judaism* 26 (Summer 1977), pp. 268-74.

Cohen, Jack. "The Jewish Day School," *Reconstructionist*, 26 December 1958, pp. 27-28.

Davis, Moshe. *The Emergence of Conservative Judaism*. Philadelphia: The Jewish Publication Society of America, 1963.

Dorff, E. "Towards a Legal Theory of the Conservative Movement," *Conservative Judaism* 27 (Spring 1973), pp. 65-77.

Duker, Abraham G. "On Religious Trends in American Jewish Life," *YIVO Annual* 4 (1949).

Eisenstein, Ira, and Kohn, Eugene, eds. *Mordecai M. Kaplan: An Evaluation*. New York: The Jewish Reconstructionist Foundation, 1952.

Fierstein, R. E. "Solomon Schechter and the Zionist Movement," *Conservative Judaism* 29 (Spring 1975), pp. 3-13.

Finkelstein, Louis. "Louis Ginzberg," *Proceedings of the American Academy of Jewish Research* 23 (1954), pp. xliv-liii.

Finkelstein, Louis. "The Underlying Concepts of Conservative Judaism," *Conservative Judaism* 26 (Summer 1972), pp. 2-12.

Gershfield, E. M. "Rebuilding the Law Committee," *Conservative Judaism* 25 (Winter 1971), pp. 59-62.

Ginzberg, Eli. *Keeper of the Law: Louis Ginzberg*. Philadelphia: The Jewish Publication Society of America, 1966.

Glazer, Nathan. *American Judaism*, 2d ed., rev. Chicago: University of Chicago Press, 1972.

Gordis, Robert. "The Ethical Dimension in the Halakhah," *Conservative Judaism* 26 (Spring 1972), pp. 70-74.

Gordis, Robert. *The Jew Faces a New World*. New York: Behrman House, 1941.

Gordis, Robert. "Toward a Revitalization of Halakhah in Conservative Judaism," *Conservative Judaism* 25 (Spring 1971), pp. 49-55.

Greenberg, Simon. "The Rabbinate in the Jewish Community Structure," *Conservative Judaism* 23 (1969), pp. 52-63.

Hammer, R. A. "The Dilemma of the Conservative Rabbi," *Conservative Judaism* 27 (Summer 1973), pp. 79-82.

Hertzberg, Arthur. "The Conservative Rabbinate: A Sociological Study," in *Essays on Jewish Life and Thought*, edited by Joseph L. Blau et al. New York: Columbia University Press, 1959.

Kaplan, Mordecai M. *The Future of the American Jew*. New York: Macmillan, 1948; republished by the Reconstructionist Press, New York, 1967.

Kaplan, Mordecai M. *The Greater Judaism in the Making*. New York: The Reconstructionist Press, 1960.

Kaplan, Mordecai M. *Judaism as a Civilization: Toward a Reconstruction of American Jewish Life*. New York: Macmillan, 1934; reprinted by Schocken Books, 1967.

Kaplan, Mordecai M. *Judaism Without Supernaturalism*. New York: The Reconstructionist Press, 1958.

Kaplan, Mordecai M. *The Meaning of God in Modern Jewish Religion*. New York: Behrman House, 1937; republished by the Reconstructionist Press, New York, 1962.

Karp, Abraham J. *A History of the United Synagogue of America, 1913-1963*. New York: United Synagogue of America, 1964.

Karp, Abraham J. "The Origins of Conservative Judaism," *Conservative Judaism* 19 (Summer 1965), pp. 33-48.

Kennedy, D. G. "A Christian Parallel to the Conservative Movement," *Conservative Judaism* 22 (Summer 1968), pp. 31-38.

Kertzer, Morris N. "Synagogue Surveys—Conservative Trends," *American Jewish Year Book* 53 (1952), pp. 155ff.

Kohn, Eugene. "Conservative Judaism—A Review," *Conservative Judaism* 2 (June 1946).

Kreitman, Benjamin Z., et al. "Further Thoughts on the Law Committee," *Conservative Judaism* 26 (Winter 1972), pp. 60-84.

Lerner, S. C., et al. "The Congregational Rabbi and the Conservative Synagogue: A Symposium," *Conservative Judaism* 29 (Winter 1975), pp. 3-96.

Liebman, Charles S. *The Ambivalent American Jew: Politics, Religion and Family in American Jewish Life*. Philadelphia: The Jewish Publication Society of America, 1973.

Liebman, Charles S. "Changing Social Characteristics of Orthodox, Conservative and Reform Jews," *Sociological Analysis* 27 (Winter 1966).

Liebman, Charles S. "Reconstructionism in American Jewish Life," *American Jewish Year Book* 71 (1970), pp. 3-99.

Liebman, Charles S. "The Training of American Rabbis," *American Jewish Year Book* 69 (1968), pp. 3-114.

Louis Ginzberg Jubilee Volume. New York: American Academy for Jewish Research, 1945. The book contains a bibliography of the work of the great rabbinic scholar of the Jewish Theological Seminary compiled by Boaz Cohen.

Mandelbaum, Bernard. "The Meaning of the Conservative Movement," *Conservative Judaism* 21 (Spring 1967), pp. 54-64.

Martin, Bernard. "The God We Worship," *Reconstructionist*, 3 February 1967, pp. 14-17, and Mordecai M. Kaplan's response, *ibid.*, pp. 18ff.

Morgenbesser, Sidney, and Sidorsky, David. "Reconstructionism and the Naturalistic Tradition in America," *Reconstructionist*, 18 February 1955, pp. 33-42.

Neuman, Abraham A. *Cyrus Adler—A Biographical Sketch.* Philadelphia: The Jewish Publication Society, 1942.

Neusner, Jacob. "Conservative Judaism in a Divided Community." *Conservative Judaism* 20 (Summer 1966), pp. 1-19.

Novak, David. "The Distinctiveness of Conservative Judaism," *Judaism* 26 (Summer 1977), pp. 305-09.

Novak, David. *Law and Theology in Judaism*, first series. New York: Ktav Publishing House, Inc., 1974.

Novak, David. *Law and Theology in Judaism*, second series. New York: Ktav Publishing House, Inc., 1976.

Parzen, Herbert. *Architects of Conservative Judaism.* New York: Jonathan David Co., 1964.

Parzen, Herbert. "Conservative Judaism and Zionism," *Jewish Social Studies* 23 (1961).

Petuchowski, Jakob J. "Conservatism—Its Contribution to Judaism," *Judaism* 26 (Summer 1977), pp. 352-57.

Porter, Jack. "Differentiating Features of Orthodox, Conservative, and Reform Jewish Groups in Metropolitan Philadelphia," *Jewish Social Studies* 25 (1963).

Rabinowitz, Stanley. "Where Do We Stand Now?" *Judaism* 26 (Summer 1977), pp. 274-78.

Rosenblum, H. "Ideology and Compromise: The Evolution of the United Synagogue Constitutional Preamble," *Jewish Social Studies* 35 (January 1973), pp. 18-31.

Silver, Daniel J., and Martin, Bernard. *A History of Judaism*, vol. 2. New York: Basic Books, 1974.

Sklare, Marshall. *Conservative Judaism: An American Religious Movement*, new and augmented edition. New York: Schocken Books, 1972. An excellent sociological study of Conservatism by one of the foremost present-day sociologists of the American Jewish community.

Sklare, Marshall. "Jewish Religion and Ethnicity at the Bicentennial," *Midstream* 21 (November 1975), pp. 19-28.

Sklare, Marshall. "Judaism at the Bicentennial," *Midstream* (November 1975).

Sklare, Marshall. "Recent Developments in Conservative Judaism," *Midstream* 18 (January 1972), pp. 3-19.

Stein, Jacob. "Promise, Performance and Problems," *Judaism* 26 (Summer 1977), pp. 296-300.

Steinberg, Milton. *Anatomy of a Faith*, edited, with an introduction, by Arthur A. Cohen. New York: Harcourt, Brace and Co., 1960.

Survey of Synagogue Membership. New York: The United Synagogue of America, 1965.

Trachtenberg, Joshua. "Books on Conservative Judaism," *American Jewish Year Book* 50 (1948), pp. 164-175.

Waxman, Mordecai. "The Basic Issues—An Analysis," *Judaism* 26 (Summer 1977), pp. 279-285.

Waxman, Mordecai. "Directions for the Conservative Movement," *Conservative Judaism* 25 (Winter 1971), pp. 1-4.

Waxman, Mordecai. *Tradition and Change: The Development of Conservative Judaism*. New York: The Burning Bush Press, 1958. A collection of essays by a considerable number of the foremost organizers, thinkers, and scholars of Conservative Judaism from its beginnings in the 1880s until the 1950s.

Weiss-Rosmarin, Trude. "Women in Conservative Synagogues," *Jewish Spectator* 38 (October 1973), pp. 5-6.

Zelizer, G. S. "Some Aspects of Schechter's Theology," *Conservative Judaism* 23 (Fall 1968), pp. 76-81.

REFORM JUDAISM

Agus, Jacob. *Guideposts in Modern Judaism*. New York: Bloch Publishing Company, 1954.

American Judaism, vols. I-XVI (1951-1966). The magazine of American Reform for more than fifteen years, containing both articles of general Jewish interest and Reform organizational news.

Bemporad, Jack, ed. *The Theological Foundations of Prayer: A Reform Jewish Perspective*. New York: Union of American Hebrew Congregations, 1967. Papers delivered at the 48th General Assembly of the Union of American Hebrew Congregations in San Francisco, reflecting the diversity of Reform views on Jewish worship by such figures as Roland Gittelsohn, Bernard Martin, Levi A. Olan, and Jakob J. Petuchowski.

Bial, David Morrison. *Liberal Judaism at Home: The Practices of Modern Reform Judaism*. Summit, New Jersey: Temple Sinai, 1967. A comparison of Reform observances (outside the synagogue) with those of traditional Judaism.

Blau, Joseph L. *Modern Varieties of Judaism*. New York: Columbia University Press, 1966.

Blau, Joseph L., ed. *Reform Judaism: A Historical Perspective*. New York: Ktav Publishing House, Inc., 1973. This volume is a collection of significant essays from the yearbooks of the Central Conference of American Rabbis.

Borowitz, Eugene. *A New Jewish Theology in the Making*. Philadelphia: The Westminster Press, 1968. A Reform rabbi analyzes twentieth-century Jewish theologians and attempts to deal with some of the basic questions himself.

Cahn, Judah. "The Struggle Within Reform Judaism," *Central Conference of American Rabbis Journal* 22 (Summer 1975), pp. 63-68.

Central Conference of American Rabbis Journal, volumes I-XXIV (1953-1977). This quarterly, containing articles written mostly by Reform rabbis and scholars, reflects the major concerns of the American Reform rabbinate during the last two decades and more.

Central Conference of American Rabbis Yearbook, vols. LV-LXXXVI (1945-1976). These volumes contain reports of officers, committees, and commissions, addresses and papers, and major deliberations at the yearly CCAR conventions.

Cohen, Naomi W. "The Reaction of Reform Judaism in America to Political Zionism," *Proceedings of the American Jewish Historical Society* 40 (1951).

Cohon, Samuel S. "The History of Hebrew Union College," *Publications of the American Jewish Historical Society* 40 (September 1950).

Cohon, Samuel S. *Judaism—A Way of Life*. Cincinnati: Union of American Hebrew Congregations, 1948. A popular treatment of Judaism from a Reform point of view written by the professor of theology at the Hebrew Union College from 1923 to 1956.

Dimensions in American Judaism (for the first year: *Dimensions*), vols. I-VI (1966-1972). The most ambitious of the magazines sponsored by the Union of American Hebrew Congregations, excluding organizational news items and concentrating on symposia, articles on Jewish subjects of some depth, and reviews of the arts.

Doppelt, Frederic A., and Polish, David. *A Guide for Reform Jews*. New York: Bloch Publishing Company, 1957. Suggested observances for holidays and life-cycle events by two Reform rabbis expressing their personal views.

Eisendrath, Maurice N. *Can Faith Survive?* New York: McGraw-Hill, 1964. Reflections on a variety of Jewish subjects, including the recent history of Reform Judaism, by the rabbi who served as president of the Union of American Hebrew Congregations from 1943 until his death in 1973.

Fackenheim, Emil L. *Quest for Past and Future: Essays in Jewish Theology*. Bloomington: Indiana University Press, 1968. A collection of important writings by the most widely known theologian associated with the Reform movement.

Fein, Leonard J., Chin, Robert, Dauber, Jack, Reisman, Bernard, and Spiro, Herzl. "Reform Is a Verb," from *Reform Is a Verb: Notes on Reform and Reforming Jews* by the above. New York: Union of American Hebrew Congregations, 1972, pp. 135-151.

Fein, Leonard J., et al., *Reform Is a Verb: Notes on Reform and Reforming Jews*. New York: Union of American Hebrew Congregations, 1972. A report on a survey of Reform Jewish beliefs and practices and the Reform laity's attitudes toward intermarriage, Israel, and the Reform congregation.

Feldman, Abraham J. "The Changing Functions of the Synagogue and the Rabbi," in *Reform Judaism: Essays by Hebrew Union College Alumni*. Cincinnati: Hebrew Union College Press, 1949.

Feldman, Abraham J. *Reform Judaism: A Guide for Reform Jews.* New York: Behrman House, 1956. A prominent Reform rabbi briefly describes the principles, practices, and organizations of American Reform Judaism.

Freehof, Solomon B. *Contemporary Reform Responsa.* Cincinnati: Hebrew Union College Press, 1974. The most recent in a series of volumes in which the chairman of the Responsa Committee of the Central Conference of American Rabbis attempts to deal with current questions of religious observance against the background of the Jewish legal tradition.

Freehof, Solomon B. "Reform Judaism in America," *Jewish Quarterly Review* 45 (1954).

Freehof, Solomon B. *Reform Jewish Practice and its Rabbinic Background,* 2 vols. Cincinnati: Hebrew Union College Press, 1944-52. A description of contemporary Reform Jewish customs, ceremonies, and observances in relation to the traditional rabbinic laws from which they are derived.

Gates of Prayer—The New Union Prayerbook. New York: Central Conference of American Rabbis, 1975. The current official prayerbook of the American Reform movement for weekdays, Sabbaths, and festivals.

Gittlesohn, Roland B. *Man's Best Hope.* New York: Random House, 1961. The case for religious naturalism presented by a Reform rabbi to the Jewish layman in simple terms—with much anecdote—but dealing with most of the relevant issues.

Glazer, Nathan. *American Judaism,* 2d ed., rev. Chicago: University of Chicago Press, 1972.

Gurland, J. S. "Should Reform and Conservative Judaism Unite?," *Jewish Spectator* 38 (September 1973), pp. 9-10.

Heller, James G. *Isaac Mayer Wise: His Life, Work and Thought.* New York: Union of American Hebrew Congregations, 1965. The most authoritative and comprehensive biography of the builder of the major institutions of Reform Judaism in America.

Karff, Samuel E., ed. *Hebrew Union College-Jewish Institute of Religion at One Hundred Years.* Cincinnati: Hebrew Union College Press, 1976. A history of the American Reform seminary in the years 1947 to 1971 is found on pp. 171-243, a segment of the major part of the work (pp. 1-283), which is a history of the Hebrew Union College over the entire span of its existence, written by Michael A. Meyer.

Knox, Israel. *Rabbi in America.* Boston: Little, Brown and Company, 1957. A biography of Isaac Mayer Wise, the great organizer and builder of the national institutions of American Reform Judaism.

Korn, Bertram Wallace, ed. *Retrospect and Prospect: Essays in Commemoration of the Founding of the Central Conference of American Rabbis, 1890-1964.* New York: Central Conference of American Rabbis, 1965. These studies deal historically with the CCAR position on various Jewish issues. The final one, by Leon Feuer (pp. 252-272), evaluates the status of the Reform rabbinate in the mid-1960s.

Lelyveld, Arthur J. *Atheism is Dead: A Jewish Response to Radical Theology.* Cleveland: World Publishing Company, 1968. A refutation of the "Death-of-God" movement, together with elements of a personal experiential theology, written in popular fashion by a leading Reform rabbi.

Lenn, Theodore I., and Associates. *Rabbi and Synagogue in Reform Judaism*. New York: Central Conference of American Rabbis, 1972. The results of a survey commissioned by the CCAR containing significant statistical data regarding the Reform rabbinate and the Reform congregation.

Liberal Judaism, vols. XII-XIX (1945-1951). The magazine of American Reform in the immediate postwar period.

Liebman, Charles S. *The Ambivalent American Jew: Politics, Religion and Family in American Jewish Life*. Philadelphia: The Jewish Publication Society of America, 1973.

Liebman, Charles S. "The Training of American Rabbis," *American Jewish Year Book* 69 (1968), pp. 3-114.

Martin, Bernard, ed. *Contemporary Reform Jewish Thought*. Chicago: Quadrangle Books, 1968. A dozen essays by thoughtful Reform rabbis that reflect the breadth of the current Reform theological spectrum.

Mervis, Leonard J. "The Social Justice Movement and the American Reform Rabbi," *American Jewish Archives* 7 (1955).

Philipson, David. *The Reform Movement in Judaism*. New York: Ktav Publishing House, 1967. This major, but tendentious, history of Reform Judaism first appeared in 1907 (rev. ed., 1933). The current edition contains a brief introduction by Solomon B. Freehof that deals with the more recent history of the movement.

Plaut, W. Gunther, ed. *The Growth of Reform Judaism*. New York: World Union for Progressive Judaism, 1965. While this reader of American and European sources does not go beyond 1948, it contains an epilogue (pp. 347-362) summarizing developments during the following fifteen years.

Porter, Jack. "Differentiating Features of Orthodox, Conservative, and Reform Jewish Groups in Metropolitan Philadelphia," *Jewish Social Studies* 25 (July 1963), pp. 186-194.

Rabbi's Manual. Cincinnati: Central Conference of American Rabbis, 1928; rev. ed., 1961. Prayers and services for circumcision, conversion, marriages, funerals, and other occasions in the life of the individual, the congregation, or the community.

Reform Judaism: Essays by Hebrew Union College Alumni. Cincinnati: Hebrew Union College Press, 1949. This volume contains essays by such prominent Reform rabbis of the mid-century as Bernard Bamberger, Levi A. Olan, Joshua Loth Liebman, Solomon B. Freehof, Abraham J. Feldman, and several others.

Reform Judaism, vols. I-VI (1972-1977). This is the current monthly publication of the Union of American Hebrew Congregations. It is popular in nature, more of a newspaper than a magazine.

Resolutions Passed by the Central Conference of American Rabbis, 1889-1974. New York: Central Conference of American Rabbis, 1975. Resolutions on specifically Jewish and general humanitarian issues adopted by the Reform rabbinate.

Rudavsky, David. *Emancipation and Adjustment*. New York: Diplomatic Press, Inc., 1967.

Schwartzman, Sylvan D. *Reform Judaism Then and Now.* New York: Union of American Hebrew Congregations, 1971. A textbook for young people containing considerable information on the structure of Reform Judaism today and the issues that divide it.

Schwartzman, Sylvan D. *The Story of Reform Judaism.* New York: Union of American Hebrew Congregations, 1953.

Siegel, Lawrence. "Reflections on Neo-Reform in the Central Conference of American Rabbis," *American Jewish Archives* 20 (1968).

Silver, Daniel J., and Martin, Bernard. *A History of Judaism,* vol. 2. New York: Basic Books, 1974.

Steinberg, Stephen. "Reform Judaism: The Origin and Evolution of a Church Movement," *Journal for the Scientific Study of Religion* 5 (Fall 1965), pp. 117-129.

Tadrikh le-Shabbat, A Shabbat Manual. New York: Central Conference of American Rabbis, 1972. A guide for Sabbath observance by Reform Jews.

Temkin, Sefton D. "A Century of Reform Judaism in America," *American Jewish Year Book* 74 (1973), pp. 3-75. A historical survey of the movement in America, concentrating on the Union of American Hebrew Congregations.

Tepfer, John J., and Kiev, I. Edward. "The Jewish Institute of Religion," *American Jewish Year Book* 49 (1947-48).

Vorspan, Albert. *Jewish Values and Social Crisis.* New York: Union of American Hebrew Congregations, rev. ed., 1971. A casebook for social action, intended especially for congregational social-action committees, which attempts to discuss in a liberal Jewish framework issues ranging from the Vietnam War and race relations to Soviet Jewry and ecology.

Vorspan, Albert, and Lipman, Eugene J. *Justice and Judaism.* New York: Union of American Hebrew Congregations, 1956. An attempt to apply certain moral values of Judaism to the major social issues in America of the mid-1950s, written in collaboration by the then executive secretary and the director of the Commission on Social Action of Reform Judaism.

Wolf, Arnold Jacob, ed. *Rediscovering Judaism.* Chicago: Quadrangle Books, 1965. Theological reflections by nine Jewish thinkers, most of them associated with the Reform movement.

ISRAEL AND DIASPORA JEWRY: AN AMERICAN PERSPECTIVE

AlRoy, Gil Carl. *Behind the Middle East Conflict: The Real Impasse Between Arab and Jew.* New York: G.P. Putnam's Sons, 1975.

Apter, David, ed. *Ideology and Discontent.* New York: The Free Press, 1964.

Arian, Alan. *Ideological Change in Israel.* Cleveland: The Press of Case Western Reserve University, 1968.

Aron, Raymond. *The Opium of the Intellectuals.* Garden City, New York: Doubleday and Co., 1957.

Avineri, Shlomo. "The Palestinians and Israel," *Commentary* 49 (June 1970).

Bell, Daniel. *The End of Ideology.* New York: The Free Press, 1965.

Ben-Ezer, Ehud, ed. *Unease in Zion.* New York: Quadrangle Press, 1974.

Ben-Gurion, David. *My Talks With Arab Leaders.* New York: The Free Press, 1973.

Brickman, William W. "Comments on the Impact of Israel on American Jewish Education," *Jewish Social Studies* 21 (1959).

Buber, Martin. *Israel and Palestine: The History of an Idea.* London: East and West Library, 1952.

Burton, William L. "Protestant America and the Rebirth of Israel," *Jewish Social Studies* 26 (1964).

Cohen, J. J. "Religion in Israel: (The Conservative and Reform 'Presence')," *Jewish Frontier* 6 (October 1967), pp. 6-12.

Davis, Moshe, ed. *World Jewry and the State of Israel.* New York: Herzl Press and Arno Press, 1977. The following essays are particularly valuable: E. E. Urbach, "Center and Periphery in Jewish Historic Consciousness: Contemporary Implications"; Gerson D. Cohen, "From *Altneuland* to *Altneuvolk* — Toward an Agenda for Interaction between Israel and American Jewry"; Irving Greenberg, "The Interaction of Israel and the Diaspora after the Holocaust"; Charles S. Liebman, "Diaspora Influence on Israel Policy"; Nathan Rotenstreich, "State and Diaspora in Our Time"; and Eli Ginzberg, "Towards an Israel-Diaspora Policy."

Davis, Moshe, ed. *The Yom Kippur War.* New York: Arno Press, 1974.

Dawidowicz, Lucy. "The United States and the State of Israel," *American Jewish Year Book* 56 (1955); 57 (1956).

Dispersion and Unity. Jerusalem: World Zionist Organization, 1967, 1971-1974.

Duker, Abraham G. "Some Aspects of Israel's Impact on Identification and Cultural Patterns," *Jewish Social Studies* 21 (1959).

Eliav, Arie Lova. *Land of the Hart.* Philadelphia: The Jewish Publication Society of America, 1974.

Eliav, Arie Lova. *New Targets for Israel.* Tel Aviv: reprinted from three articles in *Davar*, November 1968 and February 1969.

Elon, Amos. *The Israelis: Founders and Sons.* New York: Holt, Rinehart and Winston, 1971.

Fein, Leonard. *Israel: Politics and People.* Boston: Little, Brown and Company, 1967.

Forum. Jerusalem: World Zionist Organization, 1975-77. An important journal dealing with the problems of Israel, Zionism, and world Jewry.

Goldmann, Nahum. "The Future of Israel," *Foreign Affairs* 58 (April 1970).

Halpern, Ben. *The Idea of the Jewish State.* Cambridge, Massachusetts: Harvard University Press, 1961.

Halpern, Ben. "The Impact of Israel on American Jewish Ideologies," *Jewish Social Studies* 21 (1959).

Herman, Simon N. "American Jewish Students in Israel," *Jewish Social Studies* 24 (1962).

Hertzberg, Arthur, ed. *The Zionist Idea: An Historical Analysis and Reader.* New York: Meridian Books, 1960.

Herzog, Chaim. *The War of Atonement.* London: Weidenfeld and Nicolson, 1975.

Himmelfarb, Milton. "Observations on the Impact of Israel on American Jewish Ideologies," *Jewish Social Studies* 21 (1959).

Hirsch, Richard G. *Reform Judaism and Israel*. New York: Union of American Hebrew Congregations Commission on Israel, 1972. A pamphlet in which the executive director of the World Union for Progressive Judaism elaborates three theses concerning the relationship between Reform Judaism and the Jewish state.

In the Dispersion. Jerusalem: World Zionist Organization, 1964-1965.

Isaac, Erich, and Isaac, Rael Jean. "Israel's Dissenting Intellectuals," *Conservative Judaism* 26 (Spring 1972).

Isaac, Rael Jean. *Israel Divided, Ideological Politics in the Jewish State*. Baltimore and London: Johns Hopkins University Press, 1976.

Karp, A. J. "Reaction to Zionism and to the State of Israel in the American Jewish Religious Community," *Jewish Journal of Sociology* 8 (December 1966), pp. 150-174.

Kollin, G. "Israel: Anticipation and Reality. A Conservative-Reform *Bet Din* in Israel," *Conservative Judaism* 27 (Spring 1973), pp. 34-43.

Laqueur, Walter. *A History of Zionism*. New York: Holt, Rinehart and Winston, 1972.

Neufeld, Edward. "Further Comments on the Impact of Israel on American Jewish Ideologies," *Jewish Social Studies* 21 (1959).

Ofry, Dan. *The Yom Kippur War*. Tel Aviv: Zohar Publishing Co., 1974.

Patai, Raphael, ed. *Encyclopedia of Zionism and Israel*, 2 vols. New York: Herzl Press and McGraw Hill, 1971.

Polish, David. "American Jews and Israel," *Hadassah Magazine* (May 1975).

Polish, David. *Israel—Nation and People*. New York: Ktav Publishing House, Inc., 1975.

Polish, David. *Renew Our Days*. Jerusalem: World Union for Progressive Judaism and World Zionist Organization, 1976.

Rubinstein, Amnon. "The Israelis: No More Doves," *New York Times Magazine*, 21 October 1973.

Safran, Nadav. *The United States and Israel*. Cambridge, Massachusetts: Harvard University Press, 1963.

Shapira, Abraham, ed. *Siach Lochamim* (Talk of Fighting Men). Tel Aviv: Young Members of the Kibbutz Movement, 1970. Published in English as *The Seventh Day: Soldiers Talk About the Six Day War*. New York: Charles Scribner's Sons, 1970.

Sidorsky, David, ed. *The Future of the American Jewish Community*. New York: Basic Books, 1973.

Talmon, J. S. *Israel Among the Nations: Reflections on Jewish Statehood*. Jerusalem: World Zionist Organization, 1970.

Whartman, Eliezer. "Attitudes of American Rabbis on Zionism and Israel," *Jewish Social Studies* 17 (1955).

JEWISH EDUCATION

Ackerman, Walter I. "The Americanization of Jewish Education," *Judaism* 24 (Fall 1975), pp. 416-35.

Ackerman, Walter I. *An Analysis of Selected Courses of Study of Conservative Congregational Schools.* New York: Melton Research Center, Jewish Theological Seminary of America, 1968.

Ackerman, Walter I. "Jewish Education—For What?" *American Jewish Year Book* 70 (1969), pp. 3-36.

Ackerman, Walter I. "The Present Moment in Jewish Education," *Midstream* 18 (December 1972), pp. 3-24.

Ben-Horin, Meir. "Some Recent Trends in Jewish Educational Thought," *American Jewish Year Book* 60 (1959).

Berkovits, Eliezer. "Jewish Education in a World Adrift," *Tradition* 11 (Fall 1970), pp. 5-12.

Borowitz, Eugene B. "Problems Facing Jewish Educational Philosophy in the Sixties," *American Jewish Year Book* 62 (1961), pp. 145-53.

Chanover, Hyman. "Israelis Teaching in American Jewish Schools: Findings of an Exploratory Survey," in Oscar Janowsky, ed. *The Education of American Jewish Teachers.* Boston: Beacon Press, 1967.

Cohen, Samuel I. "Adult Jewish Education," *American Jewish Year Book* 66 (1965).

Dinin, Samuel. "Curriculum of the Jewish School," *American Jewish Year Book* 63 (1962).

Dushkin, Alexander M. "Common Elements in American Jewish Teaching," *Jewish Education* (November 1945), pp. 5-12.

Dushkin, Alexander M. "Fifty Years of American Jewish Education: Retrospect and Prospects," *Jewish Education* 37 (Winter 1967).

Dushkin, Alexander M. and Engelman, Uriah Z. *Jewish Education in the United States.* New York: American Association for Jewish Education, 1959.

Engelman, Uriah Z. "Jewish Education," *American Jewish Year Book* 49 (1947-1948).

Engelman, Uriah Z. "Jewish Education," *American Jewish Year Book* 52 (1951).

Engelman, Uriah Z. "Jewish Education," *American Jewish Year Book* 61 (1960).

Epstein, Melech. "The Yiddish School Movement," *Contemporary Jewish Record* 6 (1943).

Fishman, Joshua A. "Social Science Research and Jewish Education," *Jewish Education* (Winter 1957-58).

Fox, Seymour. "Toward a General Theory of Jewish Education" in David Sidorsky, ed. *The Future of the Jewish Community in America*, pp. 260-270. New York: Basic Books, 1973.

Frank, Isaac. "Teaching the Tragic Events of Jewish History," *Jewish Education* 34 (Spring 1964).

Gartner, Lloyd P. "Jewish Education in the United States," in *Jewish Education in the United States: A Documentary History*, edited by Lloyd P. Gartner, pp. 1-33. New York: Teachers College Press, 1969.

Gartner, Lloyd P., ed. *Jewish Education in the United States: A Documentary History.* New York: Teachers College Press, Columbia University, 1969.

Goren, A. *New York Jews and the Quest for Community: The Kehillah Experiment.* New York: Columbia University Press, 1970.

Hertzberg, Arthur. "Seventy Years of Jewish Education," *Judaism* 1 (October 1952).

Himmelfarb, Harold S. "Jewish Education for Naught: Educating the Culturally

Deprived Jewish Child," *Analysis.* Washington, D.C.: Institute for Jewish Policy Planning and Research of the Synagogue Council of America, no. 51, September 1975.

Himmelfarb, Milton. "Reflections on the Jewish Day School," *Commentary* 30 (July 1960), pp. 29-36.

Hochberg, Hillel. "Trends and Developments in Jewish Education," *American Jewish Year Book* 73 (1972), pp. 194-235.

Hochberg, Hillel, and Lang, Gerhard. "The Jewish High School in 1972-73: Status and Trends," *American Jewish Year Book* 75 (1974-1975).

Honor, Leo L. "The Impact of the American Environment and American Ideas on Jewish Education in the United States," *Jewish Quarterly Review* 45 (1954).

Honor, Leo L. "Jewish Elementary Education in the United States (1901-1950)," *Proceedings of the American Jewish Historical Society* 42 (1952).

Isaacman, D. "Jewish Education in Camping," *American Jewish Year Book* 67 (1966).

Israel and the Jewish School in America: A Statement of Objectives. The Commission on Teaching About Israel in America, American Association for Jewish Education, 18 May 1969.

Jacoby, Emil. *A Study of School Continuation and Dropout Following Bar Mitzvah.* Los Angeles: University of Judaism and Bureau of Jewish Education, Los Angeles Federation Council, 1969.

Janowsky, Oscar I. "The Cleveland Bureau of Education, A Case Study (1924-1953)," *American Jewish Historical Quarterly* 54 (1965).

Janowsky, Oscar I., ed. *The Education of American Jewish Teachers.* Boston: Beacon Press, 1967.

Kaminetsky, Joseph, and Friedman, Murray I., eds. *Hebrew Day School Education: An Overview.* New York: Torah U'Mesorah, 1970.

Lasker, A. "What Parents Want from the Jewish Education of Their Children," *Journal of Jewish Communal Service* 52 (Summer 1976).

Lehrer, Leibush. "The Dynamic Role of Jewish Symbols in the Psychology of the Jewish Child of America," *YIVO Annual* 6 (1951).

Levinson, Boris M. "The Intelligence of Applicants for Admission to Jewish Day Schools," *Jewish Social Studies* 19 (1957).

Levitats, Isaac. "The Organization and Management of Jewish Schools in America," *YIVO Annual* 11 (1956-57).

Lieber, David. "The Conservative Congregational School," *Conservative Judaism* 27 (Summer 1973), pp. 24-34.

Lipnick, Bernard. "An Organic Peer Community: An Experiment in Jewish Teen-Age Education," *Jewish Education* 43 (Summer 1975), pp. 38-41.

Lukinsky, Joseph. "The Education Program of the Jewish Theological Seminary—Distinctive Assumptions," in "New Models in Preparing Personnel for Jewish Education," *Jewish Education* 43 (Fall 1974).

Margolis, I. *Jewish Teacher Training Schools in the United States.* New York: National Council for Torah Education, 1964.

Myers, Lawrence, ed. *Teaching in the Jewish Religious School.* New York: Department of Teacher Education, Union of American Hebrew Congregations, 1967. A collection of essays sponsored by the Reform movement.

Nardi, Noah. "A Study of Afternoon Hebrew Schools in the United States," *Jewish Social Studies* 8 (1946).

National Census of Jewish Education. New York: American Association for Jewish Education, Information Bulletin no. 28, December 1967.

Parker, Franklin. "Jewish Education: A Partial List of American Doctoral Dissertations," *Jewish Social Studies* 3 (1961).

Pearl, Chaim. "American Jewish Education: An English View," *Jewish Journal of Sociology* 3 (1961).

Personnel Review and Trends. New York: Educators Assembly of the United Synagogue of America, 1968.

Pilch, Judah. "The Shoah and the Jewish School," *Jewish Education* 34 (Spring 1964), p. 164.

Pilch, Judah. "Changing Patterns in Jewish Education," *Jewish Social Studies* 21 (1959).

Pilch, Judah, ed. *A History of Jewish Education in the United States.* New York: American Association for Jewish Education, 1969.

Pinsky, Irving. "The Graduates of Rabbi Jacob Joseph School: A Follow-Up Study," *Jewish Education* (Spring 1962), pp. 180-183.

Pollak, George. "The Jewish Day School Graduate," *Jewish Spectator* (February 1962), pp. 11-14.

Pollak, George, and Efron, Benjamin. "Current Trends in Jewish Communal Education," *The Pedagogic Reporter* 27 (Spring 1976), pp. 2-9.

Rhodes, A. Lewis, and Nam, Charles B. "The Religious Context of Educational Expectations," *American Sociological Review* (April 1970), pp. 253-267.

Rosenack, M. "Israel and American Jewish Education," *Jewish Education* 42 (Spring 1973).

Rosenack, M. "On the Teaching of Israel in Jewish Schools," *Jewish Education* 42 (Winter 1972-73).

Roskies, Diane K. *Teaching the Holocaust to Children: A Review and Bibliography.* New York: Ktav Publishing House, Inc., 1975.

Rudavsky, David. "Jewish Education and the Religious Revival," *YIVO Annual* 13 (1965).

Ruffman, Louis L. *Curriculum Guide for the Congregational School,* rev. ed. New York: United Synagogue Commission on Jewish Education, 1959. An "official" guide for religious schools sponsored by Conservative synagogues.

Sanua, Victor D. "Jewish Education and Attitudes of Jewish Adolescents," in *The Teenager and Jewish Education.* New York: Educators Assembly of the United Synagogue of America, 1968.

Schiff, Alvin I. "Israel in American Jewish Schools," *Jewish Education* 30 (October 1968), pp. 6-24.

Schiff, Alvin I. *The Jewish Day School in America.* New York: Jewish Education Committee Press, 1966.

Schulweis, Harold. "The Holocaust Dybbuk," *Moment* (February 1976).

Schulweis, Harold, in "Teaching the Tragic Events of Jewish History," *Jewish Education* 34 (Spring 1964).

Siegel, M. "A Hebrew High School Grows in Brooklyn," *United Synagogue Review* 21 (January 1969), pp. 10-11.

Spiro, Jack. "Toward a Conceptual Framework for Reform Jewish Education," *Compass*, Commission on Jewish Education, CCAR-UAHC, no. 13 (January-February 1971).
Ury, Zalman F., in "The Shoah and the Jewish School," *Jewish Education* 34 (Spring 1964).
Vincent, Sidney Z. "Summary of Jewish Education Study in Cleveland, Ohio," *American Jewish Year Book* 57 (1956).
Weinberger, P. "The Effects of Jewish Education," *American Jewish Year Book* 72 (1971).
Weinstein, David, and Yizhar, Michael. *Modern Jewish Educational Thought: Problems and Prospects*. Chicago: College of Jewish Studies, 1964.
Winter, Nathan. *Jewish Education in a Pluralist Society*. New York: New York University Press, 1966.

HIGHER JEWISH LEARNING

Band, Arnold J. "Jewish Studies in American Liberal Arts Colleges and Universities," *American Jewish Year Book* 67 (1966), pp. 3-30. Until the long delayed publication of a 1975 study undertaken by the Association for Jewish Studies, this article remains the most comprehensive overview of the Jewish Studies field and its university setting.
Berkovits, Eliezer. "A Contemporary Rabbinical School for Orthodox Jewry," *Tradition* 13 (1971), pp. 5-20.
Berlin, Charles. "Library Resources for Jewish Studies in the United States," *American Jewish Year Book* 75 (1974-75), pp. 3-53. A competent and useful study of the development of Judaica libraries by a trained professional. Berlin, the librarian of Harvard's collection, concludes with an action agenda which suggests the need for a documentation center.
Cohon, Samuel S. "The History of Hebrew Union College," *Publications of the American Jewish Historical Society* 40 (September 1950), pp. 17-55.
Davis, Moshe. *The Emergence of Conservative Judaism*. Philadelphia: The Jewish Publication Society of America, 1968. A detailed study of the founding of the Jewish Theological Seminary which, unfortunately, does not go beyond the period of inception. This history needs to be written.
Elbogen, Ismar. "American Jewish Scholarship: An Overview," *American Jewish Year Book* 45 (1943-44), pp. 47-65. An impressionistic review of scholarship in traditional fields up to World War II.
Fasman, Oscar Z. "Trends in the American Yeshiva Today," *Tradition* 9 (1967), pp. 48-64.
Greenberg, Meyer. "The Jewish Student at Yale: His Attitude Toward Judaism," *YIVO Annual* 1 (1946).
Hartstein, Jacob I. "Yeshiva University; Growth of Rabbi Isaac Elchanan Theological Seminary," *American Jewish Year Book* 48 (1946-47), pp. 73-84.
Jick, Leon A., ed. *The Teaching of Judaica in American Universities: The Proceedings of a Colloquium*. New York: Ktav Publishing House, Inc., 1970.
Jospe, Alfred. "Jewish College Students in the United States," *American Jewish Year Book* 65 (1964).

Karff, Samuel E., ed. *Hebrew Union College-Jewish Institute of Religion at One Hundred Years*. Cincinnati: Hebrew Union College Press, 1976. A self-study by the HUC-JIR faculty which includes an extended critical history of the institution by Michael A. Meyer. The book concludes with separate notes on publications and faculty in five areas: Bible, rabbinics, theology and philosophy, history, Hebrew and Hebrew literature.

Katsh, Abraham I. "Hebraic Studies in American Higher Education: An Evaluation of Current Trends," *Jewish Social Studies* 21 (1959).

Klaperman, Gilbert. "Yeshiva University: Seventy-Five Years in Retrospect," *American Jewish Historical Quarterly* 54 (1964), pp. 5-50, 198-201. This well-written history is based on the author's doctoral dissertation and presents an understandable, if uncritical, picture.

Levine, Baruch, et al. "A Symposium on Jewish Studies in the University," *Conservative Judaism* 27 (Winter 1973), pp. 3-39. A useful collection of papers, including Paul Ritterband's statistical analysis of the growth of student enrollment and teaching opportunities.

Lewkowitz, Albert. "The Significance of 'Wissenschaft des Judentums' for the Development of Judaism," *Historia Judaica* (October 1954).

Liebman, Charles S. "The Training of American Rabbis," *American Jewish Year Book* 69 (1968), pp. 3-112. A thorough statistical study by an Orthodox sociologist of the faculty, curriculum, and student body of the major seminaries. The study is limited to seminary plans and programs which center on rabbinic training. In its time this piece raised many institutional hackles.

Lipset, S. M., and Ladd, E. L., Jr. "Jewish Academics in the United States: Their Achievements, Culture and Politics," *American Jewish Year Book* 72 (1971), pp. 89-128. An analysis of the political and social attitudes of academics who happen to be Jewish which sheds some light on their alienation from the Jewish community.

Lukinsky, Joseph. "The Education Program of the Jewish Theological Seminary—Distinctive Assumptions," in "New Models in Preparing Personnel for Jewish Education," *Jewish Education* 43 (Fall 1974).

Margolis, Isidor. *Jewish Teacher Training Schools in the United States*. New York: National Council for Torah Education of Mizrachi-Hapoel Ma-Mizrachi, 1964. A pedantic look at teacher training institutions, factual but uncritical.

Neuman, Abraham A. "The Dropsie College for Hebrew and Cognate Learning: Basic Principles and Objectives" in *The Seventy-Fifth Anniversary Volume of The Jewish Quarterly Review* (January 1967). A presidential analysis written by the school's longtime head.

Neusner, Jacob. *The Academic Study of Judaism*. New York: Ktav Publishing House, Inc., 1975. A collection of previously published papers which raise issues as to the content, range, and perspective of Jewish Studies in a university setting. Each paper concludes with some second thoughts by the writer.

Panzer, Mitchell. "Gratz College," in *Gratz College Anniversary Volume*, pp. 1-19. Philadelphia: Gratz College, 1970. A short institutional history.

Rudavsky, David. "Hebraic Studies in Colleges and Universities with Special Reference to New York University," in I. Naamani and D. Rudavsky, eds. *Doron.* New York: National Association of Professors of Hebrew, 1965. A brief, uncritical overview of Hebrew studies which traces the emergence of Hebrew language studies from a divinity school discipline into a modern language and literature specialty.

Silver, Daniel J., et al. "The Future of Rabbinic Training in America—A Symposium," *Judaism* 14 (Fall 1969), pp. 387-420. A many-sided discussion of perceived problems in rabbinical education which has the advantage of being remarkably free of institutional defensiveness.

THE SYNAGOGUE AND LITURGICAL DEVELOPMENTS

Berkovits, Eliezer."Prayer," in Leon D. Stitskin, ed. *Studies in Torah Judaism.* New York: Yeshiva University Press and Ktav Publishing House, Inc., 1969.

Birnbaum, Philip, ed. *Daily Prayer Book: Ha-Siddur Ha-Shalem.* New York: The Hebrew Publishing Company, 1949.

Blau, Joseph L. "The Spiritual Life of American Jewry, 1654-1954," *American Jewish Year Book* 55 (1955), pp. 136ff.

Bokser, Ben Zion, ed. *Ha-Mahzor.* New York: Hebrew Publishing Company, 1959.

Bokser, Ben Zion, ed. *Ha-Siddur.* New York: Hebrew Publishing Company, 1957.

Bronstein, Herbert, ed. *A Passover Haggadah —The New Union Haggadah.* New York: Central Conference of American Rabbis, 1974; rev. ed., 1975. The current Reform home liturgy for the eve of Passover.

Daily Prayer Book. New York: The Jewish Reconstructionist Foundation, 1963.

de Sola Pool, David, ed. *Book of Prayer.* New York: The Union of Sephardic Congregations, 1941.

Festival Prayer Book. New York: The Jewish Reconstructionist Foundation, 1958.

Friedland, Eric L. *The Historical and Theological Development of Non-Orthodox Jewish Prayer Books in the United States.* Ann Arbor, Michigan: University Microfilms, 1967.

Gates of the House, The Union Home Prayer Book. New York: Central Conference of American Rabbis, 1977.

Gates of Prayer: The New Union Prayer Book. New York: Central Conference of American Rabbis, 1975.

Glatzer, Nahum N., ed. *Language of Faith.* New York: Schocken Books, 1967.

Goldmeier, H. "Changing Views of God among American Jews," *Religious Education* 71 (1976), pp. 57-67.

Greenberg, Sidney, and Levin, Jonathan. *Likrat Shabbat.* Bridgeport, Connecticut: The Prayer Book Press of Media Judaica, Inc., 1973.

Greenberg, Sidney, and Sugarman, S. Allan. *A Contemporary High Holiday Service.* Bridgeport, Connecticut: The Prayer Book Press of Media Judaica, Inc., 1971.

Harlow, Jules, ed. *The Bond of Life: A Book for Mourners.* New York: The Rabbinical Assembly, 1975.

Harlow, Jules, ed. *Mahzor for Rosh Hashanah and Yom Kippur.* New York: The Rabbinical Assembly, 1972.

Heinemann, Joseph, with Petuchowski, Jakob J. *The Literature of the Synagogue.* New York: Behrman House, Inc., 1975.

Hertzberg, Arthur. "The American Jew and His Religion," in Oscar I. Janowsky, ed., *The American Jew: A Reappraisal.* Philadelphia: The Jewish Publication Society of America, 1964.

High Holiday Prayer Book: Prayers for Rosh Hashanah, volume I. New York: The Jewish Reconstructionist Foundation, 1948.

High Holiday Prayer Book: Prayers for Yom Kippur, vol. II. New York: The Jewish Reconstructionist Foundation, 1948.

Kaplan, Mordecai M., Kohn, Eugene, and Eisenstein, Ira, eds. *The New Haggadah.* New York: The Jewish Reconstructionist Foundation, rev. ed., 1942.

Kelman, Wolfe. "The Synagogue in America" in David Sidorsky, ed., *The Future of the Jewish Community in America.* New York: Basic Books, 1973.

Klausner, Samuel Z. "Synagogues in Transition: A Planning Prospectus," *Conservative Judaism* 25 (Fall 1970), pp. 42-54.

Klein, Max E., ed. *Seder Avodah,* 2 vols. Philadelphia: Maurice Jacobs, Inc., 1951 and 1960.

Koltun, Elizabeth, ed. *The Jewish Woman: New Perspectives.* New York: Schocken Books, 1976.

Laderman, Manuel. "A Love-Letter to My Congregation," *Judaism* 20 (1971), pp. 306-312.

Lenski, Gerhard. *The Religious Factor,* rev. ed. New York: Doubleday, Anchor Books, 1963.

Levin, L. "Whither Conservative Liturgy?" *Judaism* 22 (Fall 1973), pp. 433-39.

Levy, Richard N. *New Windows on an Ancient Day: An Experimental Sabbath Evening Service.* Central Conference of American Rabbis, 1970.

Levy, Richard N. *Service for the New Year: Rosh Hashanah and Yom Kippur.* Los Angeles: Los Angeles Hillel Council, 1969-1970.

Martin, Bernard. *Prayer in Judaism.* New York and London: Basic Books, Inc., 1968.

Millgram, Abraham. *Jewish Worship.* Philadelphia: The Jewish Publication Society of America, 1971.

Neusner, Jacob, and Eisenstein, Ira. *The Havurah Idea.* New York: The Reconstructionist Press, n.d.

Olan, Levi A. "A New Prayer Book—Conservative Judaism Finds Itself," *Judaism* 22 (Fall 1973), pp. 418-25.

Petuchowski, Jakob J. "Conservative Liturgy Come of Age," *Conservative Judaism* 27 (Fall 1972), pp. 3-11.

Petuchowski, Jakob J. *Prayer Book Reform in Europe.* New York: World Union for Progressive Judaism, 1968.

Sabbath Prayer Book. New York: The Jewish Reconstructionist Foundation, 1945.

Shmueli, E. "The Appeal of Hasidism for American Jewry Today," *Jewish Journal of Sociology* 11 (1969), pp. 5-30.

Silverman, Morris. *High Holiday Prayer Book.* Hartford, Connecticut: Prayer Book Press, 1951.

Sklare, Marshall. "Church and Laity Among Jews," *The Annals of the American Academy of Political and Social Science* 332 (November 1960), pp. 60-69.
Sklare, Marshall. "The Sociology of the American Synagogue," *Social Compass* 18 (1971), pp. 375-384.
Stern, Chaim, ed. *Gates of the House.* New York: Central Conference of American Rabbis, 1977. A replacement of the *Union Home Prayer Book.*
Union Home Prayer Book. Cincinnati: Central Conference of American Rabbis, 1951. Prayers and meditations for occasions of joy and sorrow in use from 1971 to 1977 in Reform Jewish homes.
The Union Prayerbook for Jewish Worship, Part I, newly rev. ed. Cincinnati: Central Conference of American Rabbis, 1940. The Sabbath, festival, and weekday prayerbook of the American Reform movement from 1940 to 1975.
The Union Prayerbook for Jewish Worship, Part II, newly rev. ed. Cincinnati: Central Conference of American Rabbis, 1945. The High Holy Day prayerbook of the American Reform movement.
Waskow, Arthur, ed. *Freedom Seder.* New York: Holt, Rinehart, and Winston, 1970.

ANTI-SEMITISM

Ackerman, Nathan W., and Jahoda, Marie. *Anti-Semitism and Emotional Disorder: A Psychoanalytic Interpretation.* New York: Harper and Brothers, 1950.
Adorno, Theodor W., et al. *The Authoritarian Personality.* New York: Harper and Brothers, 1950.
Allport, Gordon. *The Nature of Prejudice.* Cambridge, Massachusetts: Addison-Wesley Publishing Company, Inc.
Baltzell, E. Digby. *The Protestant Establishment.* New York: Random House, 1964.
Bettelheim, Bruno. "The Dynamism of Anti-Semitism in Gentile and Jew," *Journal of Abnormal and Social Psychology* 42 (April 1947), pp. 153-168.
Bettelheim, Bruno. "How Arm Our Children Against Anti-Semitism?" *Commentary* (September 1951).
Bloomgarden, Lawrence. "Discrimination in Education," *American Jewish Year Book* 55 (1954).
Cahnman, Werner J. "Socio-Economic Causes of Anti-Semitism," *Social Problems* 5 (July 1957), pp. 21-29.
Chertoff, Mordecai S. *The New Left and the Jews.* New York: Pitman Publishing Corp., 1971.
Combatting Anti-Semitism Today. A report of a conference under the auspices of the National Community Relations Advisory Council. New York: 1968.
Dawidowicz, Lucy. "Can Anti-Semitism be Measured?," *Commentary* 50 (July 1970), pp. 36-43.
Dinnerstein, Leonard, ed. *Anti-Semitism in the United States.* New York: Holt, Rinehart and Winston, 1971.
Ellerin, Milton. "Rightist Extremism," *American Jewish Year Book* 67 (1966); 69 (1968).

Epstein, Benjamin R., and Forster, Arnold. *The Radical Right*. New York: Random House, 1967. The volume exposes the anti-Semitic quotient in extreme right-wing groups of the 1960s and 1970s, such as the John Birch Society and Liberty Lobby.

Epstein, Benjamin R., and Forster, Arnold. *Some of My Best Friends*. . . . New York: Farrar, Straus and Cudahy, 1962. An Anti-Defamation League survey of social, educational, and employment discrimination against Jews in the early 1960s.

Fineberg, S. A. "Can Anti-Semitism Be Outlawed?," *Contemporary Jewish Record* 6 (December 1943), pp. 619-631.

Fineberg, S. A. "Checkmate for Rabble-Rousers," *Commentary* 2 (September 1946), pp. 220-26.

Fineberg, S. A. *Deflating the Professional Bigot*. New York: The American Jewish Committee, 1967.

Fineberg, S. A. "Strategy of Error," *Contemporary Jewish Record* 8 (February 1945), pp. 25-30.

Forster, Arnold. *A Measure of Freedom*. Garden City, New York: Doubleday and Company, 1950.

Forster, Arnold, and Epstein, Benjamin R. *The New Anti-Semitism*. New York: McGraw-Hill Book Company, 1974. A documented analysis of new forms in which anti-Semitism has appeared and of a new acceptance it has often achieved in "respectable" circles. This work also details anti-Semitism in the media and the arts, as well as among the clergy, the radical left, minority communities, and Arab sympathizers.

Gilbert, Arthur. *The Jew in Christian America*. New York: Sheed and Ward, 1966. A personal perspective on historical and contemporary problems.

Glazer, Nathan. "The New Left and the Jews," in *The Jewish Journal of Sociology* 11 (December 1969).

Glock, Charles Y., Selznick, Gertrude J., and Spaeth, Joe L. *The Apathetic Majority: A Study Based on Public Responses to the Eichmann Trial*. New York: Harper and Row, 1966.

Glock, Charles Y., and Siegelman, Ellen, eds. *Prejudice U.S.A.* New York: Praeger, 1969.

Glock, Charles Y., and Stark, Rodney. *Christian Beliefs and Anti-Semitism*. New York: Harper and Row, 1966.

Hentoff, Nat, ed. *Black Anti-Semitism and Jewish Racism*. New York: Richard W. Baron Publishers, Inc., 1969.

Leschnitzer, Adolf. *The Magic Background of Modern Anti-Semitism*. New York: International Universities Press, Inc., 1956.

Leskes, Theodore. "Discrimination in Employment," *American Jewish Year Book* 55 (1954).

Lipset, Seymour Martin. "The Left, The Jews and Israel," *Encounter* 33 (December 1969), pp. 24-35.

Liskofsky, Sidney. "International Swastika Outbreak," *American Jewish Year Book* 62 (1961).

Livingston, Sigmund. *Must Men Hate?* New York: Harper and Brothers, 1944.

Meyers, Gustavus. *A History of Bigotry in the United States*. Edited, with additional material, by Henry M. Christman. New York: Capricorn Books, 1960.

Pinson, Koppel S. "Anti-Semitism in the Post-War World," *Jewish Social Studies* 7 (1945).

Raab, Earl. "The Deadly Innocences of American Jews," *Commentary* 50 (December 1970), pp. 31-39.

Rosenfield, Geraldine. "Combating Anti-Semitism," *American Jewish Year Book* 47 (1945-46).

Selznick, Gertrude J., and Steinberg, Stephen. *The Tenacity of Prejudice: Anti-Semitism in Contemporary America*. New York and London: Harper and Row, 1969. Volume IV of the results of a five-year survey of anti-Semitism in the United States undertaken by the Survey Research Center of the University of California at Berkeley under a grant from the Anti-Defamation League of B'nai B'rith.

Shapiro, Alfred L. "Racial Discrimination in Medicine," *Jewish Social Studies* 10 (1948).

Spiegler, Samuel. "Combatting Anti-Semitism," *American Jewish Year Book* 48 (1946-47).

Stember, Charles H., et al. *Jews in the Mind of America*. New York: Basic Books, 1966.

Strober, Gerald S. *American Jews: Community in Crisis*. Garden City, New York: Doubleday, 1974. An analysis of the American Jewish community of the 1970s "under siege" and a plea that Jews solve their group dilemmas through commitment to, and in the framework of, American society.

Trachtenberg, Joshua. "Religious Background on Anti-Semitism," *Jewish Social Studies* 17 (1955).

Waldman, Lois. "Employment Discrimination Against Jews in the United States, 1955," *Jewish Social Studies* 18 (1956).

JEWISH-CHRISTIAN RELATIONS

Aronson, Arnold. "Organization of the Community Relations Field," *The Journal of Intergroup Relations* 1 (Spring 1960).

Burton, William L. "Protestant America and the Rebirth of Israel," *Jewish Social Studies* 26 (1964).

Cohen, Jules. "Religion in the Public Schools," *Journal of Jewish Communal Service* (Fall 1956).

Cooper, Charles I. "The Jews in Minneapolis and Their Christian Neighbors," *Jewish Social Studies* 8 (1946).

Croner, Helga, compiler. *Stepping Stones to Further Jewish-Christian Relations*. New York: Stimulus Books, 1977. An unabridged collection of Christian documents, with a foreword by Edward A. Synan.

Dean, John P. "Patterns of Socialization and Association Between Jews and Non-Jews," *Jewish Social Studies* 17 (July 1953).

Foerster, F. W. *The Jew—A Christian View*. New York: Farrar, Straus and Cudahy, 1961.

Frank, Isaac. "The Scope of Jewish Community Relations," *Jewish Social Service Quarterly* 30 (Spring 1954).

Friedman, Murray. "Intergroup Relations and Tensions in the United States," *American Jewish Year Book* 73 (1972), pp. 97-153.

Friedman, Murray. "Politics and Intergroup Relations in the United States," *American Jewish Year Book* 74 (1973), pp. 139-193.

Gilbert, Arthur. *A Jew in Christian America.* New York: Sheed and Ward, 1966.

Halpern, Ben. *Jews and Blacks: Classic American Minorities.* New York: Herder and Herder, 1971.

Harris, Louis, and Swanson, Bert E. *Black-Jewish Relations in New York City.* New York: Praeger, 1970.

Hershcopf, Judith. "The Church and the Jews: The Struggle at Vatican Council II," *American Jewish Year Book* 66 (1965); 67 (1966).

Hurvitz, Nathan. "Jews and Jewishness in the Street Rhymes of American Children," *Jewish Social Studies* 16 (1954).

Jones, Nathan B. "The Future of Black-Jewish Relations," *The Crisis* (January 1975), pp. 18-27.

Kandel, Alan D. *A Search for Principles in Jewish Community Relations for the Embattled World of Today.* New York: National Conference of Jewish Communal Service, 1969.

Katz, Shlomo, ed. *Negro and Jew: An Encounter in America.* New York: Macmillan, 1967.

Kirsch, Paul J. *We Christians and Jews.* Philadelphia: Fortress Press, 1975.

Lipset, Seymour Martin. *Group Life in America: A Task Force Report.* New York: The American Jewish Committee, 1972.

Maher, Trafford P. "The Catholic School Curriculum and Intergroup Relations," *Religious Education* (March-April 1960).

Olson, Bernhard E. *Faith and Prejudice—Intergroup Problems in Protestant Curricula.* New Haven: Yale University Press, 1963.

Olson, Bernhard. "Intergroup Relations in Protestant Teaching Materials," *Religious Education* (March-April 1960).

Perlmutter, Philip. "Intergroup Relations and Tensions in the United States," *American Jewish Year Book* 72 (1971), pp. 131-159.

Pitt, James E. *Adventures in Brotherhood.* New York: Farrar, Straus and Co., 1955.

Raab, Earl. "The Black Revolution and the Jewish Question," *Commentary* 47 (January 1969), pp. 23-33.

Raab, Earl. "Intergroup Relations and Tensions in the United States," *American Jewish Year Book* 71 (1970), pp. 191-216.

Ringer, Benjamin B. *The Edge of Friendliness: A Study of Jewish-Gentile Relations.* New York: Basic Books, 1967.

Rogowsky, Edward T. "Intergroup Relations and Tensions in the United States," *American Jewish Year Book* 69 (1968).

Sobel, Z. B. "Legitimation and Anti-Semitism as Factors in the Functioning of a Hebrew-Christian Mission," *Jewish Social Studies* 23 (1961).

Vatican Council II's Statement on the Jews: Five Years Later. New York: The American Jewish Committee, 1971.

Watson, Goodwin. *Action for Unity.* New York: Harper and Brothers, 1947.

Weinryb, Bernard D. "Intergroup Content in Jewish Religious Textbooks," *Religious Education* (March-April 1960).
Weisbord, Robert G., and Stein, Arthur. *Bittersweet Encounter: The Afro-American and the American Jew.* Westport, Connecticut: Negro Universities Press, 1970.
Wolfe, Ann G. *Community Relations: A New Profession.* New York: American Jewish Committee, 1954.
Wolfe, Ann G., ed. *A Reader in Jewish Community Relations.* New York: Ktav Publishing House, Inc., 1975.
Wood, James E., Jr., ed. *Jewish-Christian Relations in Today's World.* Waco: Baylor University Press, 1971.

INTERMARRIAGE AMONG JEWRY: A FUNCTION OF ACCULTURATION, COMMUNITY ORGANIZATION, AND FAMILY STRUCTURE

Borhek, J. T. "Ethnic Group Cohesion," *The American Journal of Sociology* 76 (July 1970).
Bossard, James H. C., and Boll, Eleanor S. *One Marriage, Two Faiths.* New York: Ronald Press Co., 1957.
Burgess, Ernest W. *The Family: From Institution to Companionship.* New York: American Book Co., 1945.
Carter, Hugh, and Glick, Paul C. *Marriage and Divorce,* rev. ed. Cambridge, Massachusetts: Harvard University Press, 1976.
Cohn, Werner. "Jewish Outmarriage and Anomie: A Study of the Canadian Syndrome of Polarities," *The Canadian Review of Sociology and Anthropology* 13 (February 1976), pp. 90-105.
Davis, Moshe. "Mixed Marriage in Western Jewry: Historical Background to the Jewish Response," *Jewish Journal of Sociology* 10 (1968).
Dean, John P. "Patterns of Socialization and Association Between Jews and Non-Jews," *Jewish Social Studies* 17 (1955).
Freeman, Howard A., and Kassenbaum, Gene G. "Exogamous Dating in a Southern City," *Jewish Social Studies* 18 (1956).
Glick, Paul C. "Intermarriage and Fertility Patterns Among Persons in Major Religious Groups," *Eugenics Quarterly* 7 (March 1960).
Glick, Paul C. *Some Recent Changes in American Families,* U.S. Bureau of the Census, Current Population Reports, Special Studies, Series P-23, no. 52. Washington, D.C.: U.S. Government Printing Office, 1975.
Goldstein, Sidney, and Goldscheider, Calvin. *Jewish Americans: Three Generations in a Jewish Community.* Englewood Cliffs, New Jersey: Prentice-Hall, Inc., 1968.
Gordon, Milton M. *Assimilation in American Life.* New York: Oxford University Press, 1964.
Gordon, Whitney H. "Jews and Gentiles in Middletown—1961," *American Jewish Archives* 18 (1966).
Hurvitz, Nathan. "Sixteen Jews Who Intermarried," *YIVO Annual* 13 (1965).

Kennedy, Ruby Jo Reeves. "What Has Social Science to Say About Intermarriage?" in *Intermarriage and Jewish Life*, edited by Werner J. Cahnman. New York: Herzl Press, 1963.

Levinson, Daniel J. and Maria H. "Jews Who Intermarry: Socio-Psychological Bases of Ethnic Identity," *YIVO Annual* 12 (1958-59).

Marital Status and Living Arrangements: March 1976, U.S. Bureau of the Census, Current Population Reports, Series P-20, no. 306. Washington, D.C.: U.S. Government Printing Office, 1977.

Martin, Bernard. "*Contra* Mixed Marriages: Some Historical and Theological Reflections," *Central Conference of American Rabbis Journal* (Summer 1977).

Rosenthal, Erich. "Acculturation Without Assimilation? The Jewish Community of Chicago, Illinois," *American Journal of Sociology* 66 (November 1960).

Rosenthal, Erich. "Jewish Intermarriage in Indiana," *American Jewish Year Book* 68 (1967), pp. 243-264.

Rosenthal, Erich. "Studies of Jewish Intermarriage in the United States," *American Jewish Year Book* 64 (1963), pp. 3-53.

Schwartz, Arnold. "Intermarriage in the United States," *American Jewish Year Book* 71 (1970), pp. 101-121.

Sklare, Marshall. "Intermarriage and Jewish Survival," *Commentary* (March 1970), pp. 51-58.

Warner, W. Lloyd, and Srole, Leo. *The Social Systems of American Ethnic Groups.* New Haven: Yale University Press, 1945.

CANADIAN EXPERIENCE: THE DYNAMICS OF JEWISH LIFE SINCE 1945

Ages, A. "Canadian Jewish Writing," *Congress Bi-Weekly* 40 (23 February 1973), pp. 19-22.

American Jewish Year Book. Articles on Canada in numerous issues. Of particular interest is Louis Rosenberg's study, "Two Centuries of Jewish Life in Canada, 1760-1960," in vol. 62 (1961).

Astrachan, A. "On the Broad Prairie: A Jewish Phenomenon in Winnipeg, Manitoba," *Present Tense* 2 (Summer 1975), pp. 31-35.

Beller, J. "Troubles in Quebec," *American Zionist* 62 (October 1971), pp. 16-19.

Bennett, A., and Herz, A. "Quebec Jewry's Tangled Heritage," *Jewish Observer* 19 (23 October 1970), pp. 15-16.

Canadian Jewish Congress—Fifty Years of Service 1919-1969, Montreal, 1970.

Canadian Jewish Congress, Report of the 17th Plenary Assembly, Toronto, 1974 (mimeographed and bound). Reports of earlier triennial assemblies are also available.

Chiel, Arthur. *The Jews in Manitoba*. Toronto: University of Toronto Press, 1961.

Encyclopaedia Judaica. Articles on Canada, Montreal, Toronto, Winnipeg, and other cities; see also the index, vol. 1, pp. 377-378.

Gottesman, Eli, ed. *Canadian Jewish Reference Book and Directory*, Montreal, 1963.

Greening, W. E. "The Problem in Montreal," *Anti-Defamation League Bulletin* 31 (November 1974).

Hayes, Saul. "Are the Jews of Quebec an Endangered Species?" *Journal of Jewish Historical Society of Canada* 1, no. 1 (Spring 1977), pp. 24-34.

Hayes, Saul. "Canadian Jewish Culture: Some Observations," *Queen's Quarterly* 84, no. 1 (Spring 1977), pp. 80-88.

Hayes, Saul. *Canadian Jewry in 1974.* Pamphlet, published by Canadian Jewish Congress, 1974.

"Jews in Canada—Language and Culture," *World Jewry* 10 (November-December 1967).

Kattan, Naim, ed. *Juifs et Canadiens.* Montreal: Editions du Jour, 1967.

Kayfetz, Ben G. "Canada's New Anti-Hate Law," *Patterns of Prejudice* 4 (May-June 1970), pp. 5-8.

Kayfetz, Ben. "The Development of the Toronto Jewish Community," *Tradition* 13 (Summer 1972), pp. 5-17.

"*Kulturkampf* in Canada," *World Jewry* 7 (January-February 1964).

Lappin, B. "Rehabilitation or Renaissance," *Judaism* 19 (Spring 1970), pp. 174-181.

Lappin, Ben. *The Redeemed Children.* Toronto: University of Toronto Press, 1963.

Levin, A. "A Soviet Jewish Family in Calgary," *Jewish Spectator* 41 (Spring 1976), pp. 36-40.

McGunigal, J. "Canada's Unsung Heroes of Israel's War of Independence," *Jewish Digest* 12 (May 1967), pp. 41-48.

Rose, Albert, ed. *A People and its Faith.* Toronto: University of Toronto Press, 1959. See especially the articles by Ben Kayfetz, Dennis H. Wrong, and Albert Rose.

Rosenberg, Stuart E. *The Jewish Community in Canada,* 2 vols. Toronto: McLelland and Steward, 1970.

Sack, B. G. *History of the Jews in Canada.* Montreal: Harvest House, 1965.

Solomon, M. M. "Pandora's Box for Jews," *Congress Bi-Weekly* 35 (19 June 1968), pp. 12-15. On the implications of certain political developments in Canada for its Jewish community.

Teboul, Victor. *Mythe et images du Juif au Quebec.* Ottawa: Editions de Lagrave, 1977.

Trudeau, Pierre. "A Threefold Gift: An Address," *World Jewry* 13 (March-April 1970), pp. 7-9.

Waller, H. "The Jews of Quebec and the Canadian Crisis," *Tfutzoth Yisrael* 15, no. 2 (April 1977).

Weinfeld, Morton. "La Question juive au Québec," *Midstream* 23, no. 8 (October 1977), pp. 20-31.

Wisse, Ruth, and Cotler, Irwin. "Quebec's Jews: Caught in the Middle," *Commentary* 64, no. 3 (September 1977), pp. 55-59.

"Yesterday, Today and Tomorrow—the Jews of Toronto," *Globe Magazine,* 14 October 1967.

Index ─────────────────────────────

Contributors _____

WALTER I. ACKERMAN is currently Professor of Education at Ben Gurion University in Israel and Visiting Professor of Contemporary Jewish Studies at Brandeis University. Until 1977 he was also Dean of the Faculty of Humanities and Social Sciences and Chairman of the Department of Education at Ben Gurion University. Before settling in Israel he served as Vice President for Academic Affairs at the University of Judaism in Los Angeles. He received his B.A. at Harvard University and a doctorate in education from the same institution. He is the author of *Out of Our People's Past: Source Material for the Study of Jewish History.* Among his numerous papers are "Jewish Education for What?" *(American Jewish Year Book)*, "The Present Moment in Jewish Education" *(Midstream)*, and "The Americanization of Jewish Education" *(Judaism)*.

S. ANDHIL FINEBERG is currently national consultant to the National Conference of Christians and Jews and formerly served as National Director of Community Relations of the American Jewish Committee. He received his B.A. from the University of Cincinnati and his Ph.D. from Columbia University. Rabbinic ordination and the honorary degree of Doctor of Divinity were conferred on him by the Hebrew Union College. His books include *Punishment Without Crime—What You Can Do About Prejudice, Overcoming Anti-Semitism,* and *The Rosenberg Case: Fact and Fiction.* He has also published more than forty articles on religious prejudice and interreligious affairs.

ARNOLD FORSTER is Associate National Director and General Counsel of the Anti-Defamation League of B'nai B'rith, an organization with which he has been associated for almost forty years. He received his LL.B. at St. John's College and was admitted to the bar of the State of New York. Among his many books are *A Measure of Freedom, Report from Israel* and *The Trouble-Makers, Cross-Currents, Danger on the Right* (coauthored with Benjamin R. Epstein), *Report on the Ku Klux Klan, Report on the John Birch Society, The Radical Right: Report on the John Birch Society and Its Allies,* and *The New Anti-Semitism.*

ERIC LEWIS FRIEDLAND is Harriet Sanders Associate Professor of Judaics at Antioch College, the University of Dayton, the United Theological Seminary, and Wright State University in Dayton, Ohio. He received his B.A. from Boston University and his Ph.D. from Brandeis University. He is the author of "*Olath Tamid* by David Einhorn" *(Hebrew Union College Annual)* and "Marcus Jastrow and *Abodath Israel*" in *Text and Responses: Studies Presented to Nahum N. Glatzer on the Occasion of His Seventieth Birthday.* He has also contributed many articles and book reviews to *Judaism,* the *Journal of the Central Conference of American Rabbis,* and *The Jewish Spectator.*

BERNARD MARTIN is Abba Hillel Silver Professor of Jewish Studies and Chairman of the Department of Religion at Case Western Reserve University in Cleveland. After receiving his B.A. from the University of Chicago, he studied at the Hebrew Union College-Jewish Institute of Religion in Cincinnati where he was ordained as a rabbi. Subsequently he received his Ph.D. in philosophy from the University of Illinois. The author of *The Existentialist Theology of Paul Tillich, Prayer in Judaism, Great Twentieth Century Jewish Philosophers,* and *A History of Judaism* (two volumes, coauthored with Daniel J. Silver), he has also published his translation from the Russian original of four major works of the Russian-Jewish philosopher, Lev Shestov, and twelve volumes of his translation of Israel Zinberg's *History of Jewish Literature* from Yiddish and Hebrew. In addition to holding membership in many national and international scholarly organizations, he is the editor of the *Journal of the Central Conference of American Rabbis.*

MICHAEL A. MEYER is Professor of Jewish History at the Hebrew Union College-Jewish Institute of Religion in Cincinnati. Born in Germany, he received his undergraduate education at the University of California (Los Angeles) and his Ph.D. from the Hebrew Union College-Jewish Institute of Religion. His two major books are *The Origins of the Modern Jew* and *Ideas of Jewish History.* He has written a history of the HUC-JIR and contributed numerous articles to scholarly journals in Judaica.

W. GUNTHER PLAUT is senior scholar of Holy Blossom Temple in Toronto and President of the Canadian Jewish Congress. He has also served as Visiting Professor at Macalester College and Haifa University. Born in Germany, he received the degree of J.S.D. from the University of Berlin and was ordained as a rabbi at the Hebrew Union College. His books include *Judaism and the Scientific Spirit, A History of the Jews in Minnesota, The Book of Proverbs—A Commentary, The Rise of Reform Judaism, The Growth of Reform Judaism, The Case for the Chosen People, Your Neighbor Is a Jew,* and *Genesis—A Commentary.*

DAVID POLISH is rabbi of Beth Emet The Free Synagogue in Evanston, Illinois, and a past president of the Central Conference of American Rabbis. He received his B.A. from the University of Cincinnati and was ordained at the Hebrew Union College where he also received the degree of D.H.L. (Doctor of Hebrew Letters). Among his books are *The Eternal Dissent* (also in Hebrew translation), *A Guide for Reform Jews* (coauthored with Frederic A. Doppelt), *The Higher Freedom, Renew Our Days,* and *Israel—Nation and People.* He has also lectured at the Garrett Theological Seminary at Northwestern University and at the College of Jewish Studies in Chicago.

ERICH ROSENTHAL is Professor of Sociology at Queens College of the City University of New York. Born in Germany and educated at the universities of Giessen and Bonn, he received his doctorate in sociology from the University of Chicago. Among his major publications are "The Jewish Population of Chicago, Illinois" *(The Chicago Pinkas),* "Acculturation Without Assimilation? The Jewish Community of Chicago, Illinois" *(The American Journal of Sociology),* "Jewish

Fertility in the United States" *(American Jewish Year Book)*, "Studies of Jewish Intermarriage in the United States" *(American Jewish Year Book)*, "Jewish Intermarriage in Indiana" *(American Jewish Year Book)*, "Divorce and Religious Intermarriage: The Effect of Previous Marital Status Upon Subsequent Marital Behavior" *(Journal of Marriage and the Family)*, and "The Equivalence of United States Census Data for Persons of Russian Stock or Descent With American Jews: An Evaluation" *(Demography)*.

DANIEL JEREMY SILVER is rabbi of The Temple in Cleveland and Adjunct Professor of Religion at Case Western Reserve University. He received his B.A. from Harvard University and his Ph.D. from the University of Chicago. His rabbinic ordination was obtained at the Hebrew Union College-Jewish Institute of Religion. He has also been President of the National Foundation for Jewish Culture. His books include *Maimonidean Criticism and The Maimonidean Controversy: 1180-1249* and *A History of Judaism* (two volumes, coauthored with Bernard Martin).

SHUBERT SPERO is rabbi of Young Israel in Cleveland. He received his B.S.S. from the College of the City of New York and his Ph.D. in philosophy from Case Western Reserve University, and obtained ordination as a rabbi from the Yeshiva and Mesifta Torah Vodaath. Among the institutions at which he has taught are Case Western Reserve University, the Cleveland Institute of Art, and the Cleveland College of Jewish Studies. His publications include *Faith of a Jew, God in All Seasons,* and more than twenty articles on Jewish theology in such journals as *Tradition, Judaism,* and *Perspective.*

SIDNEY Z. VINCENT is Executive Director emeritus of the Jewish Community Federation of Cleveland. Before his recent retirement he had served as executive director of the federation for more than thirty years. He holds a B.A. from Western University and an M.A. from the School of Applied Social Sciences at the same university. His publications have appeared in the *Journal of Jewish Communal Service* and other journals. He also contributed a chapter to *The Tale of Ten Cities.* He has served as president of the National Conference of Jewish Communal Service, the International Conference of Jewish Communal Service, and the Association of Jewish Community Relations Workers.